The Wolves of Alaska

Also by Jim Rearden

Hunting Alaska's Far Places
Half a Century with Rifle and Shotgun

Slim Moore: Alaska Master Guide
A Sourdough's Hunting Adventures and Wisdom

Sam O. White, Alaskan
Tales of a Legendary Wildlife Agent and Bush Pilot

Forgotten Warriors of the Aleutian Campaign

Alaska's Wolf Man
The 1915–55 Wilderness Adventures of Frank Glaser

Castner's Cutthroats
Saga of the Alaska Scouts

Koga's Zero
The Fighter that Changed World War II

Travel Air NC9084
The History of a 75-year-old Working Airplane

Jim Rearden's Alaska
Fifty Years of Frontier Adventure

All books in this list of twelve can be found in most Alaska's book stores. The above nine books may also be ordered directly from the publisher (406) 549-8488. See copyright page for address, website, e-mail, and fax number.

Arctic Bush Pilot
From Navy Combat to Flying Alaska's Northern Wilderness

Tales of Alaska's Big Bears

Shadows on the Koyukuk
An Alaskan Native's Life Along the River

The Wolves of Alaska

A Fact-based Saga

by JIM REARDEN

PICTORIAL HISTORIES PUBLISHING COMPANY, INC.
Missoula, Montana

Library of Congress
Control Number 2002104403

ISBN 978-1-57510-099-9

First Printing: April 2002
Second Printing: March 2009

COVER GRAPHICS Mike Egeler
TYPOGRAPHY & BOOK DESIGN Arrow Graphics

Wolf cover photo by Robert O. Stephenson,
Alaska Department of Fish and Game

Published by Pictorial Histories Publishing Company, Inc.
713 South Third Street West, Missoula, Montana 59801
PHONE (406) 549-8488, FAX (406) 728-9280
E-MAIL: phpc@montana.com
WEBSITE: pictorialhistoriespublishing.com

To the memory of Bob Hinman (1928–2000),
dedicated wildlife manager, lover of life,
punster par excellence, a special
Alaskan—my friend for half a century.

—JIM REARDEN

Contents

Acknowledgments

I AM INDEBTED to many people for their generous time and input on the manuscript for *The Wolves of Alaska*. My daughter Nancy Kleine made many helpful comments on early drafts. Former Alaska Department of Fish and Game wildlife biologist Dick Bishop and his wife Mary, made many helpful suggestions. Likewise, former ADF&G wildlife biologist Jim Faro spent many hours reviewing the material and made many helpful suggestions—many that weren't tied to biology.

Pat Valkenburg, ADF&G wildlife biologist and his wife Audrey—also a fine wildlife biologist—made many helpful comments that I incorporated.

Robert O. Stephenson, ADF&G wildlife biologist, was helpful in almost more ways than I can count. He not only spent days carefully reviewing the manuscript and correcting the biology—as well as my awkward syntax—he gave permission for me to use many of his published field observations as those of my fictional biologist Ren Smith. Further, it was Bob Stephenson's Anaktuvuk Pass cabin I stayed in when writing for the *National Geographic* about the caribou use by the Anaktuvuk villagers, and where Bob introduced me to the wonderful Arctic John. Without Bob's generosity, wolf knowledge, and experience, *The Wolves of Alaska* would have been much less.

Thanks too, to Grant Spearman, Anthropologist, who helped with Anaktuvuk Pass culture and language.

My long-time friend and Board of Game associate, Sidney Huntington, reviewed the manuscript and made helpful comments.

ADF&G wolf researcher Mark McNay reviewed the manuscript and insured that the wolf biology was accurate. Don Young,

ADF&G Area Biologist, was most helpful by providing accurate figures on wolves, moose, and caribou for Game Management Subunit 20A.

My thanks to Ray Tremblay for encouraging words and constructive comments.

My thanks to Governor Jay Hammond for his constructive comments on the manuscript, permission to use his writings, and for providing the comment that appears on the cover.

Jill Shepherd, Senior Editor for ALASKA magazine, made many helpful comments, and provided the gracious blurb for the front cover.

My thanks to Alaska Representative Con Bunde for permission to use the spring 1993 Alaska House of Representatives Resolution which he wrote.

My thanks to Paul Jenkins, editor at *The Anchorage Times*, for permission to reprint his editorial of December 8, 1994.

My thanks to Dr. Sam Harbo, for use of his thoughtful *Environmental Sanity: Think Globally—Act Locally."*

My thanks also to Lee Kuhn, Professor Emeritus, Department of Fisheries and Wildlife, Oregon State University, for his constructive comments on the ms. Kuhn, one of my undergraduate wildlife professors 1945–48, is still overseeing my work.

— JIM REARDEN

Prologue

The problem with wolves is how to manage them rationally—
going to neither extreme—and managing them despite criticism
of the public no matter what you do.
—ROBERT A. HINMAN, Wildlife Biologist,
Alaska Department of Fish and Game

Of all of the native biological constituents of a northern wilderness
scene, I should say that the wolves present the greatest test of human
wisdom and good intentions. The problems of rational wolf management are so complex, so beset by prejudicial extremes, so confused
by misconceptions and half truths and false moral judgments that,
to a large part of the public, the only wolf problem is one of getting
rid of and staying rid of wolves. The latter, to my way of thinking,
is an appalling oversimplification loaded with potentialities for great
mistakes. —PAUL L. ERRINGTON, *Of Predation and Life*, 1967

He's mad that trusts in the tameness of a wolf, a horse's health, a
boy's love, or a whore's oath. —KING LEAR

There are no compacts between lions and men, and wolves and
lambs have no concord. —HOMER

Under normal conditions predators generally live upon surplus
populations of prey species, and their activities have little or no
effect on breeding stock. Local readjustments are often desirable
to maintain a balance.
    Under special conditions, either favorable to the predator or
unfavorable to the prey, predators may become a real factor in
decreasing populations or in preventing recovery following a
decline in population. —IRA GABRIELSON, *Wildlife Conservation*, 1942

xi

Introduction

THIS "FACTION" SAGA (fiction based on fact) touches on the State of Alaska's attempts to manage wolves, and the work of Alaska's dedicated wildlife biologists with wolves; it characterizes the attitudes of a variety of Alaskans and non-Alaskans toward Alaska's wolves; and it attempts to present a realistic view of Alaska's wolves.

During my half century plus in Alaska my main interest has been to promote scientific management of Alaska's fish and wildlife. Of all of Alaska's varied and wonderful species of wildlife, one stands out as perhaps the most interesting, the most controversial, the most misunderstood, and the one that Alaska's wildlife biologists—and the state—have found to be the most frustrating in attempts at scientific management.

That animal is the wolf.

Extremism by environmentalist special interests now seems to dominate American society. Organizations that promote animal rights seem to me to be the most extreme. Various of these groups want to stop all hunting, fishing, use of laboratory animals for research, animal husbandry, eating of meat, fur farming and use of fur in clothing, ownership of pets, even use of seeing-eye dogs, and the existence of zoos. They are generally opposed to the science of wildlife management, preferring to let nature take its course regardless of the outcome. The wolf and its scientific management in Alaska seems to have attracted the attention of more than its fair share of these extremists.

Many of these organizations have become national and even international. They have learned how to grab newspaper headlines, how to dominate sound bites on television news, and via skillfully written letters how to bilk susceptible people out of dollars to support their causes and organizations.

Few of the dollars sympathetic people send to animal advocacy groups are spent directly for the benefit of animals; a 1990 survey of thirty-three top animal advocacy groups revealed that over ninety percent of the money raised annually by these groups was spent sending out requests to raise more money.

A recent survey characterized the typical animal rights activist: It is usually a childless white woman who annually earns more than $30,000, is in her thirties or forties, and lives in a city. She is probably a school teacher, a nurse, or a government worker with a college degree, or even an advanced degree. Most of these people—and I have encountered many of them—are sincere in their beliefs.

Through their unceasing efforts to dominate the news media, to resort to sympathetic courts, and to propagandize their beliefs in sympathetic terms, these groups have done much to paralyze the democratic process. This has impacted scientific management of wildlife in Alaska (and other states), seriously affecting wildlife populations. This has cheated citizens of the pleasure of seeing good numbers of some species of animals, and deprived those who depend upon them for food, recreation, and income. It has also encouraged development of overpopulations of some species (east coast deer for example) with attendant die-offs, habitat damage, private property damage, and highway accidents.

What makes environmental extremism different is the appalling ignorance of most of those who would bully others into adopting their skewed sentimental perspectives. Bambi is a nice story—I enjoyed it when I was a youngster—but it veers far from the real world of nature. Nature can be cruel, but many urban citizens choose to pretend otherwise. The well-spring of environmentalism, of course, is urban America and Europe.

The biography I recount for myself in this volume is true. I have invented a number of fictional characters, none of whom are based on any particular individuals, but on generalized persons I have encountered in my involvement with Alaska's wolf management. My relationships and conversations with fictional characters, of course, is made up, but it is true to my experiences with the types represented.

Most of the characters who appear on these pages are/were real people (see end pages for listings). The wolf biologist Ren Smith and the school teacher Pat York are fictional; neither of these characters is based on any actual person, living or dead. The other characters, real and fictional, revolve around them. The court cases, quotes from the press and television, are true, as they actually occurred.

The descriptions of the adventures and actions of Frank Glaser, which I have used to counterpoint modern views of the wolf and the state of Alaska's wolf management program, are true, as described to me by the real life Glaser. They are based on my book *Alaska's Wolf Man; The 1915–55 Wilderness Adventures of Frank Glaser* (Pictorial Histories Publishing Company, Missoula, Montana, 1989), for which I was named Historian of the Year 1999 by the Alaska Historical Society.

As related, I taught wildlife management at the University of Alaska for four years (that was half a century ago; no one calls me Prof any more), I served as a member of the Alaska Board of Fish and Game for five years, and was a member of the Alaska Board of Game for seven years. I was the Outdoors Editor of *Alaska Magazine* from 1968–88, a Field Editor for *Outdoor Life* from 1976 to 1996, and as a freelance writer I have written nineteen books on Alaskan subjects (including this one) and have sold about 500 articles about Alaska to more than forty magazines in the U.S. and half a dozen other countries around the world.

I have centered my story around Game Management Subunit 20A in interior Alaska because of the comprehensive record of populations and harvests of wolves, moose, and caribou for that unit. And also, in part, because in 1975 as a member of the Alaska Board of Game, I participated in launching the active wolf management program there. The population figures of wolves, moose, and caribou for Game Management Unit 20A are actual, published by wildlife biologists of the Alaska Department of Fish and Game.

The life history of wolves found throughout is based on many published accounts; of those I have used, the best and most complete is that written by L. David Mech, in his fine book *The Wolf*, The Natural History Press, Garden City, New York, 1970.

—JIM REARDEN
Sprucewood,
Homer, Alaska

Hooked on wolves: The market hunter

IT WAS THE EARLY 1950s. Alone, I was hunting moose deep in the white-peaked Alaska Range. From the Richardson Highway I had ascended five miles of the Delta Clearwater River, hand-lining my canoe over shallows, and running the outboard where it was deep.

With my canvas leanto pitched, I scouted along the bluff in the valley where the river ran slow, deep and clear, searching with binoculars for a bull moose. Near camp I stumbled onto a freshly-killed yearling cow moose. Tracks at the scene and the way the carcass had been fed upon told me it was the work of wolves. I hunted until dark without seeing a live moose or a wolf.

That September night was clear, with a full moon. A heavy frost formed. I was warm in my sleeping bag when something awoke me. I lay quiet, peering out of the leanto and saw a gray wolf walk into view. Light from the moon was so bright the wolf threw a shadow. It stopped and stood still, not ten feet from me. I heard it sniffing, and it seemed to be looking around. It must have known I was there—the scenting powers of a wolf are legendary.

I suppose the animal stood there for half a minute. Then it calmly walked away.

That was my first encounter with a wolf.

Next morning I killed a small bull moose and spent the next two days dressing it and packing the meat to the riverbank where I could load it into my canoe. I spent three full days and part of a morning in the Delta Clearwater valley. I knew wolves were there—in addition to the snooping wolf and the moose they had killed, I saw an abundance of wolf tracks. Despite my silence, and alertness, I neither heard nor saw another wolf.

Skip ahead a few years. I was a registered hunting guide, with clients Phil and Cecille Neuweiler, residents of Pennsylvania, hunting at Twin Lakes at the base of the Alaska Peninsula. Leaving the Neuweilers in camp with my assistant guide, I returned to a high peak to retrieve a backpack load of meat from the trophy ram Phil had killed. As always when returning to cached meat, I carried my rifle in the event of an encounter with an unfriendly grizzly bear.

With the meat on my packboard, I headed for camp. Half way, climbing a slope, I saw movement ahead. I stopped and peered with binoculars. It was a gray wolf loping toward me. It hadn't seen me. I dropped to the ground, rolled out of the packboard, and eased a cartridge into the rifle's chamber.

When the loping wolf was fifty yards away I shot it. I skinned the animal, and Phil took the hide—he was, of course, paying for the hunt. At the time the Territory of Alaska paid a $50 bounty for killing a wolf, but no bounty was claimed for that one.

On another hunt, this time in the arctic Brooks Range with a client from New York, I was preparing supper in our cook tent in the late evening when the howl of a wolf drifted across the ridges and lake where we were camped.

"What was that?" the hunter gasped.

"A wolf. Isn't that a beautiful sound?" I commented.

My client leaped across the tent to his rifle. He was frightened and asked, "Is it after us?"

Over the next few days we heard wolves howl repeatedly, and even saw one chasing caribou in the distance. The hunter was nervous, frightened by the presence of wolves. It spoiled his hunt, he told me at the end.

I have often seen wolves as I have flown over Alaska's wild places. My first such view was in winter, when I saw eight wolves traveling single file in deep snow. The lead wolf was breaking trail, and the following pack members were stepping in its tracks. Oscar Vogel, a long-time Talkeetna Mountains trapper, once told me that in deep snow, pack members take turns in the lead position of trail breaker. I'm not sure of that, but I had a lot of respect for Oscar's wilderness knowledge.

In common with most men in their late seventies, I enjoy dwelling on such past events, recalling adventures and the occasional achievement. I especially enjoy remembering my encounters with Alaska's wildlife, and my occasional brushes with wolves seem to stand out.

My achievements weren't great, but some gave me much satisfaction. As Professor of Wildlife Management at the University of Alaska half a century ago it was my privilege to introduce a number of talented young students to this then-relatively-new profession. I have since followed their careers with much pride and satisfaction. These gifted young men (there were no women studying wildlife management at UA then) would likely have reached the top in whatever field they chose. Nevertheless, I like to think my teachings, at least in a small way, contributed to their successes.

I didn't stay long at the university—only four years. The call of the wild was too strong. From classrooms on the top floor of the old Main Building where I lectured I could look far across the Tanana Valley to the sixty-mile-distant, sky-scraping, Alaska Range. Sometimes I broke off lecturing as my eyes lingered on winter-pink shading on the high snowy peaks as the winter sun dropped, or when I saw the great expanse of wild unpeopled land and wondered what I was doing in front of a blackboard.

I devoured books in the Alaska room at the University library, mentally joining explorer Vilhjalmur Stefansson and his Eskimo companions as they traveled across the arctic ice; with Ben Eielson and Hubert Wilkins I flew on that great 1928 exploratory flight from Barrow to Spitsbergen; I floated down the Yukon River in 1883 with Frederick Schwatka; and, with rifle over shoulder, in 1906–08 I explored the wilderness of Denali with Charles Sheldon.

I wanted to create my own adventurous career in Alaska, and I did. During my half century here I've seen millions of dime-bright wild salmon streaming into clear, gravel-bottomed rivers. I've flown in a small plane over caribou herds that stretched across the tundra farther than the eye could see. With binoculars I once counted more than one hundred bull moose scattered across a snowy Kenai Peninsula mountainside.

I've seen the skies ablaze with northern lights so bright and with color so vivid attempts at description fail. I've spent several thousand hours in my own small plane and others, soaring over rugged white-capped sky-scraping peaks and across deep rich valleys and rolling forests of spruce. I've lingered in skies above blue-ice glaciers. I've peered from on high into huge freshwater lakes and tranquil green-water coastal bays, as well as thousands of miles of clear, wild, deep rivers.

I've boated on the clear salt chuck from Alaska's panhandle to the far reaches of the volcanic Aleutian Islands and into the frigid Bering Sea.

I've seen rainbow-hued arctic grayling so abundant they blackened a river bottom. While on a November writing assignment for *Audubon* magazine, I counted from one location nearly 2,500 chittering bald eagles along the Chilkat River of Southeast Alaska; some were perched in trees, others fed on spawned-out salmon. I've had several closeup exciting (and frightening) encounters with great lumbering brown bears. One March as a passenger with hunting guide/pilot Jack Lee I flew in a small plane over the Bering Sea ice to within fifteen miles of Siberia to find and photograph the great white sea bear.

In short, I've led the kind of life I dreamed of as a boy growing up in the small northern California town of Petaluma.

Now in my declining years, I no longer hunt moose, caribou, or other big game. In my younger years I hunted for meat to feed my growing family, not for trophies. I still hunt birds with a shotgun, but only those I enjoy eating. My children are adults, gone from the six-bedroom log house I built. I no longer fly my small plane. Due to the inevitable aging process, I realized I was no longer a safe pilot and I grounded myself.

I go for long daily walks with my Brittany dog, usually on the beach of the local bay. And I have my beautiful cabin boat with which in summer I fish for salmon and halibut and simply cruise, enjoying the mountain and water scenery, the waterbirds, an occasional whale, the abundant sea otter.

I've traveled some—to Africa, New Zealand, Mexico, Canada, much of the U.S.—but I am now content to remain at home in Alaska, where I spend much of my time remembering and writing about the exciting and interesting times.

Thus, I've built a lifetime of memories, and like most old men I often indulge myself with mind games, remembering what has been. Some of my most interesting recollections are of people I have encountered who have never seen, or even heard, a wild wolf, but who insist they love wolves. It is surprising how many fall into this category. I especially remember one such lady. When I first met her she was a teacher from Boston.

⁓

PAT YORK HAD no idea her life was to pivot on an event of one August night in 1975 while she was visiting Ontario's Provincial Algonquin Park. The 29-year-old auburn-haired Boston school teacher was a lone camper amidst families and couples, but she was an independent sort, and lack of a companion didn't trouble her.

That August evening a ranger warned an overflow crowd at the Outdoor Theater, "Please be patient. With the number of cars we have tonight, the last car won't be able to move for twenty minutes after the first has left. These midnight rendezvous have become popular."

The 250 cars then moved through August darkness in the deep forest of Algonquin, a ten-kilometer-long string of head and tail lights snaking at fifty km/hour. The mysterious, bordering, dark woods and the procession of silent cars heightened Pat's anticipation.

"We get a response about half the time. We heard them last night. Remember," the ranger had said, "we'll be strung out for some distance. Please, no horn honking, and no car door slamming when you stop. Our success depends on sneaking up on them."

Pat was driving down a gentle hill when, in the distance, brake lights flared like red jewels in the darkness. Headlights winked out as the line of stopped cars progressively turned black.

She braked to the shoulder and switched engine and lights off. Excited, she shrugged into a warm jacket, stepped out, and quietly closed the door. Adjacent cars and the occupants standing beside them were dim shadows.

As her eyes adjusted she was awed by the moonless clear sky crowded with blazing stars that seemed almost near enough to touch. She didn't see stars like this in Boston. She peered into the forest but saw only dim shadows and blackness.

She stood at the front of her car, enjoying heat from the silent engine, aware of the delicious smell of spruce and balsam. The cool summer air was fresh and clean—a change from the city smells to which she was accustomed. The hooting of a distant owl fell softly on her ears; otherwise there was silence. The *who-who-who* had an eerie quality. When had she last heard an owl's call?

Would there be a response tonight? The rangers had seemed optimistic. "Forecast is for no wind, clear skies," one had announced. "If we're lucky they'll sing."

The first wails were faint, distant, unimpressive.

Is this what she had come here for? She was disappointed. Later, she realized the sound was made by a human, probably a park ranger. It was the query, "Are you there?" Or was it a challenge?

Seconds later the response came from the nearby black forest. Never would she forget that moment, or that sound—the glorious, musical howl of wolves. First one animal burst forth with a glissando that swooped up, up, and then down; in a moment the wolf howled again and as its voice soared, another joined in; then a third. Suddenly in a burst of sound came a flood of howls. Some were moan-like. One barked before howling. Others yipped and howled. Wolf voices filled the dark.Chills skidded along her spine, and hairs on the back of her neck lifted as the grand chorus rent the forest. The main singer's voice climbed, then dropped, and he (or was it a she?) repeated the wondrous sound. The wolves were close, seemingly within a few hundred yards at most, yet at times they seemed more distant. The ululations were almost ventriloquial.

The first wolf to sing had a pure, musical voice, deep and strong. The others seemed to take their cue from it. She was fairly sure the yippers were young, probably pups of the year. She was surprised to realize there were lupine sopranos, contraltos, and tenors. Some had more musically pleasing voices than others. There had to be six, eight, or more in the pack.

The surprise at hearing nearby wolves faded. The music teacher in her intruded. She suddenly realized they were harmonizing.

"They like chords!" she thought with amazement. No two sang in the same pitch. Wolves changed notes in minors. Once the wolf with the strongest voice held a long note of six or seven seconds, while the song of another danced around it.

"They're really singing; that's true music!" she whispered.

One of the rangers had said, "Howling can be a happy social function for wolves. They love to howl." She thought of this as the wild wails filled the air.

She was a city person, and nothing in her life had prepared her for these fantastic wilderness sounds. The primitive music seemed directed to her alone, and something in the spine-tingling chorus went to the depths of her being. She stood enthralled, staring raptly into the darkness, soaking up the sounds.

In her mind's eye she saw great gray animals standing and sitting among the tall conifers, muzzles pointed at the glittering stars. Later, with a secret feeling of pride, she realized she had felt no fear. At the campground next morning she heard several women admit they had scurried to the safety of their cars when the howls began.

Afterward she couldn't remember how long the wolves howled. She remained frozen in place until they stopped.

"Incredible! I've never heard anything like it," she breathed when the wild singing ended.*

Before leaving Algonquin she learned that rangers organized six or seven howlings every summer—when weather was right, and wolf participation appeared likely. Average attendance was 962 visitors. She was amazed at the public's ardor for hearing wolves howl.*

Pat carried the vivid memory of the glorious chorus and her imagined vision of wolves back to Boston and her thirty fifth-grade students. After the freedom of summer and the fascination of the wilderness of the Canadian park, she hated the thought of returning to teaching. She had agreed to teach at least until the end of the year. After that she had no specific plans; she was restless and after five years of teaching wanted to try something else.

Her father, who had been a school superintendent, and mother, a piano teacher, were both gone. She had no close relatives and only one long-term relationship with a man, and that was with Allen Potter, who had grown up next door and with her had attended primary through high school. He had once asked her to marry him, but she had told him she preferred to remain just friends. He hadn't liked it, but he had accepted, saying he was willing to wait for her.

That had annoyed her, leaving her with a faintly guilty feeling, but she had decided it was his problem, not hers. They occasionally dated, mostly having dinner out and taking in a movie. It was pleasant to have a male friend with a background similar to hers with whom she could reminisce about school events they both remembered. Whenever he began to get romantic she gently put him off. As he

---

*Public wolf howlings continue to be a summer feature of Algonquin Park.

neared thirty he was developing a pot belly and was losing some of his hair.

When school opened that fall she fell easily into the familiar routine of organizing lessons, correcting papers, attending teachers' conferences and meeting with parents.

She had taken slides during her Algonquin trip, and with them she organized several fifteen-minute stories about her summer adventures, projecting the slides for her class at mid-afternoon when they became bored with lessons. High point for the students was her story of the night she heard wolves howl.

"Why do wolves howl, Miss York?" asked red-headed, freckled Davy Foster. He was all boy and threw himself into everything, mental and physical, with an amazing intensity for a fifth-grader.

This led to a discussion of how scattered members of a pack howl so they can reassemble; and the even more complex subject of wolves howling to inform other packs of their claim to territory.

"I think wolves howl just because it makes them feel good," Davy proclaimed. Some of the other children nodded at that.

She sent for a recording of wolf howls for the children to hear, and ordered pictures of wolves which she pinned to her classroom walls. She bought a book, *Never Cry Wolf*, by Farley Mowat. The cover blurb explained it was a true story of one man's incredible adventures with a family of wolves in the Canadian wilderness. The back cover said the author was a biologist who spent many years with the Canadian government. An introduction claimed the book ". . . is a charming and engrossing scientific study that explodes many centuries-old myths about wolves."

She read aloud daily from this beautifully written book, learning with the children about the complex family life of the wolf. She especially remembered the part about wolves that lived exclusively on mice. The author seemed to challenge the belief that wolves lived by killing caribou, deer, moose, and other large animals, saying they preferred ground squirrels to caribou. But, when killing caribou they killed only the weak and sick. He intimated that wolves were unable to catch caribou fawns.

Inevitably, wolves became the topic of main interest in her classroom that semester.

Pat's studies of biology had been mostly peering at amoebae

and paramecia under a microscope and drawing them, and lectures about the balance of nature and the complexity of ecoystems. She explained to her class how things in the environment are interconnected, presenting a simplified version they could easily understand.

It wasn't only the children who were fascinated by things lupine; Pat herself often found thoughts of wolves foremost in her mind.

Ordering the tape and wolf pictures got her name listed with the Boston chapter of The National Wildlife Savers Foundation, an animal rights organization, and she started receiving flyers from the organization asking for donations and support. She completed an application and sent a membership fee so she could receive their monthly bulletin. The phone call came soon after.

"Miss York?" the caller said, "I'm Jerry Hanson from TNWSF. I'd like to introduce our ambassador to your students."

"TNWSF? What is that?" she asked, coldly. She was sure this was a salesman.

"The National Wildlife Savers Foundation," he recited patiently. "You recently became a member."

"Ambassador? I don't understand," Pat said, flustered. She hated being called from her classroom and was annoyed at this person.

"Yes, Lobo is our ambassador—he's a four-legged ambassador, a full-blooded wolf." Hanson sounded amused at her confusion.

"Oh. I didn't understand," she stammered. "I'd have to get permission from my principal."

"Could you call back and let me know?" he asked.

"Wait," she was regaining control. "Is it safe to bring a wolf into a classroom? Is he in a cage? Better tell me what to expect so I can tell my principal."

"Lobo is on a leash. He is well behaved and used to visiting schools. We allow the children to pet him, but prefer a large group doesn't gather closely around him."

The students' excitement—and the teacher's—built for several days as they awaited Lobo's visit.

The children were at their desks when Jerry and Lobo arrived. "You must be quiet so the wolf will feel welcome," Pat had warned.

Lobo, on a leash at Jerry Hanson's side, walked into the room, claws clicking on the smooth floor. Davy Foster leaped from his desk and flung himself toward the animal. As he passed her, Pat collared him; he was traveling so fast his feet left the floor. The other children gasped, Jerry Hanson grinned. He had stepped in front of Lobo and would have intercepted the boy if Pat hadn't caught him.

"Back to your desk, Davy," Pat ordered.

"I just wanted to hug him," Davy said, innocently.

"Lobo doesn't want to be hugged," Pat said, gently leading the boy to his desk.

No class exercise had ever held the children's attention like the live wolf. Every eye was riveted on the animal. They were startled by its size; even Pat was taken aback. "Why, it's as big as I am," she thought. She had envisioned wolves as German Shepherd-like, but this creature little resembled a German Shepherd dog. Though she had seen wolves in zoos she had never really looked at them; nor had she ever before been so close to one.

Lobo weighed 105 pounds, stood almost three feet at the shoulders, and stretched six feet from nose to tip of tail. Jerry Hanson's large hand wouldn't have curled around its sturdy legs, yet the animal's body was slender, aristocratic. Its broad head and tapered muzzle was pleasant, alluring. Its luminous eyes were a lovely golden-yellow, and they seemed to sparkle with intelligence. The handsome, dignified creature, alert to every classroom sound and movement, behaved like a gentleman.

Jerry, an outdoorsy, bronzed young man, led Lobo to Pat's desk at the front of the classroom, pointed and snapped his fingers. With the swiftness and ease of a cat, Lobo leaped onto the desk and stood gazing placidly at the children. The children again gasped.

"Well, kids, there's the big bad wolf!" Jerry said, dramatically.

☙

THAT AUGUST, WHILE Pat York was visiting Ontario's Algonquin Park and having her first wolf encounter, Ren Smith, a wildlife biologist with the Alaska Department of Fish and Game (ADF&G), who had studied wildlife management as one of my students, was experiencing his own pivotal wolf experience. Ren's assignment was to gather data used as a basis for management of wolves in Alaska's vast Interior. He had recently gone beyond that, and had become involved in raising a wolf pup. He planned to release the pup into the wild, and he feared other wolves would kill her. He now realized he had made a mistake by allowing himself to become emotionally attached to the puppy.

Ren was slim, dark-eyed and dark-haired, medium-tall, with tan, even features. He walked with the easy step of a woodsman. Habitually quiet, he usually spoke only when he had something worthwhile to say.

The female wolf had come to him the previous May as a week-old, pound-and-a- half, blind and deaf baby. A trapper who lived alone in a cabin a mile off the Steese Highway forty miles north of Fairbanks, said he had found a car-killed female wolf on the highway. From the condition of her nipples it was obvious she had been nursing pups.

A day later he heard a lone wolf's mournful howl a mile from his cabin. This was unusual, so he investigated and stumbled onto a hillside wolf den. It was on a warm, south-facing sidehill, oval-shaped, about twenty-five inches in diameter. Nearby he found several piles of disgorged meat. He crawled five or six feet into the den, and around a bend found an enlarged chamber holding five pups; four were cold and dead. One, a female, was barely alive. He wrapped the tiny thing in his coat and rushed it to Ren's Fairbanks office.

"Maybe you'd like to raise it as an experiment," the man suggested. He told Ren, "After I found the pups, a wolf followed me almost to my cabin and howled several times—the saddest sounds I've ever heard." He thought the mourning lone wolf had been the mate of the dead female.

Ren was suspicious of the man's story; nursing wolves with pups spend less time away from the den than other adults—they stick close to their pups for two or even three weeks after pups are born. The trappers's story put the dead female two miles from the den.

Ren explained to him that other members of a wolf pack—or the mate if there are just two—disgorge food at the den for the mother, explaining the disgorged meat the man had found. There was no way to check on the man's story, so Ren thanked him and let it go.

He put the pup on a flannel-wrapped hot water bottle. As she warmed she started to squirm; then she whined. She immediately sucked on the nipple of a bottle filled with warm milk Ren poked into her mouth. With a full belly she fell asleep next to the hot water bottle in a box in his office.

He then went to Bob Hinman, his supervisor, a burly, cheerful, experienced biologist. Few knew Hinman was a member of the Mensa Society, the international association for those with an IQ in the top two percent of the population. Hinman concealed his high IQ behind a barrage of good-humored banter. He loved puns, and while attending long boring meetings, wrote a seven page *Glossary of Wildlife Terms* (Third edition), full of in-house humor that still tickles ADF&G wildlife biologists. Examples: bear cub—Chicago ballplayer in the nude; parasites—two scenic views; bear claws—Santa in the shower; mean age of bears—from birth to death.

"A guy has just brought in a newborn wolf pup. I'd like to try raising it," Ren told Hinman.

"Why? What's the point? You know our policy. We don't issue permits for anyone to keep a wolf," Hinman said. "The commissioner won't sign a permit unless you have a damned good scientific reason for raising it."

"Let me think about it. This may be an opportunity to learn something," Ren said.

"Learn what?" Bob asked.

"I don't know, but anything we learn about wolves is worthwhile."

"Lots of researchers and zoos have raised wolf pups—you know the literature as well as I do," Bob countered.

"I'll come up with something. Give me a day or so," Ren said, rubbing his jaw in thought.

Ren lay awake for hours that night trying to think what he could learn by raising the baby wolf. He awoke with an idea, and that day poured through wolf references in the department's library. He could find no record of anyone raising a wolf pup and having it accepted by an existing wild pack.

"Is it worth trying?" he asked his supervisor after outlining the idea.

"I can't see where it would ever be of value to Alaska—we have plenty of wolves," Hinman responded. "In states where they're trying to reintroduce them, knowing how to add human-raised wolves to a pack might be worthwhile. But Ren, you know how territorial wolves are and how a pack treats strange wolves."

"Yeah. Usually they chase 'em away or kill 'em. Sometimes they eat 'em after they kill 'em. But that's usually an adult stranger. This is different. Adult wolves love pups. If I can raise this one so it's healthy and strong enough to cope with the rough-and-tumble of an existing litter, the parents might accept it. I'd like to give it a try."

"You'd have to keep it wild," Bob warned.

"Yeah, I know. I'll have to be its mother and father, and make sure it retains its fear of other people. That means I'll have to keep it isolated after its eyes open," Ren reasoned.

Thinking as he talked, Bob commented, "You know better than I—wolf pups learn complex socialization from living with litter mates, and from adult pack members. I'm not optimistic a pack will accept a man-raised pup. The pup won't know how to behave with litter mates or adults. I'd guess the younger the pup when it's introduced to a pack, the better its chances."

"Do you suppose we could plant it near a den before its eyes open and have a pack accept it?" Ren wondered.

"I doubt it," Bob answered. "It wouldn't last long outside of a den. Young pups have little ability to produce body heat. If you go near a den to leave it, you'd probably spook the pack away. By the time they returned ravens or an eagle could kill the pup, or it could die from hypothermia."

"You're right. I guess the best way will be to keep it for a couple of months, and then try to introduce it to a pack. Maybe I can find a way to start training it to be a wolf. It'll be a big leap from captivity to living with a wild pack—even if a pack will accept it," Ren said, thoughtfully.

"Ok. Outline your study, and I'll approve it. Then we'll see if the director and the commissioner will issue a permit. Be ready to fix a safe, isolated place. Also, my friend, there's no money for this in your budget. You'll have to fund it out of your own pocket. And, if you don't get a permit, you'll have to put the pup down. I'd use a lethal injection. Be prepared," he warned.

"Ok. I agree to that. I'll get back to you," Ren said, relieved. He had disliked the thought of having to kill the pup.

"One other thing, Ren," Bob said. "Remember Prof's warning about becoming emotionally involved with individual wild animals?"

"Yeah, I remember. I'll keep it in mind," Ren said.

THE ALASKA STEAMSHIP Company's *S.S. Mariposa* landed Frank Glaser, hunter/trapper extraordinaire, at Valdez in May, 1915. He was 26, single and footloose, and had been attracted to Alaska by exciting stories of its abundant furbearers and fabulous big game. He had never seen a wolf. Little did he know that his life would lead him to become one of the few living wolf experts of the first half of the 20th century. Government policy, supported by public opinion, then held that the only good wolf was a dead wolf.

It was breakup when no auto or horse team could negotiate the treacherous, bottomless muddy sections of the 371-mile Valdez Trail that led to the 20,000-person mining and commercial center of Fairbanks in Alaska's interior. Glaser walked all the way. The trail carried him through passes of the great-peaked Chugach and Alaska Ranges. The region near Black Rapids Glacier Roadhouse in the Alaska Range attracted him, and after a brief stay at Fairbanks he returned there. Within days Colonel Wilds P. Richardson of the U.S. Army Corp of Engineers arrived on horseback searching for a hunter to shoot game for meat to feed Alaska Road Commission construction crews then converting the Valdez Trail into a wagon road. Glaser convinced him he could do the job, and with a handshake he became a market hunter. It was a respected and respectable profession, and he became skilled at it. He was in almost every way a latter-day Mountain Man, and Alaskans soon regarded him as one of the most skilled outdoorsmen in the Territory.

Wild game was then the major source of fresh meat in interior Alaska. Market hunters regularly hunted Dall sheep, moose, and caribou in the wild and unpeopled Alaska Range. The meat was hauled by dog team or pack horse the sixty or more miles to Fairbanks. In 1917 a Fairbanks game warden estimated that 2,800 Dall sheep had been killed for the market over the previous four years, all within two hundred miles of Fairbanks.

Hunting near Black Rapids Roadhouse, Glaser killed mostly Dall sheep, some caribou and moose, receiving twenty five cents a pound for the meat delivered to a horse-drawn wagon on the Valdez Trail. This was big money in 1915. But there was a catch; he had to backpack the meat out of the mountains, a rugged, gut-wrenching job. An average Dall ram, gutted, legs and head removed, weighs 120 pounds. The front half of a large caribou can weigh 165 pounds; the rear half 150 pounds. Meat from a large moose can weigh 800 pounds. The rawhide-tough Glaser weighed only 160 pounds.

Grizzly bears were abundant and his first encounter with one was almost his last. Returning without a rifle to a ram he had cached to cool on a glacier while packing another out, he was within ten feet of the bear before he saw it. The bear, surprised at his feast, roared and charged. Glaser leaped a vertical twenty feet off the edge of the glacier, landing amidst a thicket of willows, which helped break his fall.

The bear stopped at the glacier's edge, chopping his teeth, growling, and swinging his head. Though scratched from willow branches and limping from a sprained ankle, Glaser sped from the scene as if the bear was nipping at his rear.

After that he carried his rifle when returning for cached meat. He commonly saw four or five of the big bears on a day's hunt, and not infrequently returned to a sheep he had cached only to find a grizzly had eaten or buried it. If he approached from upwind so a bear could smell him, the animal usually stood, looked him over, and departed. If the bear heard but couldn't smell him, it was more inclined to charge, although a loud yell or a shot fired into the ground usually sped the animal on its way.

Occasionally, even when it had his scent, a grizzly charged with the clear intent of attacking, and Glaser had to shoot it. He sold their hides, adding to his income. Later, he sent many grizzly hides and skulls to the U.S. Biological Survey for study. Alaska was a new land, rich with unknown animal species, and scientists were intent on collecting and classifying them.

Most Alaskans thought grizzly bears were dangerous nuisances; they stole meat, threatened and sometimes mauled or even killed people, panicked horses, and occasionally broke into cabins or caches for food. There was no thought of preserving these beasts, which are so cherished today.

2

The ambassador: I enlist: Savage River

"WHO WOULD LIKE to pet Lobo?" Jerry asked Pat's class.

Every hand went up. He turned to Pat, smiling. "This happens every time. Can you have them line up and come up one at a time?"

She appreciated his tact; she was still in control of the class. With the wolf perched on her desk as his prize exhibit, he could easily have taken over.

She lined the children up and allowed them, one at a time, to walk to the wolf. Lobo slowly wagged his tail as each child neared. Some of the children approached timidly, for the huge animal towered above them.

Brash little Davy tried to hug Lobo, but he couldn't get his short arms around the huge wolf. Pat was startled to see the animal "kiss" Davy by gently licking his face. Davy was in heaven, and for days afterward talked about how much his friend Lobo liked him. "He kissed me, didn't he, Miss York?" he said repeatedly.

Jerry showed a movie while Lobo lay quietly in a corner of the darkened room. One scene included views of a skinny, all-legs, playful puppy. "That was Lobo two years ago," he said. There was little resemblance between the scrawny, all-feet, dog-like puppy and the huge, magnificent adult.

Aimed at school children, the film depicted the wolf as gentle and family-oriented. "All adults of the pack commonly baby-sit pups. Wolves live side-by-side with prey animals, and they kill only the sick and the unfit," the announcer intoned. "Wolves are endangered," he also said, dramatically, "which means they are in danger of extinction."

The last scene horrified the children and Pat. On screen they saw a small plane fly low over a wolf running in snow while a gunner in the plane shot it. The dead wolf rolled into a bloody heap. "That's what Alaskans do with their wolves," the announcer said, in a tragic voice.

Lights went on. The children were silent. Jerry spoke softly. "Man has killed all the wolves in almost every state. There are some left in Minnesota and neighboring states, but they are threatened, or on the endangered list. Alaska has many wolves, but the state pays a bounty on them, and they are shot from airplanes, they are trapped for their beautiful fur, and if the killing doesn't stop, wolves will soon be gone from Alaska too."

He went on, "Wolves are an important part of the ecosystem because they kill and eat the sick and the unfit, leaving the healthy. They are beneficial for deer and other prey species.

"We need to save the wolf from extinction. It's a valuable animal that has been badly misunderstood. There is no record of wolves attacking humans in North America. Once in a while they kill a farmer's sheep, or a cow. But you must remember, the wolf lived here first, and humans have taken over the wolf's land.

"We think the wolf should be allowed to live, and we believe the wolf can exist in harmony with people."

REN WEIGHED AND measured the wolf pup, planning to keep a daily log of her development. The 15-inch-long (nose to tail-tip) pug-nosed, dark-furred puppy's ears were small, the head rounded. She could scarcely move by dragging herself using mostly her front legs. She whimpered frequently, especially when hungry.

Her blue eyes, which would change to yellow-gold in two or three months, began to open a week after Ren acquired her. His log for the day noted this. "Commissioner's permit arrived," he also recorded. Another entry read, "Name of pup Lady."

He had intended to make a dispassionate scientific study of the baby wolf. But the more he tended her, the more attached he became to the wriggling, noisy little bundle of fur. He soon realized he was sliding into the pitfall of nonobjectivity: wildlife biologists don't have to be heartless, but they do need to maintain objectivity. He was becoming emotionally attached to an individual animal.

The pup, in its box, was Ren's constant companion. He had to feed it frequently. He kept it warm with an oft-filled hot water bottle. His work sometimes required aerial surveys with his Piper Super Cub; on such flights the boxed pup rode on the back seat of the little two-place plane.

Ren was uncertain how much wolf behavior is learned and how much is inborn. If Lady were to be accepted and survive with a wild pack, she needed to know the body posturing, leg tossing, facial expressions, ear movements, and stares that signal a wolf's demands, or acceptance, of other wolves' demands or challenges.

He couldn't teach her such complex behavior. He went to his friend Garth, a professional sled dog musher and explained his need. Garth was a consistent winner of sled dog races.

"I have a year-old half-wolf bitch I can loan you," Garth suggested. "She looks like a wolf, and in many ways is more wolf than dog. I have a couple of litters of pups, and she's awfully interested in them. I think she has a strong maternal instinct. I plan to breed her next year, but I don't need her now. You're welcome to take her for a couple of months," Garth said. "She's spooky and hasn't been handled much, but she's not vicious."

Chena, Garth's seventy-pound, gray, wolf-dog, lunged against the chain attached to her stout collar when Garth led her out, appearing frightened even of her master, who, Ren knew, was gentle with his dogs. Because of her wildness, Ren feared she might kill the helpless, fragile wolf pup.

"Better that she die now than later, which she surely will if she doesn't know some wolf language," he decided.

He took Chena home and led her—now lunging in fear of him—into the boarded pen he had prepared. He released her and watched as she restlessly prowled inside the fence and poked her nose into the house he had built.

He carried the box holding the two-week-old Lady into the pen, put it down, and moved to a corner to watch. The puppy whined. At the sound, Chena trotted to the box and smelled Lady. She lifted her head and glanced at Ren, then looked back at the pup. She then licked the puppy from one end to the other, ignoring Ren.

After licking, she peered around the yard and went to the dog house. She went inside, turned around and sniffed and looked for a few moments. Apparently satisfied, she returned to the pup, gently took it in her jaws and carried it into the doghouse, put it down, and carefully coiled her body around it. The pup crawled until she lay partly on Chena and promptly fell asleep.

"She took over as if the pup were her own!" Ren marveled. "She's perfect. I know wolves love puppies, but this beats anything I've ever seen," he thought. "And to think; she's never had pups of her own."

When it was time to feed the pup he sat leaning against the dog house holding her in his lap as she sucked the bottle dry. Chena paced a few feet away, whining nervously.

With the pup fed, Ren put her back in the house. The moment he moved away, Chena dived into the dog house and again licked the pup from one end to the other, and lay down next to her.

Ren stopped taking Lady to the office. It wouldn't do for her to see other humans, even though wolf pups don't see clearly for a week or more after eyes open. He had to drive home several times a day to give the puppy her milk. Chena spent full time caring for the pup, mostly lying in the doghouse with her. She lost some of her nervousness and seemed to accept Ren as a partner in raising the baby wolf.

Lady began to hear when she was about three weeks old. Sudden loud noises startled—even frightened—her. Now she could stand and walk without staggering. She began to refuse milk and started gulping canned dog food or hamburger. Needle-sharp milk teeth appeared. She grew so fast that Ren could scarcely believe it. She spent much time crawling over Chena, playing, growling. Chena's patience with the pup seemed unlimited. Lady would also play with Ren, tugging on his clothing with mock-fierce growls.

When she was about a month old he sometimes took her into his cabin where she liked to tease by scampering off with one of his socks, or a slipper. One evening, with the pup in the cabin, Chena, alone in the pen, howled. Lady responded—her first howl. She started with a bark, then sang in a rising, high-pitched, quavering glissando. After that both she and Chena howled frequently. Ren could count on both of them howling whenever he left Chena in the pen and took Lady into his cabin. He was delighted with this; it was pure wolf behavior—members of a scattered pack calling to one another. The two, firmly bonded, disliked being separated.

Whenever Ren went to the pen he emitted a shrill whistle to identify himself. At this, Lady wriggled, whined, jumped her front feet up and down in excitement, and ran to greet him. Sometimes Lady, whose eyesight was improving but still fuzzy, didn't react when he called her. He would sit and hold his arms out in a mock hug. This she could discern, and quickly learned to accept it as an invitation for a tussle and a belly-rub. She would then leap across the yard to him.

Ren didn't want the pup habituated to other humans, and never allowed visitors. His cabin was off-road and a couple of miles from the outskirts of town. A solid board fence isolated the pup from the rest of the world, except for airplanes that constantly buzzed overhead. At first Lady was nervous at the sound, but she soon ignored all but the closest and noisiest.

Ren searched scientific literature to determine the best age to introduce Lady to a wild pack. Several scientists who had studied wolf pups concluded that friendly relations were easily established with wolf pups less than three months of age; after that it becomes increasingly more difficult. At three months, one scientist concluded, it is difficult for wolf pups to form new social attachments. Ren decided he must release her in early August, when she would be ten to eleven weeks old.

Lady became stronger and more active each day; she ran, jumped, tumbled, and played constantly. She chewed anything chewable, from Chena, to Ren's clothing, sticks, rocks, her doghouse, her own feet and tail. Her howls became more musical, although she always accompanied a howl with the yip that is typical of wolf pups. Adults drop the bark or yip.

He knew from the literature that wolf pups need much affection at an early age—affection they receive from their mother for their first three weeks, and after that from all members of the pack. Lady received an abundance of affection from both Chena and Ren.

Lady weighed thirty pounds at the end of July. Sadly, Ren concluded, it was time for him to complete his experiment and release her. She was the most delightful pet and companion he could remember—affectionate, trusting, amusing, and intelligent. He was aware that the brain of a wolf is about a third larger than that of a dog of equal size. Did this partially explain Lady's obvious great intelligence? He suspected it was so.

He would miss her. He also feared his experiment would fail, that she would be killed by wild wolves.

WHEN I WAS a boy in California, Ernest Thompson Seton's writings about wild animals had a profound impact on me. His tale "Lobo, King of Currumpaw," was one of the first ever to cast a sympathetic glow on North American wolves. Over a period of five years during the early 1890s, the 150-pound gray wolf, Lobo, and five followers, including his nearly white mate, Blanca, killed more than 2,000 cattle, horses, and sheep on the Currumpaw range ("Corrumpa" on current maps) of northeastern New Mexico (near the town of Clayton). One night in November, 1893, Blanca and another member of the pack killed 250 sheep, apparently for the fun of it, for they didn't eat any of the flesh. A bounty of $1,000 was posted for Lobo when a dollar was worth many times what it is today. Lobo repeatedly avoided traps and poison used by professional wolfers who sought to capture him and his band.

Seton, a writer and a naturalist/hunter, and one-time head of the Boy Scouts of America, using 130 wolf traps, managed to trap and kill Blanca. He then used her body and scent to lure the upset and mourning Lobo into his traps. "His heartbroken wailing was piteous to hear. It was sadder than I could possibly have believed," Seton wrote of Lobo when the big wolf discovered the place where Blanca had died. The experience changed Seton's attitude toward wolves, who, in his early life, had been an avid wolf hunter.

I thought his novel, *Rolf in the Woods* was non-fiction. Seton's oft-used phrase, "the Great North Woods" conjured visions of a vast, coniferous forest stretching across North America somewhere far north of Petaluma. I was not yet ten when I decided that was where I belonged, and that I wanted to work with wildlife.

My father, who taught agriculture in the Petaluma high school, graduated from Oregon State College (now University) at Corvallis. In 1942, after I graduated from high school, he visited Professor R. E. Dimick, head of the Fish and Game Department at OSC, to learn for me about the discipline of wildlife management, a then relatively-new profession in the United States. When he returned home he encouraged me to enroll in Dimick's department.

We were at war. I was 17, under draft age, and too young to enlist in the military. I realize now I was too young for almost any serious enterprise; I was hardly aware of the momentous world events taking place around me.

I didn't distinguish myself as a student that fall of 1942 as one of Prof Dimick's students; poor high school attitudes don't earn good college grades. But I learned enough in Dimick's freshman Wildlife Conservation class to know I wanted to earn a degree in fish and game management.

The unsettled state of the world permeated the campus and I was uneasy being a student while other males were in the military or working in war-related jobs.

I completed the quarter and at Christmas returned to Petaluma where I lived at home and worked for ninety five cents an hour unloading freight cars of bulk grain, sacking it, and piling it in a warehouse ready for sale.

In March, 1943, a month before my eighteenth birthday, with my father signing his permission, I enlisted in the navy and went off to war. Like many of the young men who fought in World War II, only in recent decades have I appreciated the significance of the colossal events of which I was a tiny part.

꩜

IN JULY 1918, at the age of twenty-nine, Frank Glaser enlisted in the army to serve in World War I. Because of his skill with a rifle he was trained as a sniper. He was issued a heavy-barreled .30-06 Springfield equipped with a telescopic sight with which he shot thousands of practice rounds on a firing range at Camp Dodge, Iowa. After that he never owned a rifle that wasn't equipped with a telescopic sight. The war ended before he was sent overseas, and he was discharged in April, 1919, at Valdez, where he had enlisted.

During the winter of 1919–20, when construction on the Valdez Trail was suspended for winter, and he had no market for game meat, Glaser hauled freight and passengers with a dog team between ends of steel on the under-construction Alaska Railroad (construction started both at Seward and Fairbanks, and there was still a gap). Passengers rode the railroad from Fairbanks to Healy . From there they paid dog mushers like Glaser $100 to taxi them the 122 miles to Talkeetna, where they again boarded the railroad for the remainder of the journey to the coastal town of Seward and a ship "Outside" (to the states).

It was here that Glaser first encountered teams of wolf-dogs and learned their potentials and shortcomings. It was probably at this time he decided he wanted a wolf-dog team of his own. He noticed that drivers of some wolf-dogs were gentle but firm with their teams, and the animals worked well. They were powerful and intelligent, but their wolf traits were always present; they often fought among themselves, and their drivers had to be wary while handling them. Wolf-dog teams owned by drivers who were quick to use whip and club were considered dangerous; other drivers avoided them.

Here Glaser became acquainted with the Malemute Kid (Frank Tondro) who was made famous by writings of Jack London. Glaser admired the Kid's dog-handling ability, and was impressed by his obvious affection for his dogs. When readying for a freight run, the Kid went to each of his twenty seven animals and put harnesses on while they were tied to their houses. The dogs howled and barked with excitement. He then turned them loose and stood by his towline, holding a big blacksnake whip, ready to stop fights. He called the leader first and hooked him to the towline. The leader leaned into the towline, keeping it taut, as the Kid called each of the other members of the team, one at a time, and snapped them into place.

The Kid's eighteen-foot freight sled could be loaded with more than 1,000 pounds, but when he yelled, "Come alive there Tony," to his leader and the team leaped into action, it skidded down the trail almost as if it were empty.

During summer 1922, Glaser helped U. S. Biological Survey field man Olaus Murie build a caribou trap out of poles in Mount McKinley National Park. The next summer Glaser, with Olaus and Olaus' brother Adolf, caught half a dozen young caribou bulls in the trap. The caribou were eventually released on Nunivak Island in the Bering Sea to breed with domestic reindeer in an attempt to increase their size.

During the two summers he worked with the Murie brothers Glaser was impressed with the great high, treeless ridges in the Savage River area near Mount McKinley National Park. No one lived there. Healy, on the Alaska Railroad, the nearest town, was eighteen miles away.

By 1923, Frank Glaser had killed about 280 Dall rams, and dozens of moose and caribou, and sold them to the Alaska Road Commission. Completion of the Alaska Railroad from the seacoast to Fairbanks now made it practical for meat to be shipped by sea from the states and on to Fairbanks by rail, ending the need for market hunting.

In the spring of 1924, with several loaded pack dogs, he walked 250 miles through the wilderness from Black Rapids Roadhouse to Savage River. His goal was to establish a trapline. To Frank Glaser, the Savage River country was paradise. It is superb caribou, moose, grizzly bear and Dall sheep range, with an abundance of furbearers. Savage River and nearby spring-fed Fish Creek run clear, and grayling were so abundant he annually dried hundreds of them he caught with a fly rod, using them to feed his sled dogs.

There, on the bank of Savage River, close by the great Alaska Range, he built a 14 by 16 log cabin. He cut spruce logs and skidded them to the site with his dog team. He chinked the logs with sphagnum moss, and covered the roof with sod. The floor was dirt, which soon compacted as hard as cement; in time he covered it with bear and moose hides. A cast-iron kitchen range, which he hauled in by dog sled, provided heat and was wonderful for cooking and baking. The cabin came under the winter shadow of the mountains on November 18. The sun didn't shine on it again until January 10.

Months often passed without Glaser seeing another person, but he was by nature a loner, and this didn't bother him. He lived largely from the land, subsisting on moose, caribou, wild sheep, and grayling. He trapped mostly red foxes in their various color phases. Trapping season opened in mid-November, closed February first.

During the trapping season of 1924–25, although he ran his traplines almost daily, he never saw a wolf track, nor did he hear a wolf howl all that winter. He had virtually no experience or knowledge of wolves. He blamed the scarcity of wolves on market hunters who, for decades, had customarily scattered strychnine baits around caches of meat. This killed not only wolves, but bears, foxes, wolverines, marten, mink, and any other animal that picked up a piece of sheep gut-fat loaded with poison.

With the end of market hunting and cessation of poisoning, wolves and other furbearers increased. A few wolves showed up in Glaser's Savage River country during the winter of 1925–26. Even more wolves were there during the following winter, and he frequently saw them chasing caribou. Remains of wolf-killed caribou became fairly common.

The campaign: The Black Pack

JERRY HANSON PHONED Pat one November evening with a request. "We need you. Can you come to an evening meeting?"

"Who is 'we'?" she asked

"The National Wildlife Savers Foundation."

"I usually correct papers and prepare class work evenings," she temporized.

"It's important. The state of Alaska is planning to kill more wolves from airplanes. We need support to stop them," he explained.

She remembered her revulsion at the scene of the wolf being shot from an airplane.

"But what can I do?"

"Come to the meeting and find out," he challenged.

Jerry, who was president of the Boston chapter, presided. About forty people attended. Most were in their 30s and 40s. All were members of TNWSF.

"For years Alaskans have been shooting wolves from airplanes," he said, emotionally. "Their Fish and Game Department is again making plans to kill wolves near Fairbanks. They tried last winter but they were stopped by a court order. They are following the same pattern of other states in trying to kill all their wolves. This has resulted in extinction of the wolf in all but two or three states of the South 48. If allowed to continue it will inevitably result in extinction of the wolf in Alaska," he said.

"Environmental and animal rights organizations such as ours are organizing a letter-writing and legal campaign to stop the wolf slaughter in Alaska. We are in touch with about 250 other animal rights groups; most are gearing up to fight the battle with us.

"We want letters from school kids (Jerry looked at Pat when he said this), and others, as well as from our members. Letters should be addressed to Governor Jay Hammond, Juneau, Alaska, or to Commissioner James Brooks, Alaska Department of Fish and Game, Juneau. It wouldn't hurt to send copies to President Ford."

"What should the letters say?" a member asked.

"Say you are opposed to killing wolves," Jerry answered. "Alaska hasn't learned from the experience of other states. The wolf is a valuable animal, and is more beneficial than harmful. It kills only the sick and weak, leaving the herds healthy. Alaska's moose and caribou are overhunted by sport hunters, and the wolf is getting the blame. We oppose hunting, which is simply an excuse for people to kill something. Can you imagine anyone wanting to kill a moose? We think all hunting should be abolished. But our concern now is with Alaska's wolves.

"Predators are at the top of the food chain, and they are vulnerable to persecution, for they are naturally less abundant than their prey. The black and grizzly bears are also under attack in Alaska. They are supposedly killing moose that sportsmen want to kill. So far they haven't started shooting them from airplanes," he said with deliberate sarcasm.

"Letters should be strong, to the point, and no longer than one page," Jerry concluded. "And one more thing to mention; there is no record of healthy wolves attacking humans in North America."

During the coffee hour that followed, Pat met two medical doctors, several lawyers, an accountant, a college professor, and many housewives. Education level was high, she concluded, after listening to the conversation that swirled around her. Feelings of indignation ran high at Alaska's brazen wolf killing policy.

She talked with other teachers and learned their classes too had been visited by Lobo. "Isn't he the most beautiful animal?" one commented, eyes bright with emotion.

Pat bought envelopes and stamps with her own money for the children's letters. Next day she told her students Alaska's wolves were being slaughtered and needed their letters to help stop it.

She made Xerox copies of her favorites: [*Author's Note: These are actual letters received by Governor Hammond; some of the names have been changed.*]

Dear Govener. My name is Jennie. Please help the wolfs. One came
to our school and we saw a movie about wolfs being extinct. The
wolf that came was nice everyone petted it. Its name was Lobo.
Wolfs are really nice if you get them trained right. And they do
not attack people. Please help the wolfs.

Love, Jennie

Dear Governor Hammond: Since I saw the program at school I
really thought about killing of wolves and I want people to stop
killing so many wolves. I know people have rights, but the wolves
are almost extinct. My favorite animal is the wolf.

Sincerely, John

Govner Hammond: We've been thinking the matter over very carefully about the wolf problem up there. And I think I have come up
with a solution. Why don't you catch some of the animals put them
on a ship and send them to Siberia? But do this at night.

Love, Davy

In mid-November Jerry called Pat again and asked, "Can you
come help us for a few hours tomorrow evening?"

"Doing what?"

"Opening letters and adding. Five or six other members will
be here."

The letters were contributions to the Foundation in response to an
emergency Alaska wolf-killing alert. Ten thousand letters had been
sent from the Boston chapter of the foundation to local sympathizers
with a message designed to pry them loose from money.

The letter read, "Despite lack of data and admitting that illegal hunting is a serious problem, the Alaska Department of Fish
and Game persists in claiming the wolf is the main cause for the
dwindling of moose and caribou, rather than owning up to the
true causes, over-hunting and severe winters.

"They now plan to kill more of these marvelous misunderstood
creatures, shooting them from the air with shotguns. All because
hunters want the fun of killing more moose. We need your letters
and contributions to help fight this disastrous state program."

She could hardly believe the pile of boxes holding unopened
envelopes on the big library table. Most held checks, but some
had bills ranging from a dollar to fifty dollars. The average check
was for twenty dollars.

The volunteers opened letters and tallied the donations. The mailing had brought an almost fifteen percent response; the 1,500 letters held slightly more than $30,000.

Pat was amazed.

"Normally, we get about a three percent response," an excited Jerry said. He was clearly pleased. "Alaska plays right into our hands when they announce they're going to kill wolves! Every time! People get emotional over wolves like no other animal, and they send money. It's wonderful!"

"You sound as if you're pleased at what Alaska is doing," she said, reproachfully.

"I'm not pleased with the wolf killing, of course," he said, hastily. "I am pleased when they announce it in advance. It puts money in our hands so we can fight them."

Pat had a disturbing, idle thought; her New England prudence nudged her conscience. This National Wildlife Savers Foundation could be a profitable business. Was it legitimate?

The cash and checks were soon stuffed into bank bags ready for deposit. As volunteers started to leave, Jerry asked Pat to remain for a moment.

"How sincere are you in wanting to save wolves?" he asked, as he locked the bank bags into a safe, turned lights off and prepared to leave.

Startled, she said, "Why, I'm very interested in wolves and I truly want to help. I thought that was obvious."

"I have a special assignment for you," he said. "You're the ideal person for it."

"Well, what is it?"

"We need a fresh face to appear before the Alaska Board of Game in Fairbanks next month. We'd like you to go."

"Go to Alaska? Me? Why me?"

"I'll be blunt. John Grant, our representative in Alaska, is supposed to be studying wolves, but he never gets results. He spends a lot of money, but he hasn't done the job we expected of him, and we're dropping him. He isn't effective. When he does get information, Alaska's authorities refuse to listen to him.

"We think a young, pretty, intelligent school teacher from the east coast—you—could make a better impression for the Foundation at this meeting. We need someone other than Grant to talk to Alaska's new Board of Game."

"Oh, I couldn't. I just couldn't," she objected.

"But you could," he said. "The meeting is during your school's Christmas vacation. We'll pay all expenses. All you have to do is sign up for the public hearing and tell the board in five or ten minutes why Alaska shouldn't kill wolves. You can read your statement. If you're sincere, the board will sense it. You can express what all of us feel."

"I can't make a decision on something that important without thinking about it," she objected. They were now outside. He walked her to her car.

"I'll give you twenty-four hours. A decision now will give whoever goes about two weeks to prepare a statement. We'll help all we can. Call me tomorrow evening," he said. "Please do this. It's very important. Someone has to speak for the wolf."

"I'll give it serious thought," she promised.

"I'll expect your call," he said, unlocking the door of his luxurious BMW. Pat wondered briefly about his expensive car, but his request for her to go to Alaska pushed the thought away.

Pat called her long-time friend Allen Potter and they agreed to have dinner together. She had talked with him about her sudden interest in wolves. Now she wanted to use him as a sounding board. Should she go to Fairbanks?

Allen was not an outdoorsman. He owned a small glass business, providing windows for homes, and replacing broken auto windshields. Bowling was his thing; he and his employees had a team and they were deeply involved in local tournaments.

Earlier he had listened to Pat's story of hearing wolves howl, and had paid attention as she enthusiastically discussed Lobo and her class's excitement over wolves. He was sympathetic, and encouraged her, although it was clear he didn't understand or share her enthusiasm.

They were sipping coffee after their meal in a quiet corner of a restaurant they often visited when Pat told him she was thinking of flying to Fairbanks to try to save Alaska's wolves.

He stared. "Pat, you've lost your mind," he said, sharply. Normally he was mild mannered.

"I don't think so, Allen," she had rejoined. "I've found something I'm really interested in, and I think I'm going to follow up on it."

"But, wolves?" he said, clearly puzzled. "Why wolves? There aren't any wolves in Massachusetts, are there?" he asked. "Alaska is so far away, and it's really none of our business what they do with their wolves."

"Allen, it *is* our business. Wolves have been wiped out in all but a few states. Alaska still has wolves, and we've got to see they aren't wiped out there too."

He shook his head. "I don't understand, Pat."

He escorted her to her doorway to say good night. "I wish you'd change your mind, Pat," he said. "You're sudden enthusiasm for wolves puzzles me."

"You don't really understand me, do you, Allen," she said, sadly.

As she prepared for bed she thought, "Poor Allen. You're locked into your little world and can't see beyond the city limits of Boston."

Later she realized it had been a final goodbye. She felt a loss, because he had been her link with the past, with her early school years, and with her parents and his as neighbors. All were gone, and memories of their school years together were fading.

⌒

"DON'T GET EMOTIONALLY involved with individual animals. Your responsibility is to populations, not individuals," I warned my students. Ren remembered, but concluded that no one, unless he had a heart of stone, could raise a wolf pup without becoming emotionally attached. He decided, from subtle wording of their reports (and unabashed wording of some), that virtually every scientist who had raised one or more wolf pups had succumbed to the wiles, innocence, and charm of their captives.

Five years earlier, while on a low-altitude June survey flight, Ren had skimmed over one of the foothills of the great Alaska Range and surprised a pack of black wolves at a den dug into the south facing slope. The four adults scattered at the sudden appearance of his plane, and the litter of five pups had fled to the den.

He later returned, landed on a lake on the north side of the hill where the den was located, and climbed to find a depression where he could remain out of sight, yet have a clear view of the den. Like many wolf packs, this one often returned to the same den to raise pups, and for three springs he had frequently returned to study the behavior and habits of this pack, which he called The Black

Pack. He spent hours with binoculars and spotting scope, lying comfortably on his belly scribbling in a notebook, often smiling at the antics of pups, and describing behavior of the adults.

This was the pack he hoped would adopt Lady. If the adoption was successful, Lady, whose color was now gray (like all wolf pups, she was dark brown at birth), could be distinguished from the blacks. He thought he could land his float-equipped Super Cub on the tiny pond a few hundred feet south of the base of the den hill.

He knew the Black Pack would leave the den in mid-July when the current litter was about eight weeks old. Their mother would lead the pups some distance to a surface "den"—a woodsy place known to scientists as a rendezvous site.

There the pups would roam within an acre or two as they matured. Adults of the pack would take turns baby-sitting them while other members sought prey—mostly moose and caribou calves—to feed the pups and themselves. The adult wolves would carry meat to the site in their jaws, or in their stomachs, bringing the food up at will for the ever-hungry pups.

Ren had found the rendezvous site of the Black Pack the first year he had observed them. They had returned to the same site each year. He was gambling they would repeat this year, and he was fairly sure the adults would be within hearing distance of the pond.

He chose a clear, calm, August day to introduce Lady to the pack. He lightened his Super Cub by removing emergency gear and draining the gas tanks, leaving only enough fuel to safely make the flight. He spread a caribou hide, hair up, on the back seat—trying to eliminate human odors—and attached a web harness designed to hold Lady in place.

With a heavy heart he prepared a hypodermic syringe with Sernylan to immobilize her, and another with Promazine, a tranquilizer, and went to the wolf pen. He had worn rubber gloves while handling Lady during the previous week, hoping to leave minimal human scent on Lady's fur. She responded to his whistle with her usual joyful leaping and capering, tail wagging, and welcoming bows. She had recently become more vocal, and she "talked" to him at every greeting.

He played with her for a few minutes, knowing it would be the last time. A few days earlier she had invented a new way of teasing him; she had discovered his baseball-type cap and had lifted it from his head and trotted around and around him with it in her jaws. When he acted cross and insisted she return it, she gently dropped it on his lap.

During this last play time, she again stole his cap and leaped and capered around and around him; she enjoyed the teasing, he enjoyed her intelligence and playful spirit. When he demanded she return it, she stopped gamboling and dropped the cap on his lap, giving him a sweeping glance, head tilted to one side as if to say, "Ok, boss, there's your silly cap, if you insist."

Finally, he firmly rolled her over onto her back into the submissive position a superior wolf in a pack might impose. He was betraying her trust, and he felt terrible. He didn't know if Chena had taught her the appropriate behavior, or if it was inborn; whatever, she froze in a belly-up position while he quickly inserted the needle and pushed the plunger. Her instant submission gave him hope. Submission is basic to wolf behavior, and each pack member except for the alpha male and female must frequently exhibit it.

She was unconscious within a couple of minutes. As he carried the sedated puppy toward the gate, an upset Chena circled him, whining anxiously.

He hardened his mind. "I can't be emotional about this," he told himself. At the plane he gently laid her on the caribou skin and tied the web around her to keep her in place, then gave her a second shot of tranquilizer—enough to last, he hoped. He hated to think how she would react if she revived in the airplane. She had not been outside her pen or his cabin since her eyes had opened.

He started the engine, filed a flight plan by radio, and eased the plane into the air; he was pleased when the lightened Cub leaped from the water in a shorter distance than usual. He would need that extra performance.

He didn't circle the pond as he normally would before landing; he wanted to land and leave with as little disturbance as possible. With engine idling and full flaps, he dropped the floats onto the water at the pond's edge. He taxied ashore nearest the secluded rendezvous site and pulled the mixture control to stop the engine. In hip boots he waded into the shallows, turned the plane, and pulled the heels of the floats ashore. Wearing rubber gloves, he carried the unconscious Lady to a dry, clear spot about two hundred yards from the pond and gently put her down. He wanted to be sure she didn't encounter the pond until fully awake; a partially tranquilized but mobile animal can drown.

Her pulse was strong. He lingered, kneeling beside her and stroking her soft fur gently.

"Goodbye, little girl. Good luck to you. I wish you a long and happy life," he murmured.

Tears welled. With an effort he straightened, wiped his eyes, and hurried to the plane. He turned and looked back at the unconscious wolf pup, memories of his weeks of parenting tumbling through his head. He hated to leave her like this. With an effort he brought his thoughts back to what he had to do. He had never before landed on such a small pond. He'd need all his skill to get the plane safely off. He mustn't let emotions affect his flying.

The warm engine started immediately. With mixture full rich and throttle wide open, the little plane skittered across the water. The floats were on step and he was almost to the edge of the tiny pond when he yanked the flap handle and tweaked the stick back. The floats left the water and brushed against low willows, but he was safely airborne. Breathing a sigh of relief, he dropped the nose to gain speed then climbed to a safe altitude. He banked and flew within a hundred yards of the sidehill wolf den, but saw no wolves there. He hadn't expected to.

He reached the lake where he normally landed when studying the Black Pack, eased the plane onto the water, beached it, tied it down, and hurriedly hiked up the hill to his observation blind.

He instantly located Lady with his spotting scope, lying, still sedated, where he had left her. He felt guilty for treating her as an experiment; she had trusted him and now he was using her. And for what? At the moment his wolf pup research program seemed frivolous. He resisted the urge to rush down the hillside to comfort her when she awoke. He wanted to take her home and keep her as a companion. But, did he really want an adult wolf as a pet? He knew it wouldn't be fair to the wolf. There is no such animal as a domesticated wolf, even after many generations of captivity. Even well-socialized wolves have the psychology of a wild animal. When handled and housed as if they are dogs, problems usually develop for both people and the wolf.

"It's people who cause the problem, but the wolf that gets the bad press," he murmured. He remembered a Russian proverb; "You may feed the wolf all you want but he will always look toward the forest." His brain told him he didn't want, and should not have, a pet wolf, but his heart sang another tune.

Lady began to stir. First she raised her head groggily, then got to her feet, only to fall. She lay quietly for a time, then again struggled to her feet. She made it this time. She appeared sharp and clear in the spotting scope, and Ren saw her looking around, becoming aware of her surroundings. She staggered a few feet then sat. She remained sitting for some time. He knew she was bewildered. Where was the fence she had known all her life? Where was her beloved Chena? Where was Ren?

She walked drunkenly for another 20 or 30 feet, then sat again. She turned her head, staring at the strange surroundings. He could tell by the way she moved she was recovering from the drug. Then she crouched, tail between her legs. "She's terrified," he thought, disgusted with himself. He again resisted the urge to rush to her.

Then Lady did what lonely wolves do. She howled. It was a sad, long, quavering howl. Ren thought it expressed fear as well as loneliness.

But he exulted. This was what he had hoped for. Would wolves of the Black Pack hear her? Would they respond? Would they come to investigate? He wasn't even sure they were at their usual rendezvous site, which lay about half a mile away in a stand of old spruces, impossible to see into from the air. He hadn't dared check it out afoot before releasing Lady, fearing the pack would move if disturbed.

Ren heard no response to Lady's howl. She remained crouched, seemingly paralyzed with fear. She had been happily playing with Ren; suddenly she found herself here, in this strange place, alone. What must she be thinking?

Again she howled, with her usual accompanying puppy-yip. Ren scanned around her, searching for any member of the Black Pack. He saw nothing. The only howls came from Lady, who sounded very lonely indeed.

"I'm going to retrieve her if this doesn't work," he had told himself beforehand. He had foreseen the possibility. He didn't know where his experiment would go from here if she wasn't accepted by a pack, but he knew with certainty she couldn't survive without being adopted.

Then, through the spotting scope, he detected subtle movements in the grass and brush near Lady. A black wolf head poked out of the brush, peering toward the lonely puppy. Another head appeared a few feet away. Then two adult black wolves trotted cautiously into the open.

Lady howled again. The two wolves stopped and stood looking at her. Lady hadn't seen them. Ren guessed she was whimpering with fear and loneliness between howls, although she was too distant for him to hear. Then, as if on a signal, the two black wolves rushed to Lady.

Ren was almost afraid to watch. One bite and Lady would be dead. But there was no biting. Instead, the two sniffed at Lady.

Lady had leaped to her feet upon sight of the wolves. "She thinks its Chena," Ren guessed. As the wolves came closer she rolled over in a submissive posture. The two wolves sniffed at her. One licked her belly and between her hind legs. "That's what a wolf mother would do," Ren thought.

The two wolves sniffed and licked at Lady. She remained frozen on her back, but Ren could see her tail wagging.

The drama ended abruptly. At some signal unknown to Ren, Lady leaped to her feet and followed the two wolves. All three disappeared into the brush, trotting toward the Black Pack's rendezvous site.

⌒

MY WAR ENDED in August, 1945, and within a month I was again enrolled in the fish and game management courses at OSC, my fees now paid by the government through the G. I. Bill. The three-year hiatus in my education, plus exposure to the horrors of war, had converted a callow 17-year-old into a more serious but still unworldly youngster. Classroom competition was stiff, for other war-weary ex-servicemen flooded OSC's fish and game courses. During the war we had gained a new perspective on life. Most of us were thankful to be alive, and we appreciated the small things. Too, we found that learning was exciting and fulfilling—infinitely more pleasurable than fighting a war.

During the postwar years, fatherly Professor R.E. Dimick, conscientious and dedicated, fashioned his department into one of the finest in the nation. He and his staff, Professors Jay B. Long and Lee W. Kuhn, both of whom served overseas in the military during the war, saw to it that hundreds of students learned the importance of the scientific method. They provided us with the tools we needed to establish sound fisheries and wildlife conservation programs wherever we might go.

"No matter how biologically sound your management program might be, if the public doesn't understand it or back it, you'll get nowhere with it," preached Prof. Long. How right he was. I have often had wry thoughts how perfectly that advice fits Alaska's wolf management program. It doesn't matter what is true; it only matters what people believe is true.

"In managing any species of wildlife, your responsibility is to the population—all the animals of that species in a given area. Many of your problems will result because the public's perspective will focus on individual animals. You must look past individuals and focus on the population. Don't allow yourself to become emotionally involved with individual animals," warned Prof. Kuhn. He too was right.

"Conservation is preservation by wise use," we learned from Professor Dimick. A simple but profound concept.

At the end of my junior year, in the spring of 1947, I landed a summer job in Alaska as a Fishery Patrol Agent with the U.S. Fish and Wildlife Service. There I patrolled with a thirty-foot boat to enforce commercial salmon fishing regulations near Chignik, a tiny village on the thrusting storm-wracked Alaska Peninsula which lies between the North Pacific Ocean and the Bering Sea. It was then I probably lost my ability to ever live in happiness in a heavily populated and developed environment.

Chignik residents are cheerful, hardy Aleuts. Beyond the village and salmon canneries are alder-clad mountains and hills, the clear Chignik River, and big Chignik and Black Lakes. To this day it is still wild and unsettled by South Forty-eight standards.

My work at Chignik introduced me to people who still lived as part of the untouched land—not on tamed land that had been "domesticated" for human use.

Chignik lies in the heart of brown bear country. The hair on the back of my neck rose at my first sight of fresh six-by-fifteen-inch bear tracks on a sandy beach. The realization that these powerful half-ton coastal grizzly bears were wandering near the cabin where I lived brought an uneasiness that lasted for days, and I kept a rifle handy. I soon realized the bears were shy, for though I lived among them all summer, I saw the great lumbering creatures but half a dozen times, and then only at a distance.

One evening I counted more than a hundred bald eagles soaring overhead in a steady wind; some were so high they appeared as specks in my six power binoculars. (Counting mammals, birds, fish, becomes an ingrained habit with wildlife biologists; it's automatic, and though I have no need to do so now, I still start enumerating whenever I see a flock of birds, or any gathering of wild creatures).

At Chignik I encountered ptarmigan, the northern grouse that turns white in winter, and a coughing, growling, grunting wolverine, both new to me. Six-to-twelve-pound Dolly Varden char swarmed under the cannery docks, feeding on the salmon gurry (waste) dumped there. No baited hook or lure tempted them; I tried, as did some of the cannery workers.

I saw dozens of huge scows loaded to overflowing with freshly caught sockeye salmon. One afternoon in Chignik Lagoon, after an hour-long fight with rod and 50-pound test line, I landed a halibut that was five feet ten inches long—exactly as long as I am tall. I took it to one of the canneries where it tipped the scales at 180 pounds. I gave it to the cook, who welcomed it as a change from salmon.

At Chignik, I also saw for the first time in numbers almost beyond belief silver-scaled salmon swimming up a clear, deep river.

That four-month introduction to Alaska changed the course of my life.

IN OCTOBER OF 1924, as Frank Glaser was building his log cabin on the bank of Savage River, the Kuskokwim caribou herd of 400,000 to 500,000 wintered on the north slope of the Alaska Range in the fifty miles between the Savage and Toklat Rivers. Their presence became an annual event during the years Glaser spent at Savage River. That first winter it seemed as if every cow caribou had a calf, every Dall sheep ewe had a lamb, and every cow moose had one or two calves.

Accustomed to the almost constant wind at Black Rapids, he was delighted at the near lack of wind at Savage River. During most of November, temperatures ranged well below zero. December arrived with temperatures of 40 below and colder. Day after day in January the temperature was 50 to 60 below zero; once it reached

72 below. Because there was virtually no wind, it seemed warm to Glaser, despite the deep cold.

He trapped for only a few weeks that winter, yet in March he drove his dog team to Fairbanks with a sled load of fox, lynx, and mink furs which he sold for $2,600, big money in 1925.

From 1925 into the early 1930s, the fur of an ordinary blond or orange red fox brought from $15 to $100, while cherry reds (trade named "Kamchatka red") brought $100 to $200. Cross fox furs brought from $15 to $100; in the early years much more. Silver and black foxes brought from $25 to $300. Lynx furs brought $25. Dog team-driving fur buyers sometimes arrived at his cabin to buy Glaser's furs, paying cash.

After he had established his traplines, he figured on making at least $5,000 a year; in some years he made as much as $7,000. That is, until fur prices took a dive in the 1930s.

His expenses were negligible. A box of shotgun shells sold for $1.50 at Smith's Hardware in Fairbanks; a .30-30 rifle, with several boxes of cartridges, cost $15. Hunting guides were paid $10 a day by the occasional trophy hunter.

With the easy availability of game meat, Glaser could have done without most of the groceries he bought at Fairbanks and Healy. A few items from one of his lists from June, 1926, included: sweet chocolate, one pound cans, five cans, $2.10; Mazola oil, two half gallon cans, $1.95. Dry dates, two five pound packages, $1.20; peanut butter, ten two pound cans, $4.80; cube sugar, two five pound boxes, $1.00; two dozen cans evaporated milk, $2.00; bacon, five pounds $1.50; beans, ten pounds, ninety cents.

For several years during the late 1920s when his income was far beyond anything he needed, he kept a room year-round at the Nordale Hotel in Fairbanks, the cleanest and best place to stay in town. Most of the trappers and miners from the bush stayed at the Nordale.

Often, at the end of trapping season, he drove his dog team to Fairbanks, sold his furs, and boarded the dogs at either Van Bibber's or Ed Day's dog livery at the edge of town. Then he'd live at the Nordale while he shopped and visited for a month or more. He often drove his dog team into the business district. Traffic was no problem; in 1924 there were only 206 privately-owned automobiles in Fairbanks, and 1,116 in the entire Territory.

Hell breaks loose: Savage River wolves

In January, 1975, eight months before Pat York's visit to Algonquin Park, Bob Hinman announced that fifty wolves were to be killed by the state in Game Management Subunit 20A near Fairbanks to allow a depleted moose population to rebuild.

All hell broke loose.

Many Alaskans said that control was two years late. Others wanted to know why the control was limited to 20A when wolves were killing moose, caribou, sheep, and deer in other areas as well. Some Alaskans, mostly in Anchorage, the most urban of Alaska's population centers, objected to wolf control of any kind, saying the wolf has a right to live and to eat moose, and man should not interfere.

Newspaper headlines howled (pun intended). Alaska's newspapers and those of other states love any Alaska wolf controversy; their sole interest seems to be to sell papers. There is never any consideration that their frenzied reporting of a planned wolf control effort might adversely impact wildlife populations. Reporters will quote anyone on the issue, any time; whether they are qualified and knowledgeable is unimportant. The more sensational the quote, the better.

Typical was the headline in the *Anchorage Times*: "STATE DECLARES WAR ON WOLVES."

Soon various anti-hunting and wolf defenders from other states started their wolf-protecting campaigns. Using the wolf control program as a wedge to pry money from contributors, they wrote a blizzard of begging letters to their sympathizers; "Send money to save Alaska's wolves!"

Next, they had their members bombard Alaska with letters, telegrams, telephone calls. Their messages to letters-to-the-editor columns in Alaska's newspapers, to the governor, and to the Department of Fish and Game, were all much alike; man has no right to interfere with other animals; Alaska should consider itself fortunate to have wolves; Alaska is making the same terrible mistake other states have made; doesn't Alaska know that wolves are endangered? Wolves and their prey have lived together for millions of years, and man has no business interfering with this wonderful relationship; wolves are beneficial because they eat only the sick and weak; animals should have the same rights as man.

Many of the writers asserted that aerial hunting of wolves, for any reason, is despicable and unsportsmanlike; wolves are intelligent animals of the highest order, with feelings, families, and complex social structure, and it is arrogant of man to even consider killing them. From the tone of their letters, many non-Alaskans seemed to think Alaska is an oversized zoo.

I wrote my former student, Game Division Regional Supervisor Bob Hinman, at Fairbanks, asking for details of the plan.

He spelled it out in a three-page letter. Severe winters, human hunters and wolves had combined to seriously reduce moose numbers in Game Management Subunit 20A which lies near Fairbanks. The aerial hunting was to be by private pilots on state contract, under supervision of state biologists. The wolf carcasses and pelts were to remain property of the state. Carcasses were to be necropsied to determine age, sex, size, condition, presence or absence of disease/parasites, and reproductive information. This would continue the long-term studies on wolves started by the federal government well before the 1959 arrival of statehood.

The 6,500-square-mile subunit (about one percent of the land area of Alaska, and a subunit of one of the twenty-six game management units in Alaska) is one of the most productive interior Alaska hunting areas. Slightly larger than the state of Connecticut, it lies between peaks of the rugged Alaska Range and the Tanana River, which flows past Fairbanks. It includes lakes, rivers, and rugged foothills of the Alaska Range. Occasional cabins, trails, and mines are scattered across it. There are no roads, no cities. Grizzly and black bear are reasonably abundant, and the area is used by several thousand caribou. It is excellent wolf habitat. It is also important as a food producer in that it provides an annual source of meat for many people in communities such as Healy, Nenana, Fairbanks and Delta Junction, who also consider their hunts an important recreation.

Hinman wrote me that in the late 1950s the unit was home to about 12,000 moose, and their numbers were increasing. At the time the federal U.S. Fish and Wildlife Service (FWS) was carrying on a Territory-wide program of wolf control. Wolves in GMU 20A were killed by poison and shot from FWS planes. Few moose were killed by hunters, because access to the unit was difficult; ATVs (all-terrain vehicles), snow machines, and jet powered boats (for shallow streams) were still in the future.

Deep snow and prolonged 40 to 60 degree below zero temperatures during winter 1965–66 killed many moose in 20A; the severe winter of 1966–67 again killed many. At this point there were an estimated 5,000 to 6,000 moose, or about half the number found seven or eight years earlier.

The next three winters were normal, and moose rapidly increased, as they will when there is abundant food and cover, and little predation. Then came the record-breaking winter of 1970–71, with exceptionally deep snow and severe cold. Moose numbers dropped to between 4,000 and 6,000.

In the late 1960s, hunters from Fairbanks and other communities started to reach into Unit 20A with snow machines, jet boats, and ATVs, and the annual moose kill increased. A domestic meat shortage in 1973, with accompanying high meat prices, increased local demand for moose meat. That year, 1,515 hunters killed 710 moose in 20A.

Department biologists recommended the one-hundred-day moose season be reduced to eighty days. The Board of Fish and Game (BFG) did the department one better by cutting it to fifty days.

About that time strange figures started popping up in reports from biologists making aerial counts of moose in the unit.

After the severe winter of 1970–71 moose numbers should have rebounded as they did after the previous severe winters. They didn't.

Because of the tough 1970–71 winter it wasn't surprising to find relatively few calves in November, 1971 (27 calves/100 cows): cows on the ragged edge of death may resorb or abort fetuses, and the calves that are born are likely to be small and weak with poor survival rates.

The November 1972 calf/cow ratio of 38:100 was encouraging, suggesting that moose numbers were rebounding.

But in November 1973 biologists found only 22 calves per 100 cows. It was apparent that moose calves were dying before their first winter. When November 1974 calf counts declined further to only 18 per 100 cows, it became even more obvious.

Bob Hinman, Ren Smith, Steve Acorn, and other department biologists who worked in 20A suspected wolf predation was the most likely cause. They set out to determine if their suspicions were correct. Was it really wolves, or some other lethal factor or factors, causing the calf mortality?

Hinman wrote me, "Our aerial surveys last winter (1973–74) resulted in an estimated wolf population in 20A of about 175, in about twenty one packs."

How does one count wolves in such a vast area? It requires experience and intimate knowledge of wolves as well as familiarity with the region in which they live. In winter, most wolves occur in discrete packs. During aerial surveys on clear days, wolves seen, and wolf tracks in snow, are counted, usually from two to five days after fresh snowfall. Fresh trails are followed until the pack is located, or at least until the pack fans out (wolves commonly travel single file), so the number in the pack can be determined. Pilots, as well as observers, must be knowledgeable in lupine habits.

If while flying you see wolf tracks in the snow, which direction are they moving? Not easy to tell without experience. To help locate packs for accurate total counts, one or two wolves in some packs were tranquilized by darting them from a helicopter and fitting them with radio collars which emitted a signal which allowed biologists with a locater receiver to home in on them. Ren also knew from years of experience in the area the approximate territorial boundaries of many of the packs.

Local trappers, hunters, and pilots also provide information on wolf numbers. Wolf harvests are closely monitored—every wolf shot or trapped must be registered with the department. Thus the population of wolves and their harvest in 20A was closely monitored.

Bob Hinman's letter continued, "Based on our early winter aerial counts of moose, which includes a cow-calf ratio, the 175 wolves in 20A are killing, annually, 300 to 400 calves and 300 to 400 adult moose. The current moose population is only 2,500 to

3,000. At these population levels this loss is sufficient to prevent restoration of moose to former numbers: not enough calves are reaching adulthood to replace dying mature moose. When more moose die than are recruited into a population, the total number of moose decreases. That's simple mathematics. Currently there is one wolf for about every seventeen moose.

"Legal trapping and ground hunting has annually removed thirty to forty wolves from 20A. If we are to effect any control on the wolves, we must remove something over fifty percent, which means during the state program we want to remove an additional fifty. This, with the normal trapping and ground hunting harvest, should result in removal of about half the wolves, or around eighty," he said.

"Our target is to rebuild the moose herd to 8,000 or 9,000 through curtailed hunting of moose, and fewer wolves. We are also concerned about the Delta caribou herd in Unit 20A. It's down to about 2,200 animals despite no hunting them for some years, and it appears to be decreasing.

"We plan to begin removing wolves February 20," his letter concluded.

From a biological standpoint, the plan for the state to remove fifty wolves from huge 20A was insignificant. There were an esti-mated 8,000 to 10,000 wolves in Alaska (although some biologists estimated as many as 15,000); the 50 wolves the state planned to remove was only .005 percent of the probable statewide popula-tion. They were to be removed from less than one percent of the land area of the state. After eighty wolves were removed (50 by the state, and the usual 30 or 40 by hunters and trappers) there would still be about 80 wolves in 20A.

Wildlife experts know that wolves replenish themselves swiftly if sufficient prey is available; thirty or even forty percent of a wolf population can be removed in the fall, only to have their numbers bounce back to the original numbers by the next fall. Adult females produce an average of five pups annually. Sometimes two litters are produced by a pack; rarely three.

The uproar resulting from the state's announcement brought repercussions from every direction. The state Senate Resources Committee scheduled a hearing, ". . .because of demands for action from the general public. People feel the Fish and Game Depart-ment's plans are not enough to solve the wolf problem," said State

Senator John Butrovich, R-Fairbanks, and Senator John Huber, D-Fairbanks, members of the committee.

Butrovich said, "I'm personally against aerial hunting of wolves, but something has to be done soon. They are getting worse and worse. I've lived here all my life, and spent a lot of time in the woods. Until recently I could count on my two hands the number of wolves I have actually seen—they always hear or smell you coming and stay clear.

"Now they're coming right into town, eating dogs and roaming in packs, cutting into the moose numbers," he continued. "Sooner or later they're going to run across somebody's little kid, and it will come right down here on us in the legislature if nothing has been done."

At the hearing, held in Juneau February 7, Bob Hinman was grilled by the committee for several hours. In the end he told the senators, "Hunters with planes can reasonably expect to kill the wolves efficiently and humanely. Weather will determine how long the job will take. We firmly believe the action complies with our state's constitutional requirement of use, development, and maintenance on the sustained yield principle for both moose and wolves."

Bill Waugaman, a long-time hunting guide of Fairbanks, testifying for the Interior Wildlife Association of Alaska, told the committee that airplane hunting probably wouldn't be able to take all the wolves necessary. "The state should be prepared to use a helicopter for the remainder of the job," he advised.

Waugaman said wolves had killed at least forty dogs, a goat, a pet moose, and two horses in the Fairbanks area during the current winter. "It's getting so bad in Fairbanks that my kids are afraid to come home from school," he said.

Darrell Farmen, a hunting guide testifying for the Alaska Professional Hunters Association, also argued for wolf control, but he said, "I can't think of anything that would stir up controversy quicker than use of a helicopter."

He said, "An airplane is the best for hunting wolves. Trapping and ground hunting are no more effective for wolf control than charging hell with a bucket of water."

The only person at the hearing who objected to the control program was Juneau resident Frederick Cohen, who said, "Winter kills, loss of habitat, and hunting is more destructive to game than wolves. Predator control upsets delicate population balances. Elimination of wolves has not helped game populations elsewhere."

Cohen argued that game populations are cyclical and that nature has its own population control programs.

On February 19, a hearing was held in Superior court in Anchorage on a motion to prevent the state's aerial hunt in 20A. The complaint, filed by the Fairbanks Environmental Center, Inc., and Friends of the Earth, Inc., plus several residents of Anchorage and Fairbanks, was a shotgun attack, listing many reasons why the control should not take place. "We fear the wolf population will suffer permanent damage and will never recover from the kill," the complaint said. And ". . . the department's program is unlawful, wrongful, arbitrary, capricious, and an abuse of their discretions and harmful to the rights to and of the plaintiffs.."

An Anchorage newspaper shrieked, "JUDGE TO DECIDE ON EXTERMINATION."

Bob Hinman was called to testify. For three hours before a packed courtroom he reviewed the situation for Superior Court Judge Edmund Burke. He summarized, "The decision for the department to remove about fifty wolves from 20A by aerial hunting was arrived at by extensive meetings and work with my Fairbanks professional staff, as well as wolf experts from Juneau.

"We need to start the program as soon as possible. We need fresh snow which makes it possible to track wolves. Our window of opportunity for this is late February and March," he said. "We intend to rebuild moose and caribou herds back to levels where they can support both hunting by humans, as well as a healthy population of wolves."

Judge Burke ordered a temporary halt to the state-sponsored hunt. He called the program sound game management, but, he concluded, there appeared to be unresolved legal questions about the authority of the department to remove the wolves.

The Alaska Chapter of the Sierra Club, in a letter to Governor Jay Hammond, charged that the department was basing its estimate of 175 wolves in 20A on a mere thirty two hours of aerial surveys taken in 1973, during which only twenty wolves were sighted.

"The controversy is a classic example of game managers bowing to local political pressure and undertaking a control program that cannot be justified by professional standards of wildlife management," a spokesman for the Sierra Club was quoted by a news reporter.

John Grant, the TNWSF wolf biologist, gained his usual newspaper headlines, mostly because he was controversial and invariably at odds with the department. He was also interviewed on a Fairbanks TV news broadcast.

"I flew several hundred hours in chartered planes over 20A," he told the interviewer. "The department's figures are all wrong. There aren't that many wolves there, and there are far more moose than they are telling the public. Also, my counts of moose calves in November are totally different from those of the department. I counted at least forty calves per hundred cows in November. They're exaggerating and making up figures so they can get the wolf kill they want. And if they get to kill wolves there, no telling where it'll stop. They'll be killing wolves all over Alaska," he predicted.

In a news release in late February, Hinman responded to charges that the program was hastily and poorly conceived and based on local hysteria. "Local hysteria, if there is such a thing, had nothing to do with our decision," he said. "The decision was based on our management goals for the area which call for maximum recreational opportunity— the opportunity to see wildlife in good numbers, and high quality hunting.

"To be consistent with these goals, we have to manage moose in 20A so the population stays near the carrying capacity of the land," he said. "It's far below that now, and the only option to us— rather than wait many years for a possible increase in moose—is to begin wolf control.

"The Department took the position several years ago that whenever there's a conflict between humans and wolves for the use of prey, the wolves will be managed to reduce the conflict. The position paper was approved by the Board of Fish and Game. This is simply the first time in this area we've come across a situation as serious as this one," he concluded.

By February the expected flood of letters from anti-hunting and preservationist groups in the Lower 48 states started arriving at the governor's and ADF&G offices.

On February 23, under the heading, "Exterminating the Wolf," The *New York Times* editorialized on the plan, although no one from the paper had called Alaska to ask about it. It referred to "... bold hunters safely perched in airplanes killing off fifty to eighty percent of the wolves in a huge area." The editor claimed that the moose decline that triggered the hunt was ". . . due to gross mismanagement by Alaska game-protectors."

The editorial claimed that a better approach would be to suspend moose hunting. It accused the state of being concerned over a drop in revenues if moose season was reduced because a shorter season would attract fewer sportsmen.

One of the silliest claims of the editorial insisted that by eliminating wolves, "The weak, old and diseased specimens that are the wolf's customary prey," would survive, and these misfits would reduce the food available for healthy moose.

"Time for a thorough study," the editorial proclaimed.

The editor had just about everything wrong, including the number of wolves to be killed, the size of 20A, and lack of a precedent. His belief that wolves kill only weak, old, and diseased had long before been disproven. And careful scientific studies by state biologists had been conducted on Alaska's wolves for more than fifteen years, and before that by federal biologists. The BFG had developed a scientifically sound policy for Alaska's wolves—one that called for management of the species throughout the state for production on a sustained basis.

Ren Smith shook his head in disgust at the editorial. "Where do newspaper editors get their information?" he asked Bob Hinman. "What in hell do people think we've been doing in the fifteen years since statehood? We have sound scientific information on wolves, moose, and wildlife habitat. Our management programs have been working. Now, suddenly, the world has decided we're a bunch of idiots.

"Look at the wording of this," he said, angrily, "Bold pilots safely perched in airplanes." "No one pretends to know how many wolves." "Extermination" "Detrimental effect that usually accompanies wiping out a predator." "Appalling, and preposterous." "Time for a thorough study." "Letting the old and diseased eat food that healthy breeding stock should get! What nonsense. A fourth grader would know better."

A hollow-eyed Hinman shook his head and answered slowly, "Relax Ren. You know and I know we're in a no-win situation. If we do manage to remove the wolves in 20A as needed, and if we don't get the expected results, the antis will say we told you so. But if moose do rebuild as expected, we'll only get increased pressure from other parts of the state to remove wolves in places where we shouldn't. We've already had requests to kill wolves on the Seward Peninsula where they're killing Eskimo-owned reindeer.

"The passion that people have for the wolf is frightening," Hinman continued. "Logic isn't involved. Wolf management in the minds of most, including the guy who wrote that editorial, has nothing to do with reality. It is people arguing their personal values, with the wolf as the symbol of their values. Probably one hundred percent of those who write or phone us from the other states have never seen a wild wolf, and ninety nine percent have never heard a wolf howl, including that editor. Virtually none have any idea of the number of wolves in Alaska, or how efficient they are as a predator. Yet they're determined that we manage the wolf their way. Whoever wrote that *New York Times* editorial is typical; anyone who knows anything about wolves will see that. But most of the public will swallow his nonsense whole.

"Sadly, the people who believe they love the wolf and who think they are influencing us to "save" the wolf, are in truth the wolf's enemies. If we give in and leave the wolves alone, they'll keep the 20A moose population low indefinitely and nearly disappear themselves because there'll be no food for them—no moose or caribou left to eat. Wolf pups will die of starvation. Adults will kill and eat each other. Then we'll be back to the scarcity of moose and caribou, as well as wolves. Noble sentiments without knowledge can lead to disaster.

"Most people seem to think that wolves and moose have always existed in balance and that if man had not intervened, they would generally be abundant. Carl McIlroy, the area wildlife biologist at Glennallen has researched the history of the area. The first historical records of the Copper River Basin describe an area sparsely settled by Natives, and game that was so scarce that hunger was common. Grizzly bears were common, but moose were rare. Written records show that the first miners probably killed more grizzly bears for food than moose or caribou. Moose did not become common until a disease epidemic in interior Alaska sharply reduced the wolf population and the bear population was probably reduced by hunting as well. The historical record suggests that if a balance between wolves and moose exists, it is at a point where moose are scarce.

"Frederick Schwatka, who drifted down the Yukon River from its source to its mouth for several summer months in 1883 saw only two or three moose the entire way. Now you'd probably see at least that many moose every day. Perhaps that was the normal state in the interior of Alaska prior to man's intervention with guns, traps and poison.

"Fish and Game Board member Sidney Huntington has lived in the Koyukuk Valley all his life. He'll tell you there were only occasional moose stragglers, and virtually no wolves in the Koyukuk country in the 1920's and 1930s. Now there are good numbers of both animals there. Modern game management *does* work.

"Under natural conditions—that is without wolf control—the record indicates that moose and wolves can reach extremely low numbers and remain that way, possibly for decades."

Ren left the room shaking his head, and Bob went for another cup of coffee.

The newspapers kept the pot boiling, with daily quotes and interviews. A Mrs. Julie Tepner, an Anchorage citizen, interviewed by a reporter from the *Anchorage Times*, claimed, "There is an awful lot of yielding to political pressures from professional hunters which has led into the plan to kill wolves. It isn't fair for the wolf to have to compete with man for food."

She claimed, "Wolves have never overpopulated an area, except where they were influenced by man. And I don't believe wolves killed forty dogs in Fairbanks. Those claims come from prejudiced people, many of whom are hunters who want a large moose herd," she was quoted as saying. She also admitted she had never seen a wild wolf.

Wolf lovers weren't the only ones who were attacking the ADF&G. Joe Vogler, a Fairbanks real estate developer, gold miner and Alaska Independence Party candidate for governor, spoke at the February Fairbanks Advisory Committee to the Alaska BFG. "We should fire the entire Fish and Game Department," he insisted. "It has utterly failed to maintain the same amount of game as when the department took over management from the federal government at statehood.

To replace the fish and game department, Vogler said, "We could hire the first three drunks we meet on Second Avenue. They could do a better job."

Vogler suggested establishing a predator control unit for the state and instituting a statewide, crash poisoning program. Without it, he said, "... there will be no big game hunting in Alaska within three years."

Further, Vogler recommended telling residents of the smaller states who were trying to interfere in Alaska's business to "go to hell." He said he was afraid to let his poodle dog out of the house for fear it will be eaten by wolves. "A wolf is going to have to kill a child before anything is done to control them," he warned.

Hinman and his staff were pummeled not only at Senate Resource Committee hearings, court hearings, and a series of public hearings, but by phone calls and a blizzard of letters, mostly from other states.

"I'll use a machine-gun on you and on the wolf-hunting airplanes if you persist in your stupid plan," an Anchorage woman threatened Hinman by telephone. An Iowa minister wrote that he, the minister, was praying for Hinman's eternal damnation.

Governor Hammond's office was flooded with letters, telegrams and phone calls. He shrugged them off. "I won't intervene," he said. "We'll either have professional wildlife management in Alaska, or we'll have political management. I opt for professional management any time."

On March 3, Judge Burke granted a preliminary injunction, delaying the aerial wolf hunt in 20A. He ruled that Commissioner Brooks exceeded his authority in ordering the hunt. Instead, the judge ruled, the order should have come from the BFG.

Burke said again that he believed the hunt as planned was sound game management policy.

Support for the program came from U.S. Wildlife and Parks Assistant Secretary Nathaniel Reed who told Alaska's Senator Ted Stevens, "It would appear in spite of adverse press, it is a well thought-out program and would pay in benefits of bringing back the moose herd around Fairbanks," he said.

Reed pointed out that Dr. Durward Allen, Professor of Wildlife Ecology at Purdue University, one of the country's experts on moose, and an expert on wolves ". . . felt the Alaska proposal was sound and should not receive opposition."

In March, after Judge Burke granted the temporary stay on the program, Jack Perkins a reporter for NBC News, with crew, arrived at Bob Hinman's Fairbanks office. Hinman and staff spent several days with Perkins, reviewing the status of Alaska's wolves, and the logic behind the need for the state to remove some of them from subunit 20A.

"Do you understand now?" Bob asked Perkins.

"Certainly. It's very clear," he responded. "Thanks for your . time, and the in-depth background. I'll be sure to include it."

ADF&G Dall sheep research biologist Wayne Heimer agreed to accompany Perkins and his photographer on a helicopter flight seeking wolf photos (it wasn't a popular assignment; other staff members shied away from it).

A couple of weeks later, viewers of the nightly NBC television news program across the nation were treated to Perkins' version of the state's planned program. To say it was distorted would be high praise.

In November 2001, Heimer, now retired from the ADF&G, described the flight with Perkins for me. He said, "We found several wolf-killed moose remains, with bones sticking out of the snow. 'Do you want pictures of those kills?' I asked Perkins.

"'No,' he said, 'They aren't very interesting.'

"We found a cow moose, which the cameraman photographed. I then suggested we head for the foothills to look for wolves.

"Flying over broken timber country in the low foothills between Wood River and Dry Creek, we blundered into a big pack of wolves. The animals scattered, fleeing from the helicopter. Some of the snow was crusted and the wolves could easily run on it. But here and there were spots of deep snow without a crust. When wolves, running all out on the crust, came to the soft snow, they stumbled, and even tumbled, sometimes end over end.

"We made a low pass and the cameraman took pictures of a running wolf on the crust. The animal came to soft deep snow and tumbled. We made a second low pass of another frightened, frantically fleeing, wolf and the photographer got more photos.

"'That's enough. You have your pictures. You're not going to harass these wolves any more,' I directed.

"On our return flight to Fairbanks I asked Perkins, 'You aren't going to use this film to screw us, are you?'

"'No. We only report the news. We don't slant it,' he answered."

Heimer told me, "I was amazed at what appeared in the nationally broadcast verson. None of the biology so carefully explained to Perkins was used. The sound of the helicopter had been dubbed out, and the engine noise of an airplane dubbed in. When the wolf stumbled and went end-over-end in soft snow, viewers heard a dubbed-in shotgun blast, and the frame of the tumbling wolf was frozen, giving the impression it had been shot," he concluded.

That scene even fooled me—I thought the wolf had been shot, and I didn't know any different until I talked with Heimer twenty-five years later.

Perkins' narration skewed the story as badly as did the phony film. He claimed the state's wildlife biologists said that stopping hunting could solve the problem of declining moose—but hunters complained so loudly that the state gave in and allowed hunting to continue. "Alaska has decided if it cannot stop hunters, it will stop wolves," he said.

He also said the state planned to kill eighty percent of the wolves, but didn't know how many wolves there were, so they wouldn't know when eighty percent was killed. "We'll guess, a state biologist says," said Perkins.

"Should man have dominion over animals? Do men end up playing God in deciding that wolves should die so moose shall live?" he intoned.

Outraged Alaskans called the Anchorage, Fairbanks, and Juneau NBC affiliates. The stations agreed to give Commissioner of Fish and Game Jim Brooks time to rebut.

Next evening, after the NBC news hour, Brooks was allowed to speak to Alaska television viewers (he was not heard by national viewers):

"I would like to comment on the NBC news short titled 'Wolf Hunt in Alaska' which was aired nationally and in parts of Alaska. The show was cleverly contrived to give the impression the state is poised to heartlessly murder wolves in response to pressure from sport hunters. Still worse, the presentation sought to arouse public compassion for a wild animal that was being persecuted to demonstrate or glorify the dominion of humans over a lower form of life.

"I'm extremely regretful that such distortions of truth is given prominent news treatment, for in reality they work against the most enlightened and scientifically based effort of professional conservationists to prevent the destruction of such valuable and interesting animals as the wolf.

"In truth the state of Alaska was the first and only government entity on this continent to take early and effective action to guarantee that the wolf would be preserved over vast areas as a vital and valuable component of the ecosystem.

"Since attaining statehood, the following positive protection measures have been taken. The federal predator program involving aerial shooting, and poisoning of wolves throughout the Territory was stopped by the new state government. Closed seasons and closed areas for the protection of wolves were established. The wolf was officially classed as a game animal rather than vermin or predator. Bounty payments were stopped. Public aerial hunting and poisons were banned. In total, the protective measures adopted to insure the welfare of Alaska's wolf population exceed the protection given to most wildlife in any part of the country.

"The program has been successful. So successful that wolf abundance throughout the state probably equals that existing before the advent of European man here. However, like it or not, humans are present in Alaska. Tens of thousands of Alaskans have for generations shared a dependence on wildlife with the wolf. These people are here today and still have a traditional dependence on wildlife for food. Even newcomers to Alaska often consider wildlife an indispensable source of support. Generally, over most of Alaska our big game animals have been sufficiently abundant to satisfy on a sustained yield basis the food requirements of both humans and wolf.

"But now we recognize acute competition between man and wolves for a limited moose resource in at least one area following severe winters that caused additional mortality among moose.

"If we are to preserve a statewide wolf conservation program it cannot be based on the philosophy that wolf welfare is of more value than human welfare. Both are important and the state's conservation program recognizes this sensible fact, in contrast to the unreasonable views projected by the NBC news commentary," Brooks concluded.

Bob Hinman wrote me about his encounter with Perkins "We explained our program in detail. He was given the facts. Obviously, the distortion was deliberate. If, in the future, helicopters are used by other news crews the way these people used the one they chartered, we'll charge them with harassment of wildlife," he wrote.

Another flood of angry letters, telegrams, and telephone calls to Alaska resulted from the NBC news segment.

Because her information was so distorted and her language so base, Ren Smith's favorite letter in that crop was from a woman from the South 48, addressed to the Department of Fish and Game,

Fairbanks. *[Author's note: This letter was actually received by the department.]*

> You rotten sons-of-bitches! Wolves kill only weak and sick prey. Hunters kill whatever they can hit. Apparently, re your wolf kill, the Fish and Game people kill everything. I am enraged and sickened by your agency and all your brother agencies, of whatever ilk, who play God, and then have the intestinal gall to call it an "experiment."
> Why not get off your duffs and learn about nature from other sources than government booklets, written no doubt by other stupid bureaucrats. Put your desks in a circle, gentlemen. May your tribe decrease.
> It might, you know, be more merciful to dispose of the human hunters who hunt wolves and moose and elk from planes. Who needs them? Up yours, Dorothy A.

The ADF&G wolf removal planned by Hinman and staff for early 1975 never got started. The temporary court injunction delayed the work until the snow was gone; good tracking snow is necessary for aerial wolf control.

⌒

BY THE 1970S, with the state's human population growth, pressure increased on Alaska's fish and game resources. No longer could the twelve-member BFG complete its annual work in a month or so; meetings now lasted nearly two months. In response, during their 1975 session the Alaska legislature abolished the twelve-member Board of Fish and Game and in its place created two seven-member boards—the Board of Game (BOG), and the Board of Fisheries.

⌒

ONE COLD CLEAR March day in the late 1920s, Frank Glaser sat on a hillside a mile or so from his Savage River cabin watching a frozen muskeg flat where several hundred caribou were scattered, feeding. A quarter-mile below him a coal ledge jutted from the fifteen-foot-high river bank. A yellow seepage from the coal smeared the blue-white river ice. Five caribou stood licking at the stain.

As he looked for wolves, he idly glanced at the five caribou from time to time, swinging his binoculars and scanning the snow-covered land. After about an hour he saw a lone gray wolf trotting across the flat. Soon three others single-filed down the river to his left. Then another appeared on his right, picking its way upstream.

The five wolves were converging on the caribou at the coal seep.

The wolf on the flat trotted to the edge of the bank above the unsuspecting caribou and peeked over at them. Then it backed off to lie down and wait. The group of three wolves left the creek and disappeared into the spruces below Frank. He lost track of the fifth wolf.

He then watched the five caribou. After about ten minutes a gray wolf streaked out of the timber and grabbed one of the cows by the flank. The remaining four caribou scattered as the frantic cow skidded and staggered, trying to shake off the clinging wolf. She tried to jump from the slick ice to the bank but immediately fell on her side, floundering with the tenacious wolf's jaws still clamped firmly to her flank. Three other wolves appeared and swarmed over her, chopping and slashing.

Then, incredibly, she pulled free. All of the animals skidded on the slick ice, but the terrified cow made it to the bank with sharp hoofs giving her traction on the ice, humped her way to the top, and hooked her front legs over. The wolf on the bank met her head-on, sinking his teeth into her nose. He hung on as the two of them rolled and flopped down the steep slope to the river ice. A red stain spread across the white ice as the five wolves then killed the cow.

Frank waited, knowing they would eat their fill and lie down for a sleep. They'd have heard him if he had tried to approach them while they were eating, since the snow was crusted enough to make walking noisy. Fortunately, the slight breeze was in his favor, so they couldn't catch his scent.

Soon they were gorged on the hot meat. Frank watched them leave their kill, climb the riverbank and trot toward a low knoll in the middle of a flat. As they trotted, their tails were higher than their backs, rolling around and around—a sure sign they had full bellies. When hungry, wolves carry their tails straight behind and down, almost dragging.

They reached the knoll and selected a spot to curl up in for a nap. Frank slipped into the snowshoes he'd been sitting on and took his time walking to a little willow-choked stream that passed close to where they were sleeping.

He was within a hundred yards of them when he got into shooting position. He carefully centered the rifle scope on one of the sleeping animals and squeezed off a shot. The wolf half rolled over as the .30-06 bullet hit, while the four other wolves leaped to their feet, staring about wildly.

As if by signal all four ran directly toward Frank and the creek. It was the nearest cover and they wanted to be in that creek. He waited until they were about fifty yards away and fired at another wolf; powdery snow flew as it skidded and lay dead.

The others split, two to his right, one to his left, as they continued their dash toward the creek. He watched the two until they were in the clear, streaking downstream, and fired three more times. At his third shot his 180-grain bullet slammed home and one of the two collapsed in mid-stride. By then the others were out of sight.

Three out of five. That gave him a feeling of accomplishment. It meant that fewer caribou would die. It would also beef up his bank account with bounties, and the sale of hides. If he hadn't known those wolves would take a nap after eating, he would probably have barged down to the river as soon as they made their kill. It would have been doubtful if he'd have had a chance to make a single shot. He was learning about wolves and their habits.

The crises: Professor Rearden: The wolf dogs

AFTER SNOW COVERED the land in the fall of 1975, Ren Smith and other biologists flew every good weather day they could, counting wolves in GMU 20A. By November Ren was confident their tally of twenty six packs, totalling 239 wolves, was reasonably accurate for the Connecticut-size subunit.

One bright October day he found fresh tracks of wolves, swooped close to the ground to determine which direction they were traveling (wolves drag their hind feet slightly, leaving a distinctive mark in snow, which indicates direction of travel), and, at the safe altitude of 500 feet, followed the tracks nearly twenty miles to the wolves. He saw them from several miles away as a line of black spots against the snow. He didn't want to spook them, so he climbed. At 1,500 feet, he banked to look down for an accurate count. He saw eight black wolves, and a gray. The gray was last in line.

"Damn! Is that you Lady?" he exclaimed, excited and pleased. The wolves were thirty miles from where he had released the pup. Wolf territories in Alaska may encompass up to 800 square miles, so it could have been the Black Pack. He descended for a better look. Young wolves reach adult size about Christmas. The gray wolf was the same size as the others, but Ren knew that by late fall and early winter it is difficult to distinguish pups of the year from adults in the field, except sometimes by their behavior.

He flew home with a happy heart and a lump in his throat.

While Ren was counting wolves, moose biologist Steve Acorn's crew was counting moose in the same subunit. Acorn's aerial counts of the big deer had been decreasing for several years and he was deeply concerned. Ren's wolf counts had remained high. Their moose and wolf counts became the subject of a tense November staff meeting.

A crises loomed, even more dramatic than that of the previous year. Research by state biologists in the fifteen years since statehood had shown that moose populations with ratios of one wolf to twenty or fewer moose usually declined. The ratio of wolves to moose in GMU 20A was now 1:10. There were 2,500 moose, 239 wolves, and 2,200 caribou in the unit. The caribou were not hunted by man—there was no open season for them. There had been 5,000 of them in 1963.

At the meeting Ren commented, "If we don't do anything, we're going to lose most of the moose *and* wolves in that unit, and soon."

Bob Hinman, doodling on a scratch pad, shook his head in frustration. "We've seen this coming for a couple of years. We tried last year, but the antis won that one. Steve, do you think bears could be killing a lot of the moose?"

"Nope," Acorn answered, "There aren't that many bears. All of our studies point to wolves killing most of the moose calves. Calf survival is way down. In the early 60s we counted more than 50 calves per 100 cows in early winter. It has dropped steadily as the moose population has decreased. This year's count is the lowest yet."

"What's the moose pregnancy rate?" Bob asked.

"Normal," Steve answered. "Nearly ninety percent for cows three years or older. In early May I tranquilized fifty-nine adult cows and checked for pregnancy by palpation. I marked them all with numbered collars. We observed those moose after calving and the initial survival of calves through about three weeks was good—nearly eighty percent. But by November, most of those calves were dead. That's when I counted only 10 calves per 100 cows."

"What about hunting pressure? Hunters from Fairbanks and surrounding areas?" Bob asked.

"Hunters are taking bulls only. That won't affect population increase. There are plenty of bulls to breed all the cows," Steve explained.

"What's the answer, guys?" Bob demanded.

"I hate to say it, but the only way to maintain good numbers of wolves and moose in that unit is to remove some of the wolves. Only that will allow moose numbers to rebuild," Ren said.

"I'm reluctant to go through that blizzard of complaints again.

Is there any other way to increase moose numbers? And keep wolf numbers high?" Bob said.

Steve answered. "Nope. Habitat is great for moose. There's plenty of feed."

"You think I want to shoot a bunch of wolves?" Ren said. "That's the dirtiest job I know. At the same time, I don't want to see a crash of wolves in that unit. If we don't do anything they'll deplete the moose, and wolves will starve or try to move. If they try to move they'll run into territories of other packs—and most will be killed in fights."

Steve commented, "The last two hard winters, plus wolf predation, have killed almost forty percent of the moose in 20A."

"Trappers and hunters are taking thirty or forty wolves every year, which isn't enough to make any real difference in wolf numbers," Ren said.

Steve finished, "At a wolf:moose ratio of one to ten, the moose will inevitably decline further or be severely reduced. Cutting back on hunting when hunters kill only bulls wouldn't change calf survival, which is the critical factor. The only answer I see is to reduce wolf numbers so more calves survive. We need to get the wolf/moose ratio back up—and the higher the ratio, the faster the moose will recover," Steve concluded.

Bob said, "Yeah, the mathematics and biology tells us that. Rural Alaskans generally support us on wolf reductions; they understand. It's those 200-plus animal rights groups that will raise hell. Whenever we talk about killing a few wolves they get up in arms and we wind up in court."

Ren said, softly, "I understand their feelings. I hate to kill wolves. Wolves are something special.They have an appeal that no other animal has. It's a little like the wild horses in Nevada and other western states. Everyone loves horses. When overpopulations of horses started damaging the range and the feds wanted to kill some, you know how the public reacted."

Bob nodded. "We all know that. We also know what is biologically sound. We also know what the state constitution says. I wish there were some way we could educate the public in the South 48."

Ren grimaced. "Wildlife management is the only profession I know with so many self-appointed experts—and critics. I should have become a dentist. Emotions rule. Science means nothing. Every citizen is an expert."

"What are our goals? How many moose will the unit support?" Bob asked.

"There were 8,000 seven and eight years ago. I'd like to see that number again. There's plenty of feed for 'em," Steve Acorn recommended.

"How many wolves should we aim for?" Bob asked.

That brought a brittle laugh.

"Pretty good, huh?" Bob smiled.

"'Tain't funny, Hinman," Ren said, sourly.

"Ok. But better to laugh than cry. How many, Ren?"

"We have 239 now. If we had 8,000 moose, the unit could support about 200 wolves, plus quite a bit of hunting and trapping pressure. But to get there, we'll have to temporarily knock the wolf population down to give moose a chance to bounce back. If we cut the wolf numbers in half, say to 120, that would give us a wolf/moose ratio of about 1 to 25. That should give moose a chance.

"If we reduce wolf numbers to 120, how long would it take the wolves to build back up to the present 239?" Bob asked.

Ren answered, "A lot of variables. But with more moose and light hunting and trapping of wolves, I'd expect at least twenty percent increase annually; probably more, even thirty percent. Of course," he said, "If we remove half the wolves, or about 120 next March, by fall wolf numbers will be back up to at least 200. Meaning we'll have to have remove another 50 to 80 after snowfall."

There was a long silence.

"God. Three or four more years of this and I'll be an old man," Bob grunted. "We know how to increase moose and wolves, but the "experts" from Outside think we're nuts when we tell 'em we're going to produce more wolves by killing wolves."

"Maybe the new board won't buy it," he said. "But I think it's our duty to spell it out. We're on solid biological ground. So, ok, we'll do it. In December we'll propose to the new BOG a wolf reduction program for Unit 20A to take place in March, or whenever snow conditions and weather allow.

"What's your recommendation—how many should be removed, Ren?"

"The more we remove, the faster the moose will recover. Don't worry about wolves—they'll recover quickly."

"We know that. We need to recommend a specific number."

"Let's propose removing fifty percent—or 120 wolves," Ren said. "We've never been able to remove the number we wanted anyway. If we manage to remove even a 100, it'll help. But it certainly won't harm the wolf population permanently if we remove half of them now."

"Ok. That's it," Bob said. "We'll propose 120 to the Board in December, to be removed in March, and another 80 next winter, provided the summer increase is as projected. Ren, you and Steve write it up for presentation. I'll include it in the package of proposals we publish next week so it won't come as a surprise to the public."

"What about long term?" Ren asked.

"I'd say it will be a three or four year program at least. We'll get a good count of both moose and wolves in 20A every year. When moose are increasing significantly, we can slack off on the wolf reduction program. We'll go to the board annually with a progress report and a request for authorization for the number of wolves we feel should be removed," Bob decided.

≈

AFTER THE MEETING, Ren salvaged Bob's doodling notes and found a few additions to the Hinman tongue-in-cheek *Glossary of Wildlife*. "Average litter size"—how big the pieces of paper are that you throw out the car window. "Board of Game"—(1) tired of all those moose, deer, etc.: (2) tired of football on TV: (3) checkerboard. "Game count"—royalty with nerve. "Game management"—point shaving. "Gene pool"—pond containing denim pants.

He left the room smiling.

≈

I RECEIVED MY Bachelor of Science degree in Fish and Game Management from Oregon State College in June, 1948, and was accepted for a two-year master's assistantship at the University of Maine, at Orono. There I did field work and wrote a master's thesis (on habitat improvements for woodcock, a bird I had never seen before I went to Maine), took advanced courses, worked as a lab assistant, and helped teach wildlife courses. In June, 1950, I was awarded a Master Of Science degree in Wildlife Conservation from the University of Maine.

I landed a position at the University of Alaska, Fairbanks where I was to organize a new wildlife department and teach wildlife management. My 1947 summer job in Alaska no doubt gave me an advantage other applicants lacked. With wife and two daughters I drove from Maine to California for a family visit in a 1941 Buick Century on which I was making payments. I then drove the Buick to Fairbanks over the all-gravel and mud—lots of mud— Alaska Highway, arriving in July, 1950.

I was broke. With no income expected until September when classes started, I worked for a couple of months as a gandy dancer (track laborer) for the Alaska Railroad, which paid the grocery bills that summer.

I started teaching that September—a young (25 years), nervous, not very experienced assistant professor. The program attracted students, and within a year I had my feet under me and my department was growing.

Students usually gained experience on summer jobs in the wildlife field with various federal agencies in Alaska. Students who completed their four-year wildlife degrees had little difficulty landing jobs in Alaska.

Providence was on the side of my students. Statehood was but nine years away, with an abundance of fine wildlife and fishery jobs with the new Alaska Department of Fish and Game (ADF&G). Those students who completed their course work, and who had a few summers of field work experience were the perfect candidates for jobs with this new agency, which replaced the federal U.S. Fish and Wildlife Service which had long managed the Territory of Alaska's fish and game.

My former students Jim Brooks and Ron Skoog became commissioners of ADF&G. Bob Hinman, and Ren Smith held top positions within the department. George Schaller, working for the New York Zoological Society, became world famous for his work with great apes, snow leopards, giant pandas, and other exotic species. Tom Cade became head of the ornithology department at Cornell University. Jim King made his mark as a Flyway Biologist for the U.S. Fish and Wildlife Service in Alaska. Others landed good positions in the wildlife field with various state or federal agencies.

These gifted men would likely have reached the top in whatever profession they chose. Nevertheless, I like to think my teachings, at least in a small way, contributed to their successes. Recently, Jim

King, now retired from his position as a waterfowl flyway biologist for the U.S. Fish and Wildlife Service in Alaska, visited me in my coastal Alaska log home. "Thanks, Prof," he said, "for the background you gave me. It made my career possible."

I choked up at that—I have become sentimental and overly emotional in my old age.

Bob Hinman left Alaska with his new bachelor's degree in wildlife management, and worked as a conservation agent in Utah while enrolled at Utah State University for graduate studies to earn a master's degree. He returned to Alaska in 1965 as a wildlife biologist and worked his way up. Ren Smith earned his Bachelor of Science degree from my department and went on to earn advanced degrees in the South 48.

I was promoted to full professor. Life should have stabilized for me, but a long-time ambition to become a professional writer intruded. Alaska, the last great U.S. wilderness frontier, is a magical place that abounds with wonderful, adventurous people. I itched to write their stories.

⤙

In November, 1926, Frank Glaser found a six-month-old black male wolf in one of his #31 kangaroo traps—a smooth-jawed trap that usually won't hold a wolf. Occasionally, however, this trap obtains a good hold above the foot of a wolf, as it did with this one.

The freshly-caught wolf was uninjured. He boldly stared at Glaser with his topaz-colored eyes and Frank had to admire him for his nerve. He decided to take the wolf home alive.

He carried a birch stick to tap trapped foxes on the nose to knock them out. He tried to tap the wolf with it, but the animal dodged every time. Glaser simply couldn't hit him on the nose. He left the wolf and went down the side of the ridge to a patch of willows and cut a short willow stick.

When he returned, the wolf came to the end of the trap chain, angry, wanting to bite. With his left hand Glaser offered him the willow stick. The wolf clamped its teeth on it and Glaser cracked him across the nose with enough force to knock him out. He tied the animal's jaws and legs, and put him on his packboard and carried him to his home cabin.

He put a collar on the wolf and chained him to a dog house, then straddled him while untying his legs and jaws. As soon as the jaws were free, Glaser jumped free, fearing his teeth. He needn't have worried; the instant he was released, the wolf plunged into the dog house.

At first the wolf refused to leave the house during the day, but at night he emerged to drink the water and eat the food Glaser left. For some time, the moment the man appeared the wolf would dive out of sight.

The black animal soon stopped being aggressive and in a few days Glaser could pull him out of his house and handle him without worrying about being bitten. But when he was about a year and a half old he became cranky, and Glaser had to watch him carefully.

When Frank went to town he couldn't leave the wolf untended at Savage River, so he harnessed him with his dog team. He always waited until the last moment to hook him in the wheel position (immediately next to the sled) where he could keep an eye on him. The wolf didn't pull much. The only time he ever really pulled was when a caribou appeared in front of the team. Otherwise he went along with head and tail down, not showing much interest.

Glaser didn't try to force the wolf to pull and was satisfied simply to be able to handle him. He had plans for that wolf.

In late January, 1927, he tied the captive wolf so he could reach Nellie, a female malemute. She had tried to make friends with him almost from the first day he had arrived. Soon she was carrying pups, and Glaser was eager for them to arrive, for he wanted a team of wolf-dogs.

Five pups arrived in late March. The four males, in varying shades of gray, he named Buster, Wolf, Kobuk, and Denali. The female, black with white throat and chest, he named Queen, which soon became Queenie. The pups were fat, warm and squirmy, and didn't appear different from pure malemute pups. The difference showed up when they got older.

Glaser again bred the captive wolf (which weighed 145 pounds at two years of age) to Nellie the following year to get another litter of wolf-dogs. When Queenie was two, he bred her to a beautiful big half-wolf/malemute that belonged to another trapper. In May, 1929 she had thirteen pups; ten females and three males. Glaser kept the three males, naming them Kenai, Yukon, and Wolf.

From 1927 until 1937, when he left Savage River, Glaser owned anywhere from seven to eleven wolf-dogs. Most were half wolf, some were three-quarters wolf, and a few were one-quarter wolf. He kept only the most promising of the various litters. Glaser said they made fine sled and pack dogs. They had great endurance and tough feet, both critical traits for sled dogs.

He started to train his wolf-dogs in summer and fall when they were four and five months old (the litters, wolf-like, were born between late March and early May). He claimed the animals had the intelligence of the wolf plus the tractability of a dog. But they were far more sensitive than most malemutes or huskies. He was fortunate, for not all wolf/dog crosses produce animals with desirable traits.

Glaser had an affinity for animals.He understood them and he cared for them. He was uniquely qualified to handle his wolf-dogs, which, of course, were work animals, not pets. He told me, "I have seen vicious, intractable wolf/dog crosses I wouldn't have kept five minutes. There couldn't be a meaner, or more savage dog than a half or three quarter wolf-dog raised or managed wrong."

Glaser knew a trapper who was attacked by three wolf-dogs in his team. He had to yank the gee pole out of his sled and beat them to death. "He brought the problem on himself. He was pretty rough on his dogs," Glaser told me.

Much of Glaser's success probably came from the way he handled his wolf-dogs. He was firm, but not cruel. When he punished a dog by voice or switch, or otherwise, it knew it had the punishment coming and there was no resentment. An angry word from Glaser was often enough; the animals hated to have him upset with them.

Owning the wolf-dogs was a major commitment. There were few people with whom Glaser was comfortable leaving them. He never allowed anyone else to drive the sensitive, intelligent animals, for they couldn't be treated like ordinary sled dogs. He had to tend them twenty four hours a day, year round. They were his family.

His wolf-dogs regarded Glaser as their leader, or the Alpha wolf, much as they would view the leader of a wild pack. He had to dominate them so they would obey and remain loyal, yet not be cowed. In the years he owned, bred, and drove wolf-dogs, Kenai, the 155-pound son of his leader Queenie, was the only one that ever repeatedly challenged him as the Alpha leader.

Fairbanks in December: Letters

PAT YORK DECIDED to speak for the wolf at the December 1975 meeting of the Alaska Board of Game. It was 30 degrees below zero, and an icy fog hung over the town on the evening she arrived at Fairbanks.

John Grant, the TNWSF representative, met her at the airport. He was about her age, dark, rough-hewn, ruggedly handsome. He wore an insulated snow suit and a synthetic fur cap. Jerry Hanson had warned her that Grant was miffed because she was replacing him as spokesman for the foundation.

He was gracious and seemed friendly as he carried her suitcase. As Pat stepped out of the terminal and the cold engulfed her she felt as if she had stepped into icy water. She hurriedly zipped her parka, pulled the hood up, and yanked mittens on as they walked to his car.

"You'll get used to it," he grinned. "This isn't bad. When it gets down to fifty or sixty below—that's when you *really* feel it."

"You're welcome to stay with me, or I can take you to a hotel," he offered.

"But, I thought you were to make hotel reservations for me," she said, surprised.

"No need this time of year. There are plenty of hotel rooms in winter. You need to make reservations in summer, when tourists are here," he said, smoothly.

His suggestion that she stay with him unsettled her; Jerry Hanson had told her that Grant was single.

"Please take me to a good hotel," she requested.

"I'll take you to the hotel where the meetings will be held," he promised.

Her impressions as he drove were of chilling cold, darkness, dazzling street lights, snow-lined streets and snow-covered houses. She was glad for the woolen slacks and down-insulated parka she had purchased before leaving Boston.

He carried her suitcase to the desk at the hotel. "After you've freshened up, meet me in the dining room and we'll have some coffee and a talk," he suggested.

In the dining room she requested,"Would you look over the presentation I'm to make to the game board"?

She wanted him on her side. His two years in Alaska should be of some value.

While they sipped coffee he scanned her paper. After the first page he looked up. "You wrote this?" he asked.

"Most of it. Jerry Hanson helped some," she answered.

She thought she detected a twinge of a smile several times as he read, but she wasn't sure. He finished reading and sat silent for long moments, apparently thinking.

"Good job. Don't change a word," he said, finally.

⁓

REN WAS AT his desk reading letters. He'd been at it for hours. Bob Hinman stood at the door for a few moments before Ren noticed him.

"How many this time?" Bob asked.

"So far, the secretaries have counted around 3,000 addressed to the governor and to the department. They're still coming."

"What are they being told this time?"

"Same old. Wolves are endangered. Wolves kill only the sick and unfit. Wolves are beneficial. Alaska is trying to kill all the wolves. Alaska pays a bounty on wolves. Over hunting and habitat destruction are wiping out Alaska's caribou and moose, and we're blaming the wolf. Illegal hunting is killing off Alaska's moose and caribou. Some animal rights outfit has warned that grizzly and black bears may be killed by aerial hunting because human hunters want more moose and caribou. Plus the usual outrage at our tampering with the balance of nature, and disrupting the perfect ecology that has evolved for millions of years.

"I'm reading every letter, and deciding which of our four responses to use for an answer. I despair of our educational system; it's surprising how many college professors and college students studying wildlife management, ecology, or biology, blindly write whatever the "save-the-wolf" organizations tell them to. Few ask for facts or have done any thinking for themselves.

"I answered one guy who was angry because Alaska was supposed to be paying a bounty on wolves. He wrote back..let's see, here it is. He said, 'If you have no bounties, you have been slandered twice by programs broadcast on PBS (July and December) concerning wolves. You might investigate.'"

Ren handed Bob the letter, who glanced at it. "Hell, if we investigated every source that is peddling lies about us it would be a full time job," he said.

"I don't know whether to laugh or cry at this one," Ren said. "Listen to this, he said, reading; 'I am a high school senior. Here is a plea from an imaginary wolverine. I am a wolf and mean no harm. My hungry pups must be nourished. I hunt and stalk the snowy hills of Alaska to get my prey.'"

"That's not funny; it's sad," Bob said, shaking his head."She thinks a wolverine is a female wolf. That's a new one. She needs to take high school biology again. I'll try to get someone to help you. I promised the commissioner and the governor we'd read and answer every letter."

"Even those that are downright unfriendly?" Ren asked, straight-faced.

Bob laughed and left.

Ren continued to read: *[Author's note: The following are actual letters received by Governor Hammond's office and the ADF&G. Some place names have been changed.]*

Dear Governor Hammond:
We protest the aerial wolf hunting which is pursued periodically in your state. The wolf is not responsible for the declining herds in Alaska. Wolf, caribou, and others have lived together for centuries and all have survived. Man is the reason for the decline of the herds. Using the wolf as a scapegoat will not solve the problem. The wolf is a useful predator. Stop the aerial wolf hunts.
An Arizona couple

Sirs: Stop the aerial shooting of wolves. Predators are vital to the balance of nature. Man is the predator taking toll on moose and caribou. I love wolves. I don't want a single one to suffer. Why do wolves take the blame when men are committing the crimes? Don't let this short-sighted, stupid, cruel thing happen.

An Illinois woman

Dear Commissioner Brooks:
Inaccurate data, insufficient study, and adherence to traditional management dogma—your department is guilty of these charges. No intensive field work by ADF&G biologists exists. Insufficient data exists to hold your latest aerial hunt. Your department has failed in its responsibilities. Healthy ecosystems produce a harvestable surplus even after predator kills. You are using the wolf as a scapegoat.

A Maine man

Gentlemen: Why are you trying to exterminate the Alaskan wolf? Is this to protect the illegal hunting in your state? Stop using the wolf as a scapegoat. Aerial hunting is barbaric. Create a habitat. Do not kill.

A Washington woman

Dear Governor Hammond:
I wish to express my concern and horror at your intention to again have aerial wolf hunting. I would think after the previous opposition you would have learned that you cannot fool mother nature. Your attempts to interfere with the natural ecology of Alaska is irresponsible, distasteful and completely without reason.

A Florida man

Commissioner Brooks, Juneau, Alaska:
The wolves are only killing weak caribou, not the strong. The pipeline is what is killing them. Wolves don't like being killed. Colorado would take any wolves you don't want.

A Colorado man

As wildlife chairman of the Milltown Women's Club, I object strongly to the aerial wolf hunting. This may be sport to some people, but it is sick. The wolf is blamed for the killing of the moose. The truth is, man is the cause of depleting moose herds.

A Washington woman

Your officials are being manipulated by special interests. You are tampering with a perfect and beautiful natural system. As an ecology major at an outstanding private college I understand fully the ecosystem system of checks and balances. Please skip the predator population studies in your reply—data can be manipulated to prove anything.

A Maine college student

Dear Governor Hammond:
How could you let those murders kill those poor, innocent, unknowing, lovable, wouldn't harm a fly, loving wolves? I hate all those bastards who kill my four-legged brothers and sisters. Stop the inhumane murdering. Animal-haters are vermin!

A New York woman

It is next to impossible for a wolf pack to kill a healthy moose calf, even a young one, and I strongly doubt that almost all of the moose calves are unhealthy. You people have the brains of a retarded rock.

A Washington woman

I like the timber wolf so much I would probably kill a human to free a wolf.

An Ontario, Canada, fifth grade boy

About one in fifty letters were in support of wolf control. They came mostly after the recipients read one of the ADF&G form letters explaining why some wolves were to be removed from 20A. These form letters went to every person who wrote to Governor Hammond or the ADF&G. A few support letter samples: *[Author's Note:The following are actual letters received by Governor Hammond or ADF&G.]*

Dear Governor Hammond:
Thank you for the memorandum regarding the treatment of the wolf problem in Alaska. It is apparent that this question is being met in your state on a humane and sympathetic basis, and we congratulate you for it.

A bank president, Connecticut.

To: Hon. Jay S. Hammond-Governor, Alaska:
I must apologize for joining the "impulsive group." There ARE two sides to the coin. You are in a better position to handle

this situation than I am. About face: you now have my full understanding and support. Regards.

An Oklahoma man

Dear Governor Hammond:

I understand you have been receiving a large amount of bleeding heart mail from uninformed residents of the lower 48 relative to the responsible programs of game management attempted to be carried out by the State of Alaska, especially relative to the wolf control program. Please consider this letter as a strong vote of support for your Game Department and your Commissioner and their efforts to produce a maximum sustained yield* of the renewable wildlife resources in the State of Alaska.

A building contractor, California

Dear Commissioner Brooks:

The Delta Fish and Game Advisory Committee would like you to know we fully endorse the Department's wolf control measures. We feel it most unfortunate that outside interests are attempting to sway the program by court action and other more devious measures.

It certainly seems a statewide predator control program might be in the best interests of Alaskans after researching areas as was done for Unit 18 and 20A.

Sincerely,
Charlie Boyd, Chairman
Delta Fish and Game Advisory Committee

Dept. of Fish and Game, Alaska:

How right you are when you said few "outsiders" knew the true state of affairs. Now I realize I should have found out exactly what was going on instead of going off half cocked. Now that I know the facts, I would like to know if there is an way I may help the [wolf control] project.

A Florida woman

A Juneau resident who decided letters could be a two-way street somehow acquired discarded official stationery of Bill Egan, Alaska's former governor, and used it to respond to letter writers in the South-48 who objected to Alaska's wolf control.

Note: Alaska's constitution requires "sustained yield," not "maximum sustained yield."

"We're delighted to hear of your interest in these animals," the letters proclaimed. "Because of your great interest you may expect one live wolf to be delivered to your address soon. Please prepare an adequate place to keep it."

Each was signed with a forged, "Bill Egan."

⌒

I HAD BEEN teaching wildlife management at the University of Alaska for a couple of years when I encountered Frank Glaser, a slim, rather small, weathered man in his early sixties. At our first encounter I was shopping at Frontier Sporting Goods in Fairbanks. He started talking as he entered the store, addressing remarks to me and five or six other shoppers, although none of us knew him. He spoke of moose hunts, charging grizzly bears, his team of wolf-dogs, market hunting, and other intriguing Alaska wilderness experiences.

After talking nonstop for ten or fifteen minutes he bought something and left.

"Who was that?" I asked Dick McIntyre, the store owner.

"He's that federal wolf hunter, a genuine sourdough, an old-timer other old timers respect."

I had heard of Glaser from Ren Smith, then one of my students. When Ren was a boy, Glaser had chartered his father's plane for a few days. For about a week the wolf hunter had been a guest at the Smith home at Wolverine, and while there the exciting tales he told about wolves had excited young Ren—enough to set him off on a home study project on wolves that a few years later pointed him to my department and a career as a wildlife biologist.

In time, I learned Frank Glaser was a living Alaska legend. A compulsive talker, he was probably making up for years of living alone in Alaska's wilderness; some called him "Silent Frank." We became acquainted and I proposed we collaborate in writing about his adventures.

I used a tape recorder at our yarning sessions (they weren't interviews; Frank didn't interview well), a new technique in 1953. I sold a dozen of the stories mostly to *Outdoor Life* magazine. Decades later I reviewed my notes and discovered many fascinating footnotes to Alaska's history among Glaser's tales. I was new to Alaska in 1953 and didn't understand the significance of many of his observations.

Forty-five years after my interviews with Glaser, based on my notes and on Glaser's diaries he willed to Dr. Lew Mayer, of Anchorage, who cared for him during his last months of life, I wrote the book *Alaska's Wolf Man, the 1915–55 Wilderness Adventures of Frank Glaser.* It was published in 1998, and the Alaska Historical Society named me Historian of the Year 1999 for it.

Glaser left Savage River in 1937 to become a predator control agent for the federal government and he held that position until his retirement in 1955. In 1952 and 1953 I invited him to tell my classes about his work.

After Glaser talked, I preached a different sermon to my students. The prevalent view in the then-new wildlife field was that predators were generally beneficial, and their inroads could not make much difference in prey numbers.

I learned much about wolf behavior from Glaser, for he was a careful observer and knew much about Alaska's wildlife from personal experience. But I didn't agree with him and the federal approach on predator control, which, in Alaska, was, simply, "kill all wolves possible." I still don't agree with that approach, nor do any professionally trained wildlife biologists I know.

I also invited U.S. Fish and Wildlife Service field agent Jay Hammond, also stationed at Fairbanks, to talk with them. He spent part of his time as a predator control agent. He had a college degree in biology (University of Alaska, Fairbanks) and his views on wolves were somewhat different from those of Glaser, being more akin to mine.

Selling the dozen adventure articles I wrote with Glaser gave me my start as a professional writer. It even gave me the courage to resign my professorship. I called myself an outdoors writer/photographer, and to augment my income, I became a registered big game guide. I thoroughly enjoyed the freedom from the structured life of teaching, although I put my family through some hungry years.

The deep-cold winters of Fairbanks plus the lure of the rich North Pacific Ocean pushed me to move from Alaska's interior to a small coastal community on the Kenai Peninsula.

For the next five years I struggled to support my family with writing, photography, and guiding big game trophy hunters. I thoroughly enjoyed showing clients the Alaska wilderness I love when they submerged themselves in the wilderness and appreciated seeing the animals. These sportsmen enjoyed the challenge of find-ing a trophy and making a clean kill. Some didn't care whether they killed anything; the hunt and being in the wilderness was their main interest. Sadly, all my clients didn't fit this mold.

To pay bills when articles or guided hunts didn't sell, I worked as a clerk in a trading post, slaved as a construction laborer, was office manager on a construction job, worked at a sawmill, and even spent one summer hunting harbor seals for their hides and the $3 bounty. Although I knew the bounty didn't accomplish anything, and I was opposed to it in principle, that extra $3 for every seal skin I collected was important to me at the time.

In 1959 I accepted an offer from the Territorial Department of Fisheries to work as a commercial fisheries biologist in Cook Inlet. It was just a temporary job I told myself.

That was the year of statehood, and shortly, to my surprise, I found myself the Area Management Biologist for the Cook Inlet commercial fisheries for the new State of Alaska's Department of Fish and Game (ADF&G), which succeeded the territorial agency. It was a high pressure job; for four summer months when the multi-million dollar salmon fishery was underway, I commonly put in sixteen hour days seven days a week. The rest of the year I concentrated on management of a four-million-pound-a-year king crab fishery, as well as Dungeness crab and shrimp fisheries.

While working as a fishery biologist for the new state, on weekends and evenings I wrote magazine articles, building rela-tionships with editors of magazines around the world.

After eleven years as a full-time fishery biologist and a part-time writer, at the end of 1969 I left my job as a fishery biologist to ac-cept a salaried position as Outdoors Editor for *Alaska* magazine, a monthly then written primarily for Alaskans, portraying "life on the last frontier."

⌒

FEBRUARY 15, 1930. Frank Glaser had his winter's catch of fox furs safely in his cache. His traps were sprung, awaiting another trap-ping season. On this night he sat near his glowing wood stove reading *National Geographic* magazines under a hissing lantern. Joseph Rock was in northern China and Tibet, and wonderful photos of the Himalaya Mountains accompanied his adventurous account, read avidly by Glaser. Near midnight he reluctantly went to bed. He was nearly asleep when the musical sound of howling wolves flooded the cabin. They sounded close, and there were so many in the various choirs that he dressed and stepped outside to listen.

The sky was clear and it was calm. A full moon flooded the snow-covered land so that it seemed almost like day. Snowy peaks and ridges towered near. The outside thermometer read 30 below zero. His wolf-dogs were awake, some sitting atop their houses, alertly peering into the distance.

A wolf howled off to the west, then another, and another, until at least half a dozen were howling. They sang for two or three minutes and suddenly stopped. Moments later a solitary wolf howled to the south. He was joined by a second, and then a third. Like the first pack, after several minutes their howls suddenly stopped, and then, far to the north, another band howled.

The wolves to the west and south sounded close, but after listening for a time he realized the still, cold, dense air carried sounds unusually well. The two nearest packs were probably a mile or more from the cabin.

After enjoying the wolf music for a time, he howled a response. That often elicited a howled "yes-we-hear-you" if wolves were near. That night it shut them up. He returned to bed.

At daylight next morning, about ten a. m., two bands of wolves howled near the cabin. The trapper sensed excitement among the big predators. He dressed in furs for a cold day in the hills, and wearing snowshoes, with binoculars and rifle, climbed a nearby ridge where he could overlook the flats where feeding caribou were scattered.

He scanned with binoculars, but saw only caribou. Wisps of fog rose from each as its body moisture condensed in the cold. A chill crept through his furs. He moved to another spot, the walk warming him. He sat on a snowshoe, and braced binoculars, holding his breath as they neared his face to keep them from fogging. Immediately he saw a pack of eight wolves, two miles away, trotting single-file across the flat. Caribou turned and stared as they passed, but the wolves ignored them.

He swept further with the glasses, and was startled to see another pack of seven wolves single-filing across the flat. The two packs were headed toward each other.

"Now I'm going to see something," he told himself. He knew wolves had territories, and that fights between packs are common. Several times he had found remains of wolves killed by other wolves; often the remains had been eaten. Wolves *do* eat wolves.

He swept the flats again, and was amazed to see a third band of eight wolves, trotting single-file. Now there were three packs bound for the same general area. As he watched, a low howl came from one band, to be answered by a low howl from one of the others. The three packs stopped a few hundred feet apart. They appeared reluctant to approach one another. Gradually, though, the twenty three wolves assembled on the open, snowy flat. The trapper had a grandstand view of this remarkable phenomenon.

The wolves milled and mixed. Yips and growls floated through the frigid air. Here and there, wolves challenged each other. Several appeared to fight. Frank was wide-eyed, thinking that eight or nine wolves would be killed in the melee. While the wolves were concentrating on each other, he decided, he would sneak close and shoot those that were bound to be crippled from the fighting. He could almost count the $15 bounties and the pile of wolf hides he would sell.

He hurried, keeping out of sight of the animals. Except for tracks and a few spots of blood, he found nothing. All of the wolves had sped off. As he stood, puzzled, some of them, now high in distant sheep hills, howled in a low, sweet chorus. He watched them for a time, realizing they had sensed his presence and fled.

Then it dawned on him—it was breeding season. Likely one or more females were in heat. The animals were simply playing around in a time of excitement; the growling, threats, bumping each other, and fussing was posturing that didn't amount to much.

Wolves had become increasingly abundant in the Alaska Range near his trapline over the previous four years, and Frank Glaser was still learning about their habits.

Board member: Pat's say: A daytime hunt

ON MY OWN time I wrote features for *National Geographic,* the German and French editions of *Geo,* as well as *Audubon, National* and *International Wildlife, Field & Stream, Sports Afield, Outdoor Life* and about thirty other magazines around the world. I wrote so many pieces for *Outdoor Life* that for twenty years my name was carried on the masthead as a Field Editor.

In early 1970, Governor Bill Egan telephoned me. "Jim, will you accept an appointment to the Board of Fish and Game?" he asked.

"Why, yes, of course, governor," I stuttered, flustered and surprised. "It will be an honor." I had no clue this was coming. "Be in Juneau Monday," he instructed. "Glad to have you aboard."

I later learned my old friend Jay Hammond, and his cohort, Clem Tillion, both in the Alaska legislature, had urged Eagan to appoint me. Hammond was the former U.S. Fish and Wildlife Service agent I had invited to lecture to my classes twenty years earlier. Tillion was a legislator from the Kenai Peninsula who had often supported my actions when I was Area Biologist for Cook Inlet's commercial fisheries.

The twelve-member Alaska Board of Fish and Game, an arm of the legislature, promulgated (a favorite word of the Juneau bureaucrats) all regulations for hunting, trapping, commercial and sport fishing, and professional guiding. Thus, unlike the system in many states, the state Department of Fish and Game does not make the hunting and fishing regulations. Instead, at statehood Alaska adopted a system that gives the public the role of establishing regulations by empowering this citizen's board to do the job. During its two annual meetings the Board of Fish and Game enacted more laws than Alaska's legislature did in several years; each regulation it enacted became law.

When I became a member of this board in 1970, a bounty had been paid for wolves in Alaska for fifty five years. A few years after statehood, the legislature had delegated to the board authority to designate Game Management Units in which the $50 bounty was to be paid.

Many studies in the United States and elsewhere had demonstrated that paying bounties for predators is largely wasted money. At my first meeting I argued that the wolf bounty was counterproductive, ineffective, and that claims were often fraudulent. Nor was the bounty effective in controlling wolves where needed. I won the battle when eight of the twelve members voted with me to halt bounty payments for wolves, and the wolf bounty was forever gone in Alaska. Allan Adasiak, a reporter friend with the *Juneau Empire*, ran a news item on my victory, heading it, "New Board Member Leads Battle to End Wolf Bounty."

Work on the board was challenging and fascinating. It took a couple of years for me to get up to speed on various regional conflicts. The knowledge that my "yes" or "no" vote could put a commercial fisherman out of business, or make it difficult or impossible for a bush resident to trap fur he needed for his entire cash income, or to bag a moose on which his family depended for food, caused me to cast my votes with great care.

The wolf control program planned for GMU 20A, which Bob Hinman had proposed, was still drawing fire in April, 1975. Many letters commenting on the plan urged Alaska to transplant surplus wolves to other states.Thinking it a way to at least partly defuse the situation, during that spring meeting I wrote a resolution offering ".. wholehearted, active cooperation of the State of Alaska to any interested and qualified agency that may wish to acquire wolves for establishment or reestablishment of wild populations of wolves ... provided the transplanting of wolves is approved by the major public conservation agency of that state or nation."

This became Board of Fish and Game Resolution Number two on April 22, 1975, with all twelve members voting "yes." It was a sincere offer. The discussion before the vote made it clear that all board members felt that transplanting wolves would be preferable to killing them.

Copies of the resolution were sent to all who inquired about Alaska's wolves, to major conservation agencies, to the Secretary of Interior, to the Alaska Congressional Delegation, and to President Gerald Ford.

That resolution was enacted more than twenty-five years ago. To date, not one state, agency, or nation has asked to acquire live wolves from Alaska. I believe the offer still stands. The only requests for live wolves have come from individuals who desired them as pets. Not acceptable.

I served five years on this board. The two annual meetings grew longer each year, for Alaska's burgeoning human population increased pressures on fish and game, requiring more detailed policies, more regulations, and more work to maintain the resource at healthy levels. The last meetings lasted nearly two months.

Few Alaskans could afford to serve four months of the year on this board; members received expenses, but no pay. Recognizing this, in spring 1975 the legislature split the board into two seven-member boards—the Board of Game (BOG) and the Board of Fisheries.

Soon after the split, ADF&G Commissioner James W. Brooks, one of my former students, telephoned me. "Prof, Governor Hammond wants to know which of the new boards you'd prefer to serve on," he told me.

Hammond, after many years in the legislature, had defeated Bill Egan for the governorship. Egan had appointed Brooks Commissioner of ADF&G in August, 1972.

Jim Brooks and I had shared many campfires on wilderness hunts. We're still close friends after half a century, and still make annual bird hunts together, even though we sometimes agree to disagree on some natural resource issues. That doesn't alter our friendship.

"The game board, Jim," I answered promptly.

We seven members of the new BOG met to be sworn in at the governor's office in Juneau.

Hammond, in office less than a year, told us, "I didn't ask any of you what your political party is before appointing you. It doesn't make any difference to the wildlife, and it makes no difference to me. I appointed each of you because of your knowledge of Alaska, your knowledge of wildlife, and your reputations as concerned Alaskans.

"You're about to take an oath to support Alaska's constitution. All of you are probably familiar with it, but indulge me and let me point out the major sections you must keep in mind as you promulgate (Hammond liked the word, too) regulations and establish policies for the Department of Fish and Game.

"The legislature is to provide for the use, development, and conservation of natural resources for the maximum benefit of the people.

"Fish, wildlife, and waters are reserved to the people for common use.

"Fish and wildlife is to be utilized, developed, and maintained on the sustained yield principle.

"Although you are an arm of the legislature, you are not elected politicians. You represent the wildlife in *all* of Alaska, not just your home districts. I expect each of you to represent the best interests of wildlife in every one of the twenty six game management units.

"I know you will do a good job and I will back you in your decisions. Keep me informed on issues that get so hot you need me to step in."

Governor Hammond was more interested in the welfare of the resource than he was in partisan politics. As he suspected, we did run into controversial issues during his two terms as governor, and as promised, he backed us every time.

Sadly, Alaska's governors since Hammond left office at the end of 1982 have not held the same view toward the state's fish and game. In contrast to Governors Bill Egan and Jay S. Hammond, both of whom were careful to appoint qualified people to the Fish and Game Boards, and who had the good sense and intestinal fortitude to back their boards decisions on even the most controversial issues, most of the governors since have used fish and game as political pawns. Personal prejudice and politics have commonly guided them on fish and game issues. Scientific management has had little standing. Some board members have been appointed as payment for vote-getting for the governor's political party; knowledge of fish and/or game has not been a prerequisite.

When Governor Bill Sheffield took office he fired the seven members of the BOG, ending my twelve years of service on the fish and game boards. One of Governor Bill Sheffield's appointees to the BOG, in Juneau for a first meeting, spotted a magnificent, antlered caribou head on the wall in the ADF&G building that had been donated by long-time ADF&G wildlife biologist Jim Faro.

"My, that's a beautiful head. What is it, a moose?" the appointee, in all seriousness, asked Bob Hinman, who was standing near.

An Alaska BOG member who didn't know a caribou from a moose?

On October 15, 1975, Dr. L. David Mech, who most professionals in the wildlife field in the United States consider to be our most experienced and knowledgeable wolf researcher, talked about his work at a meeting in Kenai. He has long been respected for his Ph.D. thesis *The Wolves of Isle Royale*, which in 1966 was printed as one of the National Parks Fauna Series. I attended the meeting, and he brought us up to date on his latest findings. His book *The Wolf*, completed in 1968 and published in 1970, was still mostly current; but he had pushed some frontiers of wolf knowledge beyond the book.

Mech, commenting on wolves in the U.S. in general said, "On one side you have people who never want to see a wolf killed. On the other side there are those who never want to see a wolf alive."

When someone asked him how Alaska should manage its wolves, he replied, "It depends on what you want to do here. If you have a religion that says wolves won't be killed regardless of what's happening, I can respect that. But if you think by doing this you are somehow going to save the wolves, you are mistaken. If you don't kill wolves, someone else or some wolf will.

"If the prey population is low and you don't control wolves, you'll have fewer prey and fewer wolves for a longer period. If you kill a few wolves, the prey population tends to increase and the wolf population comes up, too. So you end up with more prey and more wolves for a longer period than if you don't do control work."

"But what do you recommend for Alaska?" the questioner persisted.

Mech's response was classic, the response of a veteran who had dealt with the public on wolf issues for many years. "I don't advocate positions in Alaska. I have enough trouble in Minnesota," he said, adding, "But I will say decisions on wolf control should not be based on emotions or feelings. Wolves as a whole fare better if management is based on good biology and science."

It was with this background I found myself in Fairbanks in December 1975 at the first meeting of the new Alaska BOG.

⟁

"MISS PAT YORK, Boston, The National Wildlife Savers Foundation," she signed to testify at the December, 1975, public hearing of the BOG. She found a seat in the auditorium and started to glance through the thick pile of stapled papers listing proposed changes in wildlife regulations for the coming year. She noticed with surprise there were more than 300 of these, most having to do with changes in bag limits or seasons for moose, caribou, Dall sheep, bears and others. With the list was a copy of the hunting/ trapping regulations. Scanning this, she discovered a map of the twenty six game management units (GMU) in Alaska. Later she realized with awe that many of these units were larger than many of the South 48 states.

It looked complicated. She hadn't considered this. Each of these units had its own regulations. She had thought the main business at hand was that of authorizing the killing of wolves near Fairbanks. After searching she found the wolf killing proposal, an unimpressive line that read "Removal of an unspecified number of wolves from GMU 20A."

The room soon filled, and she counted nearly 200, mostly men. The crowd had an outdoorsy flavor; mostly open-at-the-neck wool shirts, warm pants, fur hats and few ties. It seemed to her that most of the participants knew one another, for there was much laughter, visiting, and apparent meeting of old friends. Included in the crowd were Eskimos and Indians. Fur parkas were draped across chairs and piled on tables. Many wore hard-soled, Eskimo-type fur mukluks. The aroma of damp fur pervaded the room.

Pat had never felt so alone. This was an unfamiliar culture. She had expected a formal atmosphere—business suits at least—at such an important meeting, but the feeling was relaxed and clothing more casual than at any public meeting she had ever attended in Boston. John Grant wasn't there. It would have helped to have at least one familiar face near. But she knew her cause was worthwhile, and she was determined to make a good impression. She had worked hard on her presentation, and hadn't Grant told her not to change a word?

We seven members of the new Game Board took our seats at a table at the front of the auditorium, each of us with a pile of books and notepads. Chairman of the Board, Dr. Sam Harbo, professor of biometrics and Chairman of the Wildlife and Fisheries program in my old department at the University of Alaska, Fairbanks, introduced us individually to the crowd. He made the required legal announcement that the public hearing on regulatory changes for Alaska's hunting and trapping regulations was now open.

First to testify was an Athabaskan Indian from Stevens Village, a Yukon riverbank village deep in central Alaska. He had long black hair, a copper skin, and wore soft-soled moccasins, wool pants and shirt. To Pat he appeared to be about sixteen. She worried for the boy—he seemed terribly young to testify at such a meeting. She was sure he would be nervous as he padded silently to the front and sat at the table holding the microphone.

To her surprise the young man calmly looked at each board member, smiled, and in a friendly voice said, "Thank you for this opportunity to testify, Mr. Chairman. My name is Esau Johnson and I speak for the Advisory Committe of Stevens Village."

His relaxed voice boomed over the public address system. "He's not at all nervous," Pat realized. "What a self-assured young man!"

"We'd like the board to change the moose regulations in our area, Unit 25," Esau said. "The regulations now allow us to kill one moose, a cow or a bull. We agree with the proposed change that has been published. It closes the cow season. We'd like to see the new regulations read, 'One bull only.' When we shoot cows late in the season we're killing the calves they are carrying, too. That's all I have, Mr. Chairman."

"Questions?" Sam Harbo asked the board.

Member Sidney Huntington called, "Mr. Chairman?"

"Go ahead, Sidney," Sam said.

"How many moose did the Stevens Village people get last fall, Esau?" Sidney asked.

"About fifteen, Sidney," Esau answered.

"Did you get yours?" Sidney asked.

"Yep. I got a nice bull," was the answer.

Sidney, an Athabaskan from the Koyukuk Valley of northern

Alaska, kept his finger on village life throughout the state. He knew the villagers of Stevens Village, and now knew there was no shortage of meat there for the winter.

That ended Esau Johnson's testimony.

Pat was impressed with the informality and first-name basis between the young Indian and the board. It wasn't done that way in Boston.

Eben Kamerak, an Eskimo in his 60s, was next. Wearing a wool shirt and pants, knee-high fur mukluks, and white gloves (traditionally worn by some elder Eskimos on formal occasions, such as our meeting), he padded to the microphone. Lee Olson, a second Eskimo, similarly dressed, but without gloves, sat beside him.

The white-gloved Eskimo calmly surveyed the seven of us on the board, and tapped the microphone to see if it was alive. He turned to look at the audience for a moment. He then began his testimony in Inupiaq, the language of Alaska's northern Eskimo. After a few words he stopped and his companion slid the microphone to himself and translated in perfect English.

The two represented one of the more than eighty Alaska advisory committees to the board. These committees, comprised of around 800 citizens scattered across Alaska, are the eyes, ears, and advisers to the boards of game and fisheries. They hold public hearings in their home districts and bring the results to the twice-a-year board meetings.

I always enjoyed the older Eskimos who chose to testify in their own language. It exemplified Alaska's wonderfully varied cultures. Few in the audience understood the language, and none of us on the board did, although at various times we had Eskimo board members. Usually, however, such members were of the younger generation who did not use their native language. Sadly, the tradition of Alaska's Eskimos using their own language for presentations at formal meetings seems to be gradually disappearing.

The Eskimos' presentation concluded. There were no questions.

Wild Animal Lovers Association representative, Gracie Bauer, was next. She seemed to be almost in tears as she pleaded with the board to not kill any wolves. "Hunters and trappers take too many wolves now," she said. "Wolves are too valuable to kill. They're an important cog in the environmental wheel," she said. "We especially condemn Alaska for the brutal use of airplanes to hunt down and kill wolves. It is morally and ethically wrong."

When she had concluded, chairman Harbo asked of the Board. "Any questions?"

Member Clint Buckmaster, from Sitka, asked, "Miss Bauer, have you ever seen a wild wolf?"

Reluctantly, she answered, "No. But I heard one howl once."

The audience chuckled. Sam tapped his gavel.

Clint asked, "You object to the use of airplanes for wolf control. If we have to remove a limited number of wolves, don't you agree the quickest, most efficient, and most humane method is for the animals to be killed instantly?"

"If you mean by shooting from airplanes, I don't agree."

Clint then asked, "Are you aware the federal government this year killed 9,645 coyotes, also called brush wolves, in California, Oregon, Idaho, and Nevada by shooting them from airplanes? And they trapped, poisoned, shot, and killed in dens another 16,654?"

Gracie shook her head. She didn't seem surprised. "No. I had no idea."

Clint asked, "What is the difference between that program, and the one we are considering, other than the fact we propose to limit the number of wolves to be killed to a mere handful, and to the area in which control takes place, while the feds try to kill as many coyotes as possible across four states? The coyote, of course, is a little brother to the wolf."

Gracie shook her head. "I don't know. I can't approve of killing either animal, especially by shooting from airplanes."

Clint then commented, "The feds are shooting coyotes from airplanes, but your organization hasn't noticed? You don't run ads saying, 'They're slaughtering coyotes in Oregon, Washington, Idaho, and Montana, shooting them from airplanes.' How come? Could it be that protesting that program wouldn't bring the publicity, and the money from massive mailings, that our wolf control proposals bring?"

Gracie didn't answer.

"It's my belief," Clint commented, "that when Alaska chooses to manage wolves by thinning a handful, it pays the rent and buys fancy new cars for a lot of environmental and animal rights organizations in New York and Washington D.C."

Gracie summoned her nerve and asked chairman Harbo, "May I ask a question Mr. Chairman?"

"Ask, and I'll rule if it is appropriate. We're here to hear comments from the public on the published proposals, and we generally keep these hearings limited to that," Sam said, not unkindly.

Gracie, rather timidly, asked, "Is there any way Alaska could have more wolves?"

"I'll allow the question. Would Ren Smith please comment," Harbo ruled.

Ren, sitting in a front row stood. "There is no single way, but mostly I'd say food is the answer," he said. "More food would support more wolves. Packs become larger with an abundance of food. Litters become larger when food is abundant. Strife between and within packs that results in mortality is lessened with more food. Survival of pups is generally higher with more food. By more food, I mean more prey animals—moose, caribou, deer, and sheep."

"Thank you, Ren," Harbo said. And looking around the board, asked, "Are there any more questions of Miss Bauer?"

There were none, and Harbo called Pat's name.

Appreciative, though puzzled, male eyes followed her as she walked to the front of the room, for she was Big-city dressed—as if participating in a public meeting in Boston. She wore a rather formal, jacketed, black shin-length dress. Heels and a pearl necklace completed the ensemble. Her shoulder-length, burnished copper hair swayed as she walked. She was tall, slim and graceful—a beautiful young woman. If she was nervous she didn't allow it to show.

Speaking with a broad Boston accent, she thanked the chairman and board for the opportunity to testify and then carefully read her presentation:

"The most bloodthirsty animals in Alaska, I'm told, are mosquitoes, not wolves. That is, unless you include the Alaska Department of Fish and Game which has repeatedly carried out a vicious program to destroy the last vestiges of one of our most wonderful animals, the wolf. That bloody program, in the eyes of many of us from the other states, is needless, and reveals a total lack of compassion for Alaska's wildlife. Among the proposals before the board today is one to continue this bloody campaign."

A murmur went through the audience. I saw people frowning and looking at one another questioningly. Several representatives of other environmental organizations, including Gracie Bauer, looked at each other with broad grins.

Pat continued. "Wolves are peaceful animals with wonderful family values. A wolf pack is made up of family members. Members of the pack bring food to the den to feed pups, and the mother of the pups. Commonly, each member of a pack baby sits the puppies while other adults are out searching for food. Each pack has its own territory and the boundaries are known by neighboring packs. A Canadian wolf biologist once established his own several-acre territory within that of a wolf pack's territory by scent marking, just as wolves do. And the wolves in that pack respected his territory. They went around it, rather than cross it.

That brought a snicker from some in the audience, and Sam tapped his gavel warningly.

"Wolves are not the vicious animals of popular belief," Pat continued. "There are friendly relationships between packs. So much so that a pack, through howls, communicates with neighboring packs, telling them where to find caribou. Through howls, they even warn other packs when humans are approaching. They make friends with foxes because they often enlarge old fox dens for their own use."

An even louder murmur and a few laughs filled the room, loud enough to interrupt Pat. Chairman Harbo rapped his gavel. The murmuring died.

I could see the laughter had shaken Pat and I began to feel sorry for her. She was obviously sincere.

"In Canada, (she pronounced it "Canader") Eskimos have such a high regard for wolves that they never kill them," she read.

Some of the audience again laughed, and Harbo rapped his gavel and sternly said. "Order please. Let Miss York have her say without interruption."

Pat continued, but she didn't sound quite so confident.

"Wolves have a bad reputation because they sometimes kill moose or caribou. But wolves always kill the sick or the weak. This benefits the caribou, moose, and deer, making the herds healthier. Usually, however, in summer especially, the wolf feeds mostly on mice. They actually prefer to eat ground squirrels to caribou. And, of course, caribou fawns can run much faster than wolves, so wolves leave them alone. Sometimes wolves feed on fish. They even use paws or nose to move rocks around in a river to catch fish hiding under the rocks. At other times they drive fish upstream and into the shallows of a river where they can more easily be caught.

"Wolves never kill more than they can eat. They never kill for fun. They are completely beneficial, and they have been needlessly persecuted, so much so they have been wiped out in all but a few of our states.

"When you kill wolves you are tampering with the balance of nature and disrupting the perfect ecological balance that has evolved in Alaska over millions of years. Wolves and their prey live in a harmonious balance; man should not interfere in this relationship.

"Canadian trappers fear wolves, as perhaps Alaskan trappers do, but there really is no reason for this. Wolves never attack humans.

"The fact that Alaska still pays a bounty on wolves is disgraceful, and it should be stopped immediately," she said.

That brought another laugh from the audience. Again Sam tapped his gavel.

"We, the 20,000 members of The National Wildlife Savers Foundation, object to and strongly oppose the proposal before you today to kill an unspecified number of wolves in Game Management Unit 20A. We believe this program has been proposed because of pressure from hunters who think wolves are killing moose they want to kill. They are mistaken. Human hunters and harsh winters are killing the moose. The fish and game department is making a terrible mistake in giving in to pressure from greedy hunters.

"Thank you, Mr. Chairman."

A loud murmur again arose from the crowd, and Harbo again rapped his gavel for silence. "Any questions of Miss York?" he asked board members.

There were none and Sam said kindly, "Thank you for your testimony."

I could see that Pat felt rebuffed. She didn't understood the reason for the laughter. She had expected at least one question. Her cheeks were flaming as she returned to her seat.

Ren Smith was nearby. I caught his eye and motioned. He came to me while Harbo was calling the next witness. "Ren, why don't you buy the lady a cup of coffee?" I suggested.

He nodded, eased to the back of the room, took a seat next to Pat, and asked "Ma'am, can I buy you a cup of coffee?"

She was uncertain. "I'd like to hear what others have to say," she said.

"The hearing will last several days. There's plenty of time for you to hear the others. I'd really like to make up for the rude way you were treated."

"Who are you?" she asked. His back had been to her when he had answered Gracie Bauer's question, so she didn't recognize him.

"I'm one of those bloodthirsty Department of Fish and Game biologists," he said with a friendly smile.

"Oh. I hope you're not angry," she gasped.

"Far from it, ma'am. I'm used to criticism. I would like to talk with you."

"You mean brainwash me?" she asked.

"Of course not. I'm just in a better position to know what's going on than you are."

"All right. But I won't change my mind," she retorted, getting up and accompanying Ren from the auditorium.

In the wake of Pat's testimony, board member Sidney Huntington spoke up.

"Mr. Chairman?" he called to Sam.

"Go ahead, Sidney."

"Me, I'm just a dumb Indian, with a third grade education who has used Alaska's fish and game resources for sixty nine years—all my life. In the five years I've spent on the Fish and Game Board and the Game Board I have listened to days of public testimony from people who consider themselves experts in game management. I dislike having to say that many of these sincere people know very little—or absolutely nothing—about the resource they testify about. They commonly repeat propaganda presented to them by extreme preservationists whose ambitions are to disrupt the proper management of our wildlife resource.

"What I hear from the preservationists is to let wildlife take care of itself. This is what we once did, and we had either feast or famine. The preservationist philosophy seems to be to pretend that man doesn't exist in Alaska.

"It seems that some people become especially emotional over wolves. There is nothing wrong with that. But emotions should not persuade interested people to believe in unfounded theories and false statements. Alaska's wildlife is too valuable to everyone to allow emotions to dictate management policy.

"I have put a lot of time and effort into studying the use of our wildlife, and in talking with others who have done the same. And I have seen our efforts bring fruitful results. I don't want to gamble on losing our game by going back to the no-management tactic. It is clear to me that the Alaska Department of Fish and Game has proven scientifically that wolf control, not eradication, is a proper and sensible management tool that benefits both the wolf and its prey.

"Surely, anyone can get the idea of a temporary reduction of wolves to allow moose to increase so there are enough moose for both good numbers of wolves, and for hunters," he said.

Sidney might call himself a dumb Indian, but to me and many others he's a self-educated genius who made such a gigantic contribution to Alaska's wildlife management during his twenty years on the two boards that the Alaska Outdoor Council established a conservation award in his name. On Feb. 3, 1996 I was honored as never before when I was presented with the Sidney Huntington Conservation Award. The beautiful presentation plaque with my name on it hangs in a prominent place in my office.

Still in the future of this 1975 meeting of the BOG was the Honorary Degree of Doctor of Public Service the University of Alaska Fairbanks awarded to Huntington in May, 1989.

Dr. Huntington. And he refers to himself as ". . . just a dumb Indian?"

Eighteen years after this 1975 meeting, I wrote with Huntington, the book *Shadows on the Koyukuk, A Native's Life Along the River*, the story of his fabulous life. He has been my close friend now for more than three decades.

~

FRANK GLASER OFTEN watched the three-by-nine-mile flat near his cabin. One day in March, 1927, from high on a ridge he watched a pack of six wolves make a rare daytime hunt. He first saw the wolves when they were about two miles away, trotting single file from a high knoll, heading across the flat, heads and tails down, looking less than ambitious. A wolf's tail reveals its mood; the higher its spirits, the higher his tail. But the tail never curls up like that of a sled dog.

They passed downwind of a lone caribou cow. Six sniffing heads came up, and six wolves swerved to head through low willows toward the caribou. When they were close, one of the six, a big black, lay down near the caribou while the other five transformed themselves into shadowy, stalking, cats.

As its companions sneaked off, the black wolf issued a low, musical howl and walked boldly toward the cow. She raised her head and stared at him. This was what he wanted. He trotted back and forth, howling, keeping her attention as he gradually worked closer. When the caribou seemed on the verge of fleeing, the wolf backed off. The nervous cow seemed fascinated. Once the wolf ran a short distance toward the caribou; then, before the caribou panicked, it stopped and retreated.

With binoculars it was all Glaser could do to occasionally spot any of the five other wolves as they expertly slipped through grass and willow clumps, keeping to low ground, smoothly working their way behind the cow. They formed a rough semi-circle around the caribou and gradually closed in.

On bellies, heads and tails low, they crawled and scooted ever closer. Occasionally a wolf raised up to peek at the cow, but she was so enamored of the howling black wolf she didn't notice.

Finally, one of the wolves got close enough and made his dash. The cow wheeled and started to run. But the other wolves rushed in, and she was surrounded. In moments she was smothered by the chopping teeth of six efficient killers. The caribou was still struggling weakly as wolves ripped chunks from her hams and gulped them down.

Normally a caribou can easily outrun a wolf. A straightforward chase of caribou on an open flat usually doesn't work, and wolves know it. That's why a sneaky, sly conquest like this has to be orchestrated for a daytime hunt.

Night hunts are most productive. One dark quiet night in late March 1932 at about eleven o'clock as Glaser was getting ready for bed, two packs of wolves howled on the nearby tundra flat. He stepped outside to listen. It sounded as if there were three or four wolves in each bunch, and he guessed they were a mile or two apart. His wolf-dogs were all awake and uneasy; several were perched on their houses looking in the direction of the howling wolves. The air bristled with tension.

Glaser had noticed that wolves make their big caribou kills at night, and he could usually tell in advance when there was to be a big kill.

The wolves lapsed into quiet for a time, but just as Glaser was dropping off to sleep, they renewed howling. This time the wolves had merged into one place. They continued howling for some time. "They'll make a big kill tonight," he told himself.

He fell asleep, thinking, "They're singing me to sleep." He awoke perhaps an hour later. The wolves were again howling. He thought they had made a kill and he was hearing post-kill howling, a behavior he had often observed.

At daylight next morning he was out with binoculars and rifle. Shiny, black, ravens flapped about, and he watched half a dozen land. He climbed to get a better look, and with binoculars saw the big birds feeding on four dead caribou, all within one hundred yards of each other. The dark birds contrasted with the white snow, clearly marking the locations. He went to inspect. The four carcasses were wolf kills from the previous night, and the wolves had eaten only from the hams of three of the kills. One caribou, and the rest of the meat on the others, was untouched.

Glaser returned to his cabin, hitched his team of wolf-dogs to a sled, and hauled the uneaten caribou meat home to feed his dogs.

Educating Pat: Nature's way

"DID THAT GAME board member tell you to brainwash me?" Pat asked, after she and Ren were seated in a coffee shop booth.

"No ma'am. Prof suggested I buy you a cup of coffee. I wouldn't dream of trying to brainwash you," Ren replied with a smile.

"Why? Was my presentation that bad?"

"No ma'am. You made a good presentation. That is, you read it very well,"

"Prof? Why do you call him that?"

"He was my professor when I studied wildlife management at the University of Alaska," Ren said. "I guess it's just a habit. We're good friends. I think he thought you had been treated rudely by the audience, ma'am, and hoped I could explain a bit."

"Please don't call me ma'am. My name is Miss York."

"Yes ma'am, er, Miss York," Ren stumbled. "Mine is Ren Smith."

She nodded, acknowledging his name.

"If I read it very well, why did people laugh?"

"Miss York, I'm sure you are sincere or you wouldn't have come all the way from Boston to appear before the board. I don't think they were laughing at you. I'm afraid the reaction was from the material you quoted."

"What do you mean? I got that information from a book by a Canadian biologist."

"I know. That's what they were laughing about."

"Do you know the book?" she asked

"About everyone here knows the information came from *Never Cry Wolf*," he replied.

"You mean the book is that popular?"

"Not exactly. Just known in Alaska for its characterization of wolves."

"Alaskans think the book is wrong?"

"Yes ma'am, I mean, Miss York. Most of us think the book, as a biological study, misses the mark. Or, perhaps Canadian wolves are different from ours."

"You don't believe that, do you?"

"No."

"You don't accept that Canadian biologist's findings?"

"Let's say we've never duplicated them," he said, dryly.

"You mean the book is no good at all?"

"I didn't say that," Ren smiled. "*Never Cry Wolf* accomplished something that needed doing. It drew attention to the wolf as something other than a varmint, or bad animal. It changed a lot of peoples' attitudes about the wolf. But I don't think it was intended to be a scientific treatise."

"You're jealous, aren't you?" she accused.

"No, ma'am, er, Miss York. The problem is, many people unfamiliar with the wolf have accepted the book as a scientific study. As a result we are often unfairly criticized by people who have read it. Perhaps the wolves Mowat studied did behave as he described, I don't know. Personally I doubt it, for I've worked with Alaska's wolves for more than ten years. They do howl, but they don't tell each other where caribou are, or when humans are approaching. They don't feed mostly on mice. Alaskan wolves need seven or eight pounds of meat daily, which they can get only from moose, caribou, sheep, or deer—large animals. To my knowledge no scientist has found wolves that rely entirely on small prey animals, although wolves will eat anything they can catch, including mice, ground squirrels, birds, and snowshoe hares.

"The Eskimos in Alaska, at least those I know, do respect the wolf, but they also hunt and trap wolves. And I don't know a single trapper or hunter who is afraid of wolves."

"I still think Mowat's study is valid," she retorted. "I don't see any need to kill wolves. They've been wiped out in almost every other state, and Alaska is trying to wipe them out too. It's not right. It's against the balance of nature. Wolves are beneficial," she retorted.

"We're not trying to wipe them out. We're simply trying to manage them. I wanted to make up for the rudeness of the audience. It wasn't polite to laugh when you made your presentation. I hope you can stay through the public hearing, and be here when the board takes actions on the proposals. The meetings are public, you know. I think it would be worth your time," he said, rather stiffly.

"I'll just do that. But I haven't changed my mind. Wolves are wonderful animals, and they shouldn't be destroyed."

"Wolves *are* wonderful animals. Destroying them is the last thing I would want," he said softly.

"Do you shoot wolves?" she asked, bluntly.

"I've had to a few times," he admitted. He didn't try to explain.

"I can't imagine anyone wanting to kill those beautiful animals," she said. It was clear she had no use for anyone who would shoot a wolf.

"No, I guess you can't," he said. "Sometimes, believe it or not, a small number of wolves need to be killed to benefit a wolf population as a whole."

"That's stupid," she retorted. "It's an excuse that doesn't make sense."

"To you, perhaps, it doesn't make sense. But it's biologically sound," he said. He hated to be defensive.

"I don't agree. I don't see how that's possible," she retorted, angrily.

That ended their coffee time. As they parted she felt patronized and resentful. Ren's feelings were mixed; he admired her fire, but was frustrated by her ignorance.

"Next time *you* buy her coffee, Prof," Ren suggested during a morning break. "She wasn't interested in what I had to say. She's a bit of a spitfire."

"Is she a replacement for the last guy?" I asked.

"I didn't get around to asking," he said, ruefully. "We didn't make much small talk."

"She's sure pretty," I commented. "And she's polite. That's an improvement over whats-his-name."

"I hadn't noticed," he said dryly.

That made me smile. Ren was single. For years his friends had tried to match him with eligible women. He dated and was sociable, but to my knowledge he had never had a serious relationship.

⤳

THE PUBLIC HEARING continued throughout the day. Most of the proposed changes in regulations had to do with adjustments in length of seasons and bag limits for moose, caribou, sheep, deer. The "balance of nature" prevalent in folklore is a myth, unless one considers a seesaw a "balance." Wildlife populations annually fluctuate in numbers, in sex, in age ratios, and in distribution, sometimes drastically. Harsh or mild winters, light or heavy predation, migratory movements, cold wet spring and summers, heavy or light hunting by man, habitat alteration by fire or settlement, and other factors, fuel these fluctuations.

For this reason wildlife populations in each of Alaska's twenty six management units are assessed annually for possible adjustments in hunting and trapping regulations. Alaska's wildlife biologists annually spend thousands of hours on the ground and in the air gathering information needed by the BOG to make informed decisions.

Aerial surveys for fishery and wildlife purposes in Alaska is not a safe activity; I can list the names of nearly twenty five wildlife and fishery biologists I have personally known who have died in plane crashes on such surveys over the past half century—and about a dozen biologists who have survived plane crashes. I had my share of close calls when I was the Area Biologist for the Cook Inlet commercial fishery, although I never experienced a crash.

The only incident of note that day came when we on the board found black crepe ribbons spread across our tables after lunch break. Since we were to consider a proposal to remove wolves from GMU 20A, most members assumed that bit of silliness was a message of sorrow for the wolves. In addition to Pat York, representing TNWSF, there were representatives of Defenders of Wildlife, Friends of Animals, and the current Alaskan group which called themselves the Wildlife Supporters of Alaska, and two or three other similar groups. We had no doubt we were indebted to one or more of these anti-hunting and animal rights organizations for the ribbons.

That evening I had a committee meeting, and phone calls to make, so it was late when I wandered into the hotel's coffee shop for dinner. The place had largely cleared out. I spotted Pat York, alone in one of the booths.

"May I join you, Miss York?" I asked her.

I think she was startled and a bit surprised that I knew her name. Then she recognized me.

"Of course," she said. "You're the board member that biologist called Prof aren't you?"

"You mean Ren Smith. Yes, he still calls me that, but I haven't been a professor for twenty years," I said. "I like to think it's complimentary, coming from Ren.

"You suggested he buy me coffee, hoping he'd brainwash me," she said, rather coldly.

"Miss York, we don't brainwash intelligent people," I said, just as coldly. "You were treated rudely by the audience this morning, and you looked upset. Ren Smith is a gentleman. I felt he could make amends for the way you were treated. Believe me, we welcome participation of the public at our hearings. And we try to be cordial to visitors from the South-48."

"Even those who are opposed to killing wolves?" she said.

"Yes, even by those who are opposed to killing wolves. Believe it or not, we don't like to kill wolves," I said. It was no time to try to explain.

As a waitress took my order, I could see she was thinking.

"Thanks for your concern. And yes, I was upset this morning. Laughter was the last thing I expected," she said, a bit contritely.

"Let's leave the wolf issue for now," I said. "I hope you will stay to hear the presentations of the staff when we take action on the proposed changes. It might help you to understand our views."

"I intend to," she said, "but I won't change my mind about killing wolves."

I learned she was a teacher, and she told me about hearing wolves howl on her Algonquin Park visit, and how her fifth graders had developed an interest in wolves.

She had yet to leave the hotel in daylight to see Fairbanks.

She relaxed as we visited, and asked the usual visitors' questions. How could we stand living with only four or five hours of daylight during winter? How did we cope with minus 50 degree cold? She was curious about ". . . the young Indian who looked about sixteen years old who first testified this morning, who seemed so self-assured."

"Esau Johnson?" I asked.

"Yes, I believe that was his name," she said.

"Esau Johnson? Why, Esau is at least thirty," I said. He's a regular at our meetings," I said. "We all know and respect him. His self assurance isn't unusual for a bush villager," I said. "From the time they are children bush residents attend village council meetings and learn to speak in public," I explained.

She wanted to know why Eben Kamerak wore white gloves when he testified, and I explained. It was obvious she was interested in Alaska and our way of doing things. She commented on the relaxed informality of our hearing, comparing it with meetings she had attended in Boston.

"Alaska is a relatively small community—there are only about 300,000 people here. Live here long enough and you'll find you have friends and acquaintances in villages and towns throughout the state," I told her. "Some of those in the audience attend every meeting of our board. Many are friends, and they contribute greatly to our knowledge of what is happening in every part of the state. That's important because we make decisions that have a major impact on the lives of Alaskans, especially those who live in the bush and depend heavily on wildlife for food."

"Are you saying that everyone in the audience supports your board's actions?"

"Heck no," I laughed. "Game management has a lot of critics. And we do make mistakes, and there are those who won't let us forget them," I said, ruefully.

"Tell me about the wolf biologist you decided to sic on me this morning," she said. "I treated him rudely, I'm afraid," she admitted.

I wasn't surprised at her question. Ren is handsome and radiates a strong personality. I answered, "Ren Smith grew up in Wolverine, a small village in bush Alaska. He went to a village school, plus he was home-schooled. He was admitted to the University of Alaska when he was only sixteen, and for four years he studied wildlife management as one of my best students."

"He entered college when he was sixteen?" she asked, surprised.

"Yep. He was a brilliant student," I said. "He earned a Bachelor of Science in Wildlife Management at the University of Alaska, then went to Oregon State College where he earned a Master of Science degree in Fish and Game Management. After that he earned a doctorate in Wildlife Ecology at Purdue," I said.

I could see she was surprised. "I didn't know wildlife biologists could earn doctorates," she admitted.

"Ren is one of the world's top wolf scientists. His field work is brilliant. The department and board rely heavily on him for information on wolves," I said.

"But Alaska seems determined to kill wolves!" she exclaimed.

"Miss York, please do a little research on Alaska's wildlife management program. Don't believe everything that you are told by the animal rights organization you represent. We've come a long way with wolves since statehood, sixteen years ago," I urged.

"What do you mean you've come a long way?"

"Are you aware that the federal government managed Alaska's wildlife until 1960, a year after statehood?"

"No," she admitted.

"During the last ten years of Territorial days, the U.S. Fish and Wildlife Service, the federal agency responsible for managing Alaska's wildlife, employed six or seven predator control agents who spent full time killing wolves. They shot wolves and spread poison bait from airplanes, trapped, and snared them, and they used specially designed cyanide "getters" to kill them. The poisons killed many non-targeted species like foxes, bears, and ravens.

"That's awful," she said.

I continued. "In the fifteen years since statehood our biologists have intensively studied wolves, their life history, and their relationship to prey. We have controlled wolves only where they have threatened to deplete their prey base. We've stopped all use of poison. Aerial hunting by the public is no longer allowed. Under the federal administration, Alaska's wolves were regarded as vermin with no closed season and no bag limits.

"As a state we have classified the wolf as a big game animal and as a furbearer—the only animal with dual classification. We now have bag limits, closed seasons, and closed areas for the protection of wolves. Wolves have repopulated the Kenai Peninsula where I live after a fifty or sixty year absence. We also eliminated the bounty on wolves, which was in place for more than half a century."

She interrupted me. "You mean, there is no bounty on wolves in Alaska?"

"There hasn't been since 1970," I assured her.

"Then I was misinformed. No wonder they laughed at me."

She frowned. "You say there are bag limits on wolves, and you treat them as big game for hunters," she said. "I can't agree with that."

"The wolf is a perpetually renewable resource, just like moose, caribou, or other wildlife. Our state constitution requires that we manage wildlife on a sustained yield," I quietly said. "That includes the wolf."

THAT EVENING WHEN Pat retrieved her room key at the hotel desk, the clerk handed her a wrapped package. "This was left for you, Miss York," he said.

Unwrapping it in her room, she found a copy of *The Wolf*, a book by Dr. L. David Mech. With it was a business card. "Ren Smith, Wildlife Biologist" it read. No mention of his degrees. Neatly written on the card was, "You can believe everything you read in this book. Best wishes, Ren Smith."

DURING HIS FIRST winter at Savage River, Glaser often took one or two of his sled dogs with him for company as he ran the trapline on the high treeless ridge to the west of his cabin. There the males lifted their legs at the occasional clump of high grass. The prevailing south wind blew the ridge bare, and the few grass clumps that were there were always visible.

This, Glaser decided, was too good an opportunity to pass up. The following summer he dug about seventy high grass clumps from the lowlands and back-packed them onto the ridge where he transplanted them on knolls where he wanted to set fox traps. He dug a hole on the south side of and about six inches from each transplanted clump. Next, he drove big steel spikes into the ground nearby. When trapping season opened, he fastened traps to the spikes, which by then were frozen into the ground, placed the trap in the hole, and covered it with dry dirt which he took from nearby ground squirrel holes.

It was a perfect set for catching foxes, and later, when they arrived, (or increased enough to trap) for wolves and coyotes. All male (and some female) members of the dog (or wolf) family habitually leave their sign on prominent landmarks, in this case the transplanted clumps of grass. Occasionally he caught lynx and wolverine in those sets, for they too like to visit and mark clumps of grass.

[Author's note: In the mid-1970s, ADF&G wildlife biologist Pat Valkenburg, working in the Alaska Range, noticed out-of-place bunches of tall grass here and there on a ridge. Investigating, he found four traps abandoned by Glaser in 1937 when he left his trapline to work for the federal government as a wolf hunter. The traps were still in working condition.]

Snow generally drifted on the south side of the grass clumps. But soon the prevailing south wind would knock the snow off. Frank thought it was a wonderful sight to stand in his cabin after a big snowstorm and watch the south wind come up. It would start at the bottom of the ridge and take the snow right on over the top. He called it "the old man sweeping the ridges." The four-thousand-foot-high foothill of the Alaska Range was cleared of snow almost as if swept with a broom. This made it possible for him to walk his twenty mile trapline without snowshoes—a wonderful advantage.

Frank Glaser gained an encyclopedic knowledge of wildlife and had a memory like one of his steel traps. Many raconteurs' stories vary with each telling. Not Frank's. He often repeated his yarns and they never varied. Though I held two wildlife degrees, I didn't have the hands-on experience with Alaska's wildlife that Frank did. I learned much of animal behavior and of their traits from the old trapper. He often told me of some trait of an animal, and then gave an example, as in the following:

Caribou don't see well in the dark; wolves do.

Frank was reading, his favorite evening recreation, one mild December night about 10 o'clock. Snow was falling. Suddenly his wolf-dogs, roaring and growling, hit the ends of their chains. He slipped into his parka and with flashlight went outside and looked around. He could see nothing, but he heard brush crackling in the nearby timber.

At daylight next morning he found fresh tracks in the snow that printed an easy-to-read story. Three wolves had chased a caribou off the ridge. It had run within twenty feet of his dogs' houses, but the wolves detoured around them. The terrified caribou fled into the nearby forest, where it had slammed into a tree and fallen. There a wolf grabbed it. Glaser found blood and a piece of caribou hide as big as his hand lying on the snow. Wolf tracks went *around* the trees.

The caribou escaped, and ran on. But soon it had hit another tree, again falling. This time at least two of the wolves pounced. Bloody tracks of the staggering caribou trailed another hundred feet to where the wolves finally brought it down. The three wolves had devoured much of that caribou (adult wolves can eat nearly twenty pounds of meat at a time), leaving the remains about 300 yards from Glaser's cabin.

During his years at Savage River, Glaser often found caribou killed by wolves during night, sometimes as many as a dozen. Usually the dead animals were fairly close together, perhaps within a few hundred yards of each other. Sign in the snow often revealed the savage tale.

Some nature writers have claimed that wolves cripple their prey by cutting their hamstring to make their kill. Glaser watched wolves kill caribou dozens of times. He found many hundreds of dead caribou and reindeer killed by wolves. Only once did he see a hamstrung caribou. It had apparently escaped after what he assumed was a wolf had cut a hamstring in one leg just above the hock. The caribou was dragging its leg, and Frank shot it to put it out of its misery, using the meat for dog food.

Hunting wolves commonly encircle a bunch of caribou, spooking them. Spooked caribou in a herd have a tendency to crowd from the edge toward the center, trampling one another, tripping and stumbling in the dark while wolves swiftly kill as many as they want simply by running up close, pulling the caribou down.

In killing a caribou, a wolf may run beside it, biting it in the flank. It can slash a five or six-inch-long gash that looks like a knife-cut. One good slash and the caribou's paunch or stomach falls out. The caribou drags itself a short distance, steps and walks on the paunch and attached entrails, and falls over within a few hundred feet. Death comes quickly. Wolves also kill caribou by gripping their throat and suffocating them.

In extreme cold, when a caribou runs at full speed for any distance, its tongue may hang out, wagging at every bound. On the infrequent occasion when a wolf manages to catch up to a caribou when its tongue dangles, it may leap and grab the tongue. One quick bite and the tongue is gone. The caribou hemorrhages and dies. Several times as Glaser watched winter chases he observed a wolf biting a caribou's tongue off, then ignoring that caribou to chase another. Seemingly, the predators realized the tongue-less caribou was done for.

Wolves are cannibalistic. From time to time packs kill intruding wolves. When food isn't plentiful, and sometimes even if it is, the dead wolves are eaten. One winter Frank was walking up the Dry Delta River on the north side of the Alaska Range. There were many caribou in the nearby timber. Ravens—one of the North's great scavengers—were flying about and landing in a clearing ahead. He investigated and found three different colors of wolf hair; gray, light gray, and black. Scouting about, he found fresh remnants of three wolves. Their skulls had been cracked open and their brains eaten; marrow was eaten from cracked bones. In fact, just about everything had been eaten but the skulls, large bones and the animals' feet.

As near as he could reconstruct, nine or ten wolves got into a fight, perhaps over territory. Wolf pack territories are sacrosanct, and intruding wolves from adjacent territories may be attacked or driven off. The three killed in the battle were eaten by the others. It seemed odd to Glaser, because there were so many caribou nearby.

During his forty years wandering the Alaska wilderness, Frank Glaser got as much pleasure out of watching wildlife as he did from hunting. As a wolf expert he often heard well-meaning people interested in wildlife claim that wolves always take sick, crippled, or otherwise misfit animals, thus benefiting the health of their prey. That isn't the way he saw it. He found that wolves take what is available. This conforms to Paul Errington's comment that, "Nature's way is any way that works." Errington was a respected mid-20th century wildlife researcher who studied predation intensively.

Glaser noticed that wolves don't go out of their way to kill infirm animals. They commonly kill stragglers. Some are weak, others are not. A pregnant caribou or moose is more vulnerable to wolves than a barren cow. The same animal at another time of year might be able to easily outrun wolves.

Moose and caribou calves are especially vulnerable to wolves. These are not "sick" or "misfit" animals that need to be weeded from the population—they are the all-important future.

It takes a large number of wolves to pull down a mature bull moose in good condition and with good footing. But two or three wolves can finish off the biggest bull moose bogged down in deep, crusted snow. Moose or caribou bulls without antlers, and tired and weakened from a long, vigorous breeding season, can be killed easily by wolves; they aren't "sick" or "misfits" either, although they are temporarily vulnerable. Since wolves commonly attack from the rear, hoofs of moose (and perhaps caribou) are more likely to cause injury to wolves than antlers.

Wolf teeth are sharp and pointed—ideal for grabbing, holding, tearing, and shearing. Once a wolf gets his teeth into its prey, severe damage takes place. A wolf's teeth work like self-sharpening shears, the upper teeth fitting on the outside of the lowers. Their large molars can crush bone. Biologists have estimated the pressure of a wolf's bite at 1,500 pounds per square inch—twice the pressure of most large domestic dogs. Their bite cause extensive internal bruising which soon causes a wounded animal to become stiff, making it vulnerable to a final attack.

A wolf's jaw muscles are extremely powerful. A large pack of wolves may consume a big moose or caribou except for the skull, the very largest bones, and the stomach. Even many of the large bones are cracked open for the marrow. Glaser's wolf-dogs, which had wolf-like teeth, could hold a caribou bone in their paws and feed it into one side of their mouths and chew off little pieces. They could even crack large moose and caribou bones to get the marrow, a feat impossible for many sled dog.

Wolves slash, leaving cuts in a moose or caribou's hide resembling cuts made with a sharp knife. The soft flank is a frequent target.

Some humans are said to "wolf" food and the word is appropriate in that context. Glaser examined the contents of hundreds of wolf stomachs and often found fist-size chunks of meat. Wolves feed weaned pups by regurgitating such chunks and he often found them at wolf dens or at rendezvous sites where older pups are raised.

The wolf's "cruelty" is not exaggerated although that's viewing it from the human perspective. The wolf isn't *intentionally* cruel; it's just being a wolf. It probably has no feeling of "otherness" for prey. The wolf thinks only of its stomach.

One September day in 1935 Frank noticed a bull moose standing in Savage River near his cabin. The next day the animal was lying on the bank with his head on the ground. He went to see what was wrong. Although alive, the moose couldn't lift his head. Wolves had eaten twenty five or thirty pounds of meat from one of his hind legs. When Glaser had first seen him, the suffering animal had been standing in water trying to cool the feverish leg.

Frank ended his suffering with a bullet in the brain. He then followed the bull's back trail across a sandy stretch of river bar where tracks were clear. Five wolves had run and pestered the bull until he became exhausted and fell or was pulled down. The wolves ate what they wanted then left, perhaps after hearing Glaser's wolf-dogs bark, or sensing Glaser's nearby cabin.

Twice after that while he lived at Savage River he found live moose with meat torn from their hams by wolves. In both cases deep snow with a light crust supported the wolves but not the moose. The moose had no chance under these circumstances.

Staff report: Pat is hired. Glaser's wolf dogs

"WOLVES WERE ONCE perceived as all bad, but as more knowledge accumulated, that judgment crumbled," Ren said. He was making his presentation to the BOG. He appeared calm, self-assured. His voice was strong and carried to the board and the audience without need of the public address system.

The public hearing had ended, and the board was tackling the more than 300 proposed regulation changes. With the high interest in wolves, we board members decided to cover that subject first. The audience had thinned. Department of Fish and Game wildlife biologists had pinned up maps and charts, preparing for their presentations to the board.

Ren continued, "Soon wolves came to be popularly viewed as all good because of their scarcity in most of the United States, and a trend developed among scientists to believe that wolf predation seldom seriously affected numbers of prey. Most recently, as our studies of wolves and other predators extended over longer periods, and new studies re-examined predator-prey relationships, it has become clear that wolves are neither all bad nor all good in terms of their impact on prey species.

"Wolves evolved into their present form about two million years ago, and they have been present in Alaska for about 500,000 years. Today they are found in more than three fourths of the state in almost every kind of habitat from the rain forests of southeastern to the arctic tundra.

"In our studies we have learned that wolves can and do affect the abundance of prey species; they can affect prey numbers a little or a lot, for a short or a long period, depending upon circumstances. It is clear that mortality from predation is usually additive to other mortality. Predation does not simply replace other sources of mortality; animals that wolves kill would often not have died from other causes. By reducing wolf kills, the survival rate of ungulates can be increased, leaving more adults to reproduce. How acceptable the effects of predation are to people also varies.

"The wolf's effectiveness as a predator can affect people's opportunities to see and to use moose, caribou, sheep, and deer. However, while it may be appropriate to regulate numbers of wolves to reduce their effect on prey species, there is no justification for their elimination. Alaska's wolf management program is designed to regulate, not eliminate, wolves and their influence on ungulate prey in selected game management units."

"I don't believe it," Gracie Bauer whispered to Pat. "They'd like to kill 'em all."

Pat had become acquainted with Gracie, a young, idealistic representative of a group calling themselves The Wild Animal Lovers Association. Both were anxious to see how the board would act on the wolf-control proposal. They hung on to every word of Ren's presentation.

Ren continued, "Research in many parts of North America, including Alaska, has shown that predation often controls the rate of prey population growth, can cause prey populations to decline, and can maintain prey populations at low densities.

"Predators must sometimes be actively managed if moderate to high numbers of moose, caribou, or other prey species are to be maintained. We have learned in recent years that without management there can be extended periods when moose and caribou numbers decline to low levels, as do the wolves that rely on them for food. If a balance between wolves and moose exists, historic records suggest it is at a point where moose are scarce. But not only do prey numbers remain low, so do wolf numbers. When wolves can't get seven to eight pounds of meat a day, they cannot thrive.

"In a simple moose-wolf system, ratios of 20 to 30 moose per wolf, or greater, are required for moose numbers to remain stable. At lower ratios, moose numbers usually decline. A ratio of more than 30 moose per wolf will usually allow moose to increase.

However, in Alaska, the use of moose/wolf ratios can be more complicated due to the presence of both black and grizzly bears, and of caribou and sheep," Ren said.

[Author's comment: Since that 1975 meeting of the BOG, much has been learned about predation in Alaska. Studies have shown that where bears are abundant they can kill a high percentage of calves born each year, and that grizzly bears also kill adult moose and caribou, as well as calves. During winter, when bears hibernate, wolves are the primary predators on herbivores in much of Alaska.]

Ren continued: "At times the ratio between wolves and their prey can fluctuate wildly, sometimes catastrophically. Wolf control can sometimes insure greater and more stable numbers of both wolves and their prey."

He then reviewed the decline of moose in 20A, information I had received in the letter from Bob Hinman. He also pointed out that in Alaska, over all, in most years, about 85 percent of ungulate mortality is due to predation by wolves and bears; 2 to 7 percent is due to human hunting, and the balance comes from disease, accidents, and weather.

Ren warned, "If wolf numbers are not reduced in 20A, we will lose most of the moose and caribou and also most of the wolves in that unit, resulting in a biological desert with few or no large mammals. If we reduce wolf numbers enough to allow moose and caribou to increase, in a few years we can have more moose and caribou, as well as about the same population of wolves we have today," he said.

"Do you believe that?" Gracie whispered to Pat. "They want to kill wolves and they say that in a few years it will give us the same number of wolves we have today. How can that be?"

"Wolves are prolific", Ren continued. "In a federal study in a 23,000 square mile area (GMU 13) in Alaska, by 1954 all but an estimated 35 wolves were killed. In 1955 wolves were protected in that area, and protection continued at statehood at which time the state took over the study. By 1965 there were 350 to 400 wolves.

"In that study, protected from hunting and trapping, the average annual increase of wolves from 1955 to 1965 was about twenty percent. Wolves can maintain their numbers, provided they have sufficient prey, even when up to 40 percent of the population is harvested annually. In short, wolf numbers can bounce back very rapidly when their numbers are reduced.

"Most packs raise four to seven pups annually. Although single litters are the rule, as many as three have been recorded within a pack. In early winter most wolf populations include 30 to 50 percent pups, or wolves of the year.

"Another example of the wolf's resilience comes from Russia, although I cannot guarantee the accuracy of the figures. During World War II, when Russians were busy killing Germans, the Soviet wolf population climbed to an estimated 200,000. Intensive control work after the war, including aerial hunting with helicopters, reduced that to about 18,000. Control was then relaxed, allowing the wolf population to soar to an estimated 100,000 within a relatively few years.

"While wolves were largely wiped out in the South 48 states to make way for the raising of domestic livestock and because of habitat alteration for agriculture, with minor exceptions, wolves in northern Canada and Alaska have remained as abundant as their available food supply of big game prey would support. For a time, under federal management, wolf numbers in Alaska were depressed. Under state management since 1960, their numbers have largely recovered.

"Each time we propose to remove a few wolves from specific areas, well-meaning people spend precious time and emotion to "save" the wolf. Actually, Alaska's wolves have already been "saved." They exist in healthy numbers nearly everywhere in the state.

"Emotionalism has replaced reason, and activism has replaced science. Some folks who comment on our proposed wolf management can be classed as professional wolf haters. At the other extreme are professional wolf lovers. There is no way we can please both extremes.

"The International Union for the Conservation of Nature, a privately sponsored organization dedicated to wildlife conservation worldwide, recently pointed out that because of the variation in wolf-prey or wolf-prey-man relationships, control of wolf numbers may sometimes be necessary," Ren concluded.

There were no questions from board members.

The board then turned to action on Hinman and his staff's proposal to remove wolves from 20A.

DURING THE DECEMBER BOG meeting, despite herself, Pat had been impressed by Ren Smith's presentation. He was obviously competent, and he didn't flaunt his education; no one called him "doctor" Smith. Board members, staff, and attending public all called him "Ren." He was obviously respected and popular.

Pat had assiduously read the book Ren had given her. He had refused her offer to pay for it. "It was a gift. I think we owe you that. Now you owe it to us to get all the facts before you judge." He said with a smile.

She felt foolish. With simplistic views, she had walked into what she now realized was a complex situation. After reading the carefully worded, scientifically documented work of Dr. Mech, she was beginning to wonder about the reliability of Mowat's book. Her head was in a whirl as she weighed facts about wolves, and listened to various viewpoints expressed to the game board by the public on the proposal to kill wolves.

During the public hearing, several older Alaskans had demanded that the board return to the program of the federal government. "Kill every one of the damned murderers," one gray-bearded woods-man almost screamed when his turn came to speak. "We had more moose, caribou, sheep, and deer after the federal wolf-killing than we've ever had since," he said.

All of the anti-hunting organization reps had opposed *any* killing of wolves. "They're too valuable an animal to kill; they are human-like in their family life, and they kill only the weak and sick. They're entirely beneficial," was the message from most.

At least Gracie and the other reps from environmental orga-nizations knew there was no longer a bounty paid on Alaska's wolves, Pat told herself. "Damn that John Grant, anyway. He knew I was going to make a fool of myself when he read my paper. 'Don't change a word' the snake had said," she anguished.

Grant had appeared briefly at the public hearing. She had ig-nored him, refusing even to speak to him. What he had done was deceitful, cruel, and damaging to Pat and to the goals of TNWSF. She was too mortified to immediately report to Jerry Hanson in Boston. She would wait and give him an oral statement when she returned home, she decided.

After several hours discussion, the board amended the staff's proposal on wolf removal, and voted six to one to direct the department to shoot wolves in GMU20A from fixed wing aircraft and helicopters, with only ADF&G employees doing the shooting. Not more than eighty percent of the wolves were to be removed. The objective was to achieve a ratio of one wolf to one hundred moose. The program was tentatively scheduled to run for three or four years.

"If the goal of one wolf to one hundred moose is achieved, moose will rebound quickly," Steve Acorn promised.

PAT WASN'T SURPRISED at the decision. Several environmental groups promised they would go to court to stop the slaughter. She was disappointed, and hated the thought of wolves being shot simply to increase the numbers of moose. "I'd rather let nature takes its course," she told herself.

She flew back to Boston after the board acted on the wolf control proposal. There she confronted Jerry Hanson. "You sent me up there totally unprepared. Why, Alaska hasn't paid a bounty on wolves since 1970. And when I quoted *Never Cry Wolf*, the book you recommended, they laughed. No one there, except maybe some of the environmentalists, believes the book. They say it's fiction, despite what it says on the cover."

"Whoa," Jerry said, holding up a hand. "I didn't know all this. My information came from John Grant."

"But you pose as an expert on wolves. You visit schools with Lobo and talk to school children and show them that wolf movie," she objected, angrily.

"I'm sorry, Pat, I haven't read a lot about wolves. I thought *Never Cry Wolf* was a good reference. And I depended on Grant to keep me informed on wolves in Alaska. Obviously, he failed me."

"They laughed at me," Pat said, angrily. "My presentation was so much garbage. I wanted to save wolves from getting killed, and I didn't accomplish a damned thing. In fact, I probably weakened the whole program of TNWSF because I was so ignorant."

"Do you still want to stop Alaska's wolf killing program?" he asked.

"Of course. Wolves should not be killed. Shooting them from airplanes, as they plan to do, is savagery," she said.

"All right," he said. "How would you like to become our permanent representative in Alaska? We have to replace Grant. The job is yours if you want it."

Pat was astonished, and for long moments she had no response. Was this the opportunity she was looking for to get away from teaching? Then she remembered the laughter.

"What would you expect of me?" she wondered, her anger cooling, "and you'd better level with me. I want to know the whole story."

"All right," he said. "Stopping Alaska from killing wolves is only one of our campaigns. You know we are an animal rights organization. We're opposed to all animal use. We want to stop livestock farming, close fur farms, halt hunting, fishing, and trapping. We are unalterably opposed to the use of animals for experimentation. Animals should have equal rights with humans. Man has too long dominated animals; it is time we realize animals have feelings, too."

She stared at him. This was a new perspective on TNWSF. She had become so involved with Alaska's wolf issue that she had missed the primary purpose of the Foundation.

"I'm not sure I agree with you. You mean I'm not supposed to eat meat?"

"That's right. Think of the terror of those poor animals that are slaughtered. You don't need to eat meat. You can get protein from other sources," he said.

"I'll have to think about this," she said. "I just wanted to stop the slaughter of wolves. I wasn't aware of your concept of animal rights."

"We know our ideas are strange to some," Jerry said. "But we believe in them. We need money to finance our program. We send requests for donations to members and to those who sympathize. We get the greatest response to requests for donations when Alaska announces another wolf killing program. You were here when we tallied the income for the Boston chapter from our last Alaska wolf-killing letter. We had a similar response from our ten other chapters. That letter brought in more than $300,000 nationwide for the Foundation. To be honest, Alaska's wolf killing helps finance our other programs. For that reason alone we need someone in Alaska to keep us informed. The more wolves they kill, the more money we receive from our mailings."

She stared at him. "In other words, you'd like to see Alaska continue to kill wolves so you can rake in more money."

"Not really. We'd truly like to see Alaska stop killing wolves," he said.

She didn't believe him. She was beginning to form a new and not very complimentary view of TNWSF.

"What was John Grant supposed to do for you?" she asked.

"Our sources in Alaska made us suspicious of the figures and information used by the state wildlife biologists. If our information was correct, we wanted him to get the true figures and make them public."

"In other words, you wanted him to dispute everything the wildlife biologists up there did?"

"In a way, yes. We figured it would weaken their position, especially if we took them to court, and give us a better chance of stopping them from killing wolves," he admitted.

"Did you really expect him to be able to get reliable figures—to compete with a state-financed bunch of professional wildlife biologists?" she asked. "That's an impossible assignment." And then, she later realized, she capitalized on her brief Alaskan experience. "Do you have any idea how big that Game Management Subunit 20A is? Why, its bigger than the whole state of Connecticut! Of course it costs big bucks to charter planes to fly over it—and that's the only way to gather the information."

She hadn't realized she had absorbed this knowledge; she simply knew it was true. If Hanson was surprised he didn't show it. She was surprised at herself.

"If I accept, what salary are you offering?" she asked.

"We'll match your teaching salary, plus ten percent. Also, we own a house at Fairbanks where Grant has been living. You could live there. You'd have to pay utilities. We'll pay all job-related expenses."

"Federal employees in Alaska get a twenty-five percent cost of living allowance," she said. "Living costs there are terribly high."

"Ok. twenty-five percent," he agreed. "Starting immediately."

"What would you expect of me? she asked, adding, "I'm not a biologist."

"Your interest in saving wolves is why we want you. With your education—you don't teach school without credentials—we expect you to look carefully at Alaska's wolf program. Check their figures. Talk to other anti-hunting and animal rights people up there. Get cozy with some of those state biologists if you think it would help."

"Are you telling me to sleep with them?" she asked, beginning to get angry again.

"Heavens no," he backed off. "Just get acquainted. Find out what is really going on and keep us informed. I've told you, every time Alaska announces it's going to kill wolves, we profit financially. Paying you to keep us informed will be a sound investment."

"Give me a couple days to consider it," she requested.

"Ok. Call me day after tomorrow," he said.

⌒

FRANK GLASER MADE half-wolf Queenie his dog team leader because she was the quickest to learn what he wanted. She was affectionate with Glaser and loved to have him pet and handle her. He frequently allowed her in his cabin. In winter when her coat was heavy she couldn't stand the heat very long, but she would stay until she was panting and uncomfortable.

The first thing Glaser taught the wolf-dogs was to come when he called them by name. Next, they learned what the harness and sled were for when he hitched them to an empty sled. They learned these steps easily.

The next step, to teach them to lie down and remain steady when he was hooking them up, required hours of patient training. He tied the sled to a tree. Then he harnessed Queenie and put her in the lead position on the towline, telling her to lie down. She learned quickly. Then he harnessed the others one at a time while they were still at their dog houses, turned them loose, and called them to their position on the towline. He made each lie down in turn and wait while he repeated the process with the others.

When the entire team was hooked to the towline and lying down, he would go into the cabin as he would in winter to warm his hands and to put on his parka and mittens. During the summer/fall training, he stood in the cabin and peeked out to see how they were behaving. Every wolf-dog would be quivering, ears up, watching the cabin, waiting for Frank, eager to go.

Often when he left the cabin during training, several of the animals would be tempted to stand. "Down," he would order, patiently pushing them down. Then he would go back to the cabin. Sometimes he worked with them that way for an hour or more, without releasing them to run. Sometimes he removed their harnesses and called them to their houses and chained them for a time. Then he'd do it all over again.

By winter he could leave them lying in place without having to snub the sled. They would anxiously wait while he went into the cabin for his parka and mittens, or anything he wanted to put in the sled. They were like coiled springs, hardly able to contain themselves. They might lie quivering for half an hour, but they wouldn't move. At his "all right," they were away like a shot, leaping into action and speeding down the trail.

In some matters he didn't know whether his wolf-dogs were especially intelligent, or were simply exhibiting wolf behavior. One September seven of his four-month-old wolf-dog pups, running loose near his cabin, encountered a porcupine. They trotted back to the cabin seeking Frank's help. Four had a few quills in their noses; three had no quills. One, the most aggressive male, also had quills in his mouth where he had grabbed the porky.

Frank yanked the quills and tied them up. Next day he took the dog that had had a mouth full of quills and searched out a porcupine. He pretended to hit the porky with a stick, and egged the young wolf-dog on. "Sic 'im, boy, sic 'im," he urged.

The animal had apparently learned his lesson, for he wouldn't get closer than three feet from the quill-rattler. Most dogs do not learn from a porcupine encounter; in fact, after being quilled, some dogs grow to hate a porky, and will tackle one whenever they can, with sad results.

Over forty years Glaser handled more than 500 dead wolves in Alaska. Only one had porcupine quills in its face, and Glaser thought that wolf was rabid. Did his wolf-dogs learn from their porcupine encounter, or did their wolf blood tell them to leave the porky alone? He didn't know.

His wolf-dogs weren't vicious with him or other people, although they tended to be one-man animals. Queenie especially disliked to be petted by anyone but Glaser. She was friendly with people as long as they didn't put hands on her. Even then she never offered to bite. When she was loose she would stand behind Glaser when other people were near. If anyone tried to touch her, she walked a short distance then stood and looked at them.

All his wolf-dogs had the peculiar odor typical of wolves. Frank often rubbed his hands through the fur of a fresh wolf skin and smelled it. He liked the smell, although some people don't. It's different from dog smell.

When loose dogs at the town of Healy (which consisted of a couple dozen buildings) where he usually shopped, smelled Glaser's team, they tucked their tails between their legs and disappeared after one whiff. Eventually the mere sight of his team arriving in town caused loose dogs to vanish.

When his wolf-dogs fought among themselves they tried to kill one another. From the time they were pups, though, Glaser worked to convince them not to fight. When a pup started a fight, he gave it just enough of a switching to sting. As adults most of his wolf-dogs weighed 120 to 130 pounds. Kenai, the biggest, weighed 155. To break up fights when they were adults Frank used a padded leather blackjack filled with a pound of lead shot. When a dog started a fight he'd tap him across the nose and knock him down. If he growled at Frank or showed any more inclination to fight, he'd knock him down again.

That broke most of them of fighting. His wolf-dogs were so powerful and their teeth so efficient they could easily have killed one another. Usually a fight started when a dog tangled his harness when running or pulling, and he'd blame the dog running beside him and light into him.

Early on, his wolf-dogs insisted on chasing caribou while in harness. When hot after caribou, they dragged the sled with Glaser on it wherever the caribou went. Too often that was high into the sheep hills. At times those powerful dogs dragged the upset sled with Frank clinging to it and cussing them for a mile or more through brush, across creeks, and over the tundra before he could stop them. His winter clothing was often torn, and he sustained many scratches and bruises. He also spent a lot of time repairing dog sleds.

He decided to break them of this habit. At the time he worked Queenie and her brother, Buster, as double leaders, running them side-by-side. One winter day when many caribou were on the flats not far from his cabin, Frank harnessed the dogs and snapped a rope between knots in the neckline between Queenie and Buster. He tied the other end of the rope to the bow on the back of the sled.

He headed the team down the trail they often traveled until half a dozen running caribou appeared. That electrified the dogs. All eyes latched onto the fleeing caribou and every animal, yipping with excitement, made huge leaps in pursuit. They left the smooth trail and the sled leaped, plunging over cut banks, and ricocheting across the bumpy ground. Frank hung on for dear life, not daring to use the jerk line on the rough ground for fear of killing himself or a dog or two. They finally came to smooth ground.

Frank hit the brake and yelled, "Whoa, whoa, dammit." The dogs knew the meaning of "whoa" but as usual when pursuing caribou paid no attention. Frank wrapped the jerk line around his wrist and with a last "whoa" leaped from the sled.

Queenie and Buster's combined weight was about 250 pounds. They yanked Glaser's 160 pounds a good ten feet through the air. Snow flew as he bounced, skidded, and rolled to a dazed stop. Queenie and Buster were somersaulted backward into the rest of the team, which rolled into a huge squirming, growling ball. The sled rammed the pile.

When Frank had them straightened and had somewhat recovered, he hunted up another bunch of caribou. The dogs ran lickety split after them. This time when he yelled "whoa," he hauled back on the jerkline while standing on the sled; he had had enough of being yanked through the air. Again the leaders were pulled over backward into a confused melee and again the team was rammed by the sled.

After that when he yelled, "whoa," the wolf-dogs slowed, whether or not they were shagging caribou, warily eying Frank over their shoulders. He made no more involuntary trips into the high sheep hills. Whenever they started to get a little hard to stop, he'd rig the jerkline. Occasionally on the first trips in fall or early winter, he had to use it again, but as intelligent as those wolf-dogs were, the mere sight of it was usually enough to get them under control.

10

Kenai: Wolf-dog problems

KENAI WAS ONE of a litter of thirteen pups Queenie, Frank Glaser's half-wolf lead dog, whelped in March 1928. His father was a great gray half-wolf sled dog. Every one of that litter of ten females and three males was gray. Frank kept the males, calling them Kobuk, Wolf and Kenai, all good Alaskan names. Kenai, the biggest of the three, was the boss from the start. When full grown, he tipped the scales at 155 pounds, twenty pounds more than any of his other wolf-dogs.

A person gets attached to dogs too easily, even to sled dogs that aren't pets. If Frank had known the trouble Kenai would cause him over the next five years he'd have killed him the moment he was born. During those five years he swore at the end of each season that he wouldn't start another winter with him in the team. Kenai was nothing but trouble. If it wasn't a fight he started, it was something else. Once he almost drowned Frank. Yet he became attached to the big wolf-dog and didn't have the heart to get rid of him.

He was difficult to understand. He was at once a clown, a hard luck dog, a working fool in harness, a foolish friendly mutt, a wonderful leader, a killer in a fight. He looked like a wolf, fought like a wolf, ate like a wolf. He wasn't all dog, and he wasn't all wolf. He was a strange mixture, and he sometimes changed from dog to wolf and back to wolf with bewildering frequency.

Kenai had big feet, and legs as thick as a big man's wrist. His canine teeth were longer than those of any wolf Frank ever killed. He could hold the frozen rib of a big bull moose with his front feet and feed it into the side of his mouth, chopping it off into little pieces. He broke caribou leg bones to get the marrow as easily as Frank could peel an orange; caribou bones are the hardest and toughest of any of Alaska's big game. An ordinary dog can't break caribou bones, although wolves can.

With his great weight and strength and his love of pulling, he could almost pull a loaded sled by himself. He was also a great pack dog, although Frank rarely loaded him with more than about thirty pounds. Occasionally in summer Frank killed meat some distance from his cabin. To get it home he'd take three or four of the wolf-dogs and their packsacks, bone the meat out and let them carry it. A few times in cool weather he loaded Kenai with fifty pounds or so for a short pack, although he didn't like to put a heavy pack on a dog. Living at a time when dogs were important work animals, he saw many dogs ruined by making them carry over-heavy loads.

Kenai loved a good fight, and no ordinary dog could stand up to him. In 1931 he killed two big malemutes in Fairbanks in almost less time than it takes to tell about it. He didn't start the fight but he sure finished it. Frank had started to guide nonresident hunters, and was organizing a hunt for a couple of clients and had left his dogs at Ed Day's dog livery at the edge of Fairbanks. He had just reached town after tying them in Ed's yard when Ed caught up with Frank, reporting that the big wolf-dog had broken loose. The dog's leather collar had rotted without being noticed, and he had lunged a few times on his chain, breaking the collar and taking off. He refused to come to Day.

Soon after, Frank found Kenai trotting back and forth across the street, head and ears up, sniffing here and there and leaving his sign at every tree, post and corner.

"C'mon Kenai," Frank called, snapping his fingers. He ran to Frank and made it clear that he had been looking for him and was glad to find him so quickly. Frank started back toward Day's with Kenai trotting at heel.

They passed a log cabin where two big malemutes were tied. They lunged at their chains and barked at Kenai. He was ready to take them on but Frank spoke sharply to him and kept walking. Kenai followed, but reluctantly. Suddenly the running wire holding both malemutes broke and they bounded across the little yard and hurdled a low fence.

Frank looked around in time to see them both dive at Kenai. Kenai staggered but didn't go down, then he turned and went to work. Frank hunted for a club to break up the fight, but he tried to watch the fight at the same time.

Kenai was a foot-fighter—that is, he would bow his neck, holding his head low and to one side, allowing the other dog to clamp down where his heavy wolf ruff protected him, and then he went for a foot. As soon as one of the malemutes had a grip on his neck, Kenai reached down, grabbed a front foot and started breaking bones. No dog can stand that. The instant the big malemute let go and tried to pull his foot free, Kenai released him, and as the dog fell backward, Kenai pounced. He slashed the malemute's belly open and yanked his guts out.

The second dog suddenly decided he had very urgent business on the other side of town and he lit out sprinting. He didn't get two hundred yards before Kenai caught him. His insides were on the ground and he was kicking his last by the time Frank got there. Both of those dogs weighed close to a hundred pounds.

Frank had to admire Kenai for his independence but cussed him for it too. He took his responsibility as a leader too seriously at times and he felt that when things went wrong it was up to him to straighten them out. Frank often used a double lead, and sometimes worked Queenie, his mother, beside him. Occasionally, when his harness tangled or something else went wrong on the trail, Kenai would reach over and grab 125-pound Queenie by the scruff of the neck, pick her up, and carry her. Kenai accomplished this without so much as breaking stride. Queenie would cry, and of course Frank would yell at him. If the dogs were moving too fast Frank couldn't do much but stop and straighten him out. If possible he kept moving and ran up alongside and cracked him across the nose with the padded blackjack he always carried.

Frank worked Buster, Queenie's brother, behind Kenai. On a steep slope, Buster growled and puffed and made a big fuss about how hard he was pulling. That always burned Kenai up. Often when this happened, Kenai quit pulling, whirled, and clamped down on Buster's nose. And it always seemed to happen when the team was less than a sled length or so from the top of the slope. The rest of the dogs had to stop then, of course, and the sled would slip back. Frank would try to hold it with the brake, but the front end usually came around sideways. The whole works, tangled dog team, sled, Frank and all, would start downhill. Frank would grab Kenai and tap his nose with the blackjack until he turned Buster loose and quieted down. Then came the job of straightening the team out, turning the sled, and getting started uphill again. After the team started again Kenai would break his neck pulling to get up the hill.

When Kenai stopped suddenly, Buster sometimes bumped into him. That too was usually good for a fight.

It was Frank's habit in the evenings when he came in off the trapline (which he covered afoot) to turn about two of the dogs loose at a time. When he turned Kenai loose, he usually let Queenie, his mother, or Kobuk, his brother, loose at the same time. They would run around the cabin, playing. They had the snow packed down in a huge circle, and chased one another having a good run. After half an hour or so Frank would tie them up and loose another couple of dogs.

If he ever made the mistake of turning Buster and Kenai loose at the same time, however, it wouldn't be any time before Kenai would run at Buster, hit him with his shoulder and try to knock him over and grab him, precipitating a big fight. Buster was a great fighter too and could defend himself. But Kenai was so big and powerful Frank always worried that he'd kill Buster.

Kenai was smart. When Frank hooked the team up he carried his blackjack fastened to his wrist with a loop. When he smelled it he wouldn't start any fights that day. But if Frank forgot and stuck the blackjack under the tarp where he could reach it in a hurry, Kenai was likely to pitch into one of the other dogs at any time, apparently just for the hell of it.

Sometimes Frank would work the dogs every day for a month or more without a fight. Occasionally he forgot to take the black-jack, and it seemed Kenai sensed that, for on those occasions, old Kenai would rip into one or more of the others, and then Frank would have a lot of trouble stopping the fight.

Kenai was more wolf-like than the other dogs in that he wasn't much to make noise. Buster, Queenie, Kobuk, Wolf—all the others—were dog-like, in that they often barked, growled, howled, or whined. Not Kenai. Of course when wolves howled, he howled back. If Frank killed a wolf near the cabin he often turned Kenai loose with one or more of the other dogs, and he'd be the first to reach the dead wolf. He would go to the rear of the wolf and sink his teeth into it, always carefully avoiding the front end. He would drag a dead wolf around and shake it and wool it for several minutes or until he was satisfied the animal was truly dead.

Kenai was a clown, too. As soon as there was enough snow each fall, Frank usually drove into Healy for supplies. He always drove down the main street— n fact the only street—in Healy, directly to the hotel. When he came into sight loose dogs always disappeared behind buildings.

He was amused at the team one day when Kenai was two, as they came pouring down the hill and into town. A stray dog running ahead ducked out of sight, and every dog in the team was looking for something else to chase, heads and ears up, and bounding into the air with every other jump. If they ever got away from Frank when in that mood they'd quickly kill any dog they caught.

Just before they came to the Baker place, Mrs. Baker opened the front door and let out her tiny Boston Bull Terrier which weighed about seven pounds. It danced into the street in front of those eight bounding wolf-dogs, screaming, "Yipyipyip!"

Frank was scared to death. He told me, "I *knew* that dog was a goner and stood on the brake, yelling, 'Whoa, boys, whoa there.'"

They stopped, and Frank's eyes just about popped. Kenai, in the lead with Queenie, lay down and sniffed at that little pooch as it came up to him. As he sniffed, the little fool ran in and grabbed one of Kenai's front legs and started to chew on it. Frank expected to see Kenai bite the idiot in two right there. Instead, that 155-pound clown cringed! Then he started to cry and whimper!

The rest of the dogs, most of which had felt Kenai's teeth at one time or other, seemed as amazed as Frank, and looked around at Frank uneasily as if to ask what was going on. Frank picked the tiny dog up, and it tried to bite *him*. Mrs. Baker came running out into the street and he gladly handed it to her, mumbling something about, "My gosh, they'd kill that little thing. One bite and that would be all." She gave him a strange look and took her pet back into the house.

After that, whenever Frank was in town and had the dogs tied behind the hotel near the Baker place, Kenai watched for that little Boston Bull. When it came into sight he coaxed it to him, and the little thing would run up, growl, then dive in and start chewing on one of Kenai's big legs. Kenai would act surprised and reel back, then scoot into his doghouse, crying as if he were being killed. It was a game with him.

And then there was the time Kenai dumped a case of canned milk into Savage River. One fall, after Frank had spent the summer at Healy, he put packs on Kenai and Buster and hiked to his Savage River cabin in order to kill his winter's meat. Kenai carried twenty four cans of Carnation milk; Buster packed spuds. When they got to Savage River Frank dropped his pack, put Buster's on the ground and started to unfasten Kenai's pack. Just then a big white-necked bull caribou trotted stiff-legged out of the willows on the other side of the river, stopped, and stood looking back. Frank was after meat, and there it was, right next to the cabin. He snatched up the rifle and held for the caribou's neck.

Wham! went the rifle, followed immediately like a peculiar echo by *kerplunk* as Kenai, pack and all, plunged into the water and started toward the caribou. The bull went to his knees at the shot, but he bounded up immediately and leaped over the bank into the river and started upstream.

Buster used his head and ran upstream along the bank, then swam out to sink his teeth into the caribou's nose. Frank watched as he held the bull's nose under water and drifted downstream. He couldn't shoot because Buster was beside the caribou. By the time the two were a couple of hundred feet downstream, Buster had drowned the caribou. The dog and caribou drifted ashore, and Buster kept mauling the caribou and chewing its throat. Frank called and he reluctantly left the bull where it had stranded on a gravel bar.

In the meantime Kenai, with the heavy pack, had a terrible time. He never reached the caribou, for he had all he could do to keep from drowning. He kicked up an awful fuss, lunging, jumping and growling.

Frank was about to jump in after the darned fool when he hit a shallow place and struggled ashore. The big waterproof dog pack must have had ten gallons of water in it and—Frank thought—the canned milk. Both pouches dragged, and Kenai's belly almost touched the ground as he walked, splayfooted. He was carrying more than sixty pounds.

Frank dumped the pack and found nothing but water. Kenai's ears drooped and he looked so woebegone it was hard keep from laughing, but Frank knew better than to laugh at Kenai. Instead he patted his head and said, "Good job, boy. You've done fine!"

That darned dog had packed milk eighteen miles only to dump it in the river at the cabin. Frank never found a single can.

He was the most sensitive dog Frank ever knew. If Frank was angry with him or even pretended to be and spoke sharply, his hair would immediately stand on end. He would walk away stiff-legged, looking at Frank over his shoulder. Several times after Frank talked roughly to him when he was loose and Frank turned his back, he ran and hit the back of Frank's knees with his shoulder, knocking Frank flat. He rolled over and jumped up each time and laughed. Kenai cringed then; he hated to be laughed at.

One early September after returning from a day in the hills, Frank turned Kenai and Kobuk loose and they started to play around in the grass. He had leaned his rifle against the front of the cabin and was watching the two dogs when a bull moose arose out of the high grass about fifty yards from the cabin. It had bedded down there while Frank was gone.

The two loose dogs saw him the same instant Frank did. He grabbed his rifle and shot. The moose dropped to his knees but got up and ran into the timber before he could shoot again. The two dogs rushed after him.

Frank crawled into the thicket and within a hundred yards found the moose with the two dogs worrying him. Kobuk would bite him on the rear end, he'd turn his head to look around, and Kenai would jump up and bite his nose. The moose's ears were pinned back and he was kicking like a mule. Frank knew if he didn't do something quickly the moose could kill or injure one or both dogs. There was little room to maneuver in the brush.

As the moose spun around Frank shot him in the neck. He dropped, dead. Instantly, the two wolf-dogs started to cut into him to eat—Kenai on his belly, the other on the front end.

Frank walked up to them and said, "Good job, boys." But Kenai would have none of it. Dining on the moose's belly, he turned on Frank, snarling, bristling up and jumping to his feet. He thought he had killed the moose and he wasn't going to let Frank have it. Then Frank laughed and he turned into a dog again. With Kenai, the wolf was never far from the surface.

After he was a year old and fully grown, some mornings Frank would leave his cabin and Kenai would be at the end of his chain like the rest of the dogs to greet him. Then, suddenly, he seemed to turn into a wolf. He would squat and stare at Frank with his wolf eyes, his tail dropping to the ground, his mane standing on end. He would growl, and back toward his house and dive into it as Frank walked to him. That bothered Frank, who thought something was wrong with him. He would grab the chain and yank Kenai's head out of the doghouse, which really took some yanking. Then he would grab both ears and pull, with him growling and snapping at Frank every bit of the way. He was always careful, though, not to bite.

Frank would rub him behind the ears and try to get friendly with him but no, the instant he let go, Kenai would dive back into the doghouse and lay there peeking out as if he had never seen Frank before. The wolf Frank kept for breeding purposes wasn't a bit wilder than Kenai at such times. Frank could never decide if Kenai just pretended not to know him, or actually didn't, when he behaved that way. He thought it was just a good act because he pulled that stunt most often after Frank had punished him, but not always.

On other days Kenai would be all dog. He would jump up and put both feet on Frank's shoulders with his head close, happy and friendly as he could be. Frank could never figure him out and never knew what to expect from him next.

Kenai almost drowned Frank once. It was late October when Savage River had frozen over enough to cross with the dog team. Frank hooked up and went to Healy for some grub and mail. When he returned the next day the ice had run, even though the temperature was 20 below zero. There was nothing but slush ice where he had crossed the previous day. Normally the channel where he crossed is narrow, but ice had jammed below, damming the river. As far as he could see up and downstream there was nothing but slush ice. He had eggs, spuds, onions and a few oranges on the sled that would freeze if he didn't get them to the cabin. He didn't know how he was going to get the dogs and himself across, much less the grub.

He unhooked the dogs, leaving their harnesses on, and started upstream looking for a place to cross. Queenie was usually very good on ice but it wasn't her day. She decided to cross the slush ice to the cabin.

"Queenie, come back here," Frank yelled as she started.

Usually she minded well, but either she didn't hear him or she had to keep going to stay on top of the half-frozen slush. She ran fifty or sixty feet and broke through. That shouldn't have been so bad, for she was a strong swimmer. Ordinarily she could have fought her way ashore, but she tried to paw herself back on the ice, and in so doing she shoved one front foot through her work collar.

That pulled her head under. She struggled, but every time she pulled with her front legs her head went under. She was spinning, her head under water, her tail whipping back and forth in the air.

Frank ran toward her, even though he knew he would break through. He was wearing a caribou fur parka and heavy winter clothes.He traveled about fifteen feet before breaking through. The water was eight or ten feet deep. Cold clamped his chest like a vice as he frantically pawed his way toward Queenie. Then he realized all the dogs were in the water with him, and big Kenai was beside him. He threw an arm over the big dog and felt his powerful muscles bunch and work at that slush. Right then Frank was mighty glad to have Kenai around.

He reached Queenie, pulled her close, and yanked her foot out of the collar. Her head came up, she blew water and chunks of ice, coughed and started swimming toward the shore from which she had started. Frank followed her, swimming, when a dog behind him put both paws on his shoulders and shoved him under. Submerged, struggling and gasping, he swallowed what seemed like gallons of water and pounds of ice. He thought he was a goner. When he came up and glanced around, guess who? Kenai, acting true to form. It looked like he was waiting to shove Frank down again. Frank continued to swim, crawl and fight the ice and freezing water, bound up by that big parka. He was seriously beginning to wonder if he would make it to shore.

When he got to where the water was normally shallow he relaxed and reached for bottom. He went clear under again, and as he came up, gasping, Kenai shoved him down again. He simply walked over Frank. Frank got another big dose of ice and water before surfacing. This time he was angry enough to wring Kenai's neck. He had turned and was waiting as Frank came up and Frank slugged him with a right to the jaw. Kenai stayed away for the rest of that icy swim. Frank finally broke his way ashore. He was numb and completely winded when he crawled up on the snowy river bank.

He stood and reached for his snus box to get a chew before his hands got too cold. It was gone, no doubt floating downriver. All he found in his pocket was a handful of ice. He was numb, but it struck him that he was unusually heavy. It was more than the soaked caribou skin parka. He was wearing a pair of loose-fitting, choke bore Filson pants, laced tightly on the bottom. He had pounds of slush ice inside them; they bulged out all the way around.

He was on the wrong side of the river from his cabin, near exhaustion, and in bad shape. His hands were numb, with water freezing on them. With that big load of ice in his pants, he clattered like a sack full of broken glass every time he moved.

He had to act quickly. He ran toward a narrow place in the river a quarter mile downstream where he thought there should be open water. He didn't dare tackle the slush again, knowing he couldn't make it across. He must have been a weird sight trying to run, water freezing on him, and ice clattering in his pants with every jump.

He found a spot where anchor ice lay on each side of the river with open water in the center. All eight dogs walked with Frank out on the ice until, about ten feet from shore, a big cake broke off, tilted, and dumped them all into the water. Frank had no trouble swimming across, but he nearly drowned getting out on the other side. Every time he put his elbows on the edge of the thin ice it broke off. He stretched for bottom and dipped clear under—it was much deeper than normal. Time and again he tried to pull himself up on the ice and it kept breaking and he kept going under. By then he was getting weak. To top it off, the dogs could get their front feet on the ice but couldn't get any further, so they struggled in the water, pawing and crying for Frank to help them.

He broke a channel and finally managed to crawl out, then yanked the dogs out one at a time and pushed them ashore. Old troublemaker, Kenai, came along last. Just as Frank was ready to grab him, he decided to swim back to the other side of the river. Frank was in a mood to leave him, but knew he would probably drown if he did, so he kneeled on the ice and coaxed him back. It took a lot of coaxing. When he finally came, Frank jerked him out. Then Frank trotted the quarter of a mile to the cabin, ice still clattering around inside his pants.

In fifteen minutes the dogs and Frank were crowding each other for space around a roaring stove. Later he dropped a tree across a narrow place in the river a mile or so downstream and carried his fresh grub across.

Such events made Frank decide every year that he was going to get rid of Kenai.

Several times in summer he turned Kenai loose, took a .22 rifle and went for a walk in the woods, each time planning to return without him. Then Frank would shoot a spruce hen and the big wolf-dog would run and retrieve it. He'd have quite a time prying it out of his jaws, and it would be pretty well chewed, but he would give it up. Frank would look at him and he would wag his tail and prance around, just a big, happy-go-lucky mutt having a good time. Frank never had the heart to shoot him.

Kenai got crazy spells every once in a while and conjured up all kinds of mix-ups. Then he would go along for months without giving the least bit of trouble. Frank never beat or whipped him although there were times when he was sorely tempted. The only time he used the blackjack was when he started a fight, picked up Queenie, or some other such thing. Then he had to be right on the spot in order to protect the lives of the other dogs. He was just too powerful a fighter for Frank to take a chance.

Frank kept Kenai five years. Sometimes he got his mail at McKinley Park, a few miles from his cabin on Savage River. Park Superintendent Harry Liek, who came out to say hello every time he drove by Park Headquarters, was completely taken by Kenai.

Kenai liked to be petted, and he knew Liek would pet him when he could. Kenai was a show-off too, because when Frank left after talking with Liek, he would throw his weight into his collar savagely, and growl enthusiastically. He was faster than the other dogs and it looked like he was doing all the work.

Liek thought Kenai was wonderful. He *was* a beautiful animal. After a couple of years Liek tried to buy him for use in the Park. He had some very fine female malemutes and thought Kenai would make a good sire for their pups. Liek also thought he would make a wonderful show dog for park visitors to see.

Time and again Frank told him, "You're wrong, Liek, dead wrong. Kenai's just a lot of trouble. The guy who gets him will be sorry. I wouldn't sell that dog to my worst enemy." He couldn't convince him.

By the spring of 1934 Frank had had enough. He had tried every trick he knew to straighten Kenai out, but it was hopeless.

As fond as he was of him, Kenai caused more trouble than he was worth. He told Liek that he would give Kenai to him if he would promise never to work him. Frank thought he would be all right for breeding purposes, and he would make a fine dog for the tourists to see and photograph. Liek agreed to take him on those terms. As a final warning Frank told him that if, in an emergency, he had to use him in a team, to be sure and put him in the lead; he wouldn't work in any other position.

Frank heard the rest of Kenai's story from Chief Ranger Louis Corbley. One day a new ranger, transferred to McKinley Park from Yellowstone Park, decided to harness the park dogs into a team to get some mushing experience. He had been told not to use Kenai.

Disregarding instructions, he dragged Kenai from the pen and snapped him into the wheel position just in front of the sled. In harnessing his dogs, Frank always turned them loose and called them to the sled, so the green ranger's first move probably upset Kenai. When he turned his back on the dogs to walk to the sled, Kenai tore into the dog beside him. The inexperienced ranger rushed up with a big club and beat Kenai on the head and the body until Kenai was dazed and almost unconscious. He then dragged him back into the corral.

Next day the ranger decided he would break Kenai of fighting. With a dog harness in hand he went to Kenai's fifteen by twenty corral and stepped inside. He then made the mistake of turning his back on Kenai to latch the gate. All that saved his life was the big fur parka he wore, with the hood up. Kenai remembered the beating he had been given and who gave it to him—it was the only beating he ever received.

Corbley ran to try to stop the ranger but he was too late. He saw Kenai lunge and put both feet on the man's shoulders and grab the back of his neck. He rode the man down, snapping and trying to chew through the heavy parka. The ranger groveled, screaming for help, trying to keep from being turned over by the angry wolf-dog. Kenai would have killed him if Corbley hadn't rushed in with a club and knocked Kenai out.

Kenai never gave Frank that kind of trouble. The big wolf-dog deserved any punishment he ever gave him, and Kenai knew it. A beating though, is something a wolf-dog can't stand.

Kenai had to be destroyed.

Frank was glad he didn't have to do it.

⁂

I ASK THE READER's pardon for departing briefly from my narrative, but as an Alaskan of more than fifty years with some knowledge of wolf dogs I feel compelled to say a few words to the unwary about these animals. I am only too cognizant of the romantic attraction of owning a part-wolf dog. After reading about Kenai and Glaser's other wolf-dogs, some readers might decide they want to own a similar animal. Not a good idea.

Frank Glaser told me his wolf-dogs were "his family," and in practical terms it was probably true. I've often heard other owners of wolf-dogs make similar claims; a good relationship with a wolf-dog, by necessity, is close, apparently much closer than a relationship between man and dog.

Glaser's wolf-dogs were work animals, not pets. He probably treated his team more gently than most trapper-owned dog teams of the time; two of his wolf-dogs, Queenie and her brother, Buster, remained with him until their deaths from old age. I don't know how Glaser disposed of the other members of the team when he left Savage River. While Glaser didn't have the training to interpret wolf behavior in the detail and depth of scientific learning of the last half century, he had an innate understanding of animals. Because of this he had a successful relationship with his wolf-dogs; even managing to handle the huge and difficult Kenai for five years.

Much of the behavior of Kenai is understandable in light of modern scientific studies of wolf behavior. While Glaser was undoubtedly considered the Alpha of the pack (dog team), Kenai, which Glaser said was "boss from the start," was probably in line for the job, and his behavior was that of a wolf eager to expand his powers. Wolf-like, he challenged Frank; as result, Frank had to repeatedly assert his dominance over the big wolf-dog.

Kenai's attack of the ranger at the very least illustrates the danger of owning a wolf dog, which can have the cunning and instincts of a wild animal that is unafraid of people. Most scientific work in the area of intelligence has fairly conclusively demonstrated that wolves have a higher order of intelligence than most dogs. Some hybrids may be included. Perhaps, as Glaser thought,

Kenai remembered the beating and was seeking revenge. Beating a wolf-dog (or a dog, for that matter) is always a mistake. For a stranger to beat one is a bigger mistake. Based on Glaser's account it appears the ranger had no business handling dogs, much less a wolf-dog.

Today (this is written in early 2002), wolf-dogs are well established and popular in the U.S. and Canada as pets, with perhaps half a million wolf-dogs in the U.S.; some estimates run as high as one million. But there is a worm in this apple. Wolf-dogs can be long-legged and yellow-eyed like their wolf ancestors, or they can resemble affection-seeking domestic dogs. But looks can be deceiving; other wolf-dogs may more closely resemble their dog parent than the wolf, but still have traits of a wolf.

Commonly, little consideration is given to the dog part of the hybrid. Some dog breeds cannot be trusted, yet they are haphazardly crossed with the wolf. Result: a real problem animal. Many people should not own a dog, much less a wolf or hybrid. In the wrong hands, a hybrid can be a disaster; a hybrid of a wolf and a vicious, untrustworthy breed of dog can put a veritable monster into unsuspecting hands.

The Humane Society reported that ten people died in the U.S. between 1986 and 1994 after being attacked by wolf-dogs. These were mostly children and toddlers. Typical, perhaps was when, in 1991, a pair of hybrids reached through the fencing of their enclosure and grabbed and severely mauled a four-year-old girl in Tabor, South Dakota. The animals were killed to be tested for rabies. The girl survived.

In December, 1997, two Black Forest, Colorado boys, ages 10 and 13, watched in horror as two wolf hybrids killed their mother, Debbie K. Edmonds, 39, who was trying to return the animals to their pen. Both animals were shot by authorities.

Reportedly, Mrs. Edmonds was in a business partnership involving breeding and selling hybrid wolves with a Colorado Springs-area man. She was the animal's caretaker.

Breeders often advertise wolf hybrid pups for sale. Usually, the more wolf blood, the higher the price. Some breeders carefully screen potential buyers for their suitability as hybrid owners, knowing that few people are suited for such ownership. Many breeders don't bother. Hybrids, like wolves and dogs, vary so widely in personality and character that structuring guidelines on breeding and sales of the animals is almost impossible. The situation also varies with the expectations of those who acquire the animals; some people can cope with the problems that can develop, most can't. Many breeders promote their hybrids as a combination of the best of the wolf and the best of the dog, ignoring the high probability that undesirable traits usually accompany the hybrid and are just as likely to be present.

Buyers cannot be sure what they are getting; that cute puppy they fall in love with might be anything from a full-blooded wolf to a dog that looks like a wolf.

Some people want unique pets, something that is different. The appeal of wolf-dogs to some owners seems to be related to the animals' reputed high intelligence and loyalty to their owner. Others who opt for these animals may feel the need to connect with wildlife and the wilderness through ownership of wolf blood.

Keeping wolf/dog hybrids is illegal in many states. These animals were once sold openly in Alaska, but in 1999 the Board of Game made it illegal (in Alaska) to possess any hybrid "game" animal, which includes wolves. Reasons for the blacklisting includes the lack of a proven rabies vaccine for hybrid wolves, the potential danger to people (including their owners) from their shearing teeth powered by exceedingly strong jaw muscles, and the danger of domestic dog diseases spreading if hybrids were to escape and join with wild animals. Kenai Peninsula and Matanuska Valley wolves, for example, now carry dog lice, believed to have been brought into Alaska in the early 1980s by a dog. When wolf hybrids escape or are allowed to run free, they have the potential to breed with wolves, which could alter the genetic integrity of wolves.

In January, 2002, the Board went one step farther and made the trade of hybrid wolves illegal if they are advertised as wolves or wolf hybrids. The goal is to get around the need to prove the animals are part wolf. The board grandfathered rights of owners to retain existing hybrids, but by July, 2002, the animals were to be registered with the Alaska Department of Fish and Game. Further, the animals had to be spayed or neutered and implanted with an identifying microchip. Owners may not transfer them to anyone other than an immediate relative. Puppies of pregnant hybrids at the time of the board's action were to be legal, but no more sales or breeding should occur.

Owners with a successful rapport with a wolf-dog almost

invariably cite the commitment and time involved in developing the relationship as being far beyond that necessary for a good relationship with a dog. Hybrids must be carefully socialized to fit in with families, and many who seek them as pets are not sufficiently knowledgeable, or don't have the time, to do this.

Hybrid wolf-dogs are not dogs, and cannot be treated as such. They are a wild animal in captivity. Close confinement in an urban setting is not an appropriate environment for a wolf-dog, and sadly, that's where many who choose them live. Most hybrids die young; they get into trouble by attacking people, by appearing (and actually being) vicious, and many owners give up on them and turn them in to a local Animal Control Agency, or to one of the thirty-some wolf hybrid sanctuaries in the U.S. Not a few hybrids are released into the wild, where they usually die of starvation, for they have not been taught by wolf parents to hunt.

Owner of one of the wolf hybrid rescue centers in Colorado recently estimated 250,000 wolf hybrids are born annually in the U.S., and that 80 percent of them never reach their third birthday because they are turned into animal control agencies or wolf hybrid rescue centers.

The policy of most Animal Control Centers in Alaska, and elsewhere, is to euthanize any wolf hybrid that is brought to them. They aren't considered adoptable. In Anchorage an ordinary dog picked up by Animal Control for biting is quarantined for ten days. But a wolf hybrid that bites is automatically euthanized, and its head submitted for rabies testing. Between 1985 and January 2002 wolf hybrids in Alaska had bitten seventy seven people, according to Don Ritter, manager of the state viorology laboratory at Fairbanks.

In 2000 the municipality of Anchorage's animal control staff estimated there were at least 200 wolf hybrids within their jurisdiction. Near Anchorage two loose wolf hybrids mortally injured a radio collared moose in January, 2000. One wolf hybrid was shot at the moose carcass. Four other wolf hybrids were loose in Anchorage suburbs; another two escaped in downtown Anchorage in March, 2000.

In 1990, in Alaska, there were five highly publicized maulings of people by wolf-dogs, one of which resulted in the death of a month-old baby. There was talk of a law banning hybrids, and about then many Alaskan owners of wolf-dogs started referring to their animals as "husky mix," a meaningless term.

Enforcing the ban on wolf dogs has been virtually impossible. Scientists use skull measurements and characteristics to identify species, but it is impossible to identify a wolf-dog skull with any certainty. Nor, so far, are there any other scientific methods that can differentiate between wolf-dogs and ordinary dogs. Perhaps the new (2002) regulation of the game board will help, but it will be an uphill fight to rid Alaska of wolf-dog hybrids.

Glaser's ownership of wolf-dogs was appropriate for him, for his time and life style, when dogs and horses were Alaska's primary personal and commercial means of transport. He had the time, the location, the understanding, the need for a dog team, and the ability to train and control them. Even then, when dog teams were common and many men knew how to handle them, Glaser never allowed anyone else to drive his team. When in town, he always left his wolf-dogs in a dog livery under professional, experienced, care.

Glaser's circumstances were far different from those of most individuals of today, who may or may not have the ability to socialize a wolf-dog, and who desires one as a companion or pet. In summary, there is no easy route to ownership of a safe, tractable, useful wolf-dog as a pet or companion for an individual or a family.

11

Snow: Captive wolf: Moose kill

THE TNWSF HOUSE, at the edge of Fairbanks, was small, built of logs, with two bedrooms. John Grant had left it in a mess. Pat hired a professional cleaner to put it right before moving in, and sent the bill to the Foundation. The furnishings were shabby, but she installed bright slip covers, new drapes, curtains and throw rugs. It was a cozy, homey place, and she loved the log walls, although she soon discovered the logs collected dust.

Before returning to Boston, Pat had visited the University of Alaska, a few miles from downtown Fairbanks. She was impressed with this small land grant college. The extensive Noel Wien public library (named for a beloved pioneer bush pilot) in downtown Fairbanks surprised her; clearly, Alaskans did a lot of reading. Despite her preconceived notion that the short winter days and long nights would be depressing, to her surprise the short December daylight hours were often bright, with light reflecting from clean snow, though the sun barely rose above the looming, seventy-mile-distant Alaska Range. She was surprised at how light it was during the twenty-hour-long nights. Snowflakes glittered with the fire of diamonds, even from starlight. One night she stood for nearly an hour staring with wonder at a display of colorful, twisting and dancing Northern Lights until, half frozen, she was forced inside.

Wearing her warmest, she had walked the icy sidewalks and trails around town with a growing appreciation for this environment, which seemed exotic to her Boston-bred eyes. Homes were mostly small, but neat. She sensed the potential for adventure, and was constantly aware of the wild land that extended for hundreds of miles in all directions from the town. The people were informal, friendly. At the time she thought only of returning for a longer visit, perhaps in summer when there were twenty-four hours of daylight. Then came the job offer from Jerry Hanson.

Although she didn't embrace or understand the animal rights doctrine espoused by TNWSF, she had accepted the job. She told Hanson she would concentrate on trying to stop the slaughter of Alaska's wolves. She didn't have strong feelings about animal rights—except perhaps for wolves. She had never hunted and hardly knew anyone who did. It seemed to her a bloody and un-necessary endeavor; after all, one can buy meat at any super market. But her feelings weren't strong. The idea of not using laboratory animals for medical research had never occurred to her. Putting the vast U.S. meat industry out of business seemed silly. In short, she gave little thought to the animal rights philosophy of TNWSF.

Before leaving Boston she spent a couple days with Beth Johnson, the teacher who took over her fifth grade class. Pat had become fond of her students, and felt a reluctance to turn them over to someone else. Beth was in her forties, and had returned to teaching when her own children reached college age. She was rather stout and motherly, with graying hair. But she was business-like in her dealings with Pat. She promised to keep Pat informed on progress of the class for the rest of the year.

Pat was settled in her new home at Fairbanks by late January. One of her first moves was to visit Bob Hinman at ADF&G. They discussed wolves, and the plan to remove wolves from 20A.

"I disagree with your plan to kill wolves," she said firmly.

Hinman, accustomed to criticism of the department's wolf manage-ment programs, smiled and said, "That doesn't mean we can't talk about it." That made her angry, but she held her temper, and thanked him for the pile of state-printed reports compiled by his staff.

She then haunted the University of Alaska and Noel Wien libraries to review everything she could find on wolves. She was browsing among the stacks at the university library one day when someone accidently bumped into her. "Excuse me," he said.

It was Ren Smith.

He didn't recognize her she realized, as he moved on. "Can I buy you a cup of coffee," she offered, with a smile.

He did a double take and smiled. "It's Miss York, isn't it? Sure. Sounds good."

"I'm afraid I was rude the last time we had coffee together," she offered when they had found a table at the nearby cafeteria.

"You were set up," he said.

"Yes, I was. I've almost memorized Dr. Mech's book that you gave me. Now, some of the stuff from *Never Cry Wolf* seems, well, a bit romanticized."

"Or Disney-ized?" he asked.

"Yes, that fits," she agreed.

"You're making progress," he said, pleasantly. "But let me warn you. The more you learn about wolves, the more you realize there is to learn."

"I'm still opposed to killing wolves, no matter what justification you use," she said.

"I don't like to kill wolves." he said. "But there are times when it benefits the resource. It's the dirtiest part of my job," he said.

"I don't understand how you can do it, if you like wolves."

"Have you ever heard of 'tough love?'" he asked.

"Yes. But I'd rather see nature takes its course without man's interference," she said.

"I understand," he said. "That's a legitimate view. We both have our views. It isn't likely we'll agree."

"No. Not as long as your department kills them. I'll never agree to that," she said.

"I take it you have replaced Grant for TNWSF," he said.

"Yes. I intend to be here for a while. I would like to have good relationships with your department even though I oppose your wolf program."

"No problem," he said. "You aren't alone. We have plenty of opposition. Don't hesitate to call on me if I can provide information," he responded. And as an afterthought he offered, "When the days get longer and it's warmer, perhaps you'd like to fly with me on a survey."

"Why, I might do that, if it's possible."

"I'll call you," he said. "It'll be March when its warmer with longer days before I do much flying."

⌒

I WAS SURPRISED when Pat York phoned me at my coastal Alaska home in early February, 1976. "Mr. Rearden, I've replaced John

Grant as the Alaskan representative of TNWSF," she said. "I'm now living in Fairbanks. I appreciated the time you gave me during your December board meeting, and I'd like to be able to stay in touch."

I smiled at that. Most of the "greenies" or "bunny huggers" as they are commonly referred to—and even called themselves— seemed to avoid contact with board members, except at formal meetings. This was a refreshing approach, and I liked it. Clearly, Pat York was better at public relations than her predecessor, who had a frosty relationship with the department staff, and who hadn't bothered to become acquainted with any of the board members. She obviously realized she would have more influence if she was on friendly terms.

"Miss York, it will be a pleasure. Any time I can be of help, please feel free to call," I responded.

She was a bit hesitant then, and said, "I do have a rather personal question, if you don't mind."

"Please. What is it?" I asked.

"It's about Ren Smith. He has invited me to fly with him on a survey flight. I've never flown in a small plane, and, frankly, I'm a bit fearful. I need to know whether you, with all your experience, think it would be safe."

That tickled me. She was buttering me up. "Miss York, I was in exactly the same position when I arrived at Fairbanks twenty-five years ago. I had flown a bit, in fact I had been a student pilot. But I wasn't so sure about flying in a small plane in Alaska. A pilot offered to take me on a flight, and I hesitated. I even asked him how much flying time he had."

"I didn't dare ask Mr. Smith that!" she laughed. "What did your pilot say. Was he insulted?"

"Far from it. He said I was wise to ask, that it wasn't smart to jump into a plane with just anyone. Turned out he was Chief Pilot for Northern Consolidated Airlines, and one of Alaska's finest bush pilots. I flew with him, of course, and we're still friends today."

"But what about Mr. Smith. Can you tell me if he's a safe pilot?"

"Let me tell you a story, Miss York. Then I'll tell you what I think of Ren Smith as a pilot. His father, Dusty Smith, has been a bush pilot at Wolverine, a Koyukuk Valley village, for around thirty years. He started teaching Ren to fly when Ren was about ten. Ren began accompanying his father on scheduled flights, and he was barely into his teens when he took the controls, while his father, sitting beside him, sometimes caught up on his sleep. He knew all his father's routes, and had flown with his father for hundreds of hours by the time he was fifteen. You realize, of course, he couldn't legally fly a plane solo until he was sixteen. Then he was caught in an emergency.

"An eight-year-old child was critically injured in Wolverine and her mother rushed her to the Smith Flight Service, begging for an immediate medivac flight to the Fairbanks hospital. But Dusty was away on an all-day charter. Weather was marginal for flying, with high wind, low clouds and rain. Ren tried unsuccessfully to reach his father by radio. He also tried to radio any other plane flying in the area, but he could raise no one.

"Although Ren was only fifteen, he rolled out one of his father's planes, loaded the injured child and her mother, and flew through a terrible fall storm to Fairbanks. He saved the child's life. When he radioed ahead to the tower at the Fairbanks airport and requested to be met by an ambulance, the controller recognized the number of the plane as belonging to Dusty, but the teenage voice obviously wasn't Dusty. When Ren landed, Civil Aeronautics Administration people were watching. The landing was perfect. The CAA inspector who saw the child lifted from the plane to the ambulance asked Ren why he was flying the plane. Ren explained.

"That was the end of it. The CAA inspector told Ren to park the plane and not fly it back to Wolverine. The story got out, of course, and Ren was a hero as a result. He passed his flight and written tests for private pilot on his sixteenth birthday.

"Ren earned his way through seven years of college by flying commercial bush routes summers for his father. He has never had an accident. I consider him one of the best pilots I've ever flown with," I concluded. "I think you'll be safe with him. Flying that is," I added, smiling to myself.

I wondered, of course, if Ren was interested in Pat York. I thought it was unlike him to invite a woman to fly with him.

"Thanks, Mr. Rearden. I think I'll accept Mr. Smith's invitation," she said.

"Good. I think you'll learn from it," I said.

This was a different Pat York from the frosty Boston teacher with whom I had dined.

⁓

REN WAS VISITING Garth at his dog yard. Since returning Chena, he had occasionally stopped to see Garth and to visit the shy wolf-dog. It had been six months since he had released Lady. "Chena recognizes your pickup," Garth said. "She comes to life, pricks her ears and wags her tail when you drive up. I think she looks forward to seeing you."

Ren kneeled near Chena's dog house, and the shy animal, head and tail down, crept to him. He gently rubbed her ears. She closed her eyes in bliss.

"She doesn't come to me like that. She's still shy, but I think she'll come around when I start working with her," Garth said. "I plan to breed her to that big male over there," pointing. "He's fast and smart," he said. "Probably in another month or so when she comes in season. I'm looking forward to seeing what her pups will be like."

"You'll probably get some big pups out of that pair," Ren said. "Do you think hybrid vigor will cause them to be bigger than either parent?"

"Who knows?" Garth shrugged. "Crossing dogs with wolves is chancy. Sometimes you get good results, more often you don't."

"Chena is a beautiful animal. I hope her pups inherit her classy looks," said Ren.

"I wonder if she associates you with the wolf pup?" Garth asked.

"I'm sure she does. She loved that pup. She was a great mother," Ren said, standing. Chena rolled over on her back. Ren kneeled again and rubbed her belly. "She's telling me I'm boss," he smiled.

Garth nodded. "Their body language is unmistakable, isn't it?"

As he was leaving the dog yard Ren commented, "Your dogs look good, as usual, Garth. How's your team look for the races?"

"Good. I expect to win some, lose some. My only problem is, I have too many dogs. I need to get rid of some of them. I get too fond of them and hate to sell, and hate worse to put surplus dogs down.

"See that Siberian over there?" he said, pointing to a blue-eyed, sharp-eared, almost-white Siberian Husky. "He's the friendliest dog in the yard. And he's smart. But he's not fast enough for me to keep for racing. I need to find him a good home. Say, would you like to have him?" Garth offered.

"Why, thanks, Garth, but no. I'm gone too much of the time to keep a dog," Ren said.

"Do you know anyone who would like to have a really nice dog as a pet?" Garth asked.

"Maybe I do," Ren said, walking to the chained animal. As he neared, the dog's plumed tail started waving and he pulled to the end of his chain, bouncing on front feet with delight. Ren stooped and the dog thrust his head onto his legs. "Why, you are a friendly Siberian!" he said, turning to Garth. "I've never seen a Siberian make friends with a stranger that fast."

"He does that all the time. He loves my kids. I sometimes turn him loose and he stays right here." Garth said. "He'd make someone a nice companion dog. He's about a year old and has reached full size. If he were faster I'd sure keep him."

"I know someone who might appreciate a good dog," Ren said. "Let me take him and make a visit. What's his name?"

"He was pure white as a pup and we called him Snow. The name stuck," Garth said.

⌒

PAT WAS SURPRISED and a bit flattered when Ren showed up at her door. "Well, this is unexpected. Come in," she invited.

"May I bring a friend?" he asked.

"Why, yes," she answered, peering around. She saw no one.

"Be right back," Ren said as he returned to his pickup for Snow.

Snow behaved well on the leash as Ren returned. "This is my friend," he explained.

"Oh, he's beautiful," Pat said. "May I pet him?"

She kneeled and Snow bounded to her, tail swishing, jaws open in a grin. She rubbed his ears.

"His eyes are blue!" she said, astonished.

"That's typical of Siberian Huskies," he explained. "It's a very old sled dog breed, brought to Alaska from Siberia around the turn of the century."

Snow explored the living room as Ren chose an easy chair and Pat disappeared into the kitchen to make coffee. Ren had once before been in this house when John Grant lived in it; it had been strewn with clothing, shoes, old newspapers, and had a sour smell. Today it was bright, cheerful, and clean with a fresh odor. Snow finished exploring and calmly chose a spot near the door, turned around a couple of times, and lay down. He remained there while Pat and Ren drank coffee and idly chatted.

"Do you mind if I call you Pat?" he asked.

"Not if I can call you Ren," she smiled.

"Ok. We're friends," he said.

"Except we agree to disagree about wolves," she said, soberly.

"Of course," he said.

He said, "I have a confession. Snow isn't my dog. He's just a friend I met today. He's looking for a good home. I thought you might like to have him."

"Oh. I haven't had a dog since I was a little girl. Why, he's an outdoor dog, isn't he? He'd be too warm to live in the house. I don't have a dog house, although there is a fenced yard out back where he could stay," she said, thinking aloud.

"I have a dog house you can have," he offered. He had built it for Lady.

Pat kneeled by Snow. The dog stood and rubbed his head on her leg, his tail furiously waving. "I think he likes me," she said.

"Obviously," Ren said. "He's unusually friendly for a Siberian. Most Siberians don't make instant friends."

"What made you think I'd like to have a dog?" she asked.

"With you living alone, it might be nice to have him around. A dog can be a lot of company. Plus, I think he'd be a good watch dog."

"That's thoughtful of you. All right, if you have a dog house I can use, Snow has a new home. It'll be wonderful to have a close friend," she said. Their eyes met and there was a long silence. Pat was the first to turn away.

"I'll leave him and bring the house this afternoon. I'll also get information you'll need on his vaccinations and the kind of food he's used to," he promised.

Later she wondered how he knew she lived alone.

FRANK GLASER'S CAPTIVE male breeding wolf and the resulting wolf-dogs gained him a reputation in Interior Alaska as a wolf expert. During summer, 1927, he was in Fairbanks when Theodore Van Bibber, owner of a boarding kennel for sled dogs at the edge of town, approached him. "I have a problem, Frank," he said, "and I think you can help me."

His problem was a female wolf he was holding in a big corral. "I've been offered $200 for her. But I can't catch her," he explained. "I've spent days trying to get a collar and chain on her, but she won't let me near. I'll give you $50 if you can get a collar and chain on her."

It was a challenge Glaser liked.

Van Bibber had acquired the wolf, a handsome, gray three-year-old, a couple of months earlier from Newton, a trader on the upper Tanana River. Newton had bought her from Indians when she was a puppy.

Frank went into the corral with her, but as long as Van Bibber was near, the wolf ran to the farthest corner where it nervously paced. Clearly, she was afraid of him.

"Do you have any pups?" Frank asked. "A little dog puppy, say three or four months old will do."

He selected a pup from one of the litters Van Bibber was keeping, and sat in the center of the wolf's corral petting it. Van Bibber kept opening the gate and peeking in. This caused the wolf to run growling to the farthest corner, her mane on end.

"You'll have to stay away," Frank told him. "I can't do anything with you here."

Frank spent an afternoon with the wolf and the puppy. From time to time he turned the puppy loose and it would run to the wolf. She smelled of it, and, after a bit, responded when the puppy wanted to play. The puppy kept jumping up and putting its paws on her and she seemed to like that.

He retrieved the puppy, and again sat petting it. He continually talked to the wolf in a friendly voice. From time to time he howled like a wolf—Glaser could imitate a wolf's howl perfectly. This seemed to interest her. Several times she followed the puppy almost to Frank. From time to time he walked around the corral continually talking to her and occasionally howling. She circled him, around and around wanting to play with the puppy, and Frank could tell she was curious about him.

She'd run one way and then the other, gradually working closer to Frank. Finally she tip-toed near to smell the puppy, and Frank touched her neck. She leaped back stiff-legged and her mane came up. By evening Frank had had his hands on her three times.

He returned to the pen next morning and took a chain with him. He had a choke collar in each coat pocket. He figured if he could slip a choke collar on her he could then snap the chain on it. He again spent much time petting the puppy, and the wolf became tamer by the hour.

Twice that day he had a choke collar almost slipped over her head but she leaped back each time.

Next day when the puppy and Frank arrived she was clearly pleased, dancing about and eagerly looking for the puppy. She came close to Frank immediately and he allowed the puppy to play with her for a time before taking it to the center of the corral where he sat petting it. He kept the choke collar handy.

The wolf came close to sniff and lick the puppy and remained still long enough for Frank to slip a choke collar over her head. She leaped back, but within minutes came close again. Snapping the chain into the choke collar was easy.

When she came up against the chain she reared back and pulled, but Frank held her, trying to soothe her. She ran around and around him, growling and making a big fuss, but she didn't attempt to bite. He put a stout leather collar on her without difficulty.

Van Bibber made his sale and Frank got his $50. At the time $5 was a good day's wage for a working man.

⟩

DURING THE LATE 1920s and into the early 1930s, wolves were so numerous in Glaser's Savage River country that he saw and heard them almost every day. Caribou were the wolves' main prey, but they also killed many moose. Even a moose doesn't have much of a chance against a persistent pack of wolves, unless it happens to be in the prime age group at a time when there is little or no snow.

One fine April day Frank was at his cabin watching coyotes

chase sheep in the high hills with his big spotting scope when a running cow moose showed up on the skyline. She frequently looked behind her. Soon five wolves appeared on her trail.

Hoping to save her, Frank grabbed his rifle and binoculars and hurried up the mountain to a lookout point behind his cabin. He watched the wolves chase the moose into a stand of spruce. She burst out of it a few minutes later, staggering from exhaustion. She was close enough that Frank could tell she was heavy with calf. He was much too far away to help her, and all he could do was watch through binoculars.

She stopped and turned to fight the wolves. As they closed in she tried to whirl and face each wolf as it attacked, but she was too slow. The swift wolves jumped in, slashed, then leaped back. For a time she stayed in one spot, standing on hind legs and striking out with her front hoofs. Then she repeatedly ran four or five steps on her hind legs while trying to cut, slash, or land on a wolf. Her head swung back and forth, ears back, mane on end. She tried, but she couldn't counter every attack. Whenever she lurched forward on her hind legs, one or two wolves attacked her rear, biting her hams. Eventually all five swarmed over her and pulled her off her feet.

By the time Frank got there she was dead and the pack had gulped steaming flesh from her hindquarters and had started feeding on her viscera, where Frank saw remnants of two unborn calves. Slashes from the wolf attack were all over her body, and big flaps of hide dangled here and there. Cuts on her shoulders looked as if she'd been ripped with a sharp knife. The wolves had heard Frank coming and had vanished.

About wolves

"... REPLENISHABLE RESOURCES BELONGING to the State shall be utilized, developed, and maintained on the sustained yield principle." reads a key component of the constitution of the State of Alaska.

Many regard Alaska's wolves as something more than a "replenishable resource." Trying to define that elusive "something more" escapes me, and, rather than try, I'll leave it at that.

For more than half a century I have collected scientific reports, newspaper clippings, anecdotes, and books about wolves. My files overflow. The more I see, read, and hear of wolves, the more respect and liking I have for the animal.

The wolf's social organization, its cooperative efforts in the hunt, its system of communication—howls, growls, squeaks, barks—draws my admiration, but none of these are greatly different from Alaska's other wild canids—the foxes and coyotes. The wolf's efficiency as a predator on wildlife man also values for meat and recreation, sets it aside from other canids. But beyond these traits, there is something about the wolf that makes it different from other wild mammals. Somehow the public has picked up on this undefinable trait. Perhaps our love for dogs explains our fascination with wolves, for dogs and wolves have many behaviorisms and characteristics in common. All breeds of our domestic dogs are descended from wolves, as strange as that may seem.

That undefinable trait is what complicates straightforward biological management of the wolf.

Many of the accounts I have collected that seem to reveal wolf traits were not written by scientists, or are even verifiable. I have, however, been selective, and retained only those accounts I believe are credible. I have concluded I'll probably never find any specific reason or reasons why wolves seem different, why the animal stirs human emotions as it does, including my own.

Wolf character is highly variable. This is probably related to their high intelligence; all wolves don't think alike. Each wolf has a distinct personality. Some are shy, some outgoing, others are aloof. As a result, all wolves do not behave alike. Nor are all of the so-called gray wolves across North America (*Canis lupus*) the same size and color. For example, in Algonquin Park, Ontario, adult wolves average less than sixty four pounds; wolves far north of Algonquin not uncommonly weigh 80 to 100 pounds; colors of "gray" wolves vary from all black to all white, with mixes of almost every color in between. I've even seen blue wolf skins.

The average Alaska wolf weighs from 80 to 100 pounds. Occasionally, however, a giant of the species is reported. Frank Glaser, the long-time Alaskan federal wolf hunter, owned a beam scale with which he often weighed wolves even before he worked for the federal government. In January, 1934, he weighed a wolf he shot at Savage River at 156 1/2 pounds. A captive wolf he owned weighed 145 pounds (live) when it was two years old. He told me he had seen the two Purdy brothers at Chicken, Alaska, weigh a wolf they had trapped that tipped the scale at 212 pounds. One January, in the early 1930s, his lead wolf-dog, Queenie, called a large wolf near enough to his Savage River cabin so he could shoot it. That animal tipped the beam scale to 154 pounds, and his cased skin was 8½ feet long and 16 inches wide.

Former Governor Jay Hammond in a letter (July, 2001) told me that while working for the U.S. Fish and Wildlife Service in the early 1950s he weighed scores of wolves. The largest he ever weighed, and the largest wolf he has ever seen, he said, was taken in the vicinity of Port Moller on the Alaska Peninsula. It weighed 165 pounds on a cannery scale. However, it had about 20 pounds of moose meat in its stomach.

The following are a few items from my wolf file.

⌒

IN OCTOBER 1955 I spent three weeks with Swedish-born Hjalmar (Slim) Carlson, an Alaska trapper, to write for *Outdoor Life* magazine about his life. Carlson lived alone for 57 years near interior Alaska's Lake Minchumina. Among the animals that stepped into his traps were wolves. Even Slim, the ultimate professional trapper, was not immune to the charm of wolves. Here is a story he told me, in his own words:

I caught a male wolf in a trap. It was uninjured and I decided to take it home alive. I jammed a stick into its mouth and tied it there, and tied its legs, and took him to where I was camped. I chained him to a tree as I did with my sled dogs.

The wolf was not aggressive; it never showed its teeth to me. I owned a big red dog that occasionally got loose and attacked the wolf. Each time, the wolf simply rolled over on his back, refusing to fight. I had to pull the red dog off or it would probably have killed the wolf.

I decided to move camp after I had held the wolf captive for two months. I couldn't kill him; it would have been like killing one of my dogs.

I released the animal still wearing a leather collar. The wolf trotted off about a hundred yards where it sat and howled for a time, then it left. He returned a few days later and sat within a hundred yards of my camp. I talked to the wolf. The wolf sat, but moved off when I tried to get close. The animal returned twice more to that camp.

I moved camp, and the wolf showed up at the second camp as well, sitting and watching. But he wouldn't allow me near. He left and I never saw him again. Some other trapper was probably surprised to catch a wolf wearing a leather collar.

Some wolves, as captives, are aggressive. Others are submissive, as was Carlson's wolf. Carlson was a soft-hearted trapper—he could have collected $50 bounty for the wolf and sold its hide for $100 or more at the time. Instead he chose to release the animal. Did that wolf's personality save its life?

⁂

HERE'S ANOTHER FROM Slim Carlson, also in his own words:

I caught a big black wolf by two toes in one of my wolf traps. It was the finest looking wolf I had ever seen. The wolf wagged his tail and whined as I sat near and talked to him for a time. I hated to kill him, but decided I had to. While the wolf was still in the trap, I tapped him on the nose with a light club, knocking it down. I then placed a pole across the its neck to hold him, and stepped on the wolf's chest [a common method trappers use to kill a live animal caught in a trap—it squeezes the heart and the animal dies quickly without damaging the fur].

As soon as I stepped on the wolf's heart, the animal lifted its head and closed his jaws on my ankle. I got kind of scared then because I couldn't reach my rifle. I leaned down and just tapped him lightly on the nose with my fingers, and to my surprise he let go. Then I gave him a good whack on the nose and killed him. I could see teeth marks on my skin, but the wolf didn't bite hard enough to draw blood.

Why didn't the wolf bite Carlson when he had his jaws on the man's ankle? Did the wolf recognize Carlson as dominant, as he would a more dominant wolf in a pack? Intriguing and baffling.

My friend David Vanderbrink was guiding Knute, a hunter from Germany, on the Alaska Peninsula, seeking a trophy brown bear. It was a nice day and they were lying on a lookout knoll watching for bears when Knute said, "I see two dogs."

The dogs were wolves. When Dave explained, Knute asked, "Can I shoot one?"

He had the appropriate tags and license, Dave told him, and he could certainly take a wolf if he wished.

As they talked, the wolves came closer. One was almost all white, with a dark area at the base of its tail—a handsome animal. The men remained hidden, watching. Soon the wolves were within easy rifle shot.

It was a year of great abundance of red voles, and the wolves were pouncing on and swallowing the little animals. Neither man spoke as the wolves came ever closer, intent on catching voles.

For more than an hour they watched the wolves as they interacted with each other, and as they stalked and caught voles.

Eventually the wolves trotted off and disappeared.

Knute told Dave, "I couldn't shoot. They are hunters like us."

Dave told me he had liked Knute's approach to hunting before their adventure with the wolves, but afterward he had liked him even better. "It was an experience of a lifetime, and both Knute and I realized it," he told me.

Did the charm of wolves again save a wolf's life?

⌒

MY SON, MICHAEL REARDEN, Manager of the Yukon Delta National Wildlife Refuge, who lives at Bethel, Alaska, in 2000 relayed to me the following, which a local resident had told him:

Two moose-hunting Eskimos, traveling by riverboat on the Kuskokwim River, saw what they took to be a sled dog swimming in the river. The man in the bow grabbed the "dog" by the scruff of the neck and lifted it aboard. Once aboard, the animal crept to the bow of the boat and remained there. The men paid little attention to it, thinking they'd find the owner when they arrived at a village a few miles away.

They beached the boat at the village and for the first time really looked at the animal, still crouched in the bow. Only then did they realize it was a five or six-month-old wolf pup. They put a rope around its neck and gave it to someone in the village, who tied it with his dogs. A few days later the animal slipped his collar and escaped. At no time did the animal attempt to bite.

It's interesting how many anecdotal accounts of close encounters of wolves and man emphasize that the wolves make no attempt to bite. In this case the wolf pup was probably about five months old. It was too young to challenge an adult wolf, and perhaps it perceived the men who captured it in the same light it would a dominant adult wolf.

⌒

MY SON MICHAEL is also the source of the following, which was related to him sometime in 2001 by a resident of the Yukon-Kuskokwim Delta:

With his pet 70-pound husky, the man was on a summer trip with his riverboat. On a Friday evening he camped on a river bar of a tributary to the Kuskokwim River, living in a tent with the dog running free. That evening, while cooking supper, he glanced out of the tent to see his dog playing with a full-grown wolf. He sat and watched the two play for half an hour, then the wolf left.

On Saturday and Sunday evenings the wolf arrived again to play with the dog. It showed no fear of the man, who made no attempt to approach it closely. He said he enjoyed watching the two animals play. He left on Monday, so he never saw the wolf again.

In some cases wolves unhesitatingly attack a dog, or dogs. In this case the wolf made friends with the dog. One wonders about the status of the lone wolf. Was it a female, and the dog a male, or vice versa? Was it a lone wolf without a pack, or a member of a pack with a defined territory? We're left with an unsolved puzzle.

MY LONG-TIME FRIEND Sidney Huntington and former BOG associate, who has lived all his life in the Koyukuk country of northern Alaska, is the source of the following:

Gilbert, one of Sidney's sons, while trapping in the Koyukuk Valley, caught a wolf in a trap. He had never seen a wolf in a trap, and he thought it was someone's big sled dog. He didn't want to kill a dog, so he walked up to the animal to release it, planning to put a rope around its neck so he could handle it and examine the foot for injuries. As Gilbert neared, the wolf lay down and made no attempt to bite, nor did it fight the trap. As Gilbert worked to open the trap, the wolf pulled as far from him as he could and turned his head away. Gilbert could have petted him.

Once released, the wolf stood up, looked at Gilbert (probably in astonishment) and swiftly ran off. Only then did Gilbert realize the animal was a wolf.

This is another example of a non-aggressive wolf in a trap. All wolves don't behave this way. Some trapped wolves are very aggressive. It would be interesting to know the age of this wolf. An immature wolf would likely be less aggressive than an older animal.

HERE'S ANOTHER FROM Sidney Huntington:

In the early 1900s, David Tobuk, an Eskimo toddler, was playing along the shore of the clear upper Koyukuk River. Suddenly a wolf darted from the riverside willows, grabbed the child by the head, and carried him screaming into the brush. A Koyukon Indian named Napoleon, working nearby, snatched up a rifle, sprinted into the brush, carefully aimed and fired, downing the wolf without hitting the child.

Tobuk survived. For the remainder of his life he carried a vivid scar on his face where the wolf had carried him. As an adult he became widely known as the captain of trader Sam Dubin's sternwheel steamer *Teddy H.* that plied the Yukon and Koyukuk Rivers during the 1920s and 1930s. Sidney knew him well.

Alaska Native elders often warn young children to be wary of wolves. It is impossible at this point to speculate about the wolf that carried Tobuk off—if it was habituated to humans, if it was food-dependent upon humans, or was simply preying on the child, assuming it was food.

⁓

Lois and Herb ("Cris") Crisler, Disney photographers, raised seven wolves from pups while filming in Alaska's Brooks Range. Two of them ran free as adults, spending time with the Crislers and hunting with wild wolves in turn.

One day one of the Crisler wolves watched Herb Crisler slide the bolt to a door of the plywood shack in which they lived, and then open the door. As soon as Cris was gone, as Lois watched, the wolf took the bolt in her teeth and tried to open it.

Would a dog have the intelligence to do this? Unlikely. The behavior of this wolf demonstrated a high level of intelligence—almost some mechanical understanding—although this seems unlikely. (Wolves' brains are about thirty percent larger than brains of similar-size dogs). More likely the animal had seen Herb Crisler open the bolt to the door repeatedly over time, and related opening the door to sliding the bolt.

Lois Crisler reported that one of the wolves she and her husband kept stood still, allowing her to pull porcupine quills out of its muzzle. Afterward the wolf (a female) "kissed" Crisler. (Probably licked her face—a common wolf behavior. Wolves are face-oriented, often licking one another's face and inside mouths, as a form of greeting and or communication).

Would any dog stand without being held to have porky quills pulled out of its muzzle? Few if any. It is extremely painful. Was this a display of intelligence by the wolf? Difficult to explain, but another intriguing side to the wolf.

⌒

Rudy Billberg, who flew for four decades as a bush pilot in Alaska and is now retired in Minnesota, is the source of the following which reveals that a wolf can exhibit curiosity, and poses questions about wolf-to-wolf communication:

One winter day, accompanied by his wife Bessie, he landed his ski-equipped Piper airplane on a snow and ice-covered lake a few miles north of McKinley National Park. They spent the night in a trapper's cabin hidden in alders about fifty yards from the lake. The airplane was tied down at the lake's edge.

Billberg went to the plane early next morning and in fresh snow found tracks of a single wolf. It had walked to the airplane's tail, then the skis, and had circled the plane, probably smelling and looking.

When the wolf finished checking out the plane, it returned almost in the same tracks it made approaching. Billberg followed the tracks, and within a hundred yards found where five other wolves had sat in the snow, apparently waiting while the lone wolf scouted the airplane. Tracks showed where the pack had been crossing the lake when they discovered the plane.

The pack must have seen the airplane and realized, what? That it was a possible threat? That it was something out of place in the wilderness? Whatever, five of the wolves had waited while the sixth wolf trotted to the plane to check it out.

One wonders what and how the scout communicated, if anything, to the five waiting wolves when it returned to them. Was the scout the Alpha wolf? Did the scout decide on its own to check out the plane? Did the five remain behind in perceived safety, while the scout accepted the risk of examining the plane? What kind of communication took place to organize such behavior?

⌒

In August, 2001, John Greenway, a helicopter pilot with years of experience in Alaska, told me the following:

The year was 1978. Greenway was aloft in his helicopter high in the Talkeetna Mountains returning to pick up a geologist he had dropped off at a small stream. When he neared the geologist, who, with a gold pan was working in the stream, he was surprised to see a black wolf lying on the bank within fifteen feet of the geologist. He veered to avoid frightening the wolf (he loves wolves) and called the geologist on the radio.

"Rob, keep doing what you're doing, and very slowly turn and look up at the stream bank to your left and you'll see one of the most beautiful black, yellow-eyed wolves you'll ever see. He's watching you work. He's just curious, I think," John said.

Rob did as suggested, continuing to pan while he slowly turned his head and looked up at the wolf. The animal was lying at the edge of the bank, relaxed, watching the strange business of panning gravel from the stream bed. Although the wolf realized he had been seen, he remained relaxed, watching the geologist, who continued to work, glancing at the wolf from time to time.

Greenway circled with his helicopter, keeping his eye on the wolf. He told me the animal watched the geologist for at least ten minutes after he had first seen it.

"He was just curious. I'll bet he was thinking, 'Now what the hell is this guy doing?'" John commented, with a laugh.

What other of Alaska's wild animals would exhibit such curiosity?

When the wolf left, which it did at a leisurely pace, it happened to travel in the direction Greenway was working with the helicopter. Over the next six to eight hours he saw it half a dozen times, traveling across above-timberline ridges. At his last sighting, he estimated the wolf had traveled fifty miles in under eight hours.

THE FOLLOWING ACCOUNT summarizes material printed by various Alaska newspapers, including the *Anchorage Daily News*, in April, 2000:

Two boys, one six, the other nine, were playing at being loggers at a logging camp near Icy Bay in late April. They were cutting down small trees within 150 feet of the house trailer where the six-year-old lived. With them was a neighbor's dog. A wolf stuck his head out of the brush near the boys.

The boys ran. The wolf swiftly caught up with them and knocked the six-year-old down, dragging him about as he bit. The dog attempted to attack the wolf, but the wolf fought it off. By then the boys were screaming. This alerted a nearby carpenter who ran to the site with the older boy's mother. They threw rocks at the wolf, and it let go of the boy.

The wolf reappeared about ten minutes later and the younger boy's father shot it.

The wolf had bitten the boy once in the lower back, and twice in the buttocks. The wounds were mostly punctures, with some tears in the back. Seven stitches and five surgical staples were needed to close the wounds. He recovered.

The wolf was a 77-pound male. It was not rabid, according to the University of Alaska Fairbanks virology lab which examined its brain.

Alaska's newspapers were full of speculation as to why the wolf attacked. The animal had been captured by a U.S. Forest Service biologist and radio-collared four years earlier as a ten-month old pup. It had reportedly been hanging around the logging camp for some time. It probably had diminished or no fear of people. Likely, loggers had fed the animal, or at least it had found easy food at or near the logging camp.

Why did it attack? It was attacking small, fleeing prey. In other words, it was a wolf. Wolves don't have a rule book that tells them not to attack small (or large) humans.

⌒

OVER ABOUT A decade at Canada's Algonquin Provincial Park four wolves became "tame"—that is, they lost fear of people, and attacked humans. All four were killed by rangers.

On one of the attacks, a 19-month-old child was playing with a toy in a campground. His father saw the wolf, but thought it was a dog and paid little attention. Next thing he knew the wolf attacked his son. The father saved the boy, and the wolf was shot.

In another instance, an eleven-year-old boy, sleeping in the open in Algonquin Park, was dragged six feet out of his sleeping bag by a wolf which clamped down on his face. He screamed and the wolf released him. His mother rushed to his aid, and his father tried to drive the wolf off. The animal repeatedly charged at the wounded boy and his distraught mother, while the father fended it off, finally chasing it into the woods.

The wolf's teeth had severely damaged the boy's face, crushing his nose, with parts of his mouth and one cheek ripped open.

He survived. More than eighty stitches were needed to close the wounds. Five days after the attack rangers killed a sixty pound male wolf at the family's camp site. Its stomach contained foods it had obviously found around human camps.

Algonquin Park policy now is to kill any wolf that appears fearless of humans. Park wolves that become unafraid of humans and dependent on humans for some or all of their food can become dangerous. A wolf attack can result in serious injury. If a pack should attack an unarmed adult or child, death could easily result.

THE FOLLOWING IS from an Associated Press release dated July 5, 2000:

At Vargas Island Provincial Park, on Vancouver Island, British Columbia, a 23-year-old college student was asleep outside his tent early in the morning when he was awakened by a dark-colored wolf tugging at the foot of his sleeping bag. He yelled and kicked at the animal. It backed up, and then lunged at the student, biting through the sleeping bag.

The student rolled over, trying to get a campfire between himself and the wolf, but the animal jumped on his back, biting at his head.

He yelled to attract companions, members of a kayaking excursion, who responded and drove the wolf off.

The student was air-lifted to Victoria's General Hospital where 50 stitches were required to close his head wounds.

Conservation officers tracked and killed two wolves in the area.

The full story isn't told in the release. It appears to be another case of a park wolf that had lost its fear of humans. As wolves receive more and more protection and as they increase, such attacks will become more common.

THERE IS MUCH evidence that wolves within a pack have a feeling of devotion or loyalty to one another. The following came from George Bishop, an Alaska trapper during the 1930's. An as-told-to story I wrote with Bishop about his experiences with wolves was published in the November 1963 issue of *The Alaska Sportsman*. The following are Bishop's words from that article:

The wolf clan has close ties within the family, or pack. I once trailed a wolf I had wounded for a long fifteen miles. Two companion wolves remained with the wounded animal the full time, prowling restlessly about while the hurt one rested. Tracks in the snow indicated the healthy ones had repeatedly urged the wounded animal on. The three were still together when I lost the trail.

⤳

DOZENS OF STORIES and articles about wolves have included the statement that "there is no record of a wolf attacking man in North America." Not true. There are authentic cases of unprovoked attacks, but they are few. However, such accounts are increasing as wolves increase, with re-introduction and natural range expansion of wolves in the South 48, and as human-wolf contacts increase in parks.

In each of the last ten years there has been an increased number of reports of wolf attacks on humans in North America. It appears likely that at any time now a wolf attack will result in the death of one or more humans in the U.S. or Canada.

⤳

BEGINNING IN MARCH 1996, members of a pack of Indian wolves in the rural northeast India province of Uttar Pradesh attacked more than seventy children, and killed more than forty, after discovering that village children were easy prey. When villagers became wary and kept their children inside, these bold fifty-pound Indian wolves slipped inside the houses at night and snatched children from their beds.

In 2001 a *National Geographic Explorer* TV presentation covered this story in detail. One wonders. Are India's wolves that much different from those of North America?

⤳

THE FOLLOWING IS based on an article that appeared in *The Alaska Sportsman* magazine of April 1943, titled "Wolves Killed Crist Kolby," by W. R. Selfridge.

In February, 1939, Crist Kolby, a bachelor about 40 years old, was trapping alone from the Hanson cabin (built by Jim and

Ulrick Hanson about 1923) about ten miles up Thorne River, on Prince of Wales Island in Southeastern Alaska. An experienced woodsman, Kolby had previously trapped the area. He was said to be in excellent physical condition.

He didn't return to Ketchikan as expected at the end of trapping season. In July, the U.S. Commissioner at Ketchikan sent W. R. (Red) Irwin and Michael Wells to look for him.

They found Kolby's camp in order. Indications were he had left it, intending to stay only a day, or possibly overnight. March 2 was the last day marked on Kolby's calendar.

The two searched near the cabin as well as they could, but the tall July grass and dense, leafy brush made an almost impossible task of it. They returned to Ketchikan with Kolby's effects. The Commissioner named Irwin administrator of the estate of the presumed dead man.

That fall, after summer vegetation had withered and before snowfall, W. R. Selfridge, who had an intimate knowledge of the area, Victor Hautop, an experienced woodsman friend of Kolby, W. A Miller, an experienced river man and beaver trapper, and Max Walker, a friend of Hautop's and an expert cook, left Ketchikan October 28 in Hautop's thirty-foot troller. In Thorne Bay, at the mouth of Thorne River, in two days they built a grid ashore where they beached the boat while on their search.

Thorne River, the largest stream on 45-by-132-mile Prince of Wales Island, flows through a beautiful valley. The men poled and lined the riverboat they had brought ten miles upstream to the ten-by-twelve hemlock-log Hanson cabin.

After several days of searching, Miller returned from upper Thorne Lake reporting the find of human remains.

"It's not Kolby," he said, explaining that he had found a .357 Magnum revolver, with cartridges in the coat pocket. "This guy was done in by wolves," he said. "There are teeth marks on the gun holster, and they weren't made by a beaver. The gun's rusty and doesn't work. Crist had a .357 Magnum in first-rate condition. Wolves could never have gotten Crist unless he lost his gun, busted it, or ran out of shells."

All four agreed the tooth marks on the holster were made by wolves. Hautop cleaned the gun and removed the wooden grips, which exposed a broken mainspring. Finding the broken spring quickly changed Miller's view. Now he decided the remains had to be those of Kolby.

On November 6 the four men went to the site and studied the scattered clothing and bones of Crist Kolby and attempted to reconstruct his last minutes. They decided that Kolby was returning to his base camp, walking on the ice of Thorne Lake. He knew his revolver didn't work. Suddenly wolves appeared, and Crist figured his only hope was to run to the woods and climb a tree.

They speculated that he discarded his knapsack on the ice and ran. A wolf or wolves met him at the edge of the ice, seizing his coat by the right shoulder. Crist struck out with his skinning knife, but lost the knife in the struggle. As he tried to fight off the wolf or wolves, his coat and the wristband of his shirt were torn off.

They thought Crist ran for two trees about fifty feet away. Just under one of the trees it appeared to the four investigators that a wolf or wolves attacked and killed him.

The men examined the scene carefully. The coat was by the water's edge, torn at the right shoulder, with the cuff of a shirt sleeve nearby. The skinning knife, with large tooth marks on the handle, lay nearby. They found bones of an arm in the water about three feet from shore. Was it torn out of its socket at the first encounter, or carried there later after Colby was killed? Impossible to say.

The clothing, all badly torn, was scattered under the two trees fifty feet inland from the lake. The belt was still buckled. They found human bones within a radius of a hundred feet. All but the skull were chewed and broken. The sheath of the skinning knife was near the clothes.

The men gathered the bones and clothing and returned to the Hanson cabin where they discussed the evidence. In their view, the only theory that explained Kolby's death was an attack by wolves. They searched carefully for bear sign, but found none. There was no indication of an accident. If Kolby had drowned, and his body floated ashore later, no wolf or other animal could have pulled the coat off the rigid body in freezing weather without tearing it to pieces.

Why would most of the bones be fifty feet or more from the torn coat and skinning knife? The knife sheath was found near the clothing. It seemed unlikely that any animal would have taken the knife from the sheath and carried it to the lake shore. It appeared that Kolby had taken it out to defend himself.

The four were convinced their conclusion was the only one possible. They believed that wolves killed and ate Crist Kolby.

The next day they fastened a sign to the tree under which Kolby met his death. It read: IN MEMORY OF CRIST KOLBY. Killed and ate up by wolves in March 1939. Found November 5, 1939 by W. R. Selfridge, Vic Hautop, W. A. Miller, M. Walker.

This report paints a convincing picture. Wolves probably ate Crist Kolby. Key words were "bones were chewed and broken," which is typical of wolves, plus identification by all four experienced woodsmen of teeth marks as those of wolves on the knife handle and gun holster.

But did wolves kill Kolby? Could he have been suffering from hypothermia? A victim of hypothermia often removes clothing. Could Kolby have taken his coat off and dropped it at the lake's edge, and froze to death under the trees, where wolves found and ate his body?

What about the shirt sleeve cuff found near the coat? That is harder to explain, although wolves in tearing at the body could have ripped it off and accidentally carried it near the coat. Could Kolby have had a heart attack? Then how explain the coat, with the torn shoulder, 50 feet away from where he apparently died?

Where was Colby's axe? A trapper afield without an axe would be like a hunter without a gun. If Colby, with a broken handgun, was attacked by wolves, an axe could have changed the odds. The article doesn't mention one.

What about a bear out of his den in March? There are no brown bears on Prince of Wales Island—only black bears. Chewed and broken bones are more typical of wolves than bears. Tooth marks on the pistol holster and knife handle appeared to be those of wolves. Bear tracks can linger for months. The men reported searching for but finding no bear sign.

Perhaps hungry wolves did kill Kolby. A pack of aggressive wolves could easily kill an unarmed man. The circumstantial evidence points that way. Evidence strongly suggests that wolves ate his body. Without better evidence though, I'd say cause of death is unknown, with circumstances pointing to the possibility that wolves did kill Crist Kolby.

13
Northway elder: The neighborhood killers

"THEY STRIKE IN the night, using the blackness and the howling wind and centuries of instinct to cover their comings and goings. They snatch their terrified prey within sight of man's lighted windows, devour their kill, and slink back into the shadows leaving bloodied snow behind."—from an October, 1975, *Fairbanks Daily News-Miner*.

Bob Hinman called me, keeping me informed as a BOG member. "Wolves in the Ester to Goldstream area [ten miles outside the Fairbanks metropolitan area] are making a business of killing dogs. We think it's the same pack of four or five. So far we've verified three dog kills by wolves, and a total of five have been reported. The last kill was within a mile of my house," he said.

"This pack has found that dogs on chains are easy prey, and they kill and eat them on the spot. One pair of dogs that wasn't chained ran down a field, barking, probably at the wolves. They didn't come back."

Most of the verified killed and eaten dogs were mixed breed huskies, although the wolves killed and ate several Labrador retrievers, another popular breed in Fairbanks. Loose pet dogs of various breeds disappeared. One Goldstream resident's beagle was gutted on his porch before he got out the door with his hand gun. The number of stray dogs which might have been killed and eaten was unknown.

Ren Smith, as the department's wolf specialist, investigated as many of the dog kills as he could. "The wolves killed some dogs and literally yanked them off their chains. They left feet, some fur, and skulls. Often even the bones were gone," he told me later.

Near Fairbanks the wolves invaded the dog lot of Harry Rasmusson, a veteran of the famous Iditarod sled dog race, where they killed one of his Iditarod trail dogs. He had heard his dogs barking late at night and had shined a flashlight toward them, but had seen nothing. He decided a moose had wandered near. Next morning he found the dead dog and called ADF&G.

Ren investigated. He found a bloody trail with an empty collar still attached to the doghouse chain. Tracks of four wolves were clear. They had yanked the sixty-five- pound dog free of its collar and dragged it into nearby woods before eating it about fifty yards from Rasmusson's house.

Ren followed the blood trail to a small spruce tree with dog hair clinging to its base, which, at first, puzzled him. He then realized that two of the wolves, dragging the dog, had gone on opposite sides of the tree. They had yanked the dog back and forth in a tug of war, rubbing the hair off on the tree. One wolf let go, and the bloody trail continued.

He found the dog's remains about thirty feet from the tree. The entire midsection had been stripped to the bone from shoulder to rump, leaving only the rib cage and spine. The skull, with meat still on it with empty, staring eyes, was still attached.

Rasmusson, who loved his dogs, was devastated and angry. "I'm going to set snares and traps all around the outside of my dog yard," he vowed. "He was one of my best dogs. I've had him for six years."

"Better think about it, Harry. You might catch one of your dogs instead of a wolf," Ren cautioned. "We're trying to catch this pack, and have traps and snares in several places where they're known to range. Can't promise anything, but we're trying."

Ren told a newspaper reporter, "Those wolves are opportunists. They've learned where to find gift-wrapped wolf food. That's wherever dogs are chained. Wolves can adapt, and they're taking advantage of an easy source of food—pets and sled dogs."

He added, "Three factors account for the upsurge in local dog kills by wolves. First, there are fewer moose for wolf food because of winter losses from deep snow of the past several years. Plus, what moose there are have good footing on bare ground and can better defend themselves from wolves. Second, the snowshoe hare population is low. Last, there's a lack of snow in the Fairbanks area, which has handicapped trappers who depend on snowmobiles to get to their traplines, so these wolves haven't had to worry much about getting caught in traps, at least this month.

"These wolves are hungry. Their normal foods aren't readily or easily available. They've discovered dogs are good, easily caught, food. They take stray or loose dogs as well as chained dogs. Chained dogs, of course, are the easiest; they don't have to run them down."

Phone calls to the department by alarmed Fairbanks mothers were fielded by Ren. "No, we don't think these wolves are a threat to children. There is very little danger of a child being killed, but we suggest you keep kids close to home, especially at night," he cautioned nervous mothers.

The ADF&G later calculated that at least thirty dogs in the Fairbanks area were killed by wolves that winter of 1975–76. Most of the killed dogs were in outlying areas, but at times the wolves slipped into suburban Fairbanks to kill dogs.

⁓

SCIENTISTS HAVE LONG held that wolves are "wilderness animals." But today wolves thrive in areas where wilderness has all but vanished, and scientists have had to redefine wolf habitat. Wolves survive and may thrive wherever they find food and human tolerance.

⁓

THAT WINTER WAS a lonely one for Pat York. She made few friends, none she considered close. She occasionally visited Gracie, the rep for The Wild Animal Lovers Association. But Gracie was single-minded; to her the world was going to hell, and she wanted to change it. Cutting a tree was, to Gracie, akin to murder. She had moaned and fretted at Christmas when many Fairbanksans had cut young spruces from the surrounding wilderness for their holiday tree. She objected to hunting, which put her at odds with most Alaskans. She worried endlessly that ADF&G was going to kill every wolf in Alaska.

Gracie's fixation quickly bored Pat. Her picture of the world was brighter, more complex, and from her studies of wolf papers, reports, and policies, she was beginning to realize that Alaska's policy was not to exterminate wolves anywhere, but to maintain viable populations statewide. She now knew that no government in North America—federal, state, or provincial—had a policy of eliminating wolves. On the contrary, all had legal mandates to conserve wolves. That conservation of wolves called for killing wolves was still beyond her. But she was slowly realizing the mammoth size of Alaska, most of which harbors wolves. Subunit 20A, and the handful of wolves the state planned to kill, she now realized, would have little impact on total numbers. She was still adamant, however, that there was no justification to kill wolves to save a few moose.

About once a week Pat called Beth Johnson to talk about progress of her students. Invariably she asked about little red-headed Davy Foster. Although he was rambunctious and needed watching, he had been her favorite. The way he threw himself into everything had impressed her. Beth soon realized Pat's special interest in Davy, and she made a point of detailing the boy's latest escapades. She told Pat that Davy had pulled the class bully off of one of the smaller students. The bully had the little kid on the floor pummeling him when Davy interfered. The bully had turned on Davy, but the little redhead had pitched into him and though the bully was bigger than Davy, Davy had him cowed before teachers separated them. Beth smiled over that for days.

Pat and Snow had bonded almost instantly. Having spent his life mostly chained to his house, the handsome husky seemed to rejoice at being free of the chain, and in the companionship of his new mistress. He knew no commands when he came to live with her, and Pat taught him to come when called, to sit, to lie down, to walk at heel.

The dog, and the attention he required, helped with her loneliness.

After many hours of patient training, Pat felt she had enough control over her new dog to allow him to run free when she snowshoed on trails near town. The pure cold air, the snow-laden spruces, the fresh snowshoe hare tracks, the scolding red squirrels she disturbed in trailside spruces, the silent-winged, friendly camp robber birds (gray jays) that followed her, and the occasional glimpse of moose, were all exciting. Having her dog as a companion increased her enjoyment.

She often brought Snow inside in the evening. He soon became uncomfortable from the unaccustomed warmth and asked to go out. Both the dog and Pat enjoyed these short visits.

The high board fence in the yard behind her house was, Pat thought, a secure and safe place for Snow, and though she was aware of dogs being killed by wolves, most of these killings were distant from her suburb. She didn't worry about Snow.

Then came the morning when she went to feed him and he didn't greet her. He was usually waiting for her, bouncing up and down, looking forward to a quick petting, and to his food. Not this morning. Puzzled, she looked to see if the gate was open. It wasn't. Then she saw blood on the snow, white fur scattered in the yard, a skull.

That was enough. "Oh, no," she moaned, dropping the pan of dog food and retreating inside. She sat, trembling. Tears wouldn't come. Could Snow have been killed by wolves? It didn't seem possible. She remembered him barking late the previous night, and then he had fallen silent. Nothing unusual.

She thought of Ren, and with trembling hands dialed his number.

"Ren. It's Pat York. Can you come right away? Something terrible has happened to Snow."

"I'll be right there," he answered.

She heard his pickup stop and peered out the window to see him walk around the house. The gate squeaked as he opened it and went into the back yard. She opened the back door and watched, as he stood over the pitiful remains of her pet.

He turned, saw her, and with a few strides was at the door. He said, "Inside, Pat," and followed her into the house. She broke down, sobbing. His hand was on her shoulder. She turned and his arms were around her, her head on his shoulder.

"I'm sorry, Pat. I thought he'd be safe inside that fence," he said.

She continued to sob and he silently held her close until she gained control.

Finally, she pushed herself away. "I'm sorry to be such a baby," she apologized.

"I understand," he said. "I've lost dogs that I loved very much, and I know how you must feel."

She dried her eyes and to her surprise saw tears in his eyes.

"Was it wolves?" she asked.

"Yes. Their tracks are everywhere in the yard. There's a big snowdrift against the outside of the fence where they jumped over."

With a plastic garbage bag, Ren picked up all that was left of the once-ebullient Snow—bits of fur, the skull, feet, several large bones—and took them away. With a board he raked fresh snow over the bloody places. A couple of hours later he phoned Pat from his office.

"You shouldn't have to be alone this evening. Let's go somewhere and have dinner," he suggested.

"No, Ren. Thanks anyway. I really don't feel like it."

"I insist. I'll pick you up at seven," he said, and hung up. She didn't call back, so he knew she had given in.

They spent a subdued but pleasant evening and talked about everything but Snow and wolves. He learned something of her life in Boston; she learned something of his life in Wolverine. The wine she drank helped her relax, and despite the sorrow at the loss of Snow she enjoyed herself.

He drove her home, escorted her to the door, gave her a quick hug, and asked, "Are you ok?"

"Yes, I'll be fine. Thank you Ren. Thank you for a pleasant evening. It helped a lot."

"I'll be making a survey flight in a week or so. I'll give you a call if you're still interested in going with me," he said.

"I'd love to go," she answered.

⌒

IN THE TWELVE YEARS (1970–82) I served as a member of the Boards of Game, and Fish and Game, I spent about one day in four or five on board work making phone calls, writing letters, studying reports, and attending meetings. In late February, 1976, I was one of a committee of three Game Board members, which included Sidney Huntington, and one other, to meet with the residents of Northway, a tiny community near the Alaska Highway about forty miles from Canada. We were there to hear their concerns, to learn something of local wildlife conditions, and to get acquainted.

Alaskans, like other Americans, are skeptical of bureaucrats. Convincing people that we as members of the BOG were seriously interested in them and their welfare was always difficult, and it was no different at this meeting. In a way, our being there was a form of entertainment for the locals, a chance to bait three bureaucrats. Northway residents, like residents of most other small rural communities in Alaska at that time, depended largely on fish and game for food. Seasons and bag limits we set were important to them, for it affected their survival.

The temperature at Northway was 40 below zero that night. The meeting room was warm, and got a lot warmer when about fifty people arrived. A table was set up with a microphone and loudspeaker, and we asked people to speak out about their concerns for wildlife and for their uses of wildlife.

The first speaker was a respected elder of the local Athabaskan Indians. His name escapes me, but I will never forget him, his face, or his demeanor. His words have stayed with me for a quarter century. He wore moccasins, a beautiful fringed gold-colored, smoked moose-skin jacket, and gray trappers' heavy woolen trousers. His long white hair was tied with a beaded buckskin band that encircled his head.

His deeply lined face was a map of his ninety plus years. His hunting years were behind him, but that didn't matter. His knowledge of the land, its wildlife, its seasons, and the almost incredible changes he had seen in his nearly a century of life, brought him respect from his people, as well as others. He was dignity itself, and clearly he was in his element before the crowd.

He spoke slowly, his voice strong and sure. "You always ignore our knowledge," he said. "We, who have been here for centuries. Our elders and their elders told us how things are and how they should be. You should listen to what we say, if no other reason than to be polite. Local knowledge is important. You are big on your scientific knowledge, from the way you look at it, but that isn't always the whole story. The moose, the caribou, and the wolf talk to us. They don't use words. Their actions tell us. When they are fat they say one thing. When they are thin they tell us something else. When they travel, they tell us one thing. When they stay in one place, they tell another story. When they are afraid, they tell us still another story.

"Indian knowledge. Local knowledge. Animal knowledge. That is what you should listen to. People are part of nature; many of you think that people should not be here on this land. But we have been here since the first, living with the moose, the sheep, the caribou, and the wolf. Our elders have told us about that in stories their elders told them.

"You take the wolf. Before we became a state, the federal government killed wolves. That was good. That way the moose and caribou increased. The wolf is an evil animal, and it should be killed. But we don't want all wolves killed, just enough to let the moose and caribou increase so we can eat too. That is what you should do. That is all."

The old man stopped speaking abruptly. He didn't give us a chance to ask questions. The applause that met him as he went back to his seat was an indication of the local respect for him, and agreement in what he said.

He said everything that needed saying that evening. Subsequent comments from other speakers more or less repeated his sentiments.

It was a meeting I have never forgotten. The old man was the only Alaska Native I have heard call the wolf "evil." His philosophy on wolf control was amazingly close to that espoused by wildlife biologists of the ADF&G, (although ADF&G biologists do not regard the wolf as evil), and to the state constitution's requirement for management on the sustained yield principle.

DURING THE SUMMER of 1928 a pair of wolves lived in an old fox den they had enlarged within a mile of Frank Glaser's cabin. He often walked along the bars of Savage River, allowing Queenie, his half-wolf lead dog, to run loose. That summer she found five big bull caribou, a two-year-old bull moose and a yearling moose that had been killed by these wolves. She would get the wind of a kill and head for it, and Frank would follow her. Without Queenie he wouldn't have found any of them. Each of the kills was in or near shallow water at the river's edge. There were probably other kills Queenie didn't find.

The kills were all near a mineral lick where game animals sometimes congregated. Reading sign, Frank figured that the two wolves ambushed the caribou or moose at the lick. Antlers are in velvet in summer, tender, and not much use for defense. It didn't appear as if the moose or caribou had given the wolves any trouble. The two-year-old bull moose was still fresh when he found it and he took some of it home for dog food.

One day Frank was on a high lookout behind his cabin about

three-quarters of a mile from the two-year-old moose remains. As he scanned with binoculars, he spotted a cream-colored grizzly shuffling aimlessly across the tussocky tundra toward Savage River. Occasionally he stopped to dig and eat a root, or swallow some other bit of vegetation. Several times he sat on his haunches like a gigantic ground squirrel, swiveling his nail-keg-size head back and forth, peering with small eyes, nose wrinkled and sniffing, then dropped to all fours and ambled on.

He came to the river and started across a gravel bar. Half way to the water he stopped, his head twisted to one side, his nose detecting the scent of rotting moose. He whirled and loped upwind, his bulky body moving surprisingly fast as he splashed through shallows, following his educated nose.

Reaching the dead moose, which was lying in shallow water, he mouthed it excitedly, waded around it a couple of times, then clamped his powerful jaws on a front leg, leaned backward, and splashily dragged the carcass to dry ground where he started to eat.

As Frank watched through binoculars, a black and a gray wolf appeared suddenly on the bar and stood watching the bear. It didn't notice the wolves until they started to close in with a mane-bristled, stiff-legged walk. They circled him. He dropped to his haunches to face them.

The wolves walked as if tiptoeing on eggs, moving slowly, heads down, hair on end, tails straight out behind. Around and around they went, the bear twisting and trying to face both wolves at once. Finally, when they got the bear between them, the black leaped in and slashed the bear's rear. As quick as a trap the grizzly whirled, bawling—Frank heard him even from his distance—and rushed at the nimble wolf. The gray wolf dashed in, snapping at the bear's heels. Bruin plowed to a quick stop, turned and swiped at the gray with a front paw. The wolf was too quick for the bear, and easily leaped out of reach.

The bear swiftly lumbered after it, but he hadn't gone twenty yards before the black wolf was again tormenting him from the rear. At one point the wolf actually leaped on the bear's broad back, slashing through his thick hide.

The grizzly skidded to a stop and reared over backward trying to reach his tormenter. For a moment he sat on his haunches, facing both wolves. The grizzly is generally boss bully of the Alaska wilds, and Frank got the impression this bear was not only frustrated, but bewildered.

The panting wolves appeared to be grinning, as they continued to bait the bear, working silently and in perfect coordination. The bear kept roaring and growling and it became clear the wolves were working him away from their kill.

Soon the battling animals disappeared into the timber, but Frank followed the fight by the roaring of the bear. He hoped they would appear again on a bar of Savage River, but they didn't. Occasionally, in breaks in the timber, he saw flashes of the moving bear and running wolves. In about twenty minutes the wolves worked the bear into the timber a full mile away from their kill.

While tormenting the big yellow grizzly the wolves didn't make a sound, but when they were satisfied, they howled a low sweet musical song and trotted off. The bear slouched off across the tundra. The dead moose belonged to the wolves who weren't about to let any waddling loafer of a bear have it.

That pair of wolves lived near Frank and his dogs for some time without Frank being aware of them. Several times that summer all of his wolf-dogs suddenly growled and made a fuss. Frank would step out of the cabin and look, and the dogs would lean on their chains looking at the three-foot-high redtop grass around the cabin. He couldn't see anything. One day the dogs kept insisting something was there, so he put a ladder up on his cache and climbed a few feet. Then he saw a gray wolf lying in the grass not far from the cabin.

He went for his rifle and climbed the ladder again, but of course by the time he got back the wolf was gone.

With his wolf-dogs, Frank went to Healy several times that summer. Each time he returned to find that some animal had dug all the dry grass out of the dog houses, and had packed the dogs' bones off. He later realized it had to have been that pair of wolves.

Two or three times during summer evenings the dogs looked out on the bar of nearby Savage River and growled. Frank would look and see the back of a wolf loping along. He never got a shot.

That fall, the gray and black wolf pair got into the habit of killing caribou on a nearby open flat. Early one mid-September morning Frank climbed a ridge overlooking the flat, hoping to get a shot at wolves—any wolves. The nine-mile-long flat was dotted with little bunches of up to twenty or so caribou as far as he could see. He stayed high, searching with binoculars.

About nine o'clock that morning, a gray wolf walked out of the red-top grass, stretched and looked around. It was about a mile away and perhaps 800 feet below Frank. Then a black wolf appeared nearby, stretched, yawned and also looked around. They started to howl softly. They were the pair from the nearby den. The gray was the female, the black the male.

Soon they started after a caribou. It was hard for Frank to believe they were the pair that had killed all the big game he had found dead along Savage River that summer, for on this day they couldn't seem to connect.

Every time they tried to stalk a caribou, another would see them and give the alarm. The two wolves would belly down like cats and slide along flattened out, now and then raising up and peeking ahead. When within thirty or forty feet of a caribou, quick as a flash they'd dash at it, but the caribou had been forewarned every time and would bound away across the rough tundra almost like a rubber ball.

On such terrain, a caribou can easily outrun a wolf. The wolf trips and stumbles, while the caribou bounds along smoothly.

After each failed stalk, the two wolves made no effort to chase caribou, but sat and howled real low. Then they'd trot off single-file, looking for another caribou.

The country was full of snowshoe hares and every time the wolves went through a willow patch, hares ran out all around them. The wolves ignored them. Not once did Frank see them even turn their heads when hares were near.

Knowing they were hungry and had big pups to feed, Frank was fairly certain they'd hunt until they killed. There were two possibilities for him to get a shot. One was to wait until they killed and gorged themselves then try to stalk them as they slept. The other was to get closer to the caribou they were stalking and hope for a shot as they hunted.

There were the pups to think of too. If he worked it right he might be able to get a crack at them. At that time of year wolf pups depend almost entirely on their parents for food. Usually, by September when the parents make a kill they'll either lead the half-grown pups to it, or they'll howl and call the pups to the kill. When pups are still very young, the adults return to the den and regurgitate food for them. These pups were beyond that stage.

All that day Frank walked back and forth on the ridge, staying back so the wolves wouldn't wind him, yet trying to keep them in sight. Occasionally he struck a match to test the wind; it remained steady from the south, and he couldn't get any closer to the wolves without being scented.

The gray wolf took the lead in all their stalks. The wolves would get downwind of a caribou and she would get down like a cat and slide along with the black right behind her. Now and then the gray lifted her head to peek. Frank frequently lost sight of the wolves, but he could tell where they were by the behavior of the caribou. One of a bunch of caribou would raise its head and stand and watch the wolves. When the wolves got too close, the caribou would run.

Once the pair stalked a big white-necked bull caribou with hard-polished, rocking-chair-size antlers. He was on a little knoll, fighting a willow bush. He'd waltz around, rub his antlers up and down the bush, then back off to rush and hook at it as if it were a rival. The bull was too busy trying to impress himself to see the wolves. When they were about twenty yards away the wolves got to their feet and *walked* toward the bull. As they neared, the black suddenly made a rush, but the puffed-up bull whirled and lowered his rack, ready for the attack.

The two wolves ran around him, howling, rushing and pestering him, trying to make him expose a flank. He simply whirled to face them, shaking his big half-polished rack in their faces. They finally howled a few times, turned, and walked away, heads and tails down. The bull had bluffed them out. He went back to dueling with the willows, probably more impressed with himself than ever.

Frank kept trying to get into position for a shot, but the wolves remained out of range. It was nearly five in the afternoon, the sun was low, and he was ready to quit and go home. He figured they'd make their kill after dark; most wolf kills are made at night.

Then a cow caribou started down the ridge with a calf at her heels. The wolves quickly scented them. The caribou were following a line of willows running down to the flat, a perfect place for wolves to make a stalk. They ran and sneaked to the line of willows to lie in wait.

This was the break Frank had been looking for all day. When the stalking wolves came to the lower end of the willows they were within 300 yards of him. As they went out of sight in the thick growth, he crawled to the willows, stopped in a little opening and sat in a game trail. The wind was right. Neither the wolves nor the caribou saw him.

He watched the brush shaking as the wolves crawled through it. Soon the cow caribou also noticed the moving willows, and stood staring. Occasionally the gray wolf poked her head up to peek, making the cow nervous. She still didn't run. Closer and closer the wolves came. Frank heard them sniffing, trying to use scent to keep track of the caribou.

Suddenly the gray wolf stuck her head out of the grass about twenty feet from Frank. She practically filled his rifle scope's field of view and all he had to do was pull the trigger. As he fired she disappeared with a growl, then the grass started twitching where she threshed about.

Frank jumped up. He saw the black wolf leap over his dead mate and run along the game trail toward him. The wolf didn't know where the shot had come from and he was so close when he saw Frank it was too late for him to turn. Frank had him in the scope, but before he could shoot, the wolf scooted past within fifteen feet, ears pinned back, feet scratching for all they were worth. Frank let him run fifty yards into the open, then fired. He swapped ends, stone-dead. The caribou cow and her calf streaked to safety.

There were still the pups to consider. Frank started howling, trying to call them. Within five minutes he had an answer from where the two adults had come out of the grass that morning. He kept calling, and soon saw five half-grown wolves through his glasses, trotting single file, straight toward him. They weighed about fifty pounds each, all head, legs, and feet—capable of eating a lot of caribou and moose.

He called them right up. When they were close he shot one. The other four ran into some willows. He walked through the willows and one by one those big pups got up to run. They'd flatten out again, hiding. He found and shot each.

He skinned all seven, mostly for the bounty, for the skins weren't worth much (wolf skins don't prime up until well into winter). Their stomachs were empty. That was hard for Frank to believe because snowshoe hares were abundant. The adults ignored them all day in order to try to kill caribou.

He had killed seven wolves with seven shots, and would collect seven $15 bounties. And there were seven fewer wolves to kill Savage River moose and caribou.

14

The flight: Glaser's new career

IN EARLY MARCH Ren called to invite Pat to fly with him. "Wear good longjohns and your parka," he warned. "My airplane can be cold."

"I won't forget," Pat laughed. "I hate being cold."

"And we'd better take your snowshoes. If we land you may need them."

"Lunch?" Pat asked.

"I usually don't bother for just a day," Ren said.

"I'll make one for both of us," she promised.

The sun had yet to appear above the distant Alaska Range when Ren parked his pickup near his tied-down Piper Super Cub at Fairbanks' Phillips Field. It was calm, without a cloud in sight. With eleven hours of sunlight ahead and a balmy (for Fairbanks) 14 degrees above, it was a perfect day for flying.

Pat watched with interest as Ren pre-flighted the plane. He removed the tiedown ropes, peeled off the two wing covers, folded them, and put them behind the rear seat. He walked around the airplane, inspecting every fitting, shook the wings, kicked the ski-wheel combination landing gear, ran his hand across the bottoms of the skis, which were in the up position. He studied the flap, aileron, elevator, and rudder hinges. Standing on a step ladder, he removed the gas caps and peered into each of the two fuel tanks. At the right tank he hesitated a moment, and studied the inside of the cap, poked his finger into the tank to make sure the tank was full. He shook his head.

"What's the matter?" Pat asked.

"That cap was loose. I always tighten it. I topped the tanks off yesterday after flying. Guess I got careless," he said, shrugging. "Anyway, the tank is full and now the cap is tight."

He filled a glass tube with gasoline from the quick drains under the wings and peered closely at it to see if there was dirt or ice. He removed the insulating cover from the cowling, unplugged and removed the small electric heater he had placed in the engine compartment the previous evening, and checked the oil.

"Do you do this every time you fly?" Pat asked.

"Yes. If something goes wrong when you're in the air you can't pull over and park, like you can with a car," he explained. "Best to make sure everything is ok before you take off."

He lashed her snowshoes to a wing strut; his snowshoes were already tied under the opposite wing.

Finally, he removed a cloth windshield cover and polished a few hazy spots on the windshield.

"We're ready," he said. "Climb in here," pointing to the back seat.

She awkwardly started to get in, afraid to touch anything. He laughed. "Grab the top of this seat and swing yourself in," pointing to the front seat and a footrest.

He fastened her safety belt. She was shivering. Was it from the cold, nervousness, or excitement?

"Relax, Pat. This is a good airplane, and I'm not going to do anything risky. You'll enjoy yourself," he encouraged.

"I'm all right. I've never flown in a small plane," she admitted. "I don't know what to expect."

"You came to Alaska for adventure, didn't you? This'll be an adventure for you," he promised. "I'm going to try to show you some wolves. At the least you'll see some pretty country."

She was surprised when, on takeoff, the acceleration pressed her back against her seat. They left the ground, and climbed smoothly, heading south, toward the mountains.

Ren turned, "We're going to notorious 20A," he shouted over the roar of the engine.

She nodded, peering down at the outskirts of Fairbanks. He banked gently, and nodded down. "There's your house," he said.

Unfamiliar with the view from the sky, it took her a few moments to make out where she lived, and by then they were almost beyond it. Soon they left all roads, houses, and other signs of civilization, and flew over frozen creeks, snow-covered open flats, scattered spruces, and later, rolling hills.

He turned and called, "Are you ok?

"Yes! It's beautiful."

He nodded. Conversation was difficult in the noisy airplane. She soon relaxed, enjoying the scenery.

"Moose ahead," he called, turning the plane slightly and heading for a dark spot on the snow. Above the moose, he gently banked and circled.

"It's a bull," he called back.

She saw no antlers. "How can you tell?" she yelled.

"Look at the neck. The top of a cow's neck forms a V-shape; a bull's neck is more straight," he explained. "His new antlers will start showing soon."

Half an hour into the flight, after circling two more moose, he banked and throttled back, slowly descending. He circled a dark spot in a snowy clearing. Tracks radiated from it.

"What is it?" she asked.

"Moose. A wolf kill," he answered. "Let's land and take a look."

He circled several times, selecting a place to land, made sure his skis were down, lowered flaps, and eased to a landing. A couple of ravens, perched on the dead moose, flapped into the air as the plane stopped. Ren shut the engine down, opened the doors, and stepped into deep snow.

"Stay there until I get your snowshoes," he said, untying his webs from the right wing strut. With his snowshoes on he retrieved hers. She slipped into them quickly. He then grabbed a saw from behind the back seat, and broke trail toward the kill.

Nearing the carcass he turned and said, gently, "Pat, don't be upset or horrified. This is nature in the raw. Wolves have to eat, and what they eat here is mostly moose they kill. It's not pretty, but there's a fascination to it. We learn a lot about both moose and wolves by examining kills like this."

He pointed. "That's where the battle probably ended. See the moose hair?" Wide-eyed, she saw a bloody, trampled area strewn with moose hair.

Ren continued, "Those are rumen contents," he said, pointing to a frozen dark pile of material in the snow."

The dead moose lay in the center of the trampled area of moose and wolf tracks. "Look where that wolf leaped—at least ten feet between bounds," he exclaimed.

"It's an adult cow," Ren said, "and fairly fresh. I'd say she was killed yesterday or the day before. Probably by three or four wolves."

Pat was wide-eyed, a bit horrified and nervous. "Why, that moose is huge. Did wolves really kill it? Will they come back?"

"Of course it's a wolf kill. Look at the tracks. And yes, they'll probably come back, unless they find an easy kill somewhere else. But not while we're here," he assured her, walking closer to the kill.

The carcass lay on its side, all four legs extended. Several trails in the snow ran from the moose toward a nearby hillock.

"They fed, then with full bellies they went to that hill for a snooze," he explained, pointing out the trails.

"What happened there?" she asked, indicating a packed area in the snow near one of the trails.

"Wolves get bloody when they feed on a fresh kill. A wolf cleaned itself by rolling in the snow there after feeding," he explained. "See, there's another over there," pointing to second, small, packed-snow spot.

They snowshoed around the carcass, and Pat gasped at the ugly sight. Blood, hair, and pieces of viscera, were on the packed snow around the carcass.

"They like to pull the innards out and eat them first," he explained. "Lot's of vitamins in the liver, kidneys, and heart. Fat on the intestines. And," he said, glancing at her, "this cow was probably pregnant. The fetuses are easy to eat, and nourishing."

Pat looked pale. "I want to check one of the long bones for marrow. If you'd prefer, go back to the plane," he said, gently. He realized this was probably the first large dead animal she had ever seen.

"No. I'll stay. I'm ok. You're right. This is nature in the raw, and I'd better know about it," she said a bit stiffly.

With the saw he cut a lower leg off and peered at the exposed marrow. "Look, Pat. See how white this marrow is? This moose was in good nutritional condition. When animals are starving, the marrow gets runny and reddish."

"I thought wolves killed mostly the sick, weak, or unfit," Pat said. "You say this moose was healthy?"

"Yep. As far as I can tell. She sure wasn't starving or weak. I don't see any broken legs or anything else to indicate she was anything but a perfectly healthy, adult moose," he said. "Her only physical disadvantage was she was pregnant."

"Pat," he added, "the common belief that wolves kill only the unfit is largely a myth. A few years ago Loyal Johnson, one of our experienced wildlife biologists, spent a winter studying fifty seven moose carcasses that had been killed by wolves. He determined the age and sex of each. Most of them, about fifty six percent, were calves, which is expected; they're easier for wolves to kill than adults. But, of course, removing them from the population doesn't benefit the health of the herd. Actually, just the opposite. The young are a key element—they're the future of the herd.

"Loyal found the sex ratio of the adult moose killed by wolves was nineteen bulls to one hundred cows. Average age of adult bulls was three years, and about eight and a half years for cows. That was almost exactly the sex ratio and age structure of the moose herd as a whole.

"In other words, the theory that wolves kill only the disabled and inferior animals didn't hold up in that study. To cap it off, of the calves killed by wolves, animals that were apparently healthy appeared to predominate," Ren said. "It was a deep-snow winter, and moose were unusually vulnerable to predation, which probably influenced results of the study. Most studies do find old, young, and infirm predominate in the prey of wolves."

"But everyone says that wolves kill mostly the sick and unfit, and weak. They're supposed to be good for the health of their prey species," Pat objected.

"Yeah. Everyone says a lot of things about wolves that aren't necessarily true," he said. "Some of the evidence to the contrary is in front of you. Paul Errington, a great wildlife scientist, once said, 'Nature's way is any way that works.' That makes sense to me. Wolves are intelligent and adaptive. Results of research one year, or in one area, do not necessarily apply to other years or other areas. Or other wolves."

"Suppose moose and caribou in an area are all strong and healthy, without any sick, unfit, or infirm members. If wolves ate only the sick, unfit, or infirm, they would have nothing to eat. It doesn't really work that way," he smiled.

"The more I learn about wolves, the more confused I get," she said, soberly.

"I warned you, didn't I?" he reminded.

He pointed to the lower parts of the hind legs. "See the blood in the hair around the hocks, and all that chewed area above it?

That's where wolves usually attack moose—there and in the flanks. Sometimes we find remains of a kill in which everything has been eaten but the lower hind legs. In that case a bloody lower hind leg is strong indication of a wolf kill.

"While one or more wolves attack from the rear, another wolf will grab the moose by the nose and hang on, even when the moose lifts it off the ground."

They returned to the plane and flew for another hour, circling several more moose, but they didn't find any more wolf kills. Once Ren flew low, studying tracks in the snow. He shook his head.

"I hoped they were wolf tracks. A lynx, I think," he said, climbing again.

They flew over a tiny log cabin. Smoke rose from the stove pipe. Ren circled, and a man stepped out and waved.

"A trapper friend," he explained. "Would you mind stopping for a visit?"

"Of course not," she answered.

Ren eased to a landing near the cabin and stopped the engine. Before opening the doors he turned to Pat and warned, "He's a good friend, but he has an attitude about wolves. Don't let it bother you."

Ren reached behind the seat for a small insulated bag he had placed in the plane at Fairbanks. He had stopped the plane near a packed trail and they didn't need snowshoes.

Herman, the trapper, had a full, graying beard and wore insulated coveralls and insulated boots. "Why Ren, you have a lady friend," he said, almost accusingly.

"Herman, meet Miss York. She's a friend of mine from Boston. I'm giving her the Super Cub special tour."

"Welcome Miss York," he said, shaking her hand. "Any friend of Ren's is a friend of mine." His hand was hard, calloused. He was tall, slim. The part of his face visible above his beard was tanned, weathered, and wrinkled. His eyes were sparkling blue.

"How'd trapping go this winter, Herman?" Ren asked, as they shook hands and slapped each other on the back.

"Fair to middlin', Ren. Got half a dozen wolves, a pretty good bunch of marten, a couple of wolverine, and three lynx. Getting ready for beaver season. Should get my limit of twenty five," he said.

"How'd you like to take another wolf or three? An hour ago

we stopped at a fresh wolf kill—a cow moose. It's at the head of Clear Creek in that big flat where you shot your bull moose last fall. You've got another three weeks of season and you might want to set a trap or two there," Ren told him.

"I'll do it, and you can count on it. Thanks. Them damned devils have been howling every day and night for weeks. They've run all the moose off around here. I don't know why your department doesn't kill 'em all off. They've sure raised hell with the moose and caribou here. Oh, excuse my language miss. Here, you two come in and let's have some coffee," he invited.

His cabin was neat and clean. They chatted as they drank strong coffee and ate dry, round pilot crackers with strawberry jam. Herman showed Pat some of his winter's catch. She rubbed her hands across the fur of several velvety marten skins, and was amazed at the huge size of the wolf skins. She thought of gentle, friendly, Lobo as she ran her hand through the soft fur of one of the six-foot-long pelts.

Ren handed Herman the insulated bag. He opened it and poured fresh oranges, apples and bananas onto the only table in the cabin.

"Thanks, Ren. You sure know how to please this old trapper," Herman said, handing the bag back to Ren. "You can fill that bag and bring me fruit any time you come this way. I'll be happy to pay."

"You know better than that, Herman. Don't insult me," Ren said, humorously.

Back in the plane, Pat asked, "Why did you tell Herman to set traps at that wolf kill?"

"I'd rather trappers or hunters take the wolves. If they don't, the department will have to," he said

"Oh," she said. In her excitement of the flight she had almost forgotten the plan to kill wolves in this area.

Ren flew farther into the foothills, toward the snowy, towering peaks. He studied the snow below, and kept mostly above openings in the spruce forest where he could watch for tracks.

"There," he exclaimed, banking and descending for a closer look at a line of tracks. He lowered the wing flaps and flew slowly over the line of dimples in the snow.

"Wolves," he announced. "Fresh tracks. They were going that way," pointing. "We should catch up with them pretty quick."

He climbed and followed the tracks. Within ten minutes a line of dark spots appeared on the snow ahead. As they neared, the spots turned into a pack of wolves travelling single file. Ren stayed high to avoid spooking them.

"See 'em, Pat?" he asked.

"Yes," she said. "They're all black, aren't they?"

"Maybe," he said, wondering if they had come across the Black Pack, and hoping he'd see a gray wolf among them.

He circled, banking gently..Pat stared at the first wild wolves she had ever seen. "Ren," she called, "there's a gray one with them. I count seven blacks and a gray! The gray is second from last."

He smiled, delighted, wondering if the gray was Lady. He'd never know, of course, but he was near where he had seen the pack of eight blacks and a gray the previous October.

The wolves ignored the circling plane, continuing to travel single-file through the deep snow. Ren circled them several times.

"Time to head home," he called, turning toward Fairbanks. He glanced at the sight gauge for the left wing fuel tank, saw it was down to about a quarter, and switched to the right wing tank.

Ten minutes later the engine sputtered, then caught again. He glanced at the sight gauge. Plenty of fuel in the right tank. His instruments were ok, except perhaps for temperature. It appeared to be climbing a bit. That was strange and unusual. He watched it carefully and it continued to edge upward.

Then, abruptly, the engine quit. No sputter, no warning. It simply quit, with the prop horizontal.

The sudden silence when the engine quits in a small plane aloft is one of the most attention-getting sounds a pilot ever hears. Automatically, Ren dropped the nose to keep flying speed. He hit the starter button. The prop didn't quiver. It remained horizontal. There were plenty of places to land. He chose a flat near a tongue of spruce trees; if they were going to be stuck overnight, they'd at least have firewood, and the timber would provide shelter.

"What's happened?" Pat called.

"I don't know. Engine quit, and I can't get it started. Don't worry. I'll land near those trees."

He called Fairbanks on the radio without getting a response. "Too far," he muttered. He tried again, while guiding the plane down. Again no answer. By then he was nearing the ground and he concentrated on landing. The skis whispered in the loose snow, and the plane stopped on the snow near the stand of spruces.

They sat in silence for a few moments.

"Are we stuck here?" Pat asked.

"Afraid so. At least for a while," Ren said. "I'll check the engine. Maybe I can figure out what happened. Stay where you are," he suggested as he climbed out and buckled on snowshoes.

Making sure the magneto switch was off, he tried to pull the prop through. It wouldn't budge. He raised the engine cowling and peered about, but he could find nothing out of place.

"I don't know what it is, Pat. One thing is sure. The engine won't turn over, and if it won't turn over, it won't start. We aren't going anywhere," he said.

"Maybe when it cools off?" she asked.

"Nope. The engine has seized. I don't think it'll change when it cools," he said. "Please don't worry. We'll be all right. I filed a flight plan this morning, and I told Herman where I planned to fly. It might be tomorrow before we're picked up, but we're safe. We have emergency gear."

She decided to make light of it, and laughed. "When I was in high school I went for a ride with a boy. His car stopped on a lonely road and he told me he was out of gas. He had plenty of gas. It was just an excuse. Is that what you're up to?"

He grinned, relieved she wasn't upset. "No, but it's not a bad idea," he answered.

Turning serious, he said, "We'd better set up camp for the night."

With a snowshoe Ren shoveled snow down to the ground in a sheltered spot at the edge of the spruce grove, spread a light tarpaulin, and pitched a two-person tent on it. With a saw and small axe he cut dry lower branches from several spruce trees and dragged them to a spot near the tent and soon had a cheerful, crackling fire. They sat near the fire on two tiny aluminum folding camp stools and ate the lunch Pat had prepared.

"I promised you an adventure today, and you got it," he said wryly.

"I'm enjoying myself. I'm also glad I wore longjohns," she said. "I was getting cold in the plane. It was time to land and light a fire."

"Yeah. But I didn't plan it that way," he said.

"Ren, when you checked your gas tanks this morning you said the cap was loose on your right tank. Do you think that has anything to do with the engine stopping?"

"I don't know. I've been thinking about it. I'm careful around the plane and check myself all the time. I'm sure I tightened that cap when I topped the tank yesterday. I've been wondering if someone put something in my gas."

"Oh, no. No one would do a thing like that, would they?" she said.

"My job makes me vulnerable. There are crackpots who wouldn't be sorry to see me gone."

"You mean environmentalists—wolf lovers?" she asked.

"Yeah," he answered, but he would say no more.

Changing the subject, he asked, "What did you think of Herman's furs?"

"They were beautiful," she replied.

"You realize, your TNWSF is opposed to trapping and wants to stop it entirely. They'd even close all fur farms if they could," he said.

"I know. I'm confused about that. I like to think I'm an environmentalist, but I have a problem understanding it all," she confessed.

"Let me give you my two-bit lecture on furs," Ren said.

"All right. I'll listen," she said, poking a stick at the fire.

"Fur is renewable, biodegradable, and non polluting," he said. "This gives us an incentive to manage furbearers on a sustained yield basis and to protect wildlife habitat. Animal rights groups like yours advocate the use of fake fur. But synthetic or fake furs are manufactured from petroleum, a non-renewable resource. That involves the use of vinyl chloride and other toxins. Pollution often results. Oil has to be transported to industrial centers where it can be converted into various products. You're no doubt familiar with the death and suffering to wildlife and damage to the environment when there's an oil spill. Oil is not an ecological, harmless alternative. End of lecture."

"Oh, I'd never thought of that," she said. "But you have to kill animals to get their fur," she said. "I don't like that."

"I know. But you wear a leather belt and leather shoes. You have leather purses, you eat chicken, turkey, beef, pork, lamb. All of those products are from animals that have been slaughtered," he said.

"I know," she said. "I guess I'm a struggling environmentalist."

"What is the difference between fur and leather?" he asked.

"Why, none, I guess," she answered, after a moment's thought.

"Of course not. And leather is an important commercial product, accepted by just about everyone in our society for everything from clothing to upholstering car seats and furniture. Why should fur be viewed any differently?" he asked.

Ren kept feeding the fire as the evening darkness slowly arrived. They were enjoying each other's company. She was surprised at his depth of knowledge. He gave her something to think about. She couldn't help but enjoy the romance of the day—seeing firsthand the snowy wilderness, the wildlife, visiting a remote trapper, and then being forced down in a small plane. Ren didn't seem concerned for their safety, and she had confidence in him.

As darkness settled, the chill night air pushed them into the tent and the two down-filled sleeping bags atop insulated pads. Ren handed her a small bleached and washed flour sack. "Fold your parka and put it in this for a pillow," he advised. "And leave your socks on. They'll dry overnight and your feet will be warm in the morning."

Leaving most of their clothing on, they zipped into sleeping bags, and resumed their conversation. "How many moose did we see today?" he asked.

"Six, plus the wolf kill," she said.

"Remember that. I have another area I want to show you—after I get my airplane flying again. You do want to fly with me again?" he asked.

"Depends. How often does your engine quit?" she teased.

"Believe it or not, this is the first total engine failure I've ever had," he told her. "I'm really sorry."

"You didn't stop the engine on purpose," she said, knowing how badly he felt.

"Listen!" Ren hissed.

She raised her head out of the soft folds of the sleeping bag. In a moment she heard a wail, then another. "Wolves!" she said. "I know that sound."

"It's a beautiful sound, isn't it?" he said.

"It's true music," she commented.

The howls continued for about five minutes. The distant sounds reminded her of Lobo, and she told Ren how the big wolf had visited her classroom. "It was really educational for the children," she commented.

He said nothing.

"Ren? Don't you think its good to have a live wolf visit classrooms?"

"I don't want to spoil it for you, Pat," he said, after a moment. "But there are two sides to it."

"What do you mean?"

"I think it's great to teach kids about wolves," Ren said. "I'd like to see honest and sound scientific information presented, instead of what most preservationist organizations present. Seeing a captive wolf in a classroom can give kids the impression that wolves make good pets. They don't make good pets. They can turn violent in an instant. You can never tame a wolf. Your Lobo might have looked like and behaved like a well-trained dog. If he was pure wolf, even if he was born in captivity, he was still a wild animal and potentially dangerous.

"I read various newspapers, and keep a scrapbook of clippings on wolves. Last July a one-year-old child was bitten in the face by one of those 'ambassador' wolves being displayed in New Jersey by The Fund for Animals. The child survived, but she had to undergo plastic surgery. Supposedly, the wolf closed its jaws on the child's face. Her father pulled her away, while the owner of the wolf pulled on the wolf's leash. The wolf hung on. It tore the girl's cheek open." Ren said.

Pat was skeptical. She thought he was wrong. Lobo had seemed placid and friendly. She couldn't imagine him being dangerous.

Before falling asleep she almost giggled, thinking, "I've never slept with a man before."

Remembering that I had once told her, "Ren Smith is a gentleman," she thought, "Thank God."

⁂

FUR PRICES DROPPED in the 1930s, and fox furs especially, lost value. Frank Glaser's income plunged. He had depended on the sale of fox furs, and suddenly they weren't worth trapping. He had to find other ways of making money, so he turned to guiding trophy hunters for grizzly bears in the spring, and for grizzlies, sheep, moose, and caribou in the fall. He sold some of the rifles he had collected. In the summer of 1935 he worked as a temporary park ranger in McKinley National Park.

His reduced income forced him to live more and more off the land. There was no longer money to maintain a year-round room at the Nordale Hotel, or to buy every new rifle model that interested him. When visiting Fairbanks he could no longer give lavish handouts to down-and-outers as had been his custom.

Over the years, Frank had sent many hides and skulls of wolves, bears, foxes and other mammal specimens to the U.S. Biological Survey, precursor to the present U.S. Fish and Wildlife Service. He was acquainted with Frank Dufresne, Executive Officer of the Alaska Game Commission, which represented the Biological Survey in Alaska, who was aware of Glaser's reputation as a wolf hunter.

In April, 1937, he was hired as an Agent Hunter, working for the Predator Control Branch in a cooperative program between the Territory and the Biological Survey. His annual salary was $2,000. He was to hunt and trap wolves and coyotes, and teach trappers how to take these predators. His first assignment was to try to reduce wolf numbers in the central Alaska Range where for several years they had been decimating wintering caribou.

Frank Glaser was starting a new career at the age of forty-eight.

He wasn't the only federal employee in the 1930s campaign to kill Alaska's wolves. While researching Glaser's life I came across the following in a July 24, 1937 issue of the *Fairbanks News-Miner*. "As part of the Alaska Game Commission's campaign to save wild game from the increasing packs of wolves and coyotes, Warden Sam White has brought in six and one-half barrels of wolf traps for distribution among Fairbanks and Fort Yukon trappers.

"'These big traps will be sold to trappers at cost price—and no charge is being made for freighting them to Fairbanks,' said Mr. White. Warden Peter McMullen left Fairbanks yesterday with a load of these traps to be distributed from his headquarters at Fort Yukon."

Glaser abandoned his Savage River cabin, and on April 22 left Savage River driving his wolf-dogs on his first federal wolf hunt. His sled was loaded with a tent, stove, food for himself and the dogs, extra harness, rifle, ammunition, and other items for an extended trip. He headed west along the north slope of the Alaska Range, looking for wolves and wolf dens.

Snow was deep even when May arrived. Days were warm, and

snow was melting with every little creek running beneath the snow. In some deep drifts he could push a pole down seven or eight feet into slush. He was on snowshoes, of course.

He reached the Toklat River, fifty miles from Savage River, and found a three-quarter-mile-wide overflow of water running about two feet deep atop the ice. He followed the riverbank upstream, avoiding the water. About ten miles upstream he found dry ice to travel on. An inch or so of fresh snow had fallen during the night, and he soon ran into a set of fresh wolf tracks.

He made camp and hunted wolves on foot. He loved to hunt and to outsmart wolves and now, in his new federal job, he was being paid to kill them. While trapping at Savage River he hunted wolves as a challenge, for the bounty and hides, and, in his mind, as a way to protect the moose and caribou. But he wasn't the heartless hunter one might assume. He had a strange love-hate relationship with wolves. In a 1934 letter to Frank Dufresne, he wrote, "I don't mind shooting wolves, but every time I find one in my traps I feel ashamed and can hardly get up nerve to shoot it. Wolves are the real gentleman of the predatory animal family."

During the hunt near the Toklat, he killed with a rifle a gray female that had a litter of six young pups. He dug out the den and killed the pups too. The black mate escaped. Frank had the skin of the female drying in his camp. For several days the black male repeatedly sneaked up to his camp, searching for his mate.

When he wasn't creeping up to Frank's camp, he howled forlornly from a distant ridge. When Frank waited for him with a rifle, he didn't show up. But the minute Frank tried to get some sleep, he'd creep close and the wolf-dogs would hit the ends of their chains and roar at him.

Frank felt sorry for the black wolf, and told me he had asked himself, "How can I break up such a happy home and family?"

At their den he had found parts of two calf caribou and the remains of two Dall sheep lambs killed by the wolves. He realized that by November those cute little wolf puppies he had destroyed would have been adults, killing moose and caribou. He thought of the times he had found bloody caribou remains on the flats near his cabin after a night of killing.

He reminded himself of the suffering of the three live moose he had seen with their hams partly eaten by wolves. He had seen mourning mother moose and caribou stand for days over remains of their young that wolves had killed. He thought of the years when thousands of caribou had wintered near Savage River and how their numbers had dwindled as wolves increased.

For the next several years Glaser hunted and trapped wolves and coyotes mostly in the Fairbanks area. He taught his methods to trappers around Fairbanks, Palmer, and Anchorage, and on the Kenai Peninsula.

The March 24, 1938, *Fairbanks News-Miner* reported: "Frank Glaser, professional wolf hunter, left Fairbanks this morning for a three-month campaign against predatory animals in the White Mountains. Roy Lund took Mr. Glaser to Olnes, and from there the wolf hunter drove a team of four dogs provided by Carl Anderson. Mr. Glaser is an agent of the U.S. Biological Survey's All-Alaska campaign against wolves and coyotes. He plans to seek the dens of the pests."

This 1938 solo trip with a leased dog team (his wolf-dogs were mostly gone) required three hard-working weeks in deep snow for him to reach his goal, the White Mountains, forty-five miles north of Fairbanks. He spent months there without killing a wolf. When the snow was gone that spring he and his leased sled dogs walked to the Steese Highway, and he hitchhiked back to Fairbanks. He left the dog sled and camp gear in the White Mountains for later use.

In the fall of 1939 in a chartered plane he flew to the Mount Hayes area in the Alaska Range where he spent most of a winter alone, managing to kill five wolves.

These Quixotic attempts at wolf control had no significant biological impact. Perhaps 10,000 to 15,000 wolves lived in the Territory.There was no way a lone man with traps, snares, and rifle could make an impact on these predators, no matter how skilled he was. Frank Glaser's greatest success as a federal wolf hunter was yet to come.

15
The governor speaks up: Park observations

PAT AND REN WERE awakened by the whistle of wings and the roar of an airplane flying low above the trees that sheltered their tent.

"Damn! We overslept," Ren yelped, crawling out of his sleeping bag, hurriedly putting on boots and parka, and rushing out.

Dawn was breaking. It was cold, near zero, Pat guessed as she left the tent, buckled on snowshoes, and followed Ren. By then the airplane had landed and was beside Ren's Cub. The stocky, grizzled pilot climbed out.

"What's goin' on here?" he asked, gruffly.

"Got tired of flyin' and landed to spend the night," Ren answered, deadpan.

"You pulling a Bob McCord?" the man asked.

"Dad, you know better than that," Ren answered, sharply. "Say hello to Pat York. Pat, this is my father, Dusty."

"You're the lady who loves wolves, aren't you," he said. "We've heard about you. Nice to meet you." There was no irony in his tone. He was simply direct, Pat decided as she shook hands.

"Glad to see you're ok," Dusty said emotionally, as he briefly hugged Ren. "You had us worried. Got a call from the FAA last night that you hadn't closed your flight plan. I left Wolverine this morning before daylight. What happened?"

"Pull the prop through on the Cub," Ren suggested.

Dusty buckled on snowshoes and walked to the Cub, peered inside to make sure the magneto switch was off, then pulled on the prop. It refused to move. He tried harder. It wouldn't budge.

"What do you think?" Dusty asked Ren. "Did it quit suddenly?"

"Sputtered a bit, then quit. Right after I switched tanks," Ren explained. He then told Dusty about the loose gas cap.

"Someone trying to do you in?" Dusty asked.

Ren shrugged. "I'm going to take the cap to Jim Gates to see if he can find any strange fingerprints on it. And I'll send some of the gas to a lab to have it checked."

"Sugar?" Dusty asked.

"We'll see," Ren answered.

"Your other engine ready to go?" Dusty asked.

"Yep."

"I'll fly you two back to Fairbanks, we'll pick up the engine and tools, and come back and make the switch. I arranged for Andy Anderson to fly my mail routes for a couple days."

"Ok. Thanks, Dad. I think we can have it done by tomorrow," Ren said.

Pat didn't understand everything they were talking about, but she was impressed by the quick decisions these men made.

"We'd better get in the air and call the FAA. The Civil Air Patrol was organizing a search," Dusty said.

"Tired, Dad? You probably didn't sleep much last night. I've had a good night's sleep. I can do the flying."

"You sure about that good night's sleep," Dusty asked, with a sly smile.

"Yes, Dad. Dammit, lay off," Ren said.

"Sure. You fly, I'll catch up on my sleep," Dusty said, not a bit abashed by Ren's testiness.

Dusty's airplane was a four-place Cessna 180. Dusty climbed into the back, and Ren helped Pat into the right front seat. He started the engine, checked controls and magnetos, and took off in a cloud of flying snow.

The Cessna seemed luxurious to Pat after the stark practicality of Ren's Cub. The cabin was warm, engine noise was muted, and she had room to stretch. Dusty snoozed in the back seat.

Ren climbed for altitude and radioed Fairbanks to put a stop to search efforts.

"Do you think someone put sugar in your gas? Would that stop an engine?" Pat asked.

"I don't know. It's a possibility, and the only logical thing I can think of, unless something major broke in the engine, which isn't likely. And, yes, I think sugar in a gas tank will stop an engine."

Ren landed at Fairbanks and taxied to his pickup.

"I'll drive you home, Pat," he said. "Dad, I'll be right back. The engine's over at Hutch's hangar. We can load up there. I'll bring my tools from the house."

"Sure. I'll refuel while you're gone," Dusty said. To Pat, he gave a quick hug and whispered, "You're the first girl he's taken a shine to in a long time. Thanks for being nice to him."

"What did your dad mean by asking if you had pulled a Bob McCord?" Pat asked as Ren drove to her house.

"Oh, it's an old bush pilot story. It's not very nice. You wouldn't want to know."

"Now you really have me curious. Tell me."

"You sure you want to know? Dad has kind of a rough sense of humor. He was so glad to find us all right he said the first thing that came to mind."

"Tell me," Pat insisted.

"Well, it's an old yarn. Bob McCord was a greedy bush pilot who, many years ago, picked up two passengers at McGrath, a young man and a young woman who were strangers to each other. Bob was to fly them to Anchorage. On the way he got a radio call through his headset that another passenger had shown up at McGrath to charter him for a flight downriver. He decided to collect charter money from all three passengers.

"It was fall, just before freeze-up. His plane was on floats, and he landed on a lake, telling the man and woman he had an emergency flight and would be back shortly to pick them up to fly them on to Anchorage. Just in case he was delayed, he said, he'd leave them a sleeping bag and some food.

"So, he dumped these two at the lake with one sleeping bag. He didn't get back until the next day. It got very cold that night, and to keep warm both of them got into the sleeping bag. Well, you know what happened. A few weeks later the couple had to get married, as people did in those days.

"It's not very funny, but supposedly a true story that most long-time Alaska bush pilots know," he said, apologetically.

Pat threw her head back and laughed. "So, your dad thought you had planned to do me a bit of no good. That's what he was needling you about. I suspected it."

"I'm sorry, Pat. Like I say, he has a lousy sense of humor."

"I think he's delightful," she said.

He looked at her in puzzlement as he stopped in front of her house.

"I'll call you," he said. "Busy time for flying coming up. If you're game, there are a few other areas I'd like to show you."

"I'm game," she said. And with a twinkle, "Just so there are two sleeping bags for emergencies. And thanks for the adventure."

He grinned, waved, and drove off.

⌒

REN AND DUSTY made a tripod of spruce poles, and with block and tackle removed the locked-up engine and replaced it with Ren's spare. Using the left tank and fresh fuel he had brought, Ren flew the Cub back to Fairbanks. At Fairbanks he drained and flushed the right tank and sent a sample of the suspect gasoline to a lab at Anchorage.

Alden, an aircraft mechanic friend who worked at the airport, came by as Ren worked. "What's doin', Ren?" he asked. "Get some bad gas?"

"Yeah, Alden. Bad gas." He then explained about the loose cap and the seized engine.

"Jeez, Ren, I haven't heard of anything like that around here for years," Alden commented. He then looked puzzled, trying to remember something. Ren continued working.

"Ren, I don't like to point fingers. But I remember when you topped your tanks off the other day and parked. After you left I saw that bunny hugger guy who always flies with Thompson walking around near where you tie down. I thought he was looking for Thompson and didn't pay any attention."

"You mean John Grant?"

"Yeah, that's his name."

"Thanks for the tip."

He took the tank cap to his friend, FBI agent Jim Gates, at Fairbanks. Gates was a tall, hawk-nosed, slow-talking southerner. To some he appeared a bit slow of mind; he was just the opposite. He simply liked to take his time and mull things over.

After Ren told Gates of his suspicions, including the presence of John Grant near the plane, the agent commented, "This could be a case for the State Troopers. On the other hand, since it involves an airplane, it is possible a federal law has been broken and I could be involved. I'll see if our Washington lab can find prints on the cap. Since you handled it, any strange fingerprints will likely be smudged, but we'll see what the lab can find."

He took Ren's fingerprints for comparison and promised to call in a few days.

That March was a busy time for Ren. Staff biologists, working from small planes and helicopters, killed 67 wolves from 20A. Hunters and trappers killed 78. Thus 145 wolves were removed from the population of about 239.

Wolves killed by ADF&G staff were taken to the department lab at Fairbanks where they were skinned. Ren then necropsied the carcasses, measuring and weighing each, and determining sex. He aged them by horizontally sectioning and staining canine or premolar teeth, and under a microscope counted the cementum annuli rings—each representing a year of growth. He counted the developing embryos of females. He also counted placental scars, which revealed the number of pups from previous litters. He searched for parasites, and preserved some stomach contents for a later food habits study.

His work was a continuation of that accomplished in the 1960s by ADF&G biologist Robert A. Rausch, who, between 1959 and 1966 collected and necropsied approximately 4,160 interior Alaska wolf carcasses taken mostly by trappers. Rausch determined that most of Alaska's wolves reach sexual maturity at twenty two months, and that ninety percent of the sexually mature females breed every year. Litters average 6.5 pups, with the litters of first breeders averaging about 5.5 pups. Subsequent studies showed that in less heavily harvested populations the pregnancy rate is somewhat lower.

As every young, gray, female, arrived at the lab, Ren wondered. "Is it Lady?" for the Black Pack lived in 20A where the control work was taking place. The emotional involvement with Lady still affected him. He often reminded himself that his responsibility was for the health of the wolf population as a whole; he couldn't let his involvement with Lady affect his judgment.

⊂⊃

SOME EXTREME ANIMAL rights groups swore they would do "whatever it takes to stop" the March, 1976 ADF&G wolf removal program. Most responsible conservationists (as opposed to preservationists), after reviewing the facts, recognized the program was not a threat to Alaska's overall wolf population. Yet animal rightists continually propagandized the program as a mass killing, saying that Alaska wanted to destroy as many wolves as possible. Lawsuits were threatened. Federal legislation was planned, claiming that ADF&G was incapable of properly managing Alaska's wildlife. Misinformation and sensationalism were common tactics used to solicit public support. The livelihood of these organizations depends upon controversy, which generates donations, and they well know how to create it.

Animal rights fanatics apparently do not believe humans are part of nature. They do not believe we should try to manage wildlife. Many believe in letting nature take its course, even if it means animals being wiped out by starvation or disease—or by each other.

Mailings went out portraying Alaska's wolves as "endangered" and "persecuted," with emotional wording like "slaughter," "decimate," "kill thousands," "exterminate," "cruel," and "barbaric." These and advertisements in many major newspapers across the country brought a flood of donations to various animal rights organizations.

One preservationist group boycotted Alaska. Their pickets marched in major cities with placards denouncing the "mass killing of wolves in Alaska," and urging tourists to stay away. Space was purchased in major newspapers with ads denouncing Alaska.

A full-page ad in the *Anchorage Daily News* advertised a "Rally opposing wolf control" and a panel discussion at a local auditorium. Bold letters asked, "Why are we killing Alaska's Wolves?"

The news media loved it. There were television sound bites of comments of pickets, with interviews of animal rightists denouncing Alaska, and editorials in many newspapers, mostly sympathetic to the cause of those who claimed to be protecting the wolf. Without the news media, the effectiveness of these organizations would be lost, and many demonstrations were staged for television. Once the cameras stopped, the demonstrators left the scene.

Janet Lidle, editor and publisher of *Wolf!*, a quarterly compendium of world news of wolves she published in Clifton Heights, Pennsylvania, popped the bubble of boycotting animal rightists with her common sense editorial. "A tourist boycott is divisive," she wrote. "The wolf's constituency covers a far broader range than the instigators may allow. It includes hunters, trappers, guide-outfitters, wildlife managers, biologists, non-hunters, anti-hunting/trapping activists, animal rights advocates, and people concerned about the humane aspects of human exploitation of wildlife.

"There is a broad consensus on keeping the wolf as part of Alaska's wild ecosystems, but no consensus on how to achieve this, whether through active management or letting nature take its course.

"The boycott over wolf management is misdirected. The argument is with the Alaska Board of Game, not the state operated ferries, private air carriers, the keeper of a roadhouse in Chicken, or the wilderness guide taking people out to hear wolves howl. A tourist boycott hurts the wrong people, people who are not responsible for the policies and programs being protested.

"Economic retaliation against uninvolved parties, whether legal or not, is ethically and morally wrong."

Sadly, circulation of her fine publication didn't reach the large numbers of the gullible public that newspapers and television sound bites did.

In my job as Outdoors Editor I wrote in *Alaska* magazine, "If one accepts that moose are important to Alaskans and others as food and as a source of recreation, a temporary, small reduction of wolves should be acceptable. If one doesn't agree that moose are important to man, wolf control may not be acceptable. If moose are to again increase in 20A in the near future, some wolves must be removed."

I then quoted Bob Hinman. He said, "Wolves are an important part of Alaska's environment. So are moose and humans. Our decision to remove in a humane and efficient manner some wolves from 20A was made after careful consideration of the values and needs of all three."

That March I was pulled out of bed by a 2 a. m. phone call. "You'll pay for your vote to kill wolves, you bastard," the male caller announced. Then he hung up. I learned later other board members also received threatening calls.

Another man called half a dozen times, threatening to kill me. "You'll find out what it feels like to be shot," he said on one call. On another, "You'll die like a gut-shot wolf." I tape recorded some of his calls and played them back for the local police chief, who suggested I carry a revolver. I dusted off my .357 Magnum revolver, bought a shoulder holster, and got used to wearing the gun. Happily, I never had to use it. An article on the controversy, written by Governor Jay S. Hammond, arrived on my desk. "Use as you see fit," he wrote me. (In a tongue-in-cheek aside, he commented, "Perhaps we could defuse this by reporting that a lot of wild dogs are killing moose. The same people who oppose killing wolves would be furious and demand that we do something about those ravaging wild dogs)."

I edited the piece, titled it "The Wolves and the Furor," wrote an introduction, and sent it on for publication in *ALASKA* magazine where it appeared in the June, 1976, issue as an editorial.

In my introduction I wrote: "Last December, Alaska's BOG authorized the Department of Fish and Game to reduce wolf numbers in Game Management Unit 20A in an attempt to assist a moose population to recover from heavy wolf predation.

"National television coverage of this project was, to be charitable, distorted. And, as has been the case where wolves have been involved in recent years, the public reacted.

"Between January and early March more than 2,000 letters commenting on the program were received by the Alaska Department of Fish and Game, while another 1,000 letters poured into the governor's office. Based on what they had been told in mass mailings, and by television sound bites, most writers of these letters believe Alaska is trying to exterminate every wolf.

"Governor Hammond, author of this article, holds a degree in biology from the University of Alaska. He was a U.S. Fish and Wildlife Service agent in Alaska for many years before serving for twelve years in the state legislature. He was a professional bush pilot, and is a Master Guide. He was elected as a conservation governor on a platform of environmental protection and planned growth.

"Hammond served as chairman of both the state House and Senate Resources Committees, has been a member of many appointive conservation agencies. He has published numerous articles on conservation subjects."

Hammond's article is reproduced here with his permission:

Cry "wolf" and listen to the "experts" howl. Understandable. I used to be a wolf expert myself. That was almost thirty years ago, before I'd trapped and hunted wolves professionally for several years. Though I hung up my guns and traps long ago, I've observed, photographed, spied and speculated on wolves ever since.

Some think that because I've seen more wolves than most that perhaps I'm an expert. Sorry. I lost my expertise somewhere along the trail.

For example, before I spent much time among them, I "knew" wolves took only the lame, the sick and the halt—until studies of scores of wolf kills indicated that if selectivity for caribou is exercised by wolves, it seems to be for the fat and healthy. True, selection among moose favors younger animals; but at some stage all moose are lame, sick, halt or calves.

I "knew" wolves killed only what they needed—until one day I found twenty seven wolf-killed reindeer from which had been scissored only tongues and livers.

I "knew" that aerial wolf hunting was despicably unsportsman-like, akin to shooting ducks in a bathtub, until I started trying to shoot them while flying solo. I then learned why mortality of aerial wolf hunters is so high.

I "knew" predators did not significantly affect prey popula-tions—until I noticed that almost everywhere where wolves were controlled in Alaska big game increased remarkably.

Though today I know less about wolves than I once did, I'm pleased that there is no shortage of "experts" to take my place and that the pendulum has swung from where it stood thirty years ago. Now, the case for predator control must be made from hard data and over public protests. Then it was made from public pressure. Wolves were "vermin" to be exterminated. Politicians made points promising to raise bounties.

Then, as usual, I was one phase out of cycle. Twenty years before he wrote Never Cry Wolf *I made noises like Farley Mowat: "knock off poison"; "eliminate bounties"; "wolves take nothing but the feeble". Of course, that was when I was still an "expert." Later I ended up somewhere between the "wipe 'em out" school and those who say "kill not at all." The truth, I suspect, roams this middle ground.*

The latest Alaskan wolf flap came when biologists found that in many areas, though normal numbers of moose calves were born, almost all were gone within weeks. Wolves were so abundant and bold that forty dogs were killed by wolves near Fairbanks.

Most biologists agree that in some cases predators must be reduced if healthy game stocks are desired. They believe, as I do, that a few areas of the state should be managed for maximum game production; just as other areas should not. Surely there's room enough for both hunter and wolf lover; but not on each and every acre.

Accordingly, biologists recommended to the BOG that control be undertaken in Game Management Unit 20A—less than one percent of both Alaska's land and our estimated 8,000 to 12,000 wolves. Ninety-nine percent of Alaska's land and Alaska's wolves remain unaffected.

Unfortunately, few know this outside of Alaska. Instead, projected nation-wide is an image of bloodthirsty Alaskans, intent upon "exterminating" the last of an "endangered" species. Frankly, if I believed propaganda presented by such "experts" as those on NBC, I'd bombard Juneau with hate mail too.

Truth is, wolves are not endangered in Alaska. Everyone I know— biologists, trappers, guides, hunters—who have spent years in the field agree wolves are more abundant now than twenty years ago.

We did not open areas to aerial wolf hunting as many Alaskans demanded. Instead, the hunt was to be conducted by the most selective and humane means possible, using professional biologists and airplanes. Results will be closely monitored. Had we simply issued aerial permits to all comers, the spin-offs would have been horrendous. I can just hear some Congresswoman from New York reading a sheaf of news reports describing in gory detail a fleet of airborne bandit guides gleefully exterminating the last remnant wolf for a fat fee from some rich blood-lusting dude. "Can we permit those barbarians to have any say at all in managing Alaskan lands or wildlife?"

I was tempted to override the board's decision to conduct control. I did not because management people convinced me selective control was necessary. To have overridden the board would be a political decision motivated more by my concern for image than intellectual honesty. Not even my Alaskan image at that, because for each wolf lover (I confess I'm one myself) who feels betrayed that I did not override the board in their behalf, there is at least one Alaskan hunter who would feel betrayed had I done so.

As governor, I've tried to take politics out of fish and game management. Most agree with that—unless, of course, they disagree with our professional game managers and they wish then to insert their brand of politics.

Members of professional game management and wildlife organizations in the lower forty-eight support the department's program. These include the National Wildlife Federation, Campfire Club, Association of American Foresters, and John Gottschalk, Execu-

tive Secretary of the International Association of Fish and Game Commissioners. Many Interior Department people agree that some reduction of wolves is warranted.

We have their support only because this would be a closely monitored program conducted by professional game management people. Had we opened the hunt to everyone, we'd have lost that support. Only with such support, can we possibly offset assertions that we do not know what we're doing.

Ironically, the feds conducted predator control through selective aerial hunting in Alaska for years. However, they, too, are suffering shell shock from flak fired at them by persons mostly misinformed. To shift the line of fire back to us, they have revoked some $10,000 in federal aid to the Alaska Department of Fish and Game asserting that no environmental impact statement has been recorded. Not mentioned is the fact they have never filed an EIS for their control activities.

Some have suggested that instead of killing wolves, we should simply curtail trophy hunting of prey species. The problem is, calves are not surviving, and so far as I know, hardly any "head hunters" lust for calves.

Uniquely as governor, I'm a target for those who love wolves, just as I am from those who loathe them. After all, a quarter of a century ago, my partner and I shot more than a hundred wolves in about a three-week period. Yet, later, I was instrumental in curbing the use of poison and the bounty system. So, take your choice. I happen to like wolves and believe it would be a sorry day if there were none about.

I hate the idea of having to kill any; just as I hate the idea of a moose calf being flayed alive. But a game herd wiped off the map wipes out both the hunter and the wolf. Far preferable that we try to provide for both.

Frankly, I'm glad the pendulum has swung from where it was back in the forties. Never again will predator control be undertaken lightly. Never again will we engage in such all-out war unless, of course, repression of any wolf management whatsoever causes that pendulum to swing back too far the other way.

What was it like before? Federal agents with a small armada of light aircraft ranged the entire Territory and by gun, trap, and poison significantly reduced wolf numbers. There also was a $50 bounty, and anyone could take by aircraft all the wolves they could *possibly get. Even then, while they took many, wolves remained in fair supply.*

Today, the state is closed to aerial wolf hunting by the public. Poison and the bounty system are curbed. The wolf is recognized as a trophy animal. A tag fee is charged for nonresidents, and there's a limit of two per hunter. Under these constraints, you can be sure that wolves will be here after we wolf lovers have long gone.

Meanwhile, this offer stands: We'd far rather tranquilize and export live wolves than kill them. However, this takes money and willing recipients. To date, both have been in short supply. Had all the sound, fury and postage promoted by this hunt prompted instead acceptance of our offer, we could have sent the entire pack "Outside" [to the states] *parcel post!*

IN 1940 FRANK GLASER was assigned by the U.S. Fish and Wildlife Service (which in 1940 replaced the U.S. Biological Survey) to observe summer wolf behavior in Mount McKinley National Park. He spent several weeks watching six adult wolves and a litter of young pups at a den. One day the six adults were sleeping near the den when a big gray wolf, a stranger, arrived on a nearby ridge and trotted toward them.

When he was about a hundred yards away, one of the six, a female, ran to meet him. The other five quickly joined her, running full speed. When the female in the lead reached the gray stranger she struck it with her shoulder, knocking it sprawling. Then all six wolves, growling fiercely, grabbed the stranger from different sides. There was no snapping and letting go. They stretched him out and banged him up and down on the ground. After a few moments, they released him and stood watching.

The stranger got up and hobbled off several hundred yards and bedded down. Though Frank watched the den for some time afterward, he never saw the strange gray wolf in the vicinity again. The message, apparently, was, "This is our territory. We don't want you hangin' around here Mr. Gray."

The presence of a strange wolf is rarely tolerated. Acceptance of a strange wolf by a pack is the exception. The home pack usually attacks and sometimes kills intruders. The intruder may also be eaten, for wolves are sometimes cannibalistic. Skirmishes between packs may take place, resulting in serious woundings or death to individuals. Most wolf killings by wolves occur close to the edges of adjacent wolf territories.

He made another interesting wolf behavior observation while on that McKinley Park assignment. Glaser and park ranger Harold Herning were eating lunch on a little hill overlooking a fork in the Teklanika River. In the vee of the fork 350 or so caribou, mostly cows, yearlings, and calves were congregated.

The wolf family Glaser and Herning had been observing, led by a small black female, trotted up the river, and upon smelling the caribou, dashed over the bank toward them. The caribou fled.

The little black female was much faster than the other wolves, and soon left them behind. Some forty or fifty two-and-three-week-old calves bunched up and dropped behind the main body of caribou, and the black wolf was soon among them.

She grabbed a calf by the middle of the back, reared up, shook it, flung it aside, and continued the chase. She bowled over the next calf with her shoulder. Before it could get up, she grasped its back, shook it three or four times, and dropped it. She knocked over a third calf, grabbed it, and shook it. The fourth calf she seized happened to be on soft ground where a wolf is clumsy. She hit the calf with her shoulder, knocking it down, but at the same time she stumbled and rolled end over end. The calf was first to its feet, and as it started to flee again, it accidentally bumped into the just-recovering wolf, knocking her flat.

That seemed to anger the wolf. After half a dozen jumps she caught the calf by the back and raised it high in the air, shaking it. Then she slammed the calf down, putting both her front paws on it, and biting out large chunks of flesh, which she tossed aside as fast as she could.

The wolves didn't eat any of those calves, at least while Glaser was there, and he watched for their return for several days. Each of the dead calves suffered bites through the backbone and into the lungs and heart.

Davy's arm: Lord Balmar: Saving reindeer

Pat looked forward to her Friday afternoon calls to Beth Johnson, for Beth always had interesting and amusing stories of the children in Pat's former class. Beth told Pat what the students were studying, and brought her up to date on progress. She never failed to mention Davy Foster, for she too had become fond of the red-haired, freckled boy.

Beth had never called Pat. Thus when her phone rang on a Wednesday afternoon in April and Pat heard a subdued Beth on the line she instantly realized something was wrong.

"I'm sorry to have to tell you this, Pat," Beth said. "It's bad news."

"Oh. What is it?"

"It's about Davy Foster," Beth said.

"What is it, Beth?"

"Well, you know how proud he was of his 'friend' Lobo? He's told me a dozen times that his friend Lobo kissed him. He was simply crazy about that wolf."

"What happened, Beth?" Pat asked, with a sudden chill.

But Beth was not to be rushed. She continued, "Somehow Davy learned where your friend Jerry Hanson lives and where he keeps Lobo. He pestered his parents to take him to visit Lobo. They finally gave in and found the house. According to Davy's father it's in a plush, big bucks neighborhood. When they arrived, no one was home. Davy insisted on opening a gate and going into the back yard where Lobo is kept inside a high fence. His parents followed in time to see him run to that fence and stick his arm through it to pet Lobo.

"Pat, it's awful. That wolf bit Davy's right arm off," Beth said.

Pat didn't remember the rest of the conversation, except that Beth said the boy's arm was off just below the elbow. His parents had rushed him to a hospital. Davy survived, but his arm was gone.

For a time she was too stunned to even cry. But as the truth sank in, tears came. "It's all my fault," she told herself. "I got him interested in wolves. I arranged for that wolf to come to my classroom."

Pat had made friends with half a dozen women in Fairbanks, but she didn't feel comfortable asking any of them to share her grief. She remembered what Ren had said about there being no such thing as a domesticated wolf.

"He was right. I was wrong," she thought. "Poor Davy," she repeatedly said, picturing his freckled face and remembering his enthusiasm for life.

She needed someone to talk to and remembered how Ren had consoled her at the loss of Snow. She dialed his number.

"Can you come, please," she said, her voice trembling. "Something awful has happened."

He was there in fifteen minutes. She threw herself into his arms sobbing so hard she couldn't speak. He quietly held her for a long time. Finally the paroxysms let up and she sat and told him about Davy and Lobo.

"You were right and I was wrong about that damned Lobo. It's all my fault," she wailed, sobbing again. "I thought Lobo was tame. He was so gentle and well behaved in the classroom," she anguished. "That poor boy."

"The fault isn't yours, Pat," he said. "The fault lies with the person keeping that wolf where the boy could get to him."

"Yes, but Davy wouldn't have known about wolves if I hadn't started it all," she wailed.

"Davy isn't the first child to have his arm bitten off by a fenced-in wolf. The fault lies with the person owning the animal. No one would leave a tiger or a lion in a pen that kids could walk up to and stick their arm through. But, for some reason, people don't think the wolf is capable of such behavior."

"You mean it has happened before?" Pat asked, peering at Ren through teary eyes.

"Yes. I have half a dozen clippings describing almost identical circumstances—a child sticks his arm into a wolf's pen—or a wolf-dog's pen—and it is badly mauled or is bitten off," Ren said.

"I don't think there is such thing as a domesticated wolf. A wolf is, well, a wolf. Their behavior is built in. They instinctively protect their territory. And with its strong jaws and shearing teeth, a wolf can take a child's arm off with ease."

He knew he had made a mistake in saying that, and bit his tongue as Pat again started to sob. He pulled her to her feet and again held her close without speaking for a long time.

Finally, sobbed out, Pat pulled away. "How about some coffee," she suggested.

"Sure. I'd love some. How about dinner tonight?" he invited.

"With my red eyes? No, thank you," she said. "People would think you'd been beating me."

Pat was still sniffling as they drank coffee. "I apologize for dragging you into this, Ren. With Snow you were involved. But this is my problem."

She smiled wanly at his response. "My job is wolves. When people have problems with wolves they call me. Let's call this a professional visit," he said.

"Are you going to bill me?" she asked, trying to inject a little humor.

"Don't worry. You'll pay," he said, catching her eye. She was the first to look away.

"Our Washington D.C. lab found one smeared fingerprint on the cap that wasn't yours," Jim Gates said. He had asked Ren to come to his office. "The print wasn't enough to positively tie to anyone, but it had the characteristics of a fingerprint of John Grant. It's pretty certain he had his hand on that cap."

Ren nodded. "The lab report from Anchorage was positive for sugar in the gas. The tank holds eighteen gallons, and they calculated a pound of granulated sugar was poured into it."

"There's more, Ren," Gates said. "Grant has a record. That's why we had his fingerprints in our files. He was a suspect in a half million dollar vandalism case in Boston. He and several others, believed to be members of The National Wildlife Savers Foundation, broke into a medical research lab, released about fifty monkeys, wrecked office machines, poured chemicals over files of research papers, and stole records. According to our Boston office, the research was for a specific kind of cancer shared by humans and monkeys, and some promising drugs were being tested. It set the program back five years."

"Animal rightists, then," Ren sighed.

"Yeah. I guess that's what they call 'em," Gates agreed.

"Do you think there's enough to nail him for sugaring my gas?" Ren asked.

"Doubtful," Gates said.

"He's not going to get away with it, you know. I'll see to that," Ren said, angrily. "If that engine had quit at the wrong time I could have been killed, and so could my passenger. We were lucky it stopped when it did."

"Ren, don't do anything crazy," Gates warned.

"Yeah," Ren said. He then had a thought. "How good is the information that he was involved in that vandalism case?"

"I haven't seen the file, but I was told by phone there was a leak in the Wildlife Savers Group. A former member fingered Grant. And Grant's car was seen near the building on the night it was broken into. There were no fingerprints; whoever did it wore rubber gloves," Gates said.

"That's enough for me," Ren said.

"What do you have in mind, Ren? I hope you aren't going to go off half-cocked."

"Don't worry. I have connections that friend Grant would be surprised to know about," Ren said. "I think he'll be leaving Fairbanks in the near future."

IN HIS DECADES of flying from the Koyukuk Valley village of Wolverine, Ren's father, Dusty, earned a reputation as a reliable and safe pilot who knew the land intimately. During fall hunting season he often flew hunters into the vast, nearly uninhabited California-size arctic Brooks Range that sprawls east and west across northern Alaska.

In August 1959 a lone Englishman calling himself John Balmar arrived in Wolverine and asked Dusty to fly him into the Brooks Range where he could hunt for a trophy-size Dall ram.

"Are you a resident of Alaska?" Dusty asked.

"No," Balmar answered.

"You need a guide, then," Dusty told him.

"Guide?" Balmar responded. "But I'm an experienced hunter. I don't need a guide. I have a non-resident license and a tag for sheep."

"It's the law," Dusty explained. "A non-resident hunting sheep in Alaska must be accompanied by a registered guide. I'm sorry. I can't take you without a guide."

While they were talking, Ren arrived, preparing to fly a scheduled trip for Dusty. At the time he was working toward his Ph.D. degree at Purdue. He was introduced to Balmar. "He wants to hunt for a Dall ram, but he doesn't have a guide," Dusty explained.

"How much hunting have you done?" Ren asked Balmar.

"I've hunted in Africa, India, in the Himalayas, in Borneo, and South America. I also hunted for a month in British Columbia some years ago. I prefer to hunt alone when I can," the Englishman explained.

Ren glanced at the hunter's well used camp gear. It looked professional. He made a sudden decision.

"Mr. Balmar, I'm a licensed guide as well as a pilot. I'm due back at college in a week, but I could register late. I would enjoy the break and I could give you a week. And I know a place where we might find a trophy ram."

The deal was struck, and Ren flew them to a tiny high, timberline, mountain lake. Instead of having to live in a tiny tent, as Balmar had planned, they stayed in an abandoned prospector's cabin that Ren knew about. At first the Englishman resented being burdened with a guide he felt he didn't need.

During their first evening, Ren was straightening the cabin. He hung Balmar's gun case on a nail in the wall and noticed "Lord John Balmar" written on it.

"Does this mean what I think it does?" Ren asked. "I've heard of a Lord Balmar who finances wildlife conservation programs around the world. Is that you?"

"Yes," the Englishman answered. "But don't let it bother you. I prefer that people don't know who I am. Being an English Lord can be a burden, you know. You're to call me John, and forget the rest, please."

Shortly, after they had eaten their evening meal, Balmar

asked, "How is it you know about my wildlife conservation programs?"

When Ren explained that he held two degrees in wildlife management and was working on his doctorate, Balmar exploded in laughter. "We're both involved in wildlife conservation. What a coincidence. And what is the subject of your doctoral thesis?"

"The ecology of an Alaska wolf pack," Ren told him.

That led to a discussion of Alaska's wolves and the Territory wide efforts of the U.S. Fish and Wildlife Service to reduce wolf numbers.

"I think your government is making a mistake," Balmar said. "Wolves have been all but wiped out in Europe, and, of course, there are none left in England. It would be nice to see wolves treated with the respect other Alaskan animals are. It should be considered a trophy animal, and appreciated for what it is. An Alaska without wolves wouldn't seem right."

Ren agreed with him. "Yep. I'd like to see wolves managed like we manage bears, for example. They're valuable and interesting animals. Perhaps if we get statehood things will change."

Of course, when statehood came in 1959, the changes Balmar and Ren wanted did come about.

Daily, Ren accompanied Balmar high into the mountains searching for a trophy ram, and he was surprised at how tough the older man was. Balmar was also selective; he turned down several rams that didn't measure up as trophies. On the fourth day of their hunt the hunter downed, with one shot, a fine old ram with horns that measured forty inches around the curl. He helped Ren pack the meat and trophy out of the mountains.

"The old boy wouldn't have lasted through many more winters," Balmar commented. "He's done his biological duty. His genes are no doubt now in many generations of sheep in these mountains."

Ren liked the Englishman's approach to hunting, and he and Balmar became fast friends. After that hunt the Englishman often returned to Alaska to spend a week or two with Ren camping in some remote site. Sometimes they hunted, sometimes they didn't. Both loved the wilderness, and their common interest in wildlife conservation led to interesting discussions over evening campfires.

In the 1960s and early 1970s Ren's work with wolves for the new state of Alaska fascinated Balmar, and he asked Ren if he thought an investment in creating a conservation fund to study Alaska's wolves would be worthwhile.

"Sure, a well-trained researcher, given a free hand, could do a lot of worthwhile work with wolves. My work is aimed at management of wolves. I don't do in-depth studies of such things as the social lives of wolves, genetics, interactions between packs, and so on. Anything we learn about wolves is helpful in their management and conservation."

It was then that Lord Balmar created the Wolf Lovers Association of Great Britain (WLAGB), and in 1976 the executives who took care of the details of his various conservation trusts hired John Grant, recently fired by TNWSF. The credentials Grant presented looked good. Unfortunately, no one in England had checked further.

Ren was sure that Balmar was not aware that when Grant accepted the position with WLAGB, he had continued to push the TNWSF animal rightists program, which opposed any use by humans of animals, including hunting; so far his work for the English group had been mainly attempts to discredit the ADF&G. Lord Balmar, then, was the connection Ren referred to when talking with Jim Gates.

⌒

IN THE FALL of 1940 Frank Glaser was loaned to the Alaska Native Service, but continued as an employee of the U.S. Fish and Wildlife Service. His new assignment was to remove wolves that were reportedly decimating Eskimo-owned reindeer herds in northwestern Alaska.

He arrived in Nome October 3 and met with Sidney Rood of the Reindeer Service, an arm of the Alaska Native Service, to review his file of reports from reindeer herders.

Between 1891 and 1902, 1,208 reindeer were brought to Alaska from Siberia by Dr. Sheldon Jackson, General Agent of Education for the Territory of Alaska, to ". . . advance them [Alaskan Eskimos] in the scale of civilization . . . change them from hunters to herders . . . utilize hundreds of thousands of square miles of moss-covered tundra . . . and make these useless and barren wastes conducive to wealth and prosperity . . . to take a barbarian people on the verge of starvation and lift them up to comfortable self-support and civilization . . ."

Jackson meant well, but he ignored or wasn't aware of the rich eons-old Eskimo culture. He judged the Eskimos against his own background. Eskimos of northwestern Alaska have always been hunters. It was asking a great deal of a hunting people to abandon their traditional way of life to become herders. Why should a skilled hunter, proud of his ability to feed his family and his village, spend his time in the boring occupation of driving reindeer? The rewards of reindeer herding, while they might be substantial, are always in the future, while the rewards of hunting are visible and edible daily, and bought status in the community.

Alaska's northwestern Eskimos are not acquisitive. If a man has a satisfactory house, a good rifle, a boat, a dog team, and can get enough food by hunting, what else could he want? When seals are plentiful, or when the cries of migrating walrus float on the soft air of an arctic spring, how can a man whose deepest instincts urge him to rifle and harpoon turn his back on the excitement of the chase in favor of the dreariness of following reindeer?

Reindeer, closely related to Alaska's wild caribou, were domesticated from the wild reindeer of Europe and Asia. Shorter-legged than caribou, they may be white or spotted, and have other minor differences. When herded they become tame, but quickly grow wild when left alone. They will breed with caribou, and the offspring are fertile.

By 1914, Alaska had sixty-five reindeer herds, totalling 60,000 animals. Two-thirds were Eskimo-owned, while the remainder belonged to the U.S. government, various missions, and Lapp herders who had come to Alaska with the reindeer.

Reindeer numbers peaked at 641,000 in 1932. Many were owned by whites. But by October, 1940, when Glaser arrived to try to save them from ravaging wolves, there were only about 250,000 left.

The crash resulted partially from passage of the Reindeer Act— a law passed by Congress making it illegal for non-Eskimos to own reindeer in Alaska. This was in response to pressure from the western cattle industry when high quality reindeer meat started arriving in U.S. markets in the mid-1930s.

For several years after passage of the Reindeer Act, deer owned by non-Natives were purchased by the U.S. government to transfer them to Eskimos. Chaos reigned as the Bureau of Indian Affairs tried to interest Eskimos in accepting them.

That October Glaser arrived at where a reindeer herd was

supposed to be, thirty-five miles from Unalakleet, a seventy-five-person Eskimo village on the shore of Norton Sound. He hired Henry Nasholik, an Eskimo with a dog team, and drove to the area to find the herd scattered, many missing. Herders had left it on its own for some time. For a couple of weeks Frank searched around the herd for wolves and found no sign of wolves. Animals from that herd were lost from neglect, not wolves.

In mid-December, 1940, he searched for a reindeer herd at Battleship Mountain, fifty miles from Golovin, on the Seward Peninsula. To get there he hired Mischa, another Eskimo with a dog team. There he found reindeer on nine bald mountains where wolves had driven them. They were afraid to come down because of wolves. The deer were terribly thin, for the only feed for them were a few rock lichens. Soon after he arrived, in the distance he saw eight wolves chasing a small bunch of reindeer, but they were too far away for him to do anything about it.

As Glaser and Mischa returned to the cabin where they were staying, a lone wolf howled to the north. Frank knew it was a pup because its deep wolf howl ended with "bow-wow."

"Let's get out of sight," Frank urged. "I'll call that wolf and shoot him."

The two ducked into a low depression, and Frank started howling. The wolf answered and ran toward them, then stopped. Frank called again. The wolf answered and ran closer and stopped. Frank, his .220 Swift rifle ready, called again. They saw the back of a wolf, and then tips of his ears, as it trotted over a ridge. Suddenly it was standing on a snow drift about fifty yards away.

The wolf dropped dead at Frank's shot.

Mischa left the next morning to return to Golovin for more grub. "I'll be back in a couple of days," he promised.

He seemed anxious to leave. Frank learned later that he told people at Golovin that Frank was a nice man but he could talk like a wolf. He wanted to get away from Frank so he could think for a few days. Eventually he accepted Frank, but for a while his superstitious nature made him uneasy when with Glaser. There were things about the wolf hunter Mischa didn't understand.

In a few days Frank counted 280 dead reindeer lying around Battle Mountain. Many had starved. Their deaths could be attributed to wolves that had driven them onto the mountains where there was no food.

Wolves had killed many of the reindeer, but ate little from them. With all the dead deer lying around and the easy availability of live ones, the wolves weren't hungry.

A few days after Christmas Frank hid near a bunch of reindeer carcasses and started howling. In about an hour he lured a pack of eight wolves within rifle range. Using the Swift rifle and its 48 grain bullets is o.k. when there isn't any wind, but a strong wind tossed the light bullets around; some hit as much as twenty feet from the running wolves. He killed two out of the pack, but said he should have killed four or five.

Siegfried, an Eskimo at Golovin, who had herded reindeer from the time he was a boy, agreed to take the herd. With several other Eskimos, Frank and Siegfried drove 4,500 reindeer off of the barren, icy mountaintops to within ten miles of Golovin. Frank then left Golovin.

In early February, 1941, Henry Nasholik, the Eskimo Frank had hired at Unalakleet, wrote to Frank. "Our herd has been moved into the mountains about ten miles from Unalakleet. Wolves are after them. Come and get the wolves."

Henry drove Frank to the herd of 2,000 animals where they were grazing high on a big mountain. Frank pitched a tent close to that of the herders, at the edge of timber. Frank's official field diaries tell the story best:

February 19, 1941: I climbed a high divide and saw three black wolves about half a mile away eating a reindeer. They soon had my wind and ran. Temperature today 20 to 30 below zero.

February 20, 1941: I made a trip to the divide and stayed on the highest ridge. Found a deer that wolves killed last night, and another 12 that had been killed in the last month. The recent gale also uncovered several old kills. The dead deer I found today are very thin. 40 below zero today. Miles on foot 15.

Feb. 21: Last night wolves were around the herd. This morning I found one deer that four wolves had killed. They were hungry, for they ate all of the hindquarters. I stayed on the high ridges all day trying to locate these wolves, without results. Miles on foot 15.

Feb. 22: Saw tracks of four wolves close to the herd. It was a terrible day to be out as the wind was so strong that in places I had to crawl. The temperature was way below zero. It is hard to keep warm in a tent in such weather. Miles on foot 12.

Feb. 23: Today the wind is still blowing hard and it is more than 30 below zero. The herd has been gone two nights. I went with the herders to look for them. We found them about six miles from our tents. Wolves killed one animal last night and they ate most of it. This is a tough life living in tents in this kind of weather. The wind has blown every day since I have been with the herd. That's what makes it a fine range. There is lots of feed, and the wind keeps the snow blown off. Butchered a deer for camp meat. Miles on foot 14.

Henry Nasholik arrived to take Frank back to Unalakleet for a break after he had been with the herd for three weeks. It was a fine, calm moonlight night at the reindeer camp. "Let's leave now," Frank suggested. "It's good traveling weather."

They moved swiftly and were traveling down the Unalakleet River about six miles from the village when they ran into a solid wall of clouds, fog, and strong wind. It turned pitch dark and they could barely see the dogs. Then it began to snow, cutting visibility even more. Frank, trotting beside the sled, constantly stumbled because he couldn't see the ground.

"Wait," Henry called. "I turn Almosholik loose."

He stopped the team. To Frank's amazement he unharnessed a small female malemute. She disappeared into the howling snowstorm and Frank figured she was gone for good. The team waited, and Henry calmly stood at the rear of the sled.

In about ten minutes Frank saw a blur through the snow as Almosholik reappeared. The leaders turned and followed as she headed back into the storm. Frank had heard of mushers using a loose leader, but he had never seen one until that night. From time to time the team stopped and waited as that little dog disappeared into the storm. She'd return in a few minutes and again the team would follow her. Time after time she ran ahead, scouted the route, and returned to lead the team. Henry and Frank were just passengers; Almosholik did it all.

Frank had no idea where they were as they traveled in the blinding snowstorm on that blackest of nights for what seemed hours, guided only by Almosholik.

"Maybe we pass the village and go out to sea," Henry finally said, worriedly. "Some people have done that."

Then the sled ran into something solid. Frank groped along the sled and discovered it was the corner of a log building. They had reached Unalakleet.

Without the guidance of Almosholik they couldn't possibly have found the village in the storm.

During March and April wolves killed more than twenty reindeer in the Unalakleet herd. Frank stalked them with a rifle, set traps on carcasses, and did everything he could to get the four wolves responsible. He walked up to twenty-five miles some days patrolling around the herd, but the killers were clever and managed to avoid him and the traps. They made their kills at night, repeatedly stampeding the herd. The head herder, Reuben Paniptchuk, and his two or three helpers had to walk miles to round them up again. Frank often helped.

March 8, 1941: It must be 50 below. A stiff breeze is blowing, and one cannot stay long on the ridges before one starts to freeze. I was out for about six hours, stayed up on the highest points. See no sign of wolves. At this temperature a cloud of steam hangs over the deer herd when they bunch close. 12 miles on foot.

A church convention was held in Unalakleet starting March 27. More than 200 Eskimos arrived from villages around Norton Sound and from the Seward Peninsula. Frank counted 55 dog teams, with a total of 609 sled dogs. Dogs howled and barked day and night during the week-long meeting.

The reindeer herders cut about a thousand reindeer from the herd, drove them near the village and held them on a big open flat. Visitors were told to help themselves to whatever animals they wanted. A constant stream of dog teams kept going to and from the herd. Each driver would shoot two or three deer, load them on his sled, and return to the village. The deer meat fed the visitors as well as their sled dogs.

Eight or nine big wash tubs were placed over outdoor driftwood fires and shoveled full of snow. The reindeer were skinned, the carcasses chopped up with an axe, and the meat tossed into the tubs. All parts of the deer were included except for the intestines. Anyone who wanted to speared a big chunk of meat with a hunting knife and ate it right there.

Frank counted 220 reindeer slaughtered from the Unalakleet reindeer herd during March to feed the church conference people and their sled dogs. Frank left the herd that June, a little better educated than when he arrived. Four years later, the Unalakleet herd was down to 200 animals. Wolves had killed a few, but losses from other causes had more to do with the decline.

Grant leaves: My caribou article: Amaguq Frank

REN AND JIM GATES called on John Grant. Grant let them into his small house and seated them. Gates did the talking. "John, someone put sugar in the gas tank of Ren's Super Cub. I think you did it. A mechanic saw you near the plane, and our Washington D.C. lab has found a fingerprint on the gas cap of the Cub that could be yours."

"Why would I do anything like that?" Grant said, looking surprised. "I don't operate that way."

"Are you aware that you are under suspicion for vandalizing a medical research laboratory in Boston?" Gates said, quietly.

"I don't know what you're talking about," Grant said.

"Be aware that we're still working on the both of these cases, and you could be charged for either or both if and when we get more evidence," Wilson said.

"You have the wrong guy," Grant protested, shaking his head. "I don't do things like that. I'm a scientist doing a research job."

Within a week of Ren's letter to Lord Balmar, John Grant again found himself without a job. He left Alaska, and, to fill the vacancy, with the Wolf Lovers Association of Great Britain. Ren recommended a promising young wildlife researcher who was working on his Ph.D. degree. Lord Balmar himself hired him.

෴

AMONG MY PERKS while working as Outdoors Editor for *Alaska* magazine was owner/publisher Bob Henning's generosity in allowing me to write for other magazines while on his payroll. Some assignments happened by chance, as when writer Mike Edwards of the *National Geographic* arrived at my door, requesting that I take him to a newly transplanted group of Russian expatriates who, seeking religious freedom, had settled in Alaska. Their tiny, new, raw village was near my home, and, by chance, I had become acquainted with some of these people.

After we visited the village, Edwards said, "There's a fine *National Geographic* story here. Would you like to write it?" Silly question. Every free-lance writer wanted to write for the *National Geographic.* My article, "A Bit of Old Russia Takes Root In Alaska," illustrated by Charles O'Rear's photos, appeared in the September, 1972 issue.

That opened the door, and I wrote several other articles for that magazine. My next *National Geographic* assignment was "Caribou: Hardy Nomads of the North." I was both author and photographer. To get the caribou observations and photos I needed, I took advantage of biologist friends of the ADF&G.

I flew in a helicopter into the Wrangell Mountains with ADF&G wildlife biologists Loyal Johnson and Greg Bos. It was March, and I photographed and observed as they lay on a high ridge with spotting scopes peering at the distant caribou to gather information on their reproductive rate, based on the adult cow/calf ratio.

On another trip, I drove to my guide/pilot friend Bill Ellis' place at the end of the Nabesna Road in the Wrangell Mountains and arranged to use one of his cabins, which was even deeper in these rugged mountains. On my snow machine, I followed the wending Nabesna River about ten miles to the cabin, and lived there for a week, photographing and watching caribou feeding in the Nabesna canyon and on the nearby ridges. Some of the animals, 2,000 feet above the cabin, made the snow fly as they dug for food with front feet. Wind whipped the snow they dug into the air, where the low-lying sun tinged it with pink. Thus I could see tiny pinpoints of pink scattered along the top of the ridge where caribou fed.

After shivering for two or three days in the chinkless log cabin, I realized what a dummy I was and shoveled snow into the gaps on the outside of the cabin. After that the little wood stove kept the cabin cozy. I often thought about the caribou high on the windy ridges—they kept warm by depending upon energy from the sun which was stored in plants they ate. I also depended on energy from the sun stored in plants to keep warm—by burning the spruce chunks I tossed into the stove.

A small pack of wolves howled near the cabin each night. One day I watched a lone gray wolf as it attempted to catch a caribou. It climbed a high ridge, following a hard-packed caribou trail, and rushed at a cow on the steep hillside where she was digging through the snow for food. The cow saw the wolf at the last moment and leaped down the side of the steep ridge in huge bounds, landing in deep snow each time. The wolf attempted to follow, but it became hopelessly buried in deep snow and was immediately left far behind. The longer legs of the caribou gave it the advantage. Each time it landed and jumped the caribou was almost hidden by loose, flying snow.

The wolf was a slow learner, for this performance was repeated three times as it attempted to catch other feeding cows on the steep slope. I took pictures, of course, but even with my 500 mm telephoto lense, the wolf appeared as a small dot on the film. It finally gave up, returned to the frozen river, and trotted around a bend upstream, head and tail down.

In his early studies of wolves, Ren Smith had turned to the Nunamiut (Eskimos) of Anaktuvuk Pass in the arctic Brooks Range whose knowledge of Alaska's wolves is unsurpassed. For many years the main cash income for Anaktuvuk residents came mostly from the sale of wolf hides and the $50 wolf bounty the Territory, and later the state, paid.

Anaktuvuk Pass is a natural route through the mountains that has been used for centuries by caribou, man, and other animals. The inland Eskimos who live there still depend mostly on caribou for their food, using almost everything of the animals but the grunt and hoof-clicks. Where there is an abundance of caribou, there are almost invariably wolves.

Ren Smith owned a sod house in Anaktuvuk Village, which he acquired while learning wolf lore from the villagers. I called him to ask if I could stay in it while visiting the village to document how the Nunamiut depend on caribou for my *National Geographic* article.

"Sure, Prof. You're welcome to use it. But you might be sharing it with Pat York, me, and Arctic John."

That was fine with me, and interesting besides. I had heard of the Eskimo, Arctic John, or *Italook* (his Eskimo name), a renowned hunter and mountain wanderer. Robert Marshall mentioned him in his classic book *Arctic Village*, a 1930s portrait of Wiseman, an early day Brooks Range mining village. I felt the old man would have much wisdom to impart about caribou. As for Pat York, I had heard via the grapevine the good news that she and Ren had been keeping company.

Ren and I chatted for a time and he told me about his misadventure with the seized engine of his Cub, and his near-positive identification of the culprit.

"He's long gone from Alaska," Ren said, satisfaction in his voice. "I saw to that."

I then told him of the threatening phone calls. They had suddenly stopped.

⌒

"HOW'D YOU LIKE to go where it's still winter?" Ren asked Pat one day in mid-April. She was enjoying the seventeen-hours of daylight and the promise of spring. Snow was mostly gone, ice was leaving creeks, lakes and rivers. Plants were exploding into green life.

"I'm enjoying the warmth!" she exclaimed.

"Yeah, but the mud isn't any fun, is it?"

"What's on your mind?"

"I'm going to visit friends in Anaktuvuk Pass. I have a sod house there."

"No sugar in the gas?" she asked.

"Better not be," he said. "I keep the plane in a hangar now."

"Two sleeping bags?" she asked, sweetly.

"You can count on it," he promised.

"I'd love to go," she said.

Early next morning Ren pushed his Super Cub out of the hangar, and did his usual pre-flight inspection. As Pat watched she realized that in four months her knowledge of the Alaska way of life had increased exponentially. Ren's pre-flight inspection made sense to her now. And she understood why the rear of the little plane was filled with emergency gear. Though it was a mild 20 above zero on the ground at Fairbanks, she knew her multiple layers of clothing and insulated boots were essential for her comfort in the plane's back seat, even in April.

Before they climbed into the ready Cub, Ren shuffled a bit, looked slightly embarrassed, and hesitatingly spoke. "Pat, I should prepare you a bit for Anaktuvuk Pass."

"Oh. What should I know?"

"It's just that, well, you're a city girl. Your meat has always come from a super-market. The people at Anaktuvuk Pass live from the land. Their food is almost entirely caribou they shoot near the village. If you're not used to it, it might seem, well, kind of bloody."

"You mean, someone else has always done my killing and butchering for me? Now I'm going to see it in technicolor," she said. "I've thought about it a lot lately. Don't worry, I won't faint."

"I didn't think you would. I just don't want you to be upset."

"Thanks, Ren. You're thoughtful to warn me. I'll be ok. I'm looking forward to seeing how bush villagers live."

She enjoyed the rush of the plane leaving the ground, and peered down as houses and roads became ever smaller. They climbed over the nearby ridges, and droned northward.

After an hour, "Yukon River," Ren yelled back at her, pointing down.

The great river was still frozen over, with snow atop the ice. It was much wider than she had envisioned. Smoke rose lazily from a cluster of cabins on the north bank.

"What's that place?" she asked.

"Stevens Village," he called back.

She recalled Esau Johnson, the Indian from Stevens Village, who had testified before the game board in December. "What a tiny island of civilization," she thought. "It's miles from anywhere. What kind of lives do people there live?" she wondered.

Ren gradually descended after crossing the Yukon, and Pat could tell he was looking for something on the ground. She soon learned what it was.

"Moose," he called, turning the plane slightly to fly over a group of about a dozen moose standing and lying about. Shortly he called out again, and then flew once more over a handful of the animals. Soon moose seemed to be in sight all the time, with the dark animals standing and lying about in singles, pairs, and small groups.

There were still snow drifts, and the land was still partially in the grip of winter. But the number of moose was incredible—there were far more than she had seen on her first flight with Ren into 20A.

Ren banked the plane steeply, and she felt her weight increase with the sharp turn. She gasped, and clung to the seat in front of her. Ren must have felt her hands on his back, for he turned with a grin, "Sorry. I see something I think you'll enjoy," he said as he straightened the plane to fly in a new direction.

Soon he dipped the right wing. She looked down and saw a line of trotting animals. Wolves! She counted twelve, six blacks, and six grays. Ren yelled, "That's what you came to Alaska to save!"

"They're beautiful," she yelled back, over the loud engine noise.

He nodded agreement, and resumed course. Moose continued to be abundant. Newly forming antlers on the bulls were bulbous and misshapen. They wouldn't be fully formed and the velvet wouldn't be shed for another six months, in September, she realized.

They flew over another pack of ten wolves traveling single file. Ren circled. The pack broke up, with various wolves plunging in different directions. The plane had spooked them.

"I didn't mean to do that," Ren said. "They've probably been shot at by someone in an airplane."

They were back on course and in level flight when, suddenly, Ren climbed steeply, and then nosed into a shallow dive. Pat grabbed Ren's seat. "What was that?" she asked, her heart racing.

He turned to face her, "I had to climb over the Arctic Circle," he explained with a straight face.

"I suppose you do that to every cheechako (newcomer)," she shouted, half angry, but laughing at the same time.

"Nope. Just the pretty ones," he replied jauntily.

Ren landed at Bettles, a roadhouse and a tiny cluster of log and frame homes, where he topped his gas tanks. "Hi, Ren," the attendant greeted. "Long time no see."

Pat walked about, stretching her legs. "That's what I wanted to show you, Pat," Ren said. "Good moose numbers and good wolf numbers. We were lucky. It isn't often we see two big wolf packs that easily. They don't travel much after a kill, so catching two packs out like that was a fluke."

"I thought you said wolves keep moose numbers down," Pat said. "I don't understand. We've seen lots of moose and lots of wolves. In fact, the moose look about as abundant as cattle on a ranch."

"It's really simple," he explained. "The critical factor is the ratio of wolves to moose. We use it as an indicator on the effects of predation. There are three general types of moose-wolf relationships where moose is the primary prey and the wolf the primary predator.

"When there are fewer than twenty moose for every wolf, predation usually leads to a decline in moose.

"At a level of twenty to thirty moose for every wolf, predation can be the primary force affecting numbers of moose. Whether moose numbers remain stable or declines depends largely on the effects of such things as hunting, food supply, and winter severity.

"When there are more than thirty moose per wolf, moose numbers may remain stable or increase if food is adequate and if other sources of mortality are minor.

"These ratios are only crude guidelines, but they often help where long, expensive studies aren't possible.

"Simply put, a large moose (or caribou) population is essential for supporting a large population of wolves.

"My point? Wilderness filled with wildlife is a delight to everyone; wilderness without animals is so much dead scenery," Ren concluded.

She nodded, but she was still confused.

Ren flew up the John River from Bettles. Craggy peaks rose on each side of this spectacularly beautiful river valley. Winter still held this land in its icy grip, and here and there were ice-sheathed cliffs. Under a clear blue sky snow dominated the land below as well as on the peaks above.

Suddenly, the plane shuddered. Then again. "Turbulence, Pat. Don't worry. It's common here," Ren called.

The little plane bounced about frequently for the rest of the flight as it fought a brisk north wind blowing down the John River canyon. Ren seemed relaxed. Pat was nervous, and, after tightening her seat belt, she clung tightly to Ren's seat back. At times the plane seemed to drop out from under her; next it would surge upward, pressing her firmly into the seat. Occasionally one wingtip or the other dropped as the Cub rolled about. She was frightened and kept reminding herself of my comment, "I think you'll be safe with him."

⁓

IN THE FALL OF 1942, Frank Glaser found himself in the 400-Eskimo village of Noatak, sixty miles above the Arctic Circle, where wolves were reported to be killing reindeer. On the day he arrived in the village, three large boats arrived. They had come from far up the Noatak River and carried many bales of caribou calf skins, which make wonderfully warm parkas. The hunters had been gone for months. The skins were sold in the large coastal village of Kotzebue. Both the hunting and sale of skins was illegal, but Noatak was so remote that such activities by Eskimos were largely overlooked. Glaser said nothing about it.

One of the hunters described for him the area in which they had taken the skins. Where there are caribou, there are wolves. Were the caribou herds close enough to bring wolves to the Noatak reindeer? How abundant were wolves around the caribou herd? Glaser decided to go see.

For $50 Glaser hired Gordon Mitchell, a Noatak Eskimo, to take him one hundred miles upstream on the Noatak in his outboard-powered, forty-foot-long umiak, a walrus skin boat. They traveled up the icy, clear river for three days. Frank peered into the water and saw huge schools of whitefish and grayling in almost incredible numbers. In places ling cod (burbot) lay on the bottom so thickly he could scarcely see the gravel. He saw vast schools of two kinds of char, running from three or four pounds to at least twelve pounds.One kind was round, long and slim; the other was heavy and deep, salmon-like, and tinted with the most gorgeous colors he had ever seen on fish—red, orange, purple, green, pink. Char spawn in fall, and these fish were in full spawning color.

There were chum salmon, too, but they had mostly spawned and were dying, their bodies drifting downriver and piling up on the bars. The water was so clear he could see fish ten feet down as if they were floating on air.

It turned cold when Glaser and his Eskimo boatman were about ten miles above the Kugurorok River. Here the Noatak River was shallowing, with the water level dropping fast. Four inches of slush ice was running on the river, and ice was coming out of the riverbank. It was October 8, time for Mitchell to hustle back downriver with his umiak before the river froze over.

Frank piled his tent and supplies on the beach. As he unloaded he saw tracks in the frozen wet sand where a wolf had chased a caribou. Ten feet further was the frozen track of a large grizzly bear.

"You will kill lots of caribou, Mr. Glaser," Gordon said, after seeing the caribou track.

"I just want one, for meat," Frank said.

Glaser had arranged with Noatak villager Saul Shield to come for him with his dog team some time in November or December. That gave him a month, maybe two, to scout out the region and trap or shoot wolves.

He built a square foundation three spruce logs high the exact size of his 8×10 tent. On that he erected a spruce pole frame on which to hang the tent. With the tent pitched atop the square of logs, he could stand up straight against the side walls. He sodded up around the logs and tent for additional insulation.

Before he left Noatak, Frank had Austin Stalker make him a wood burning stove. Starting with a new fifty gallon oil drum, Stalker worked for three days, cutting it to size with a cold chisel. He built a fine door and damper, with a good stove pipe hole. It burned two-and-a-half-foot-long wood, and was about fifteen inches high, with a flat top for cooking. When he delivered it, Frank asked, "How much, Austin?"

"Do you think $5 is too much?" he asked.

Frank paid him $10 and got a bargain. That little stove heated his 8×10 sod-insulated tent beautifully.

A couple of days after he got his tent set up and a good pile of wood cut, the temperature dropped to 26 below zero, with a strong east wind blowing downriver. The Noatak froze up overnight.

He was alone in the Arctic, seventy or eighty miles from the nearest person. It was the kind of life he loved. He searched the country for about fifteen miles in all directions from his camp, but never saw a caribou. The herd had passed through; all their tracks led northwest.

From Glaser's Diary: *October 16, 1941: Late this afternoon while returning from downriver, when I came out of the timber near my tent I saw a gray wolf on the far side of the river. It was eating on a salmon. I shot at him with the .220 Swift and missed; blew a geyser of sand up right under him. It was 300 yards, and I had thought it*

*was 200 yards. The wolf looked around, and went back to eating. I
corrected my aim and killed him with my next shot.*

*With binoculars I saw three more wolves downstream. They
saw me and ran before I could shoot when I came out of the timber
across from them.*

*From my tent I could see the dead wolf with binoculars. Just
at dark another wolf started to eat the dead one. I shot at him, he
dropped, but got up and ran off. Saw a total of five wolves today—
four grays and one black.*

Frank crossed the river the next morning and found where
wolves had eaten most of the wolf he had shot. He found a few
drops of blood where he had hit the other wolf, but there was
no snow, so he couldn't trail it far. Wolves had been eating old,
spawned-out salmon all along the river. The ice went out while
he was on the far side of the river and he had to walk a couple
of miles upstream to find a riffle he could ford. He had to wade
through swift waist-deep water with slush ice running to return
to his tent.

A few days later he was at the mouth of the Kugururok River,
about ten miles below his camp. Spawned out chum salmon had
washed up on the bar and two wolves were feeding on them. They
saw Frank and went into the brush, and he sat down on a bar trying to figure a way to get close to them. As he sat there a red fox
ran out of nearby willows, looking back. Its tongue was hanging
out, and it looked tired. Frank sat perfectly still and it loped on
by, still looking back.

Moments later a gray wolf came out of the same place in the
willows and trotted down a dry slough toward him. Clearly, it
was trailing the fox. The wolf trotted along, head and tail down.
Occasionally it stopped and looked back. When it was about
twenty yards away Frank called, "Just a minute."

The wolf threw its head up and jumped, but it was too late.
His bullet was already in the wolf's chest.

The wolf, a female, was trying to catch the red fox for food.
Later Frank sent its skin and skull to a museum that had requested
a wolf specimen.

About October 20th Frank walked twenty-five feet out on the
ice of the river and peered into deep water and saw a school of
arctic char swim by. He was without fishing tackle, but a day later
he found, lying on a bar below his camp, a sixty-pound chunk

of ivory mammoth tusk. With a wedge-shaped rock he split off a piece and filed a small lure out of it. He bent an eight penny nail, and sharpened it to make a hook, and lashed it to the ivory lure. For line, he used a six-foot piece of reindeer back sinew he had for patching mukluks.

He cut a willow pole, attached the sinew line to it, walked to the edge of the ice, and dragged the plug through the water. A big char sucked it in. Frank lifted its head up and slid it out onto the ice. The fish didn't know what was happening, and didn't even struggle until it was out of the water.

He caught several hundred pounds of fish that day. That evening, using a packboard, he carried a few fish to his tent. Next morning after breakfast he saw four river otters busily carrying fish he had caught into the water. They had taken only a few by the time he rushed down and stopped them. He packed the rest home. They froze, and Frank ate from them for the rest of his time there.

On October 27, Frank saw two Eskimos, Enoch S. Sherman and Henry Harris, with two dog teams, camped on the far side of the river. He showed them a safe place to cross on the ice. The Noatak is swift, and ice often forms, is washed away, and reforms, so crossings are always hazardous. That night he cooked a big feed for them, for they were low on food. They had been hunting but had found no caribou. They agreed to haul him and his gear back to Noatak for $50. He had decided the few local wolves where he had been hunting were no threat to the Noatak reindeer herd. It was time to leave.

When the two Eskimos and Frank pulled into the village, a crowd gathered around, as they always did when travelers arrived. Enoch reached into his sled and one at a time pulled out the three wolf hides Frank had collected. "Oh, big!" everyone exclaimed as he flourished each hide. Frank didn't think they were big, and it embarrassed him.

He was in for even more embarrassment. Next morning as he left his cabin, six old Eskimos who made up the village council were laying for him. As he neared, one called, "Stop, Mr. Glaser." As he stood wondering what was going on, they surrounded him, holding hands. One announced, "You're just like an Eskimo, Mr. Glaser. You go out in the hills and you stay. You're not afraid of Indians or anything. And you kill wolves. Now we give you Eskimo name. You are now *Amaguq* Frank (Wolf Frank)."

It was a high honor, but Frank was so embarrassed he later realized he didn't express his appreciation as he should have, but the Eskimos didn't seem to notice.

On Sunday, December 7, 1941, Frank's 52nd birthday, in his Noatak cabin, on his battery radio, he learned of the bombing of Pearl Harbor. Shifting stations to JOK, Tokyo, where reception was perfect, he heard a Japanese announcer, speaking English, read off the names of the American battleships Japanese planes had sunk. He heard Japanese laughing in the studio, and even the crinkling of paper as script pages were turned.

For three more years Glaser continued to kill wolves around reindeer herds at Eskimo villages in northwestern Alaska. He spent time at Kivalina, Candle, Noatak, Selawik, Unalakleet, Teller, Golovin, and elsewhere. Then he was assigned to Anchorage and Fairbanks for a time.

In January, 1944, he was sent to Walden, Colorado, where he was taught the use of poison for controlling predators. This included the use of the cyanide-loaded "getter" gun. The getter, or gas gun, is a foot-long metal pipe-like device driven into the ground or hard snow. An attractive scent is placed on a tuft of fur or wool and left protruding from the ground. When a wolf (or any other animal) picks up the scented wool with his mouth, it triggers a firing pin, which explodes a .38 caliber blank cartridge loaded with a powder which on contact with moisture in the animal's mouth turns to cyanide gas. Death is almost instantaneous.

After a year in Colorado, in February 1945 Glaser was assigned back to Alaska where he was again loaned to the Bureau of Indian Affairs. He was sent to Nome in northwestern Alaska where he continued his program of controlling wolves killing Eskimo-owned reindeer.

18
Anaktuvuk: Ren's wolf notes; Pat's fur parka

"HELLO, DOC," I WAS greeted by bright-eyed, excited Eskimo children who were among the villagers meeting the flight as I climbed from the Wien plane at Anaktuvuk Pass. The Anaktuvuk people have been endlessly studied by medical researchers and anthropologists; many visitors can legitimately be called "doc."

Ren's friend Bob Ahgook met me and I piled my camera cases and sleeping bag into a sled towed by his snow machine. As we left the still-parked Wien plane I heard rifle shots nearby, and looked around warily. Seeing my concern, Ahgook, a handsome young man with an excellent command of English laughed, "Don't worry. He's just sighting in a new rifle."

Several thousand caribou had been near the village the previous day, and Ahgook told me villagers had made a good kill. Because of this, excitement was high. Eleven-year-old Timothy Ahgook, trotting beside the snow machine, told me, "We'll eat good now. Lotsa caribou in drying racks."

As a boy in northern California, I "knew" an igloo was an Eskimo house made of snow. As an Alaskan, I learned igloo is a general term meaning "house," whether it be made of snow, wood, or skins. Most of the twenty five or thirty igloos of Anaktuvuk Pass were insulated plywood houses. While on a caribou survey flight in 1952 with Clarence Rhode, Regional Director of the Fish and Wildlife Service, I saw the village when the people still lived in caribou-skin tents, and, of course, depended upon dog teams for transportation.

Ren Smith's cabin was built of logs and sod. Sod was piled outside the logs to provide additional insulation, making it a cozy refuge from the constant winds that whistle through the wide pass.

After leaving my sleeping bag and pack at Ren's cabin, with camera I wandered about the village snapping shots here and there, working on my *National Geographic* story. I was greeted with smiles and friendliness everywhere. Most villagers seemed to know I was a friend of Ren Smith.

I watched Ellen Hugo butcher several caribou her husband had shot the previous day. She stood, legs straight, bending from the hips, working on the animals as they lay on the snow. Over her fur parka she wore a brightly colored washable cotton print, called an *atig*, which functioned as a kind of full-body apron. Blood stained the snow for twenty feet around her butchering site, yet her *atig* didn't have a drop of blood on it. I don't know how she did it.

Her husband had hauled the animals to the village on a sled towed by his snow machine. With her ulu, the half-round Eskimo woman's knife, she slashed swiftly, accurately severing rib ends, cutting through femur sockets, filleting meat from bones. The anatomy of a caribou was no mystery to her. There was no waste.

"We use the leg fur for *kammiks* (fur boots)," she told me, as she neatly stripped the skin from the legs. She removed strips of sinew from the back and scraped them clean. "We use sinew for sewing. It's stronger than thread," she said.

When she was done she invited me into her tiny, neat home, where we drank scalding cups of tea and chewed on dried caribou. She told me she remembered living in caribou skin tents and using caribou-fat lamps (hollowed out rocks) for light as her people wandered through the mountains before building their wooden igloos and settling in this high pass.

Her husband was out again, caribou hunting. "He doesn't speak English," she said. "He's a good hunter," she added, with pride.

"My cousin, Arctic John, stays with you," she pointed out. "Now he and his wife live in Fairbanks, but he comes home to get caribou so they can have meat."

Arctic John, also known as *Italook*, my fellow guest at Ren's cabin, was also out hunting caribou.

I thanked Mrs. Hugo for her hospitality, and continued to wander about taking pictures. On the other side of the village

Jack Morry was changing a snow machine engine. He worked at it like a professional mechanic, smiling when I asked where he'd learned to be a mechanic.

"We have to be mechanics," he said. "We can't send our machines to Fairbanks to be fixed every time they quit."

I crossed the trail used by the hunters where they left and entered the village with their snow machines. It was red with the blood of caribou they had brought home. Late in the afternoon an Eskimo with a dog team arrived, his sled holding three freshly killed caribou. He was a rarity; most Anaktuvuk residents had switched to snow machines.

Arrival of snow machines, and the disappearance of most of the sled dogs, meant that the villagers didn't need to kill as many caribou; dog teams, of course, were fueled with caribou meat.

Dusk came about 7 o'clock. I returned to Ren's cabin and lit the oil heating stove and Aladdin lamp. At dark, sled dogs were howling, and a chill wind whispered around the cabin. Shouts of playing children drifted across the village. Snow machine engines muttered in the distance. Pinpoints of their lights crawled across distant mountain slopes.

Arctic John arrived, weary from his day of hunting. He was tall, ruggedly handsome, with a weathered face, large ears, and gray hair. I greeted him and told him my name. "I have little bit, not much, English," he apologized.

He was overly modest. His English was good. "Bad weather today. Pretty wet," he said. "I kill two caribou. My back—something wrong," he said, bending and hold his back with one hand. "Too many skidoo (snow machines), make lotsa noise. Everybody scare caribou," he said "Once noisy snow machine make caribou come to me," he said, with a laugh.

He had a strong personality and the manners of a prince. I was impressed by his sense of order, his cleanliness—he washed his hands and face several times a day—and his constant good cheer. He often picked up after me, and I don't consider myself disorganized. Each morning this "Hill's Man," as he sometimes called himself, who didn't encounter a white man until he was an adult, shaved with a disposable razor, and finished by slathering on a pungent aftershave lotion.

He sat drinking hot tea, talking. "We got no calendar when I born. Maybe I be around 80 years old. One man made me 82," he said. "Pretty soon I go someplace," he remarked, meaning his life would end soon. It was a casual remark without self pity.

He showed me his Model 721 Remington rifle. "Bought twenty years ago from Johnson's store in Wiseman," he explained. He had recently put a 4× scope on it because of his failing eyesight. The rifle looked new. He carried it in a soft case, even when hunting.

"Warm enough for you?" he asked. "Stove not strong," he said, pointing to the small oil stove. He was right, it didn't throw much heat. It didn't burn much oil, either, which really was the point; fuel for it had to be flown from Fairbanks. In Anaktuvuk Pass, where there are few opportunities to earn money, priorities are different; cool indoor temperatures can be the norm. One simply wears more clothing. "I used to live here," he said. "But life is easier in Fairbanks. But Fairbanks has too much big timber. Can't see far," waving a hand. "Here I can see long way."

He was right about that; the nearest trees are about twenty five miles from the village.

About nine o'clock Arctic John left, saying, "Don't wait up for me. I like to walk around and see my friends."

He had scarcely left when the door opened and four 10 and 11-year old boys burst into the cabin. They fired questions at me, asking about my cameras, where I lived, my family. They rattled on about the village—they were used to nosy visitors and knew answers to the most obvious questions. Bright-eyed as squirrels, they wanted to know what kind of doctor I was. They asked to see pictures of my family. In my visits to bush villages I always go well supplied with candy for the kids, and this gang would have cleaned me out if I had let them.

They left and I stepped outside. A full moon lit the snowy land; it was almost as bright as day. A pink, purple, red-tinged, and green aurora danced above. Sled dogs howled and moaned. In the distance the tiny light of a snow machine inched across a mountainside. Back inside I noticed frost had formed on the inside of the windows.

Another gang of six children arrived, with more questions. They were full of giggles and exploring hands. I asked one little lightly dressed girl, "Don't you have a parka?"

"I'm an Eskimo. I don't need one," she said, shyly. More candy went out the door when they left.

Next morning it was snowing lightly, and a brisk north wind

blew. I was taking photos in the village when Ren's Cub flew over, circled, and landed. I met the plane almost before it stopped sliding.

"Welcome to the arctic, Miss York," I said, helping her out of the plane.

"Thanks, Prof. It's good to see you again," she said.

"Hi, Prof," Ren greeted, shaking hands. "You look like a *cheechako* with that camera hanging around your neck," he teased.

Two villagers arrived with snow machines and sleds to haul Ren, Pat, and their gear to Ren's cabin. I joined them there. Arctic John was washing breakfast dishes. Ren and Arctic John were old friends, and greeted one another with gusto, speaking in both English and *Inupiaq*.

Ren introduced the old man to Pat.

"You are Ren's woman?" he asked, in his direct way.

Ren laughed, as Pat squirmed, looking this way and that, not knowing how to answer the question. "We're just friends," she finally managed.

"Maybe," Ren told Arctic John, looking at Pat in amusement.

"You better get busy make sure," the old man said, with a loud laugh.

Pat blushed as we all laughed.

Pat remained quiet and seemed shy, but her eyes were big as she stared about. I realized it was her first close encounter with Eskimos, and her first visit to a bush village. I smiled inwardly, thinking her encounter with the real world of rural Alaska would educate her more quickly than all the books, public hearings, and talk she had encountered in her few months in Alaska.

One of the Eskimos who had hauled Ren and Pat to the cabin cornered Ren and talked earnestly with him. Ren nodded and asked questions, while frequently glancing at Pat. I overheard him say, "Maybe. Just a minute."

Pat and I had been chatting. She had noticed the log wall interior of the cabin, and asked me how the logs had gotten there. I told her.

"Hauled twenty five miles from the nearest timber by dog team?" she repeated, surprised.

Ren interrupted. "Pat, would you mind if I left you with Prof for today? Yesterday one of the hunters located a new wolf den high in the mountains, about forty miles from here, and I'd like to go check it out. There's no place nearby to land the plane, so I have to go by snow machine. It's going to be a long hard trip, and it will be windy and cold. I don't think you'd enjoy it."

"Why, no, I don't mind, if Prof doesn't," she said a little hesitantly.

Earlier, I had arranged to accompany Arctic John on an afternoon hunt. He wanted to return to skin two caribou he had killed, and to see if he could collect another animal or two. He overheard Ren, and turned to me. "We take her with us," he said.

"Me, go on a hunt?" Pat said, with surprise, when I explained.

"Yep. You'll enjoy it," I assured her. "Hunters here commonly take their wives and kids with them. It'll be just for the afternoon."

Ren rushed off on his snow machine, accompanied by one of the men on another machine.

"Let's wander around the village a bit," I suggested to Pat, picking up my camera.

It was educational for both of us. I was amused by Pat's reaction to the racks of drying caribou meat. "That's their pantry," she concluded. She even chewed on a piece of dried caribou one of the village women offered.

Ellen Hugo was working on two more caribou her husband had killed. She greeted Pat like an old friend, and pointed out the various uses she made of caribou parts—the skin, the sinew for thread—as she swiftly skinned and butchered the two animals. I took pictures and Pat stared in amazement as the capable woman swiftly butchered the 150-pound animals. Pat didn't seem to be horrified by the blood-stained snow or piles of raw meat.

Mrs. Hugo finished and invited us in for tea and talk. I sat back and listened to the two women whose lives and cultures were so different. Pat was fascinated with stories the older woman told of her early nomadic life.

"Once our family nearly starved," she said, matter-of-factly. "My father killed our sled dogs, one at a time, for food. There were only two left when a skinny cow caribou wandered by and father shot it. The meat gave us strength to walk fifty miles where we found a few more caribou. My father killed three, ending our starvation days.

"We're lucky now. If caribou don't come, we go long way after them with snow machine," she said. "You know, we (meaning the villagers) need 400 to 500 caribou a year. Caribou are like cattle are to you," she told Pat. "They're our life. This is one big caribou farm," she said, waving her hand at the surrounding mountains with a laugh.

Pat was silent and appeared thoughtful when we left the Hugo house and returned to Ren's cabin, had lunch, and with Arctic John headed out for an afternoon hunt. A frigid north wind greeted us. Arctic John, his cased rifle over a shoulder, carried a five-foot walking stick to prod snow to locate a packed snow machine trail which we followed for easy walking. We moved single file, Arctic John in the lead. I noticed the skimpy coyote fur face ruff on Pat's down-filled parka. She had trouble facing the wind, but she didn't complain.

As we climbed the shoulder of a mountain near the village, high scattered clouds scurried past on the brisk wind. Arctic John pointed about three miles ahead to a low ridge. "My caribou there," he said. For an 80-year-old, he moved well. Pat stopped occasionally to stare through the crystal air at the high snowy mountains.

"I've never seen anything like this. Why, these mountains are vast. They make me feel insignificant," she commented.

Arctic John stopped to rest. Half a dozen snow machines were in sight, some more than ten miles away. They looked like ants crawling on the mountains. A distant shot echoed among the canyons and peaks. "Someone shoot caribou," Arctic John said.

Black spots appeared here and there on the snow in the pass and on the hills fronting the great peaks. They were huge northern ravens—two feet from beak to tip of tail—feeding on viscera of the Eskimo's caribou kills. More ravens constantly wheeled about the sky, croaking. One flew near and we heard the swish of his wings in the cold, dense air. When directly overhead it called with a deep tone.

"Why, that sounded like a bell," Pat exclaimed.

"*Tulugak*," Arctic John said. "Smart bird. He know everything. He call like that sometime. Makes lotsa different sounds."

He turned to look at me, and said, quite seriously, "If you shoot *tulugak*, it bring bad weather."

We reached the two caribou Arctic John had killed the previous evening. Working bare-handed in the raw wind, he quickly skinned them, working carefully to preserve the skins. He handled the meat carefully, keeping it very clean. He was patient, and took his time. There were no wasted moves.

The skinning done, he dug into a frozen gut pile he had left, found a kidney, and ate it raw, one bite at a time as I snapped his picture. "Eskimo lunch, long before white man came," he said. "Liver good too," he said.

Pat's eyes widened as the old man munched on the raw, half frozen organ.

She had said scarcely a word. All of this—the vast land, the hunting, the way of life, the dependence of people from the land—was new to her, and I guessed it was a lot to take in all at once.

While working, Arctic John, enjoying himself, humming an Eskimo tune. When his two caribou were skinned and butchered, he covered the meat with the hides, and piled the small cow antlers atop as a marker. A friend with a snow machine was to retrieve the meat and hides for him. Caribou may be left in the hills like this for weeks or even months during winter. The frozen hide and antlers protect the meat from ravens.

Next he sat on the snow and scanned for caribou with binoculars. "Caribou stop at noon. Move in afternoon," he commented. "Maybe we wait here."

Pat sat with her back to the wind and I saw her put her hands on her cheeks. "Is your face freezing?" I asked, pulling her mittened hands away and looking intently for white spots.

"I don't think so, but my face is cold. And this down parka isn't as warm as I thought it would be," she admitted.

"Would you like to go back to the village?" I asked.

"Oh, no. I'm all right. I want to stay," she answered.

We sat silently for some time as John studied the pass and the mountains with binoculars and an old fashioned brass telescope he must have carried for years. "Caribou there. Won't come this way," he said, pointing to the mountains at least ten miles across the pass. "Caribou travel into wind."

With the wind from the north, the caribou he had seen would travel away from us.

We sat quietly for some time. The frigid north wind continued, and the scattered clouds flew by overhead. Sun occasionally dappled the pass, and the snow sparkled with its rays. Once we saw a golden eagle swoop from on high and a couple of hundred yards away capture a white ptarmigan on the ground. He fed on it for a few minutes, then carried it off, flapping vigorously in the north wind.

"What do you think of wolves?" Pat asked Arctic John. It was the first direct question she had asked him, and he looked at her, puzzled.

After some thought, he answered, "Wolf like Eskimo. He lives on caribou. Most wolves smart, a few not smart." And, with an impish grin, "Eskimos are like that too."

"What do wolves eat?" she asked.

"Wolves eat everything. Whatever they catch. Here in mountains more caribou than other things," he answered. "I killed six wolves one day. That long ago. I got three hundred dollars bounty. Sold hides for another three hundred dollars. All for one day hunt. But no more for me now. Now I walk slow. My back no good," he said, not complaining, simply stating facts.

"Do you hate wolves because they eat caribou?" she asked.

I could see the question puzzled the old man. He slowly answered, "Hate wolves? No. Wolf and Eskimo always live together. Wolf partner to Eskimo—his fur keeps our face warm," he said, pointing to the fine wolf ruffs on his parka and mine. The long guard hairs of the ruff surrounding our faces broke the wind. "Wolf skin parka also warm," he said. "Wolf fur make warm blanket for sleeping."

The old man staggered with fatigue as we slowly returned to the village late that afternoon. He didn't complain. "Fine afternoon, eh boy?" he smiled at me as we arrived at Ren's cabin. Since he was three decades older than me, I didn't mind being called a boy.

"How you like hunt?" he asked Pat. "Sorry we didn't kill caribou," he apologized.

"Thank you for taking me. I enjoyed it very much," she said. I noticed she stood for a long time close to the small stove after we lit it. She had been cold most of the day.

Ren arrived. "Sorry to have abandoned you," he apologized to Pat. "I hope Prof and Arctic John treated you right."

Pat chattered throughout our simple evening meal, detailing for Ren what she had seen during the day. She didn't notice when Ren smiled and winked at me. "We'll make an Alaskan out of you yet," Ren said.

Pat laughed. "I've learned more about how people live from the land in one day than in all the rest of the time I've been in Alaska."

She asked Ren about the wolf den he had gone to look at.

"It's a new one," he said. "Wolf dens are often used by the same animals every year, and the hunters here know where most of them are. Several of the hunters have shown me dens which I've measured, and on which I've recorded other data. It was clear wolves intend to have pups at this new den within a few weeks, so we didn't go close. We didn't want to disturb them."

"I thought the people here hunted and killed wolves," Pat said, surprised.

"They do," Ren said. "But they practice good wildlife management. Next winter the pups from the mother wolf in that den will be adults and their skins will be prime. If they killed the mother now, the pups would all die. That would be a loss. Also, the skin of the mother wolf isn't very good right now—she has shed a lot of fur around her nipples. It's better to harvest wolves when the skins are good.

"Remember, Pat, the wolf is a valuable renewable resource."

"Most people where I come from don't look at the wolf that way," she said, frowning.

"I know," Ren said. "We hear that all the time."

Ren laughed. "The hunters here are far ahead of most scientists who study wolves. I learn something every time I come here. For example, today I asked one of the hunters if he had seen wolves in the area near that new den. 'Yes, tracks of eight,' he told me.

"As a joke, I asked, 'What color were they?'

"'All gray,' he answered.

"'How do you know that?' I asked.

"'The biggest wolves are usually black. The tracks we saw were made by small wolves,' he said."

"How fascinating," Pat said.

This encouraged him to describe more experiences he had had while studying wolves at Anaktuvuk Pass.

"One summer, with Bob Ahgook and Justus Mekiana I spent much time high in the mountains near the village, using spotting scope and binoculars, watching wolves and studying their behavior. We watched one wolf for eighteen hours straight; another for fourteen hours.

Ren said, "One of the wolves we watched that summer had

lost two toes from a front foot. It often traveled with the damaged foot held up. But when it needed four feet in rough going, or for speed, it could and did use the injured foot just fine.

"One female wolf the villagers have known for several years, has a crippled and useless rear leg, yet she has raised two litters of pups.

"We watched one wolf backtrack another to meat the first wolf had fed upon. It traveled several miles, sniffing the tracks, right to the meat. I had often wondered how wolves found distant meat other wolves had killed.

"Wolves are incredible travelers," Ren said. "I tagged one wolf here that traveled 110 miles in five days. Several times we watched wolves successfully catch and kill caribou in chases of from four and a half miles, to eight miles. Bob Ahgook says that's fairly common."

He continued, his enthusiasm for the subject and admiration of the Anaktuvuk people obvious, "In May, 1972, Bob Ahgook and I were walking up a boulder-strewn mountainside in an area where Bob knew of two dens used in previous years. We had already spent several days there attempting to locate an active den, and observed two different wolves whose movements and behavior suggested that one of these dens was being used.

"When an all night watch at one den revealed no wolf activity, we decided to investigate the other den in an adjacent valley. As I followed Bob through the rocks and dwarf birch up the steep hillside, he suddenly stopped and pointed to the vague outline of a narrow trail leading up and across the slope, saying it looked like a wolf trail.

"Following the trail with his eyes he added, ' . . . there's a wolf.'"

"A hundred meters away, a tan wolf hurried up the mountain, climbing almost vertically between segments of a sheer escarpment before it disappeared, after a final glance back.

"Bob said the wolf was a female which had just had, or would shortly have, pups. He had seen her dark abdomen where the hair was shed around her nipples. Certain we were near the den, we retreated to avoid disturbing it further. At a safe distance, we looked back for some indication of the den location. As we watched, a robin landed about thirty meters above us and quickly flitted away. Bob immediately said, 'The den is there, where robin landed.'

"'How do you know?' I asked.

"'Saw it pick up wolf hairs for its nest,' he explained.

"When I looked closely, I saw freshly exposed soil—evidence of digging—around a boulder where the robin had landed.

"Bob Ahgook's observations and knowledge sometimes make me, with all my scientific training, feel like an amateur," Ren said, wryly. "At a glance he spotted the wolf trail and the wolf. He immediately identified the wolf as a female by her dark abdomen. He located the den by observing the robin."

Pat and I were fascinated by Ren's account.

We finished supper and started to clean up. "Rachel's done," Arctic John told Ren. "You go now. I wash dishes and clean floor," he said. I didn't understand what he meant until later—there are few secrets in a village where most of the 120 residents are related either by blood or marriage.

Ren nodded, "Thanks *Italook*," he said. Then, "Pat, let's go visit one of my girl friends. Prof, you're welcome to come too."

I happened to see Pat's fleeting expression as Ren said "girl friends." It was then that I realized how close was her attachment to Ren.

Her name was Rachel, and she was expecting us. "How are you, Rachel?" Ren asked, as she hugged him. "Good, Ren. Please come in."

Though we had just eaten, we followed social custom and had tea and hard, dry, round pilot crackers with jam. Rachel was of indeterminate age. Her two children, 8 and 9 years old, were playing a board game in a corner of the tiny house, which was lit by two Coleman gas lanterns. Flame flickered in a tiny oil stove in a corner. Pat was quiet, but polite, as Rachel and Ren discussed the recent success of the village hunters. The caribou meat supply had been low when the animals had arrived.

Pat perked up when she heard Rachel apologize, "I'm sorry my husband isn't here. He should be back tomorrow. He followed the caribou north and decided to stay overnight."

Rachel looked at Ren questioningly, and he nodded. She uncovered something from a corner of the one-room house and handed it to him.

"Stand up, Pat," Ren requested. She stood and Ren said, "Let's see how this fits you," as he slipped a magnificent fur parka on her. The soft gray fur, frosted with white-tipped hair, shimmered in the lantern light. A decorative strip of arctic animal cutouts was sewn around the bottom of the garment. The hood had a beautiful wolf ruff.

She looked down at the glossy fur, ran her hand over it, and stared at Ren.

"It's for you," he said, gently, with a smile.

"Ren, I can't accept this," she protested.

"I think you can," he said. "*Italook* and the Prof told me you were cold today," looking at me for confirmation. I nodded and said, "She shivered all afternoon."

"That parka will keep you warm. Rachel made it for you. She needed to see you this morning to know exactly what size it should be. She worked all day to finish it. Please. It's a gift from me. Rachel is one of the finest skin sewers in Alaska, and she'll be insulted if you don't accept it."

"But a parka like this must cost hundreds of dollars," she protested.

"It cost me nothing. Rachel made it to pay what she considered to be a debt," he said.

Rachel nodded her head. "It's small payment for what I owe Ren," she said, simply.

"Let's try the hood for fit," Rachel requested, slipping it over Pat's head. It was perfect. Rachel then said, "When you need to protect your face, you roll the ruff forward, like this," rolling the wolf ruff so that long guard hairs surrounded Pat's face. "On a windy day, or when you travel on a snow machine, this will keep your face from freezing," Rachel explained.

"You wear it tomorrow. If it doesn't fit, you bring it back and I'll fix," she said.

Pat was almost without words. She did ask, "What kind of fur is it?"

I think she feared it might be wolf. Ren grinned, and I'm sure he thought the same. "It's *sik-sik-puk*—marmot." he said. "*Sik-sik* is the ground squirrel—that's the sound he makes. *Puk* means 'big.' So, *sik-sik-puk* literally means 'big ground squirrel.' The marmot, which is a cousin to the ground squirrel, can weigh twenty or more pounds. It's about the size of a Cocker Spaniel dog. He's a big, mountain-living relative to the ground hog that you probably knew in Massachusetts."

I complimented Pat. "You're a lucky woman. That parka is a work of art. You'll never see finer fur work anywhere."

When she nodded I saw tears in her eyes.

We returned to Ren's cabin. Arctic John had slicked the place up and was gone. We had no sooner lit the Aladdin lamp than Pat insisted Ren tell her about the debt Rachel thought she owed him.

"She has long insisted it was a debt. I didn't look at that way. It was a simple courtesy. It happened when she was in labor with her oldest son—you saw him playing in the corner while we were there. His name is Ren," he grinned.

"What?" she asked. Then, almost severely, but with humor, "You'd better explain."

Ren grinned, enjoying her suspense, then said, "I flew a geological survey party to the North Slope, left them, and was returning to Fairbanks through Anaktuvuk Pass. Weather was lousy, so I landed here to wait for it to improve. Rachel was in labor—and had been in labor for something like two days. The local women were worried about her. They said she had to get to a doctor and a hospital.

"I flew Rachel and her husband through the storm to Fairbanks. Remember the turbulence we hit coming here? That was nothing compared to what we flew through that day. I radioed ahead and an ambulance met us at Phillips Field and took Rachel and her husband to the hospital. I went to a hotel for the night—I was beat from flying through the storm.

"Next morning I went to the hospital. She had undergone a Caesarean section, and she and baby Ren were just fine. She's convinced I saved her life, and perhaps I did. I wouldn't let her pay for the flight—I was flying to Fairbanks anyway. Over the years she has insisted she wanted to make me a parka in payment. Last time I was here I agreed to have her make a parka—for you.

"Satisfied?" he asked.

"Oh, Ren, of course. I'm overwhelmed. Thank you very much," she said, with a hug and a brief kiss.

Late the next day I was taking pictures in the village when Ren and Pat, on snow machines, returned from an all-day trip. Pat had never previously ridden a snow machine.

"Well, Pat, were you warmer today?" I asked.

"Yes, Prof. It was heavenly. Why, it's unbelievable how much warmer my face was, even in the wind. The thick fur ruff makes all the world of difference. And the fur parka is much warmer than my down-filled parka," she answered.

Her lovely face, framed with the nearly half-foot-long wolf guard hairs in the ruff, was rosy and animated. Her eyes sparkled.

I couldn't resist a slight needle. "You can thank a wolf for the ruff on your parka," I said. "Remember, Arctic John told you the wolf is a partner to the Eskimo."

She nodded. "I've been thinking about that all day. I realize the ruff is made from wolf fur. Believe me, I'm grateful to be warm, and I have a little better understanding of what it takes to live off the land."

The Alaska education of Pat York was progressing.

My caribou article appeared eventually in the *National Geographic*, accompanied by my photos of caribou, Arctic John, and Anaktuvuk village. In one photo Arctic John is eating the raw caribou kidney.

19

Wolf den: Moose kill: Lady: Aerial wolf hunt

"How would you like to visit a wolf den, and maybe see some pups?" Ren asked. It was his first call to Pat in the three weeks since they had returned from Anaktuvuk Pass. He had been away, much of the time on flying assignments.

"I'd love to. How do we get there?" she asked.

"We'll fly. I'll pick you up at six tomorrow morning."

"Lunch?"

"Won't need it. We'll be back before noon," he promised.

It was May, and Pat had been luxuriating in the nearly twenty four hours of daylight, often finding herself lingering long after midnight over some chore, or a long walk, simply because it was still light and didn't seem time to go to bed.

Ren had just wrapped up his studies of the wolf carcasses that had been taken by the ADF&G in the control work in 20A. His last project was to arrange for a public auction for fifty raw wolf pelts. The state took in $13,769 from a crowd of 200 who bought every last one at prices ranging from $140 to $280. Many were purchased by local skin sewers who use strips of wolf skin from the area of longest fur (the roach) for making ruffs on winter parkas similar to the one Ren had given Pat.

"Thanks for asking me," Pat said when he arrived at her door the next morning.

"My pleasure," Ren answered with a smile.

Ren had replaced the wheel-skis on his Cub with floats. Pat had never been in a float plane and clung nervously to the back of Ren's seat as, full throttle, the little plane skittered across the water and lifted off. Ren pointed the nose of the plane toward 20A, where he had taken Pat in March when it had been locked in winter snow and ice.

Pat could hardly believe the changes that had taken place. Ponds and lakes which had previously appeared to her as flat snow-covered land, now dotted the area. The melting of snow and ice, and the green explosion of late April and May, had transformed the land into a lush, rich, scenic Paradise.

An hour after takeoff Ren eased the Cub to a landing on the lake north of the Black Pack den and taxied ashore. He hadn't told Pat about Lady, holding his emotional attachment to the wolf pup close, not willing to share it, even with her. He wondered if he would see a gray wolf with the Black Pack on this day.

"I can't promise they'll be here, but there's a good chance they will be. This way," he said, shouldering a tripod for his spotting scope and starting off. His binoculars hung around his neck and were tucked inside his shirt.

They climbed the hill to his observation point. It had been nine months since he had released Lady. About half of young wolves die in their first year, so there was only a fifty-fifty chance that Lady had survived, even without the control program—that is, if she had been adopted, which it appeared she had. And if she had survived the first critical weeks in the wild. Even with adult wolves natural mortality is annually about twenty percent in each age class; most wolves in the wild die before they reach five years of age.

He was pleased to find the slight breeze came from the direction of the den; the wolves, if they were there, wouldn't catch their scent.

Near the top of the hill he placed his fingers across his lips. "Quiet now, Pat. The den's not far."

They crawled the last few yards to the depression he had previously used as a lookout. With binoculars Ren saw an adult black wolf lying near the mouth of the den. He attached the 30X spotting scope to the tripod, and squinting through it, saw a black pup, then another. They were playing and wrestling not far from the den. The adult was keeping an eye on the pups.

"Ok, Pat. Take a look," he said, in a low voice. "These wolves are old friends. I've been watching them now for four seasons. Each year they've returned to this den to raise pups. There are usually five or six in the pack, and so far, they've all been black.

The adult you see near the den is a baby sitter, guarding the pups. The others are probably away hunting. So far I've seen two pups. There are probably more."

Pat was unfamiliar with a spotting scope and it took her a few minutes to get her eye placed properly, to focus it, and to recognize what she was seeing. "Oh, I see four pups," she breathed. "They're chewing on something—and dragging it around. They're all tugging on it from different directions," she whispered.

"Remnants of a kill," Ren said. He peered at the animals through his binoculars, and started to take notes.

"Oh, this is marvelous," Pat said. "Now I see another pup. I think there are five altogether. They're all black. One is chewing on a leg of the baby sitter."

"Wolf pups are born all the same dark color. Their adult color shows up by mid summer," Ren explained.

For the next hour they watched the active wolf pups play in the soft morning sunlight. They were all legs, awkward, and full of energy. There were mock battles, wrestling matches, and tug of war with bones and remnants of skin and body parts near the den. The patient adult moved from time to time to escape pups that climbed over it, or tried to chew on its legs, tail, ears—whatever they could reach.

Ren took notes, and occasionally handed Pat the binoculars so he could use the scope. Pat was peering through the scope and Ren had swept his binoculars across the flats beyond the den.

"Wow!" Ren exclaimed.

"What is it?" Pat asked.

"I'm not sure. I saw something flash through an opening in that stand of birches. I think it was a moose and wolves," he said.

He continued to peer intently. Suddenly a cow moose burst into the open from screening trees, followed by one gray and four black wolves. The cow was staggering. As he watched, two of the black wolves leaped in and slashed at her lower hind legs. She whirled to face them. She appeared weary; her movements were not the swift, graceful actions of a fresh moose. The wolves before her retreated. But a black and the gray wolf leaped to slash at her rear. She fled. The five wolves followed, one on each side of the moose, three strung out single file behind.

Ren's mind was in a whirl. Was the gray wolf Lady? He kept an eye on it, noting that the gray was as aggressive as the others.

"Pat, wolves are attacking a moose! This is a rare opportunity to see how they do it." His voice was filled with excitement.

He quickly turned the spotting scope to the besieged cow and focused it. "Here, Pat, you use the scope. I'll use my binocs," he said.

The fleeing moose with the following wolves was soon on an open tundra flat within a hundred yards of their blind. Two black wolves leaped in and ripped at her hind legs. The gray leaped in and clung to her flank. She kicked hind legs at the wolves, but they dodged and she missed. The gray at her flank clung for a time as she continued to run. The weight of the clinging wolf caused her to stagger; she kicked at it with her hind leg and the hoof appeared to brush the predator off. She stopped running and turned to face the five wolves and briefly ran forward on hind legs, attempting to drop onto a wolf with her front hooves. The wolf dodged easily. Two of the blacks rushed to her rear and leaped and again slashed at her hindquarters. She turned and fled again, with the five wolves crowded around her. The attacking wolves were swift and silent.

Ren frantically wrote notes. Pat, horrified and fascinated, kept the moose centered in the scope as it ran, stopped to fight, and ran again. The 30X glass showed every detail—patches of loose or missing skin where the wolves had slashed, many dark patches of blood on the cow's body, the red tongues and gleaming white teeth of the panting, grinning wolves. When not leaping and slashing, the wolves' tails wagged with excitement.

"I think it's a pregnant cow," Ren said. "They've probably been harassing her all night. She's worn out. She staggers even when she runs. We may see them finish her."

A black wolf leaped and grabbed the moose's nose and hung on, while two others tore at its neck and throat. The gray and the other black slashed at the hocks and lower legs. The besieged cow tried to run, but she stumbled. She tossed her head, trying to rid herself of the wolf clinging to her nose. The wolf stubbornly hung on, even when she lifted it free of the ground. The moose managed to run a few more feet, then she stumbled and fell. The wolf clinging to her nose continued to hang on, while the other four swarmed over her. Her legs waved wildly in the air, and now, for the first time, Ren and Pat heard the cow's frantic bleats—almost screams.

"I can't watch this," she moaned, pushing the scope away and turning her head.

Ren lowered his glasses and turned to her. "You came to Alaska because you said you love wolves," he said, in a steely voice. "You wanted to learn all about them. Well, you're seeing wolves in action, which is a privilege few people have. This is nature, it's life. I'll be disappointed if you quit now."

Ren had never spoken to her like that before. The tone of his voice and the words shocked her.

"All right," she muttered, pulling the scope back into position and once more peered at the carnage.

Again the cow blared a cry of fear and agony. There was no mistaking the suffering of the besieged animal.

Pat shuddered, but grimly continued to watch as the five wolves swarmed over the downed and still living moose. They ripped chunks from the hams and sliced into the belly. Through the scope she could see great bloody gashes all over the moose. The cow raised her head one last time and groaned as the wolves greedily tore at her. Then she remained silent and lay still.

Pat suddenly lost it and turned away, saying, "I'm sorry. I can't handle this."

Ren felt ashamed, dropped his binoculars, and put a hand on her shoulders. "I'm sorry. I didn't mean to be so rough on you."

She shook his hand off and moved away. He sat next to her. "Pat, I'm sorry. Please forgive me."

"I don't mind what you said," she said. "You were right. I don't know what I thought about wolves when I came here. Everything has changed. I had no idea that wolves could be like that. I've never seen anything so horrible. Oh, that poor moose."

Ren suddenly realized that Pat had probably never before seen a large animal die.

"They were so cruel," she exclaimed.

"No, Pat. That's a human concept. Wolves are not deliberately cruel. They were simply being wolves. They have to eat. That's the way they get their food."

"Well, I don't like it!" she exclaimed, turning and looking him.

He pulled her close when he saw her tears. "Ren, please forgive me," she managed, wrapping her arms around his neck.

He didn't know what he was supposed to forgive her for, but he was willing to do so. They clung to one other tightly as they lay in the depression. Ren was the first to break off.

"Pat, I want more of this—lots more," he said, softly. "But now isn't the time. Let's see what the wolves are doing."

Slightly miffed because the wolves seemed more important to Ren than she was, she nodded, and reluctantly returned to the spotting scope.

The wolves were now tearing at the moose in a more leisurely manner. They watched the animals feed for another fifteen minutes until three of them left the carcass and wandered off, tails raised high and rolling around and around—a sign of full bellies.

"They'll go sleep it off. One or more of them will take meat back to the den," Ren said. "I want to go check on that moose carcass," he said. "But for now I want to try something. Would you mind if I left you alone for a little while?"

Pat wasn't sure. The savagery of the wolves had frightened her. "Will I be safe?"

"You mean from the wolves?" he asked. "Of course. They won't bother you. In fact, I want you to lie low and stay quiet. If they see or smell you they'll likely disappear," he reassured.

"I won't go far. In fact, you'll be able to see me. I'll leave my binoculars here. You can use them or the spotting scope to watch me. I'm going to slip down the hill and try to keep out of their sight," Ren said.

He crawled out of the depression and, crouching, ran down the hill, keeping to low trees and brush. He soon reached the place where he had released the three-month-old Lady the previous August.

If the gray wolf in the pack was Lady, and he was almost sure it was, would she respond to his whistle? Would she remember him? His heart was pounding with excitement.

He sent a piercing whistle across the tundra—the whistle he had always used to identify himself when approaching Lady in her pen.

He waited several minutes, peering about, hopefully. He whistled again.

"Pat must think I've lost my mind," he thought.

There was a rustle in the brush and a blood-covered gray wolf trotted into the open thirty feet away. It stood, looking warily at him.

"Lady. It is you, isn't it," he said, softly. The wolf seemed about to flee. He realized he was still standing; a wolf reads the lowering of your body as friendliness. He quickly sat, whistled again, and held his arms out in the old invitation for a tussle and a belly rub.

Ren would never forget the next few minutes. The wolf dashed to him, and when close it performed the exquisite greeting postures of the wolf, with head tilted to one side, back humped, neck bowed, paws spread far apart, neck almost touching the ground—a quick, graceful, fluid action. A wolf, like some dogs, demonstrates its joy with its entire body.

As she moved, her topaz-colored eyes met his. A wolf's eyes are among the most expressive in the animal world. Afterward he remembered that meeting of eyes as a climactic moment. Somehow, he felt she perceived his emotions, as he did hers. There was real communication.

And then she was in his lap, whimpering, licking his face, tail wagging, head bowing. She leaped up and went around and around him, head low, ears laid back, tail whipping in excitement. He ignored the fresh moose blood as he ran his hands through her full coat, and talked. "Lady, Lady, it is you. Oh, but you're beautiful. I'm so happy to see you."

She lay next to him and rolled onto her back for him to rub her belly. Her coat was heavy and beautiful, and as he ran his hands over it he estimated her weight at 80 pounds. There were several scars on her muzzle, which is common; they probably came from disputes within the pack.

She leaped to her feet and lifted his cap off his head and carried it as she danced around him, teasing. She then dropped it on his lap without his having to demand it. She remembered her latest trick!

He didn't know how long the reunion lasted; afterward he remembered it as one of the most emotional times he could recall.

It ended abruptly.

Lady suddenly stopped moving and stood listening as a low howl came from a few hundred yards away. An answer came from another direction.

Lady instantly dropped her excited greeting behavior, and became a different wolf. Her tail dropped and her ears pricked up. Her eyes met Ren's for a long instant—another climactic moment—and without a backward glance, she quickly slipped back into the brush from whence she had come.

Lady had made her choice.

He sat for some time, exulting. "What an experience this has been," he kept telling himself. "I'd never have believed it."

༄

PAT HAD WATCHED Ren sneak down the hillside wondering what he was up to. He stopped in a small clearing and whistled. Was he whistling at her? He wasn't looking in her direction. Why was he whistling?

She centered him in the binoculars, puzzled. Then, suddenly, a blood-covered gray wolf appeared. Ren flopped onto the ground, and she gasped as the wolf leaped at him. Was it attacking? She almost jumped to her feet to go to his aid, for he seemed to be rolling and tumbling with the wolf.

But wait. Ren was grinning, and he was talking, although she couldn't hear him. *He was petting the wolf.* His hands were all over it. The wolf lay on its back and Ren vigorously rubbed its belly. Was she seeing things? How could this be?

The wolf snatched Ren's cap from his head and trotted around with it, then dropped it in his lap. The damned wolf was trained. Where would a wolf learn to do that?

Pat's bewilderment was complete.

Then she heard low howls from nearby wolves, and the gray wolf ran into the bushes and disappeared.

After the wolf left, Ren sat for a while, then slowly got to his feet. For some time he stood looking at the brush where the gray wolf had disappeared, then he motioned Pat to join him.

༄

WHEN PAT NEARED, Ren laughed at her bewildered expression. "Pat, you've just seen the climax and conclusion of a scientific experiment—and probably one of the biggest mistakes I've ever made as a biologist. And yet it was one of the most satisfying projects I've ever tackled." He was almost giddy with excitement.

"I thought that wolf was attacking you!" Pat said, accusingly. "I almost rushed to help you."

"Why, Pat. I'm sorry. I didn't mean . . . well, frankly I didn't really expect Lady to . . . what I mean. . . Forgive me. It must have frightened you," he apologized.

"When I saw you grinning I realized you and that wolf were buddies. Now, I know you're a wolf biologist and all that, but this beats anything I've ever heard of," she said, half humorously, half accusingly.

Ren hugged her and she hugged back. Both had just been through deeply emotional experiences, and the mutual hug was a wonderful release. Suddenly they were involved in a long, eager kiss—their first truly emotional physical joining.

The kiss ended, and Ren simply held her tight for a long time, his arms around her and her arms around his neck, her head on his shoulder.

It ended, they smiled at one another, and Ren, holding her hand, suggested, "Let's go check out that wolf kill."

"Ren Smith, you simply *have* to be the last of the great romantics," she laughed.

He smiled sheepishly, relieved that she saw the humor in it.

"You have blood all over you, including your face" she said, "And you've gotten me all bloody, too," looking down at her soiled clothing.

"Sorry about that," he smiled. "I guess it won't hurt us."

As they walked to the kill, Ren told her about Lady, choking up a bit when he told how he felt when he had released the wolf pup. Pat put a hand on his shoulder in sympathy.

"Prof warned us. 'Never get emotionally involved with individual animals; your responsibility is the population,' he said. "I got caught by that one for sure."

Pat was determined she wouldn't go queasy at sight of the kill, and she didn't. However she was pale, and didn't say much.

They stared at the multiple bloody slashes. Chunks of hide as large as a man's hand were missing; large skin flaps hung loose. Meat had been eaten from the hams. The belly had been cut open and viscera was strung out. Remnants of two fetuses could be seen; wolves had eaten most of both, leaving hooves and heads.

"She'd have dropped her twins within a few days," Ren said. "And she was in good shape. Look at all the mesenteric fat," pointing.

"Was she crippled?" Pat asked.

"No. She was vulnerable because she was pregnant—heavy with calf, awkward, and slow. As I've told you, wolves don't kill only the sick and crippled. If anything, pregnant cows and calves are the most valuable to the herd," he said.

Pat nodded. "I see what you mean. But you didn't have to prove it this graphically," she said, ruefully.

"Pat, this is the first time I've seen wolves kill a moose when I was on the ground. I've seen them attack moose when I was flying, but I never had a grandstand seat like we did this morning," he said.

Pat looked around nervously. "Will they come back?" she asked.

"Not with us here," he said. "But they'll be back. They won't waste this much meat so close to the den and their pups," he said.

Ren stopped examining the kill and faced Pat. "Now do you understand that the wolf is a killer?" he asked.

She nodded.

"In winter an adult wolf needs eight to ten pounds of meat a day. One wolf consumes the equivalent of about one moose every forty five days or so. A pack of nine needs a moose every five days, or more than seventy moose annually," Ren said.

He continued. "Humans are also killers. We eat meat and use a wide variety of other animal parts. But wolves don't have the luxury of leaving the butchering to a few individuals while the rest of the pack righteously looks the other way. Every pack member must help with the killing."

"It's cruel," she burst out, near tears.

"Yes, nature is cruel, and life can be cruel," he agreed, pulling her close, adding, "but it is dishonest to pretend it is otherwise."

⌒

THERE WERE MORE than a million caribou in Alaska during the 1920s. Three decades later, during the early 1950s, caribou numbers were at an all-time low of 140,000. Predation was likely the primary cause for the decline; human hunting didn't cause the reduction.

For years Glaser was the only full-time predator agent in Alaska, but gradually through the 1940s others were hired and put to work controlling wolves. One of the early success stories for the FWS predator control division in Alaska was with the Nelchina caribou herd, which ranges the vast Nelchina basin between the Wrangell and Alaska Ranges. In the 1940s, because these caribou were accessible by highway, about sixty five percent of the caribou legally killed by hunters in the Territory were taken from the Nelchina herd. But the herd was hard hit by wolf predation. For a time there were only seven calves per hundred adults in the fall counts.

Then Bob Burkholder, a federal predator agent at Palmer, and his cohort, Buck Harris, at Anchorage, started trapping and aerial hunting wolves in the Nelchina. Over a three year period they killed more than 300. Calves per hundred caribou jumped to fifteen—more than double the previous figure. As caribou increased in response to wolf reduction, the hunter kill (by humans) doubled. With good numbers of caribou in the herd, wolf hunting was halted, and wolves swiftly increased. The end result of wolf reduction was a land rich with both wolves and caribou.

Another area that suggested itself for reducing wolf numbers to benefit caribou was the treeless arctic slope north of Alaska's Brooks Range. In the early 1950s, wolves existed there in large numbers and caribou had decreased alarmingly. In March, 1952, the FWS organized an aerial wolf hunt using Umiat, on the Colville River, as the main base.

With three airplanes, all seven FWS predator agents in the Territory gathered at Umiat. Two of the planes were new 125-hp two-passenger (tandem) Piper Super Cubs; the third was a World War II three-seat Piper J-5 the crew called the "Gray Ghost."

Maurice Kelly, director of the predator control division, oversaw the operation and also flew as a gunner. Jay Hammond, a WWII ex-Marine fighter pilot with many hours of flight time (who later became Alaska's governor), flew the Gray Ghost, usually with Bob Burkholder as gunner. Buck Harris and Joe Miner flew the new Super Cubs, with, variously, Kelly, Doyle Cisney, or Frank Glaser as gunners. Glaser was by far the oldest of the crew at the age of 63.

In the first three weeks this crew killed 161 wolves, shooting them from the planes. By May, wolf numbers had thinned and only three or four wolves a day were being killed.

The arctic slope is a land of strong winds, and, in winter constantly drifting snow. In March, when the hunt started, most of the willow patches were covered by hard snow drifts, and there were few places for wolves to hide. Wolves of arctic Alaska have a variety of colors, including coal black, light gray, white, dark gray and, rarely, bluish.

Most packs had one or two blacks, which could be seen for miles on the snow. Often the hunters saw a black spot, flew to it, and found a black with several grays.

Flying the ski-equipped planes, they searched for wolves at an altitude of about 400 feet. When they spotted a wolf or a pack (generally from five to ten animals) they circled a mile or so away, dropped to within 40 or 50 feet of the ground, and flew directly toward them. The wolves usually ran straight away in single file. The pilot would fly on their left, and the gunner, using a shotgun loaded with buckshot, shot the wolves out of the right side of the plane, often at ranges of twenty or thirty feet.

The wolf is Alaska's brainiest wild animal. He learns well, and he learns fast. Usually the first pass at a bunch of wolves was easy, and shooting simple. But the second pass was often another story. By then surviving wolves would have learned a lesson, and some would weave back and forth on a dead run away from the plane.

Occasionally an unusually intelligent (or lucky) wolf learned to dodge sharply left when the plane neared, putting him under the plane and out of the gunner's sight. The wolf didn't know this, of course; he usually learned by accidentally dodging left and discovering he wasn't shot at.

One quick-learning wolf Glaser shot at was on the edge of a high mountain rim. The terrain forced pilot Joe Miner to fly at him from above, but each time the plane neared, the wolf leaped from the rim and out of sight, making him hard to see and even harder to hit.

Glaser fired eight or nine shots at that wolf as Miner made pass after pass over him for at least half an hour. Finally, Miner made a dangerous approach from below and pushed the animal into the open where Glaser finally dropped him.

Temperatures dropped to 40 and 50 below zero nights, and the hunters spent several hours each morning pre-heating the airplane engines. Each night engine oil was drained, and kept warm overnight. Mornings, after the engines were heated, the hot oil was poured back in, and the engines started.

While flying, Glaser wore a heavy seal skin parka, fur pants, and fur socks inside fur mukluks. Heavy gloves were essential to keep fingers from freezing. This made it awkward to handle a shotgun, which had to be thrust into the 60- or 70-mile-an-hour slipstream.

April 12, 1952, was a typical day of aerial hunting for Glaser. He and Joe Miner had been following movements of a caribou herd about fifty miles south of Umiat. Wolves had been killing its members. They flew to the herd and within fifteen minutes Joe pointed ahead to a lone gray wolf. He circled and flew about forty feet above the ground. As they neared the wolf, Joe unlatched the upper half of the Cub's door on the right side of the plane, Glaser opened the lower half.

Glaser released his safety belt and knelt with his right knee on the seat and poked the shotgun out the open door. The below zero air swirled into the airplane and he felt its bite on his fingers despite heavy wool gloves. The wolf was running from the plane, and he snapped the safety off.

Suddenly the wolf bolted left. Glaser couldn't shoot; if he had he'd have hit the propeller.

Joe swung the plane around and made another run at the wolf, this time flying within twenty feet of the ground. The plane was moving faster than the wolf, so Glaser had to hold *behind* it in a reverse lead. At his shot the wolf rolled end over end in the snow.

Joe circled, looking for a place to land. They recovered the hides of the wolves shot from the planes when possible, examined stomachs to determine what the animals were eating (mostly caribou), and checked females to see how many embryos they were carrying.

There was no safe place to land near this wolf, so they flew on, heading up the canyon of Chandler River. The valley was more than a mile wide as they approached five-mile-long Chandler Lake in a 4,148-foot-high pass. Near the lake they found a pack of five wolves feeding on a caribou they had just killed. After five passes and ten shots three dead wolves lay on the snow. The other two escaped. Glaser had to remove gloves to reload, and the slipstream sucked his right glove out of the plane. He continued to shoot without the glove and as a result, froze three fingers. He knew better, but in the excitement of the hunt, he was determined to continue shooting.

They landed within two miles of the wolves and snowshoed to them and took their skins. Two were black. The third was a gray female carrying seven unborn pups.

They then flew sixty miles west to the Killik River valley, where Glaser saw several running caribou high on a steep mountainside and tapped Joe on the back and pointed. Joe banked and climbed until they saw a black wolf chasing the caribou.

Glaser's shot was good on the first pass and the black wolf rolled over and over, dead. Joe made a hazardous landing; the plane stopping near the edge of a dropoff into a canyon. They skinned the wolf. Glaser then held the plane in place to keep it from sliding while Joe started the engine.

As the propeller bit into the icy air the skis started to slide and Glaser couldn't hold the plane any longer. He put his left foot in the step and threw his weight on top of the wing strut, holding onto the back of Joe's seat with his left hand. Suddenly the plane was moving swiftly, and became airborne with Glaser still outside the cabin, clinging to the lift strut and to Joe's seat.

The icy slipstream whipped the fur ruff on his parka into his face. He tried to yell at Joe, but the slapping fur all but stopped him. Then Joe saw him. He had the plane in a steep climb to avoid a mountain ahead, but he rolled the plane into a left turn and with his right hand grabbed the wolf ruff of Glaser's parka and yanked him into his seat.

Returning to the north slope, they found new snow, ideal tracking conditions. They soon crossed a fresh wolf trail. But which way were the wolves traveling?

Joe flew within ten feet of the ground and they examined the tracks. He saw where some of the animals had dragged their hind feet, revealing the direction of travel. In this case they saw where the wolves had left their trail to urinate on a lone clump of grass. The pack appeared to consist of five wolves. Joe followed the tracks east, and suddenly, there they were, five wolves curled up atop a low ridge, tails over faces, asleep.

They scattered. After three passes, three dead wolves lay on the ground. All were males, they found, when they landed and skinned them. One weighed an estimated 120 pounds. All had caribou meat in their stomachs, and all were fat.

Low on fuel, they headed for Umiat. Within five miles they located tracks of a lone wolf, determined its direction of travel, and followed it. Glaser killed it with one shot. They made a rough landing and skinned the large female, which carried five unborn pups.

They landed at Umiat late in the afternoon. Glaser's frozen fingers put him out of action for several weeks. The other agents continued the hunt until 259 wolves had been killed. Of these, 102 were recovered for their skins and biological information.

This was probably the largest scale wolf hunt ever conducted in the United States, and with the possible exception of modern Russia, probably in the world.

The results? Caribou increased exponentially on Alaska's North Slope.

Today (2002) two major caribou herds and one small one use Alaska's North Slope. The Western Arctic herd numbers about 430,000, and migrates north and south along the western end of the Brooks Range. The Porcupine herd—named for the Porcupine River which it often crosses in its annual migrations—numbers about 130,000. In recent years the Porcupine caribou herd has traditionally calved in Alaska (usually on the North Slope) and migrated deep into Canada's Yukon Territory in late fall and winter. The Central Arctic herd moves north and south generally to and from the Prudhoe Bay region.

Some of these caribou frequently spill through passes in the Brooks Range, including Anaktuvuk Pass.

Wolves recovered quickly from the 1952 kill; they are common today on Alaska's North Slope.

20

The Teller wolf

MOST WOLVES CAN be trapped, shot or killed in one way or another if a hunter knows his business. Once in a great while though, a wolf becomes wise to the ways of man and somehow manages to evade capture. At the same time it might kill many valuable livestock or game animals.

The Custer Wolf that lived near Custer, South Dakota, killed $25,000 worth of livestock. Despite a $500 bounty, it evaded hunters and trappers for at least six years. A government hunter finally killed this wolf in 1920 after hunting it full-time for six months.

As mentioned in an earlier chapter, another famous wolf was the 150-pound Lobo, made famous and dubbed "King of Currumpaw" by writings of Ernest Thompson Seton. For about five years this wolf killed many cattle and sheep in the Currumpaw region of New Mexico.

Three Toes of Harding County, South Dakota, was a livestock killer for thirteen years, destroying $50,000 worth of livestock. At least 150 hunters sought Three Toes before a government hunter caught him in the summer of 1925.

There have been others; the Aguila Wolf of Arizona, which for years killed a calf about every fourth night; Old Lefty of Burns Hole, Colorado, accused of killing 384 head of livestock over an eight year period; and Old Whitey, of Bear Springs Mesa, also in Colorado, known as a livestock killer for a reported fifteen years (a fifteen-year-old wolf would be the equivalent of a 105-year-old man). His track could barely be covered by a large man's hand.

Because of their depredations and because they had identifying color, marks, size, defects, or unique habits, these wolves earned their nicknames and became famous.

During Alaska's Territorial days, the goal of the federal government was to reduce wolf numbers because of their inroads on moose, caribou, deer, Dall sheep, and, of course, reindeer. During Frank Glaser's forty years as a private and government trapper in Alaska he encountered only one especially clever wolf he thought was on a par with some of the famous livestock killers of the Old West. He came to call this animal "The Teller Wolf," after the area in which it lived and hunted.

For nearly six years Glaser hunted, trapped, and finally, poisoned, wolves around reindeer herds. More times than he could remember he helped Eskimos gather scattered reindeer herds which had been stampeded by wolves. He couldn't eliminate all wolves around reindeer herds, but in the years that he spent trying to protect these deer he made an impact. He had removed many wolves, and he had taught Eskimos how to take wolves themselves. Wolf problems around reindeer herds decreased.

In early 1945 Glaser went to Teller, ninety five miles south of the Arctic Circle, on the Seward Peninsula, where the Native Service told him wolves were raising hell with reindeer. Teller, on the treeless, windswept tundra, was (and is) a tiny Eskimo village of sod and log igloos, some frame buildings, and a trading post.

He hired John Komak, an Eskimo who had a dog team, and they headed out, looking for the reindeer herd. They drove across wind-packed snow for twenty five or thirty miles and found both live and dead reindeer scattered everywhere. In one day Glaser counted more than 400 reindeer wolves had killed. They were lying atop the snow, some partially eaten, some killed and left without any part eaten. There was no telling how many reindeer carcasses were covered by drifting snow. Whenever deer saw the dog team coming they lit out running, spooky from being chased by wolves.

Frank returned to Teller, angry at being asked by the Native Service to go to this herd to kill wolves and finding that the herders weren't taking care of the deer. What he learned at Teller didn't help. Local Eskimos were helping themselves to the deer, both by killing them, and by using those the wolves had killed. They were feeding reindeer to their sled dogs, and eating the meat themselves.

He went to the trading post and asked Mrs. Marks, the owner's wife, "Where are the herders?"

"Aren't they out with the herd?" she asked.

"No."

"They must be playing cards," she said, pointing to a cabin.

Frank found five young Eskimo men sitting on the floor in the cabin playing poker.

"Are you fellows the reindeer herders?" he asked.

No answer. They looked at one another and started talking in Eskimo.

"Let's talk English," Frank said, getting more angry by the minute.

No answer.

Soon, in came Maggie Topkok, an Eskimo girl who worked for Mrs. Marks at the trading post. Her father owned an interest in the reindeer herd.

Glaser told Maggie what his troubles were, and she spoke sharply to the boys in Eskimo. They then started to answer his questions.

"Why aren't you with the herd?" Frank asked.

"Oh, Mr. Glaser, the wolves keep the herd scattered. No one can keep them together."

"All right," Frank told them, "I can kill the wolves but not with the deer scattered all over the country. You fellows round them up and get them within ten miles of town, and I'll go to work on the wolves."

They agreed to that, but Frank could see they were reluctant. He didn't realize why.

Next day the herders hooked four or five dog teams to a little plywood house on runners and dragged it ten miles or so from town, giving them a warm place to headquarter. They then started to round up the deer. Two or three days later Frank went out and found the animals bunched at Dese Creek, a willow-fringed stream in a shallow basin.

He pitched his tent near the herder's cabin, planning to stay close to the herd. That night he learned that the young Eskimos were half-afraid of the wolves, and he soon understood their reluctance to go back to herding. As he lay in his tent trying to sleep, wolves moved close to the herd and howled and howled. He had spent twenty five years living among Alaska's wolves, and he had never heard anything like it. A wolf song is beautiful, and he had always enjoyed hearing it. But that night, after a few hours, the continuous howling began to get on his nerves. Those wolves were unusually bold. They were aware of his and the herders' presence, but that didn't dissuade them. The continual howling also got on the Eskimos' nerves; the deer, also frightened by the howling, scattered into the black night.

That night wolves killed half a dozen reindeer and drove an unknown number into the hills.

The herders had to start all over again.

Wolves are difficult to trap in that open windy country, because traps are soon covered by drifting snow. Snares can't be used because there are no trees from which to hang them. Glaser had walked literally thousands of miles around reindeer herds with a rifle, trying to shoot wolves, with scant results. Strychnine baits and cyanide gas guns, commonly called "getters"—which he had learned to use the previous year in Colorado—were the only practical control methods, and he had started using them.

He picked his spots, his years of observing wolf habits telling him the most likely places, and put out bait stations and getters. He instructed the Eskimos to travel to and from the herd by a certain creek where he had made no sets, for he didn't want them to lose any sled dogs.

Glaser worked around the Teller herd all that winter of 1945-46, keeping getters and poison baits out and he pretty well cleaned out the wolves. Very few deer were killed by wolves after he had been there a while, and the herders kept the deer pretty well under control.

That summer passed without any wolf trouble at the Teller herd. In the fall of 1946 before it snowed, whenever the Eskimos butchered reindeer Frank hauled the entrails and heads out to knolls all around where the herd was kept. When winter came he asked the herders to keep the herd where he could surround it with bait stations. By November he had twenty five bait stations, reindeer guts and heads piled on windswept knolls with poisoned lard baits and getters around them.

Whenever a pack of wolves moved in, they would hit one of these knolls, and they would die. In December, a group of Eskimos traveling across the sea ice from Wales, a village on a peninsula sixty miles to the northwest, saw nine black wolves heading toward Teller. The animals were on the sea ice, about ten miles offshore. They told Glaser, who paid little attention, thinking the wolves had found some dead walrus on Point Spencer and it was unlikely they would ever get to the Teller reindeer.

But ten days later he found nine black wolves dead at one of his bait stations.

It went that way until January 1947. Every pack of wolves that arrived hit one of his stations before they reached the herd. No deer were killed, and the herders were pleased.

To add to their joy, Frank and his helper, Tony Bernhardt, a part-Eskimo with a lot of savvy (who, in the early 1970s served for a time with me on the Alaska Board of Fish and Game) found around 500 stray deer and drove them back to the herd, bringing it up to about 1,200 animals.

One day in January Frank went with Tony and his dog team to the herd on a routine check. They were met with three long-faced herders. "Six deer were killed by wolves last night, Mr. Glaser," one reported.

He looked at the carcasses and found by the tracks that a lone wolf had killed them. The wolf's tracks showed on the hard snow where it had dug in its toes. It had used the technique common to wolves in killing caribou; it ran beside a fleeing reindeer and slashed its flank. The stomach of the reindeer fell out, pulling the entrails with it. The deer traveled maybe fifty or sixty yards, pulling itself along with its front feet, with the hind quarters dragging, until it died. He found the six reindeer scattered over a stretch of perhaps half a mile, each with its stomach and entrails strung out behind.

While he was looking at the dead reindeer, Frank saw ravens rising and falling in the wind at a nearby knoll where he had a bait station. When he got there he found seven dead wolves, some black, some gray. As he stood looking at them, a gray wolf howled forlornly about a mile away on a nearby mountainside. He looked at it through his rifle scope and watched it run east toward the Sawtooth Mountains.

At the time he had no idea of the trouble that wolf would bring. To Frank it was just another wolf. He was sure it had been a member of the pack of seven killed at the bait station. Frank thought it saw the others die from the poison and it learned from that. He couldn't think of any other explanation for the behavior of that wolf that followed.

This was the Alaska of the mid-1940s, when wolves didn't have much of a chance to learn the ways of man. The Seward Peninsula was sparsely settled. Some of the famous wolves of the Old West learned about man where there were far more people.

Glaser learned a lot about that lone gray wolf during the next six or seven weeks.

A few days later, during a blizzard, six deer in the Teller herd were killed by a lone wolf. Each had been slashed in the flank, allowing the stomach and entrails to fall out. The right front foot of the killing wolf didn't spread normally; the killer was crippled.

The Eskimos hauled three or four of the deer home for dog food. Frank put poison baits around the others, using methods he had learned in Colorado. He also put poison in the ears of the slain reindeer, and cut some pieces of hide off and scattered them around with poison baits under them.

A few days later he found the crippled wolf's tracks all around the dead animals where it had circled and walked up to them. There hadn't been much wind for several days and the poisoned lard baits were lying on top of the snow. The wolf had cracked two or three of the frozen baits open.

He was sure it had eaten some of them, so he circled and found its tracks and followed them for about a mile. It never faltered. It hadn't eaten any of the baits. Frank began to wonder what kind of wolf he had come up against.

He set a bunch of cyanide getters around the dead reindeer. Day after day they remained untouched.

During a howling blizzard a few days later, seven more reindeer were killed by the same wolf. It ate a little out of one hind quarter, pulled a few tongues out to eat, and cut a few throats to lap up the blood. Again Frank put out lard baits and getters. He was now worried.

Wind blew all the next night, and he returned to find that the wolf had returned after the storm and circled the baits, but this time it hadn't cracked any open. It pawed some out from under pieces of hide, and had rolled them around on the snow, but it hadn't eat any.

That happened several more times over the next two weeks. Frank finally realized he was up against a wolf far more clever than any he had ever encountered. The Eskimos too, soon realized the wolf was different. One day when Frank arrived at the herd he found the four herders in their little shack, with the deer scattered. The Teller Wolf, as he had come to call it by then, had made a kill the previous night and the herders didn't want to go into the hills to round up the deer.

Loss to the herd came not only from the reindeer the lone wolf killed, but from those it scattered and were lost. The reindeer were now difficult to herd, for they were jittery from the wolf's depredations.

Frank had orders to leave Teller February 2 to go to Nunivak Island to count musk oxen, and he simply had to get that wolf before he left or it would wreck two winters' work. That lone wolf was capable of wiping out the Teller herd. It already had the herders intimidated.

The lone wolf with the crippled paw continued to kill reindeer, preferring to work in a blizzard and at night, and there were plenty of blizzards that winter. Day after day the wind blew, with temperatures ranging from zero down to 40 below.

From the wolf's tracks Frank learned that most of the time it stayed in the Sawtooth Range, otherwise known as the Kigluaik Mountains. It would leave the mountains to kill reindeer, then it would high-tail it back into the mountains. It didn't howl much, or at least the herders didn't hear it often, nor did Frank.

One day Frank found where the wolf had crawled up to one of his getters, put a paw on each side, and then very carefully licked the scent off. The least pull and the shell would have detonated, resulting in a dead wolf.

He could understand how a wolf might have learned of the danger from lard baits. Perhaps when it opened one it got a taste of the strychnine, or it saw the others in its pack die from eating the baits. But licking the scent off of a getter was hard for him to believe, and harder to understand. He was using the two most efficient methods he knew for controlling wolves, and the animal apparently wasn't going to be taken with either. He didn't know what to try next.

He kept putting out the standard scents with the baits, and setting getters, and the lone wolf continued to terrorize the herd. The herders were ready to quit and go back to the village and their cards, and he had to keep after them to stay with what deer were left. Secretly, he didn't blame them.

One day as he was making rounds of his sets he suddenly remembered that many years earlier he had experienced some unusual successes when he had used the scent of skunk to lure wolves.

That night he wrote to the government bait station at Pocatello, Idaho, requesting they airmail him some skunk musk.

On January 27 he made a trip around the bait stations with Tony Bernhardt and his dog team. There was no sign of wolves. The reindeer were scattered miles from the herders' camp, and Frank went to the camp to tell them where the deer were. The herders told him a wolf had killed three deer the previous night. It was 18 below zero, with drifting snow all day.

That day a box containing the skunk musk arrived in a foot-square carton. Inside was a wide-mouth quart jar packed in shredded paper. Inside the closed jar was a little jar, also packed in shredded paper. There wasn't a trace of skunk odor when he opened the box.

He was in his warm cabin and he thoughtlessly unscrewed the lid on the inside jar and the odor of skunk poured out, smelling up the cabin. Frank started coughing. He immediately screwed the lid back on, but it was too late. He had to live with that smell for days.

He added a few drops of the skunk musk to one of his regular scents, and put the rest in an outside cache.

Next morning Tony Bernhardt, driving his dog team, picked Frank up just before daylight. The dog team was lively, it was crisp and cold, and the sled banged up and down over hard snow drifts along the trail at a dead run. Tony began to cough.

"Mr. Glaser," he said, "what kind of scent have you made up now?" he asked, with a wry look.

Frank had spilled a drop or two of the skunk odor on his gloves, and the scent was strong in the cold heavy air. With the sled moving up and down, it hit Tony in waves. It was an unfamiliar smell to Tony; there are no skunks in Alaska.

When they arrived at the herd, Frank found two freshly-killed, blood-spattered reindeer stretched in the snow. The distinctive wolf tracks were all around. As usual, the killer with the crippled foot had come from the Sawtooth Range and had returned the same way after having its fun. The wolf had taken only a bite here and there from the two deer.

By then the lone wolf had killed fifty two reindeer from the Teller herd. It had driven at least that many away from the herd, so Frank figured a loss of at least 100 deer to that one animal.

On January 31, 1947 he found two more wolf-killed deer, with the signatory tracks of the cripple. He hauled a dead deer to the top of a high hill and made a bait station set—a getter with skunk scent. He also put lard baits on top of the snow with a little of his regular scent, made from rotten brains. He peeled a piece of hide back from the brisket and cut three holes in the frozen fat. Into each of the holes he put a poisoned skunk-musk-treated lard bait, then pushed the fat over each bait, covering them.

He went back to Teller to wait. Several Eskimos in the village spoke to him about the crippled wolf. "You've got to get that wolf, Mr. Glaser. There won't be any reindeer left if you don't get him."

He had to leave in two days.

The next night a wind came up, and the temperature was 20 below. Snow filled the air, streaking parallel to the ground. It was impossible weather.

Frank stayed in the herders' cabin near the reindeer herd and didn't sleep well, but lay awake off and on most of the night as wind rocked the little hut. He suspected the lone wolf would kill again during the blizzard.

The wind let up somewhat toward morning, the sky partially cleared, and there was fair light from the moon. Before dawn he decided to slip out to the herd to see if the wolf had been there. He put on his reindeer skin parka and sealskin pants, slipped into his snowshoes, and started off, rifle slung over his shoulder.

The wind was still gusting. Sometimes wind-blown snow blotted out everything; other times it would die and the moon gave enough light so he could see pretty well. As he neared the herd the wind picked up a bit. Through the blowing snow he saw a dark blob. It was just coming light, and when he reached the blob he found it was a dead reindeer, still warm, its bloody stomach and entrails strung out behind. Wolf tracks, still visible in the swirling snow, told him all he needed to know. The crippled wolf had killed again and it was somewhere near.

The wolf's tracks went upwind and Frank figured it was hunting for another reindeer. He unslung his .220 Swift and followed the tracks. They were clear and fresh. He could see about twenty feet through the flying snow. After a hundred yards of cautious walking he found another dead reindeer, also still warm. The wolf had killed it moments earlier.

From that dead deer he followed the wolf tracks up a knoll,

not even able to hear his snowshoes creak in the gusting wind and swirling snow. When he reached the top of the knoll, ahead perhaps twenty five or thirty yards he saw a moving, dim shape. It stopped, apparently to stare at him, and then it moved again. It was too small to be a reindeer, but in the blowing snow he couldn't see what it was.

As it started to disappear into the storm Frank suddenly realized it had to be the lone wolf he had been trying to kill. He pushed the safety off his rifle as he lifted it to his shoulder, centering the scope on the vague, moving blur. He snapped a Hail Mary shot, knowing his chance of connecting was small.

The movement stopped, and the blur remained in one place as he ran toward it, working the bolt, hoping for another shot.

It wasn't needed. His first shot had connected, and the wolf lay dead before him.

It was a gray female weighing about eighty pounds. One front foot was crippled; two toes and about half of the foot was missing—perhaps from a trap.

Frank had killed the Teller Wolf through pure luck. He hadn't outsmarted her at all.

21
Pat resigns: Love prevails: Moose John and Punyuk

"I'M NOT SURE I'm earning my keep with TNWSF," Pat told Jerry Hanson. She had flown to Boston to get her car out of storage and drive it back to Alaska. It was June, when nothing was happening with Alaska's wolf control program. It was a good time to get her car and have a talk with Hanson.

"You're watching what Alaska does with its wolves, aren't you?" he countered.

"Yes, but the state doesn't plan to kill any wolves until next winter, so there's no activity now. Also, my views have changed a bit about Alaska," she said.

"How have they changed?" he asked, a bit sharply.

"When I went to Fairbanks I was convinced Alaska wanted to kill as many wolves as possible, shooting them from airplanes. That view came largely from what I heard at your meeting, and the letters you sent out. I believed it all.

"I no longer believe that Alaska wants to kill every wolf, although it is true the Department of Fish and Game killed sixty seven wolves by shooting them from airplanes this past spring. I kept you informed about that, of course. But they killed only what they were authorized to by the game board, and that only in Game Management Unit 20A. I haven't heard any talk of the state killing wolves elsewhere, at least for now," she explained.

"Sounds to me as if you've been brainwashed," Hanson said.

"I'd say I've been educated," she said, slowly.

"Do you approve of shooting wolves from airplanes?" he asked.

"No. I don't agree with that, and I never will," she retorted.

"In your reports you've said you've become friends with one of the state biologists," he said. His voice insinuated her relationship was more than friendly.

"Yes, I have. And I don't like your insinuation," she retorted, hotly. She knew she was blushing, which only made it worse. "You told me to get friendly with the wildlife department biologists," she said, weakly. "I've gone flying with one of them several times, and I've seen wolves each time," she said. She hated to be defensive.

"Well, it's up to you, of course, how you do your job. Your assignment is to keep us informed on Alaska's wolf killing programs. You've kept us up to date on the program in 20A, and we've capitalized on that. Letters we've sent out asking for funds to fight Alaska's wolf-killing in 20A have more than paid your salary," he said, with satisfaction. "Don't worry, you're earning your keep."

"Let me show you something," he said, rummaging in his desk. He handed her a form letter. "This one really pulled in the money," he said with satisfaction.

A photo of a cute, tiny wolf pup appeared next to the TNWSF letterhead. She read, "Dear Friend of Wolves: Please look at this cuddly little wolf puppy. His name is Freedom, and he was born in Alaska where the state is shooting wolves from airplanes, claiming they kill too many moose. Actually, hunters and severe winters are killing most of the moose.

"When Freedom leaves his den and grows up he could be killed by a load of buckshot fired by an employee of the Alaska Department of Fish and Game flying in a small plane. We must stop this practice so Freedom can live up to his name, and his brothers and sisters can be freed of the fear of dying from a load of state-sponsored aerial buckshot.

"You can 'adopt' Freedom by sending a generous contribution to TNWSF and we will use it to fight Alaska's deadly wolf-killing program.

"Wolves are wonderful, gentle, animals that live in close-knit families, called packs. All members of the pack share food, and care of the pups. They are cuddly, warm, and affectionate. Wolves avoid humans. No healthy wolf has ever been known to kill a human. These animals are an important part of Alaska's environment.

"To justify slaughtering these marvelous, beneficial fellow creatures, Alaska has demonized the wolf as vermin that need to be destroyed. They even pay a $50 bounty for every one killed by citizens.

"We appreciate your commitment to the survival of Alaska's wolves. To thank you for your support of $15 or more, we'll send you a free tote bag and a poster of Lobo, our ambassador who accompanies us on our educational visits to schools throughout the northeast."

The letter was signed Jerry Hanson, President, Boston Chapter, TNWSF.

"But this isn't true," she protested. "Alaska doesn't pay a bounty on wolves. That ended six years ago. And where did that name 'Freedom' come from; is that just an imaginary pup you have dreamed up, or is there a pup somewhere named that?"

"It's imaginary, of course," he said. "But people who get our letters won't know that. And most people here don't know there is no bounty," he rejoined. "And the fact is, Alaska did pay a bounty on wolves for many years. If telling people they still do helps save wolves—and helps bring in dollars for our overall program—what harm does it do?"

"It's dishonest," she said. "I don't like it."

"It pays your salary," he reminded her.

"I don't care. I still don't like being dishonest," she exclaimed. "And this letter gives the impression the state of Alaska is killing wolves by shooting them from the air statewide. Their program, for now anyway, is limited to Game Management Subunit 20A, which is only one percent of the state."

"Do you want to stop them from shooting wolves from airplanes?" he demanded.

"Yes. But I want to do it honestly," she said. "And another thing. Are you still taking Lobo to grade schools, after what he did to poor Davie Foster?"

"Yes, of course. That wasn't our fault. The kid was trespassing. He had no business at Lobo's pen."

"I hear you're being sued by Davy's parents," she said.

"Yeah, but we have a good lawyer. We have a good chance of winning in court. If not, we'll probably settle out of court. It's no big deal."

Hanson's callous attitude as well as his dishonesty upset Pat. She fumed about it while having her car serviced in preparation for the long drive back to Fairbanks. Should she go back and have another round of arguments with him? She decided against it.

Pat called Allen Potter at work. He was surprised to hear from her, but he wasn't very cordial. She explained that she was driving to Alaska.

"You mean, you haven't moved home?"

"Not for a while, Allen," she said. "I rather like Alaska."

"I'd better tell you," he said in a formal voice, "I've found someone else, and we plan to be married."

That lifted a small burden, but she didn't let on. She had felt a bit guilty ever since he had told her he would wait for her when she turned down his marriage proposal.

"That's wonderful, Allen. It's time you got married. Congratulations. I wish you every happiness," she bubbled.

She didn't dare try to see little Davy. She knew she would break down at sight of his disability, and she still felt responsible. Nor did she try to see Beth. School was out for summer, and the class that was once hers was ready to move on.

It was fun to drive her little car again. She was relieved to get out of Boston traffic and be driving west. It reminded her of her exciting trip to Algonquin Park the previous summer. Though only twelve months had passed, so much had happened it seemed much longer.

Afterward Pat had little recollection of driving across country. Driving was automatic; she simply followed the long winding road, putting miles behind, stopping at motels overnight, eating at restaurants. Her mind was too busy to notice the passing land.

Six days after leaving Boston, when she entered Canada from Montana, with another 2,000 miles ahead of her to Alaska, she knew she could no longer work for TNWSF. But what should she do? Did she want to make Alaska her home? If so, how could she make a living? Where was her relationship with Ren Smith going? Was he seriously courting her, or was he simply doing his job as an employee of ADF&G trying to educate a "greenie" who opposed the state's wolf control program? If that was the case, what about her feelings? She was strongly attracted to the wolf biologist.

When she had first approached him as a newly assigned rep of TNWSF, she hadn't dreamed they would become close, as they apparently had. She was only trying to establish friendly relations with the enemy so she could do a better job. That had changed as she became acquainted with Ren; her feelings had become personal.

How would she feel if he dropped her? It was a bleak thought.

She passed Calgary and Edmonton and reached Dawson Creek, the beginning of the Alaska Highway, once called the Alcan Highway. As the miles rolled by and she reached the mountains, she began to appreciate the stirring scenery, and often stopped to snap pictures of spectacular mountains, valleys, and wild rivers. As she narrowed the distance to the Alaska border, there was a growing excitement within—a feeling of returning home.

Pat York, born and raised in Boston, excited over possibilities in Alaska? It didn't seem possible. She now knew her subconscious had made a decision. Come what may, she would remain in Alaska, at least for the foreseeable future.

She had a feeling of pride once she crossed the border into Alaska. She smiled when she saw and crossed the fast-running, silty, Tanana River, knowing it snaked passed Fairbanks—her home. She felt a smugness and a proprietary feeling for the magnificent scenic land around her and she ignored the abundant frost-heaves on the highway, as she drove the last couple of hundred miles home. Her mind was at peace. She knew what she had to do.

REN RETURNED FROM a ten-day assignment of flying a fellow ADF&G biologist on a count of caribou calves on the North Slope. He called Pat, but she didn't answer phone calls, nor was she home when he went to her house.

He checked every two or three days, and was disappointed each time. After a couple of weeks he became alarmed. Had something happened to her?

He checked with Gracie Bauer, but Gracie told him she hadn't heard from Pat, and didn't know where she might be.

He called the office of TNWSF in Boston.

"Can you tell me how to reach Pat York?" he asked.

"No," a man answered. "She's in Boston somewhere I think, but I don't know where she's staying."

"Will she be returning to Fairbanks?" Ren asked.

"I can't say. I don't know," the man said.

He spent a bad week living with the thought that he might never see her again.

He was relieved when she called.

"I missed you," he said. "I tried to call, but there was no answer."

"I called to let you know I was leaving for a while, but you were gone. I went to Boston to get my car," she explained. And then she said, "Ren, we need to talk. I have a few things I need to tell you."

"How about dinner tonight," he suggested.

"I'll expect you about seven" she agreed.

⌒

THEY CHOSE A QUIET booth in a small restaurant. She told him about her drive from Boston. He told her about his caribou-counting flights. They talked about the weather. Both had serious things to say, but each was reluctant. Finally Pat decided it was time.

"Ren, I want to talk seriously to you. I've resigned from TNWSF," she said.

She told him about her talk with Jerry Hanson, the lies in the letter he had sent out, and her objections to his callous attitude toward the lawsuit by little Davy's parents.

"I have to be honest with you," she said. "When I invited you to have coffee with me when we met at the University Library, I was doing my job for TNWSF. I wanted to use you to get information, and I wanted to try to persuade you to change. You were a public relations challenge."

He was smiling.

"Yes," he said. "Go on."

"You aren't angry?" she asked.

"Not yet. Is there more?" he asked.

"Well, as I came to know you and you were so kind in helping me, in giving me Snow, and showing up when I had all those silly crises, and you took me flying, and we spent a night together (he smiled at that), and you introduced me to your friends at Anaktuvuk Pass, and gave me that beautiful parka, well, my feelings toward you have become personal," she blurted in a rush of words.

"Now that I'm no longer with TNWSF, I hope we can continue to be good friends," she finished.

Ren tipped his head back and appeared ready to laugh. Instead he smiled broadly.

"So, you were willing to get friendly with me, to use me to your advantage," he appeared serious.

"Yes. I'm not proud of it," she admitted.

"How far were you willing to go?" he asked, leering.

"Not *that* far," she retorted, beginning to blush.

"Ever hear the saying, 'Hoist by one's own petard?'" he asked.

She nodded.

"I think both of us have been hoisted," he said with a broad smile. "When you invited me for coffee, I figured it was my job to try to convince the new bunny hugger she was wrong, and I made a special effort to be helpful. I took you flying, gave you a dog, bought you dinners. I even slept with you one night," he said, with a mischievous grin.

"But long before you went with me to Anaktuvuk Pass, my reasons for taking you flying and taking you out to dinner and all had changed. I worried when you disappeared. I finally realized something."

He went silent and gazed out a window for long moments. He then looked into her eyes and took the plunge. "I'm afraid I'm in love with you, Pat," he said.

Tears rolled down her cheeks. "I'm *afraid* I have the same problem, Ren," she said. "I'm *afraid* I'm in love with you." She giggled her relief, then teased as she wiped her eyes, "And, as usual, you simply *have* to be the last of the great romantics. What do you mean 'You're *afraid* you're in love with me?'"

In answer he held her eyes with his, and in a serious voice said, "I'd like to ask you to marry me, Pat, but I'm afraid you'll turn me down."

"You'll never know until you ask," she said, feeling guilty for baiting him, but unable to resist.

"Ok. Will you marry me?" he asked in a husky voice.

She smiled through her tears and answered, "Yes, Ren, I'll marry you."

☞

MOOSE JOHN MILLOVICH, 60, left Fairbanks in April 1933 to trap beaver at Beaver Creek in the White Mountains, sixty miles to the north. Without dogs, he pulled a sled, bucking spring snow through the rolling hills and low tundra to the big bend on the Beaver, a route that Frank Glaser followed on his trek to the White

Mountains in 1938. Moose John was an experienced outdoorsman who had previously lived on the banks of the Beaver. Neither he nor any of his many friends foresaw any danger there.

He was expected back in Fairbanks in late May, but July rolled around, and he hadn't returned. Two of his Fairbanks friends, George Bojanich and Sam Hjorta, hiked to the Beaver to look for him.

They found the door to Moose John's cabin open. Dates on a calendar were marked off through May 9. There were burned hotcakes and burned bacon in a pan on the wood stove. The table was set with clean dishes and silverware. But there was no Moose John.

The two men searched upstream and down for several miles, thinking their friend might have fallen into the river and drowned. After three or four days of fruitlessly scouting along the river they were ready to give up. About the only sign they'd found were wolf tracks all around the cabin. Wolves occasionally howled from the hills as they made their search.

They finally reasoned the missing man must be somewhere near the cabin, since he obviously wouldn't wander far while cooking breakfast, so they started circling the cabin, covering ground inch by inch.

Less than thirty feet from the cabin, in a stand of knee-high redtop grass, one of the men found a human thigh bone under some large spruce trees. It had been cracked open by a powerful-jawed animal. Soon they found a human skull with part of the hair and scalp still attached. Other human bones were found near.

George Bojanich told Frank Glaser later that all they found of Moose John just filled a five-gallon can. Ribs and all the small bones were missing. His clothing had been widely scattered through the gloomy spruces, with an occasional bone clinging to the cloth by bits of dried flesh.

Bojanich and Hjorta decided that wolves killed Moose John. There were certainly plenty of wolves in the White Mountains at the time. Moose John had trapped the region for marten the previous year, and the howling of wolf packs had made him so jittery he was glad to leave in the spring. Wolves get hungry when there are few or no caribou or moose, which was the case in the region at the time, and wolves *do* become bold.

Did wolves kill Moose John? No one will ever know. Wolves

almost certainly ate him, for his bones were cracked open, strong evidence that wolves chewed on them. They were not buried. If a grizzly had eaten from the body chances are it would have covered the remains with vegetation and dirt. Also, wolf sign was all around the cabin a couple of months after the apparent date of Moose John's death.

Glaser thought about that incident for a long time. George Bojanich told him every detail when he and Sam Hjorta returned after burying Moose John's remains. Also, in 1938, five years after Moose John's death, Glaser lived for many months in the Fossil Creek cabin where Moose John died. Bojanich and Hjorta had buried the can holding the trapper's remains about twenty feet from the door, in front of the only window. Glaser spent hours sitting at that window, eating, writing, and reading and every time he glanced out he saw Moose John's grave and the cross over it.

Although Bojanich, Hjorta, and others believe wolves killed the trapper, Glaser didn't think so. He said there are many possible explanations for his death. Moose John was 60, and might have died of a heart attack while throwing out garbage near the cabin. Wolves could have found and eaten his remains.

While Glaser was in the White Mountains on one of his patrols searching for wolves, he was crossing a rock slide when a thin, mouse-colored old grizzly charged him, jumping down the slope toward him. Glaser fired at it, and the bear passed not more than six feet away, turned, and started back for him. He then shot the bear in the neck, putting it down for good.

Others have had similar experiences with grizzlies in the White Mountains. The bears there, for some reason, are unusually aggressive. Glaser didn't know why, unless because it's hungry country grizzlies *have* to be aggressive if they're going to eat.

Moose John had trapped eight or nine beavers before he died and he didn't have dogs to eat the carcasses. He had probably tossed the skinned beaver in the snow in front of the cabin. Bears usually have been out of hibernation for a week or so by May 9, when he stopped marking his calendar, and Glaser suspected that one of those aggressive spring-hungry grizzlies was feeding on beaver carcasses when, for some reason, Moose John walked near and was swatted down. Glaser believed that was much more likely than wolves killing him.

YEARS LATER, AND far to the north, Glaser investigated a case in which there was no doubt that a wolf had attacked a man. It was January when Glaser received a message from Marge Swenson, teacher-nurse at Noorvik, an Eskimo village on the Kobuk River, who had a daily radio schedule with Kotzebue, where Glaser was then living. "Please come to Noorvik. A wolf has attacked a local resident."

Glaser hired a dog team and drove the fifty miles to Noorvik, taking two days for the trip. It was cold, stormy, and mostly dark, as the North is at that time of year. He arrived four days after the wolf had attacked an Eskimo named Punyuk.

The evening Glaser arrived, Marge Swenson went to Punyuk's house to change his bandages and Glaser went with her to hear the story from the old Eskimo himself. He lived in a small, crowded, log cabin, which is unusual in that mostly treeless country where logs have to be hauled many miles. Punyuk was lying on a low couch when Glaser and the nurse entered the lamp-lit, smoky cabin.

Punyuk, 63, knew only a few words of English. His married daughter, who assisted Swenson at the school, interpreted his story for Glaser.

Punyuk had been living in a stove-heated tent and trapping on a ridge between the Kobuk and Selawik Rivers. His sled dogs were tied to willows near the tent. During early evening he heard his dogs growling and making a fuss. Stepping outside, Punyuk saw what he took to be one of his dogs running loose. It was dark, but the moon and stars reflecting from the snow gave fair light. He picked up a chunk of ice from a pile he kept to melt for cooking and drinking and tossed it at the "dog" and ordered it to come.

When the ice hit the animal it rushed Punyuk, jumped up with its front feet on his shoulders, and bit at the top of his head. Punyuk realized instantly it wasn't one of his dogs, both from its behavior and its size. It was twice as big as any of his dogs. He was dealing with a wolf.

The animal knocked him down and started chewing on his head. It ripped three or four places clear to the skull, and tore the whole length of his scalp before Punyuk grasped the animal's throat and managed to get his knees on it and choke it down. He got a small pocket knife out after the animal had relaxed a bit from being choked, and slashed with it a few times. He didn't stab.

He stood up, looked closely, and saw for sure it was a black wolf. He didn't try to finish it off.

Figuring that a trapper normally would have a pile of wood outside his tent, Glaser asked his daughter, "Did he have some stove wood there, or an axe?"

"Yes."

"Then why didn't he hit it with a piece of wood or axe and kill it?"

She talked with him for a long time then, and he seemed reluctant to tell her. Finally she said, "My father cannot kill a black wolf."

That puzzled Glaser at the time, but he learned later that many Eskimo elders believed that when some old village grandmother died, her spirit would go into a wolf, preferably a black wolf. To kill one was like killing a respected old woman.

Punyuk stood over the black wolf he had choked into unconsciousness until it revived, making no move to harm it.

"You have hurt me enough, grandmother," he said. "Now go and leave me in peace."

As his daughter translated, Glaser tried to picture simple old Punyuk standing in the arctic moonlight, his scalp loose, blood running down his head and face, talking to the wolf.

Marge Swenson dressed his wounds as Punyuk told his story. It was a strange setting in the dim light of the tiny cabin, and the old Eskimo's gutteral tones emphasized the bizarre tale. He didn't wince as Marge pulled the blood-stuck bandages free and probed to drain his wounds.

The wolf recovered after the old man had talked to it. It got up and sank its teeth deep into Punyuk's right thigh. The Eskimo wore a pair of overalls, having just stepped from the heated tent. If he had had his regular outdoor wear of sealskin pants he'd have had better protection.

The wolf lifted him clear of the ground and threw him down, then placed his forepaws on him and pulled, trying to tear a chunk out of his thigh.

Glaser could see bone in the two main holes in his leg where the wolf's upper canines had entered. On the opposite side, where the two lower canines had penetrated, he saw a couple of ligaments or cords the teeth had caught as the animal tried to pull out a chunk of meat. They were terrible wounds.

When the wolf found it couldn't yank a chunk out of Punyuk's leg it let go, and Punyuk struggled to his feet. But the wolf jumped up and grabbed his shoulder, biting twice clear to the bone. Then it tried Punyuk's head again, driving one tusk in just above his ear. If it had been a little lower, it probably would have killed him.

Evidently Punyuk passed out then, for his daughter said, "My father didn't know any more."

When Punyuk revived, the wolf was gone and his dogs were barking. He dragged himself into the tent and washed the blood off, bandaged himself crudely, and put on his fur clothes. He crawled around harnessing his dogs, and crawled into his sled and the dogs pulled him to Noorvik.

When Punyuk told the story to his two sons, they immediately harnessed a dog team and left to track down the wolf. The old beliefs didn't mean anything to them.

As they followed the wolf's tracks they found a little blood, and saw where it had staggered and fallen a number of times. Several times it went out of its way to attack a lone spruce tree and to chew limbs from it.

The trail zigzagged to the village of Kiana, about twelve miles from Punyuk's camp. When his sons arrived there they learned that someone in the village had killed the wolf as it was eating some malemute puppies.

The day after Punyuk told Glaser his story he went to Kiana. The wolf had been skinned, but he found the carcass and cut off the head. The animal was an adult in good condition, weighing more than a hundred pounds.

Glaser turned the wolf's head over to Dr. Bauer of the Native Health Service in Kotzebue who sent it out to a laboratory. For some reason the lab report didn't get back to Kotzebue for several months, too late to help Punyuk. In March word reached the reindeer camp where Glaser was working that the old Eskimo was dead. He had apparently recovered from the wolf's attack, then had died suddenly while lying on the ice and fishing for sheefish.

The laboratory confirmed what Glaser suspected; the wolf had rabies. By then, of course, all the excitement had died down and many people, in saying Punyuk was attacked by a wolf, let it go at that. One account published in a national magazine said that Punyuk died of his wounds shortly after being attacked by a wolf. Rabies wasn't mentioned.

Glaser didn't know of any proven instance of a healthy, normal wolf attacking a human. He tried to learn as much as possible about every reported attack in Alaska during his years as a federal wolf hunter.

In the 1940s while Glaser lived in Nome during his wolf-controlling assignment among reindeer herds, he made a trip to Fairbanks. As he started to walk into the Nordale Hotel for a room, he was astonished to see a big gray wolf crouched in front of the doorway. A woman was holding it by a leash.

"That's a nice wolf you have there, lady," he said, as he took the leash and skidded the animal aside so he could walk through the door.

"It isn't a wolf. It's a dog," she shouted after him as he went to the desk to register.

He read in the paper that night that the city council had called a special meeting to warn two or three people who had young wolves from the same wild litter to get them out of town or they'd order them destroyed. They were a danger to kids and even to adults who might encounter them.

The half-tame wolf Glaser dragged out of the doorway at the Nordale Hotel was frightened. Glaser saw fear in its eyes, and it was flattened out on the sidewalk, afraid to move. A half-tame wolf is dangerous. There's no telling how it might react if a youngster pulled its tail or tried to pet it. Glaser told me the city council had made the right decision.

But a wild wolf is different. Glaser believed humans are safe from attack by healthy, normal wolves in the wild.

22

Wolverine village: Uncle Toby: Glaser retires

REN ARRIVED AT Pat's home carrying a box of candy and a large bouquet. She laughed when she saw the gifts.

"Isn't this what a man is supposed to do when he calls on his best girl?" he asked.

"Yes, Ren. Thank you. You're very thoughtful."

Once inside he wrapped his arms around her, and after kissing her held her for a long time.

"This weekend I'd like to take you home to Wolverine to meet my family and have you see where I grew up," he said.

"Two sleeping bags?" she asked, sweetly.

He laughed. "How about one sleeping bag?"

"Sure," she said, "provided it comes with a license."

"License?" he asked.

"A marriage license," she laughed.

"Deal," he said. "We'll take one to Wolverine with us. I'll bet we can get Pop Rainey to marry us there. He's the local Episcopal priest. He has ministered to our family for as long as I can remember."

"You'd like that, wouldn't you?" she asked, softly.

"I was hoping you'd like the idea."

"I love it," she said. "I've always thought if I ever got married it would be in June."

"I'll bet you never dreamed you'd marry a bunny-hugger," she teased.

"Leave the bunny off, and you can hug me all you want," he shot back.

PAT WAS NERVOUS in Ren's Cub on Saturday morning as they flew from Fairbanks to Wolverine. Flying with Ren didn't worry her; it was the thought of meeting his family. What if his mother didn't like her? She was a *cheechako*, and she had arrived as an adversary to Ren. She realized it would take years for her to absorb the culture of Alaska; now she would be faced with trying to understand and absorb the culture of his Athabaskan people. She thought of the tiny one-room houses she had visited at the Inupiat village of Anaktuvuk Pass. Would the houses in Wolverine be so small? Would the villagers accept her?

Two hours after leaving Fairbanks Ren pointed ahead. "Wolverine," he called, as he reduced throttle to descend. He circled the village twice. Pat looked down on the neatly arranged log cabins on the spruce-forested west bank of the clear Koyukuk River. Wood smoke rose lazily from stovepipes, and she actually smelled it. Boats were pulled up on the beach. Several float planes were tied to small docks at the river's edge. She saw an aircraft runway with a hangar at the end nearest the village. Several wheel planes were parked near. Then she saw a small crowd gathering at the water's edge near one of the docks.

Ren glanced back at Pat and grinned. "That's the welcoming committee. They recognize my plane and they've heard you were going to be with me. I'm related to half the people here."

Ren eased to a landing on the river and taxied to where the crowd stood waiting. He killed the engine, allowing the plane to drift close. Eager hands caught the Cub and tied it to the dock. Ren was out of the plane in an instant and helped Pat out.

Dusty stepped from the crowd and hugged her. "Welcome home, daughter," he spoke quietly into her ear. "We're pleased to have you in the family."

"This is Ren's mother, Hannah," Dusty introduced.

Pat turned to see a beautiful, slim, youthful looking woman. Her skin was the color of old ivory, and her dark hair was beginning to gray. She wore slacks and a man's wool jacket, which emphasized her femininity. She immediately hugged Pat after exclaiming, "Oh, you *are* beautiful. We're so happy Ren has brought you home. We were afraid he was never going to marry. Welcome to Wolverine, Pat York."

Then followed a confusion of hugs and handshakes as Ren introduced her. First was Ren's sister Blanche, a matronly woman with a warm smile. Her husband Roger, who appeared to be full Athapaskan stood shyly near.

"You never told me you had a sister," she accused Ren.

"You never asked," he replied.

Next came Ren's brother Bill, in appearance a smaller edition of Ren.

"He lives in Seattle," Ren said.

"You know, it's not too late to back out," Bill told her, smiling. "Are you sure you want to marry this bum?"

She laughed, relieved by the overwhelming welcome.

Most of the others in the crowd were cousins, aunts, uncles, nephews, nieces, and friends. How could she ever remember all their names?

"Come. Let's go up to the house," Hannah urged after Pat had been introduced to what seemed to be everyone in the village.

Ren called to one of the teenagers, "Timmy, would you bring our bags from the plane, please?"

"Sure, Uncle Ren," he said, cheerfully.

The Smith home was a large, two story, gracious log house, with a huge rock fireplace in the main room. There were half a dozen fine paintings of wildlife and spectacular Alaska scenery, a mounted full-curl Dall ram trophy head, and a large grizzly bearskin rug, with comfortable overstuffed chairs and couches. Book-filled shelves lined one side of the big room.

"This used to be Blanche's room," Hannah said, showing Pat to an upstairs bedroom. "When you get freshened up, come down and we'll have coffee."

It was a family gathering, with Dusty, Hannah, Blanche, Bill, Ren and Pat. Conversation was filled with teasing and laughter. Pat was included, and she was grateful for their consideration.

During a lull she asked Bill, "What do you do in Seattle?"

Ren jumped in to answer, answering Pat, kidding Bill, "Oh, he's an ambulance-chasing sawbones."

"Ren," Hannah scolded. "He's an orthopedist, and you know it. He came home just for your wedding, and you shouldn't insult him."

"Yes, Mama," he said. "I'm sorry. I just don't want him to get a swelled head."

"It's all right, Mama," Bill said, "He's just jealous because he got the wrong kind of a doctor's degree."

Later Ren took Pat on a tour of the village. "We should visit Uncle Toby first," he said. "He's regarded as the chief, or the village elder. Uncle Toby knows more about what is happening in Alaska—and the world—than any other person I know. He has a shortwave radio and gets news from everywhere; he reads *Newsweek* and *Time*, and a dozen other magazines, as well as *The Fairbanks News Miner*, the *Anchorage Times*, and the *Wall Street Journal*. He practically memorizes the ADF&G bulletins and reports I bring him.

"As a boy he was sent to the Eklutna Vocational School, run by the Bureau of Indian Affairs, near Anchorage. While there he won an essay contest and as a reward he was sent to a specialized high school and after that to a small eastern college. None of those school exist now, but at those schools Uncle Toby learned to read and speak like a scholar. We're all in awe of him.

"Please don't be upset if he quizzes you on your views on hunting and animal rights," he warned.

Pat remembered meeting tiny, wizened, gray-haired Uncle Toby at the dock. He wore bifocal glasses perched on his wrinkled face and spoke slowly in a deep, cultured voice.

She was nervous as Uncle Toby welcomed them to his modest log cabin. His wife, Aunt Molly, almost as wrinkled as Toby, obviously expected them, for she had fresh coffee brewed and there was a hot, freshly-baked loaf of bread with blueberry jam on the kitchen table where they sat. Pat realized she was learning something of the protocol in this village; a courtesy visit to the village elder was the first order of business.

After talking about the weather, the current high level of the Koyukuk River, the possibilities of the season's salmon run, and Ren and Pat's flight from Fairbanks, Uncle Toby got down to business.

"My sister Hannah tells me you have resigned from your job with The National Wildlife Savers Foundation. Is that true?"

She was amazed that he knew the name of the organization, and blurted, "You know the name?"

"Of course," he said calmly. "We must keep track of the various organizations that would destroy our way of life. Nowadays there are many of them."

"Oh," she exclaimed, "I had no idea."

"Miss York, my nephew has told us you are a fine person, that you are learning about Alaska, and that you have an open mind. That he has brought you home to marry you is proof of that. You have many things to learn, and we want to help you all we can.

"Thank you Uncle Toby—may I call you that?"

"Of course. You are now to be a part of our family. Now let me tell you a few things about our lives. Today eighty percent or more of U.S. citizens live in urban or suburban areas. These city folk have little understanding or compassion for those of us who live off the land, and even for the farmers who also make their living from the land.

"They buy everything they eat. They hunt for their meat in super markets. They have little idea what takes place when an animal is raised, shipped to a slaughterhouse, killed, and butchered. To them "beef," "pork" or "lamb" is a piece of meat wrapped in plastic that is ready to cook. Some probably don't even know that meat comes from living animals."

He smiled at that, making clear he knew he was exaggerating.

"One of the strange results of the urbanization of America has been the formation of anti-hunting groups, and even worse, environmentalists and animal rights organizations whose members seem to believe that mankind has no place in this world. Those who live in cities are so far from the land they hardly know where food comes from. Because they live in a plastic world they want everyone to live in a plastic world. They believe fools who tell them what sounds pretty to them. The more removed people are from the land, the more susceptible they are to environmental extremism."

Pat was amazed. She had come across an intellectual in the remote village of Wolverine. She hardly knew what to say.

"If Ren has been talking about me, and he apparently has," she said, looking at Ren, "you must know I grew up in Boston. My six months in Alaska have been very educational. I am learning, and I want to learn more."

"Good," Uncle Toby beamed. "By now you may have learned it's tough nowadays being an Alaska Native. Anti-hunting groups get angry at us because we endorse aerial wolf control. We know it works. Animal-rights groups like the one you worked for get angry with us because our lives are tied to wild animals and the killing of those animals. These people would stop us from hunting and trapping, which has been our way of life for centuries, and the only way we can survive. Without hunting and trapping we would die as a people.

"The organization you worked for is one of the most radical. They would stop use of animals for anything—food, clothing, medical research, pets. That would mean no milk, no wool, no way to test new surgeries or new drugs, no seeing eye dogs, no family with man's best friend, a dog. No zoos. In our view they are insane.

"Such people ignore biology; if animals are not harvested, they can destroy their environment. Look at the suburban deer in the eastern states. They overpopulate, then die of starvation. Yet urban people oppose hunting them. Do you think ranchers would allow their livestock to overpopulate their valuable grazing land? They also ignore the fact that wolves reproduce rapidly; they complain that wolves will never recover if even a few are removed to allow depressed moose and caribou herds to rebuild.

"The true agenda of animal rights is not to give rights to animals, but to take rights from people.

"Such a view is, simply, illogical. To give in to these views would be foolish—you cannot compromise with people who value animals more than humans."

Pat wanted to tell him she had never embraced the non-use of animals advocated by TNWSF, but thought it better to listen. Clearly, he loved to talk. He was obviously knowledgeable, she decided, and she could learn from him.

"I understand you came to Alaska because you objected to the state killing wolves," he said.

She nodded.

"Everyone has an opinion on how wolves should be managed. This, of course, depends on one's interests. Some view the wolf as all good. Some view the wolf as all bad. Trophy hunters have their own agenda. Wildlife photographers also. In Alaska, those who depend on moose and caribou for food—the rural residents and many Native and non-Native hunters in urban areas—have a much different viewpoint from that of non-hunting residents. Tourists have their view—they want to see abundant wildlife, including wolves. Those who like to hike in the wilderness usually have a similar viewpoint to the tourists. All want their particular view to be the primary one to determine how the wolf is managed.

"The peculiar aspect of this is that most want the same thing—an abundance of moose, caribou, wolves, sheep—whatever—as well as a healthy population of wolves. The disagreement on how to achieve this comes largely from an ignorance of biology."

Pat asked, "But, does the wolf have to be managed? Can't we just leave the wolf alone and let nature take its course?"

Uncle Toby nodded. "Of course. That is one option. You have touched upon the very heart of the argument. Now, let me give you my viewpoint, which comes from a lifetime here in the Koyukuk valley. I freely admit that my view differs from that of many others. But then, I live with wolves, and I depend upon moose for food."

He sat thinking for a few moments, then continued in his slow, deep voice. "Only in recent years have our Koyukuk wolves been managed. Long ago nature took its course because there was no choice. Bows and arrows and deadfalls were not efficient in taking wolves, and wolves sometimes became too abundant. As a result, we had either feast or famine. But today we have a choice. The wolf is no different from other wildlife; it needs to be managed. Modern game management works—when it is given a chance.

"When I grew up in the 1920s and 1930s there were no moose here in the Koyukuk valley. Oh, one occasionally wandered in, but it was hungry country, and when anyone found moose tracks, they followed the moose until they killed it. The family then moved to the moose and remained there until the moose was eaten to the last scrap.

"We have oral traditions that have been passed from generation to generation telling of Koyukon people often starving before the white man arrived. Our people were constantly on the move, always going to where they could get food—animals they could catch, fish they could trap. In my younger years we depended mostly on fish, small game, and caribou, for our meat. There were few moose.

"Moose began increasing in the Koyukuk Valley in the late 1930s. By the 1940s moose were a dependable source of food. They were our livestock—as important to the people in the villages along the Koyukuk River as cattle, sheep, and hogs are to people who live in the South 48 states. When a family kills a moose in the fall, it has the same importance to them that money in the bank has to a city-dweller. It means, simply, food for winter.

"Raising wild animals isn't much different from raising farmed or ranch animals. The advantage is, you don't have to change the natural environment. There are no fences and there is little use of fossil fuels, no fertilizers to run into streams and lakes, no man-made hormones—and the meat produced is lean and healthful. In other words, when we 'ranch' moose, we have virtually no impact on the environment. By 'ranching' I mean modern game management. And, of course the moose, like other animals, including the wolf, is a perpetually renewable resource.

"Are you aware that Alaskans statewide annually harvest around 15 million pounds of high quality protein from moose, caribou, Dall sheep, mountain goat, deer, bison, and elk?"

"You are well informed, Uncle Toby," Pat said

"Yes. I read a lot. And my nephew," with a glance at Ren, "provides me with reports and bulletins from ADF&G. It is important that we stay informed."

He continued, "Wolves increased as moose numbers grew in the Koyukuk. At first there was no problem—there were enough moose for us, and for the wolves too. We were happy to trap and shoot the wolves for their fur and for the bounty the Territory paid. We used the furs for our winter clothing, and sold or traded them for things we need from stores like rifles, ammunition, and flour.

"Please understand, Pat, we do not hate the wolf. That would be like hating ourselves, for the wolf and our people both belong to this land. We admire the wolf for his intelligence, and for his ability to kill.

"But when the wolf becomes overabundant and game is plentiful, he can be wasteful. There is more to tell you, then I'll stop. I know I talk too much. Please forgive me."

"Oh, no, Uncle, please continue," Pat said.

The old man was a wonderful story teller, and she realized she was learning much from him about the Koyukon people and their home region.

It all seemed like a dream to her—to be in this tiny arctic village, in a log cabin, surrounded by thousands of square miles of wilderness, 200 miles from the nearest road, being lectured to by this intelligent village elder. He was doing it kindly, but she got the message; she, a city person, had come to the frontier state of Alaska with preconceived ideas. To this old man and his people, reducing wolf numbers could insure food for winter. She remembered too vividly watching wolves kill the cow moose. He was telling her about a world she hadn't even known existed.

"All right," he said. "One last story. By the mid-1950s wolves seemed to be everywhere in the Koyukuk Valley and our people began finding moose they had killed and had only partly eaten. In 1956, Donald Stickman, a Koyukon who owned a small air charter service on the lower Yukon, saw dead moose scattered across many gravel bars of the Dakli River, a tributary to the Koyukuk.

"He landed and found that wolves had killed the moose. They had eaten some of the tongues, and had ripped the moose open to get at the fat, kidneys, and livers. Much of the red meat was wasted.

"Stickman remembered the hungry years, when there were no moose in the Koyukuk. When he found those dead animals, moose was the single most important source of meat for the Koyukon people. It angered him to find those wasted animals.

"How would you feel if you raised beef cattle for food and found dozens of them slaughtered with most of the meat left to rot?

"Stickman then flew up and down the valley and saw wolves almost everywhere.

"At the time a citizen could get a permit to hunt wolves with an airplane. Stickman got a permit, and with Jimmy Huntington, another Koyukon Indian as his gunner, started hunting wolves, shooting them from an airplane.

"In the winter of 1956–57 Stickman and Jimmy Huntington killed 149 wolves in the Koyukuk valley. During the next winter they killed another 150.

"That was enough to change the balance, and they stopped hunting. They didn't want to kill all the wolves, but they had killed enough so the moose were no longer threatened with decimation. Now there were enough moose to satisfy the needs of both our people and the wolves. Their aerial hunting was a form of wildlife management. Those two, on their own, established a reasonable balance between wolves and moose in the Koyukuk Valley. Because of their efforts we still have a good moose population, as well as more modest numbers of wolves.

"The TNWSF, which you worked for, would halt all aerial hunting of wolves. That could be disastrous to us. Last December the proposal before the Board of Game to remove a few wolves was for Game Management Unit 20A. Next time it could be Unit

24—the Koyukuk Valley. Thank God we have a governor who appointed good people to the board, and who backs the board and the department in their decisions. If we ever get a governor who appoints board members who are animal rights advocates, or if we get a governor who doesn't have the backbone to stand behind the board and the ADF&G in their decisions, we rural residents could be in deep trouble.

"End of story," Uncle Toby said. "Now that's enough lecturing. I'm sure my nephew will teach you how to be a true Alaskan. You will learn more from him how we live from the land."

"Thank you, Uncle Toby, for helping me understand something of village life," she said.

Nevertheless, she still had a horror of wolves being shot from airplanes. She didn't dare mention it to this old man.

"We're pleased that he has found you," Uncle Toby said, "and that he is finally getting married. Welcome to our family, Pat York."

⌒

PAT AND REN were married on Sunday, June 22, 1976, by The Reverend Roland ("Pop") Rainey in the beautiful log church at Wolverine, so Pat's dream of being married in June came true. Since she had no family, and Bill was to become family, she asked him to give her away. The church overflowed, for the wedding was attended by all the residents of Wolverine and many of Ren's relatives from up and down river. For their honeymoon Ren flew them to a cabin he owned on a remote lake in the Brooks Range.

Saturday evening as they loaded the Cub, preparing for the honeymoon flight, Pat watched Ren stuff two sleeping bags into the back of the Cub.

"Two sleeping bags?" she asked.

"Yep," he responded with a grin. "You didn't know it, but those two bags zip together to make one. We've been flying with one sleeping bag all along."

⌒

DURING THE FIRST decade after statehood, Alaska's moose, caribou, sheep, and deer reached unheard of population highs. Many Alaskans believe the wolf control program of the FWS during the

1950s brought about the sudden and almost explosive increase. Did it?

No one knows for sure, for no long-term Territory-wide scientific evaluation studies accompanied the federal wolf control program. North Slope caribou increased dramatically after the aerial wolf kill there in 1952 when 259 wolves were killed, and it is difficult to argue this increase didn't result from wolf control. Caribou also increased dramatically in the Nelchina Basin after the FWS removed most of the wolves there about 1950. Governor Jay Hammond told me (in 2001) that when the FWS started wolf control on the Alaska Peninsula in the 1950s, they could account for only about 1,200 caribou from an estimated high of 50,000 plus 10,000 reindeer. After 250 wolves had been removed over a number of years, "Caribou increased ten-fold," Hammond said. "At the same time, wolves also increased far behyond previous levels, indicating selective control of predators can ultimately increase *their* numbers as well."

In huntable areas in Alaska in most years about 85 percent of the annual ungulate mortality (mostly the young) is due to predation by wolves and bears; 2 to 7 percent is due to hunting by man (all adult animals); and the rest is from accidents, disease, old age (few wild animals die of old age) and weather.

Alaska's wolves increased rapidly after statehood, and by the late 1960s and early 1970s they were probably as abundant as they were in the 1930s and 1940s when the human population was under 75,000. Though traps, poisons and rifles were used without restriction during territorial days, wolves managed to remain present over much of their natural range. Now, after the turn of the century, Alaska's wolves are abundant, and they still occupy nearly all of their original range.

Frank Glaser retired from the FWS in June, 1955. He was 68. For his outstanding service Interior Secretary Douglas McKay presented him with the Meritorious Service Award of the Department of Interior. It read, in part: "He spent most of his adult life in the wilderness of Alaska studying and observing wildlife. His primary responsibility was the control of predatory animals. However, his inquisitive mind led to an unequaled store of information as to the previously unexplained causes of behavior of wild animals.

"Working under almost inconceivable hardships in difficult terrain and severely cold weather, Mr. Glaser, far from communication lines and other methods of assistance and protection, traveled in the Arctic by dog sled, teaching the Eskimos how to protect their reindeer from wolves. Through his undaunted courage, physical durability, and spirited concern for the Natives, he withstood the extreme physical hardships encountered in his work."

Frank and his wife Nellie left Alaska about 1957 and for the next 15 years they lived in Idaho, California, and Oregon. Frank showed his Alaskan movies to audiences but bookings were difficult to get, and he eventually abandoned the effort.

In their old age the Glasers returned to their beloved Alaska. For a time Frank lived in the Anchorage home of his stepson, Calvin Osborne. One evening he became upset, insisting he heard wolves howling. "They don't belong in town. They'll kill dogs, and a lot of kids are running around too. I'm worried about them. Those wolves have to be killed."

He became so agitated that Dr. Louis Mayer was called. Mayer made a house call, talked with Frank, and gave him a sedative.

Mayer told me that on the next day he learned the ADF&G was holding captive wolves nearby. Frank Glaser knew a wolf howl when he heard it, even though his aged mind wandered some.

Ray Tremblay, one of Glaser's long-time FWS associates, visited the old wolfer several times at an Anchorage nursing home. Frank would know Ray for a time, then he'd drift off and forget Ray's name. Once when his mind cleared he told Ray when he gained strength he was going back to Savage River to the life he had left 37 years earlier.

Perhaps Frank did go back to Savage River, for that wild and lovely region was his idea of the Happy Hunting Ground. He died May 16, 1974, at the age of 86. Nellie, with him at the nursing home to the last, died 15 days later.

Oscar Vogel, the Talkeetna Mountains guide and trapper told me, "Although it was well attended, there were only two wolf trappers present at Frank Glaser's funeral. I was one of them."

Success in 20A

"We fear the wolf population will suffer permanent damage and will never recover from the kill," read part of the legal complaint that in 1975 resulted in a court decision that temporarily stopped the removal of wolves from Subunit 20A. The complaint was filed by the Fairbanks Environmental Center, Inc., Friends of the Earth, Inc, and several residents of Anchorage and Fairbanks when Bob Hinman announced plans for the program.

Was the wolf population permanently damaged? Were these environmentalists' fears realized?

Hardly.

The program for the state to remove a limited number of wolves from 20A got underway in 1976 and was suspended in 1995, with no wolf control between 1983 and 1992. During the years 1975-1976 through 1994-1995, ADF&G and hunters/trappers removed 963 wolves from 20A—an average of 48 per year. There were 239 wolves at the beginning of the program, and 180 when the program ended. Wolf numbers increased after wolf control was suspended and exceeded precontrol levels by 5 wolves by the year 1998 (the 1998 population was 244). Wolf count in the fall of 2000 was 191, the latest figure available as this is written.

This is, simply, another example of the ability of wolves to reproduce and/or to fill vacant habitat.

The goal was to increase moose numbers from a low of 2,500 to at least 8,000 or 9,000 to provide for an increased human hunter harvest, and to support a reasonable number of wolves.

Moose increased at an annual rate of about 15 percent. There were 2,500 in 1976 and 11,100 in 1998—a nearly four and a half-fold increase. The moose population peaked at 13,800 in 1994. In November, 2001, there were 11,500 moose in 20A.

There were 5 more wolves and 8,600 more moose in 1998 than at the beginning of the program.

Caribou in 20A likewise benefited. From 2,200 in 1976 their numbers peaked in 1989 at 10,690. Hunting was allowed after 1979, although it was stopped in 1992 when their numbers decreased to 5,900. There were 4,300 caribou in 1994. In June, 2001, there were 3,000 caribou (latest figures). ADF&G biologists believe that two back-to-back severe winters were responsible for the decline—not wolves.*

Consistent removal of some wolves, plus light predation on moose and caribou by bears, and mostly mild winters, all helped to produce these favorable results in 20A.

While moose and caribou in 20A were increasing, in the immediately adjacent McKinley Park and Preserve, which is similar habitat exposed to essentially the same environmental conditions, moose and caribou numbers remained stable at low levels, or actually declined. The only major factor that differed was the removal of a limited number of wolves in 20A.

⌒

IN 1984 THE BOG asked the ADF&G staff for a cost-benefit analysis of the 20A wolf reduction program. Oliver ("Bud") Burris, ADF&G Regional Game Coordinator at Fairbanks, calculated that in the first eight years (1976–84) the state spent $824,200 to kill 1,313 wolves in the area where moose and caribou had been reduced (this calculation included portions of adjacent game management units, not only 20A). The return on that expenditure, according to Burris, was an increase in moose and caribou numbers that allowed an increased harvest by hunters with a total meat value of $3,352,972, using $2.74 a pound—comparable to the then-current price of domestic meat. The cost-benefit was calculated for meat production only. It did not include the value of increased recreation, and increased business to

---

*The figures through 1994–95 are from "Increases in Moose, Caribou, and Wolves Following Wolf Control In Alaska," by Rodney D. Boertje, Patrick Valkenburg, and Mark E. McNay. *Journal of Wildlife Management*, Vol. 60, No. 3, July 1996. Figures for more recent years were provided in January 2002 by the Fairbanks office of the ADF&G.

guides, pilots, and merchants, or the value of increased photographic opportunities and tourist viewing of wildlife.

Presumably, even those opposed to killing wolves to increase moose and caribou, as well as wolves, want an abundance of wildlife. In the 20A instance, opposition to the program by mostly animal rights advocates worked against achieving that abundance. Without removal of some wolves, moose, caribou and wolves would have inevitably declined, leaving a scarcity of large mammals, a condition which could have remained for decades, judging from historical records.

The Nelchina mystery: Wolf summit: Harbo's plan

THE NELCHINA BASIN (Game Management Unit 13) is one of Alaska's great wildlife ranges. It is surrounded by rugged mountains, dotted with lakes and crossed by rivers and creeks. Caribou and moose roam there, and Dall sheep peer down on the huge valley from the upper foothills and surrounding Alaska Range, the Talkeetna Mountains, and the coastal Chugach Mountains. Wolves, grizzly bears, and black bears are the major predators.

Moose numbers peaked there in 1960. They started to decline over the next decade. Were severe winters killing them? No. Mild winters brought no improvement. ADF&G investigations indicated it wasn't poor range conditions, nor was it disease or parasites. Overhunting? No. Hunters were allowed bulls only, and all breeding age cows were having calves. Moose calves were arriving in abundance, but November aerial moose surveys revealed most calves weren't surviving the summer.

Wolves? The twelve wolves that survived FWS Bob Burkholder's and Buck Harris's aerial hunting and trapping there in the 1950s had increased to about 450 by the 1960s, yet another example of their tremendous reproductive potential and ability to fill wolf-vacant habitat. Bears, which had also suffered from the anti-wolf poisoning campaign of the federal government, had also recovered. Thus, as moose decreased, predators increased.

To learn what was killing Nelchina basin moose calves, ADF&G wildlife biologist Warren B. Ballard tackled the problem in 1975—about the same time that wolf control started in 20A. He, and other ADF&G wildlife biologists suspected wolves were killing the calves in summer. To check this diagnosis, starting in 1975 wolves were killed by aerial hunting in a part of the study area. By 1978, sixty had been removed.

The calf mortality continued.

More than one hundred adult moose were captured, marked with ear tags, canvas collars, or a radio collar. Blood studies indicated they were healthy.

To learn essentials about wolves in the study area, between 1975 and 1980, more than 150 were captured by darting from a helicopter. Each was equipped with a radio collar and ear tag.

Ballard developed great respect for the wolves, commenting that, "Most have their own personality. I could often identify individuals in a pack even without a radio collar. I had to be on guard to keep my personal feelings for the animals from interfering with the design of the research program."

Over a five year period, radio-collared wolves were located from airplanes on more than 4,000 occasions, resulting in almost 10,000 individual wolf sightings. Wolf territories varied in size from 268 to 864 square miles. Wolf packs where the fewest moose and caribou lived had the largest territories; where moose and caribou were abundant, territories were smaller.

Dispersing wolves—generally the younger animals—traveled an average of about fifty miles before forming a new pack or joining an existing pack. In one case, at least two, and perhaps as many as four, wolves from the Nelchina traveled 455 air miles to the eastern Brooks Range of arctic Alaska—one of the longest movements known for wolves anywhere.

By late August or early September, when wolf pups had started to travel with adults on hunting trips, Ballard and his crew visited thirty den and rendezvous sites to gather information on dens, and to collect scats (droppings) to learn the types and quantities of food eaten while these areas were in use.

Evidence of what wolves eat—primarily hair and pieces of bone—remains in their droppings. In 3,624 scats, calf moose was the most frequently identified food (44%), followed by snowshoe hare (14.2%), beaver (10%), and adult moose (9.2%). Based on these data alone one would conclude that calf moose were heavily preyed upon by wolves.

Research by Dr. Dave Mech and T. Floyd in Minnesota suggested that because of volume to size ratios, relatively small prey such as calf moose are proportionately covered with more hair than larger prey animals. Thus the small prey like moose calves and snowshoe hares are over-represented in wolf scats if one relies solely on percentage of occurrence of food items. Because of this, Ballard converted the scat data to actual numbers of prey.

This analysis, with wolf population estimates, allowed him to estimate that from mid-May to mid-July during the years 1975–79, at the most, wolves preyed on 1,013 moose calves, and 132 adult moose.

Sound like a lot? Not really. Even these maximum figures represented a small proportion of the prey available to wolves.

An estimated 10,000 or more moose calves were annually produced in the Nelchina Basin during these years. Therefore the maximum estimated kill of about 1,000 moose calves based upon scat collection represented ten percent or less of the moose being born.

From moose counts made each November it was fairly clear that around eighty percent of the calves were dying. If the scat data generally represented what wolves were killing and eating, an additional 7,000 calves or so needed to be accounted for.

The low estimated number of calf moose killed by wolves was supported by aerial observations of radio-collared wolves.

From April 1975 through June 1980, radio-collared wolves were observed on 360 kills. On thirty eight of these, brown bears were also present. Interestingly, during May through November, when most calf mortality occurs, wolves were observed on 172 kills, of which only 21 were moose calves.

From these results it was apparent that predation by wolves on newborn moose calves in this area was not as important as had first been thought.

Because wolf scat analysis and aerial observations of radio-collared wolves failed to explain the large calf moose losses, it became clear to Ballard that he needed a different approach.

The best way to study moose calf mortality was to radio-collar moose calves. Ballard used a collar that would expand as the calf grew. Each collar contained a radio that sent a pulsed signal similar to that used on collars attached to wolves and adult moose. But there was an additional feature—if the calf wearing the collar stopped moving and was presumably dead, the signal tripled its pulse rate.

To apply the collars, cow-calf pairs were located form a fixed-wing plane, and a helicopter was called in to fly low over the cow-calf combination, forcing them to separate. The tagging crew leaped from the hovering helicopter, grabbed the calf, and slipped the radio-collar on. Next, the sex of the calf was determined.

Sometimes that was all that could be done because the cow would return and drive the taggers away. Usually the helicopter pilot hovered near the cow, trying to keep her from attacking the biologists. If the cow didn't push too hard, a blood sample, weight, and measurements were taken. Results: the calves were generally found to be healthy.

Cow moose are capable of killing with their sharp, pile-driver hoofs. Ballard and crew always carried a rifle for last-resort defense. Once Warren and his partner were measuring a calf when his partner, with the rifle and watching the cow, shook Warren vigorously, yelling "She's coming, she's coming!"

Ballard knew the moose was very close when he heard his partner's footsteps receding, fast. He dropped the calf and hastily followed to safety.

During spring, 1977, Ballard radio-collared 48 newborn moose calves, and monitored their radio signals twice a day. When a fast-pulse signal was heard from the searching plane, he tried to spot the dead calf and any nearby predators. A helicopter was then called in and the study was continued on the ground.

Think of Ballard and crew approaching a freshly-killed moose calf in heavy brush, not knowing what killed it. Was it a grizzly ready to defend its kill? Or was the predator a wolf, which would probably flee? On the first dead calf they investigated, Ballard and Ted Spraker, following a radio signal, were very close, and took off their earphones (needed for the radio-direction finder). As they did, a gray jay leaped from the brush, startling the on-guard biologists, who were half-expecting a grizzly bear.

After their pulses dropped back to normal, they found fresh bear scats, hair, and big-clawed grizzly tracks near the dead calf remains. Fortunately, the bear was gone.

Of the 48 calves radio-collared in 1977, 30 were dead by mid-July. Most (24) had been killed by grizzly bears.

Ballard's study was the first to scientifically demonstrate that bears can be a major predator on moose.

During the period when bears were killing moose calves, radio-collared wolves were preying largely on adult and one-year-old moose. Thus it appeared the high mortality of newborn calves could be attributed to bear predation. But more data were needed to prove conclusively that bears were the main problem.

In the spring of 1978 Ballard radio-collared 72 newborn moose calves. In the study area he also captured and equipped 23 adult grizzly bears with radio-collars. Each bear was weighed (using a scale hung from a hovering helicopter); average for males was 550 pounds, and for females about 275 pounds.

Once Ballard and his assistant John Westlund were picking up equipment after processing a sow grizzly when she recovered from the tranquilizing drug and came to her feet. She stood looking at the two biologists, who fell backwards in four-foot deep snow, frantically reaching for their pistols. Then the bear ran off. Warren said it took the two of them—and probably the bear—an hour to stop shaking.

Of the 72 calves radio-collared in 1978, 36 were dead within six weeks of birth. Of these, 28 were killed by grizzly bears, and only one was killed by a wolf.

In summary, 55 percent of the 120 radio-collared moose calves died within the first six weeks of study, with predators of all types killing 79 percent.

During the spring and summer 1978, Ballard, assisted by ADF&G wildlife biologists Ted Spraker and Ken Taylor, monitored the 23 radio-collared grizzlies. From late May until November when bears began to den up, these bears were seen on 78 kills, most (69) of which were moose (88 percent). Moose calves comprised nearly half of the kills (47 percent).

All of the kills of moose calves were seen between late May and mid-July, which corresponded precisely with the timing of mortality of the radio-collared calves. Not only were bears significant predators on moose calves, but the limited data suggested they were a significant predator on adult moose as well.

Would reducing the number of bears cut down early losses of calf moose, or would some other mortality factor intervene?

In May and June 1979, Ballard had the help of ADF&G wildlife biologist Sterling Miller, who helped in capturing and transplanting 47 adult grizzly bears from the study area. This was about 60 percent of the estimated bear population. Each of the bears was slung under the helicopter and flown to a field station where it was measured, weighed, and samples of teeth, blood, and hair collected. From there they were moved by truck and airplane to release sites from 87 to 160 miles distant.

The 47 bears were monitored by telemetry-equipped airplanes. About 7 out of 10 of the bears returned to the capture area in an average of 58 days. The bears were expected to return—experience by ADF&G in removal of nuisance bears had demonstrated this. But the high rate of return of the bears showed that transplanting grizzly bears for any reason is a temporary measure—a significant conclusion for bear management throughout Alaska.

Bingo! Removal of the bears protected moose calves during their first weeks of life, confirming that grizzly bears were the main predators on newborn calf moose in the Nelchina study area. Surveys the following November produced the highest survival records recorded for the area—52 calves per 100 cows. When corrected for sightability (biologists never see all calf-cow pairs during aerial surveys) and for young moose which were not of reproductive age, Ballard found the ratio to be about 70 calves per 100 cows.

This step-by-step solving of the unknown causes of the decline of moose in the Nelchina Basin, with the answers slowly wrung out after years of work, gave biologists new insights into the intricate workings of predator-prey relationships.

Ballard's ground-breaking study reinforced a comment made by Paul L. Errington in his 1962 book *Of Predation and Life*: "The study of predation is no field for snap judgments. Cause-and-effect relationships have, on occasion, their own ways of turning out to be quite different from what they may seem to be at first."

That was certainly the case in the Nelchina Basin. The wolf, which at first appeared to be the guilty killer of moose, in the end proved to be only slightly guilty.

Could the answers to the Nelchina puzzle be applied elsewhere in Alaska where moose numbers are in decline? Unfortunately, no. However, the answers found in the Nelchina, provided valuable clues and basic information. Subsequent studies elsewhere have shown both black and grizzly bears can be important predators on moose calves in many parts of Alaska.

By 2002, ADF&G wildlife biologists had found evidence of significant bear predation on moose calves in the Galena, Fort Yukon, middle Yukon, and McGrath areas. Often, popular local belief had fixed the guilt on wolves. Only in-depth studies similar to that made by Ballard and his staff can determine positively the main causes of mortality in moose and other prey species.

DESPITE THE SUCCESS of wolf control in 20A, animal-rights and anti-hunting groups continued to challenge the state's wolf control programs, regardless of the supporting information. The ADF&G has long been confronted with the problem of trying to manage wolves to satisfy increasingly polarized user groups. When there have been public votes on wolf-management issues, urban-oriented Anchorage, the major population center of the state, has usually voted with the animal-rightists. The average Anchorage resident has been in the state less than ten years.

An exception came in 1998 when animal-rightists managed to obtain signatures enough to get a proposal on a statewide ballot that would have ended the use of snares to capture wolves in Alaska. Professional trappers, rural and urban wildlife users and others mounted a major campaign and defeated it.

Nevertheless, the popular view on appropriate management of wolves in Alaska did not, and still does not, agree with the views of most of Alaska's professional wildlife managers.

In 1990 the ADF&G formed the Alaska Wolf Management Planning Team consisting of twelve members with a broad range of interest and values, including animal-rights advocates. The Team hammered out recommendations to the ADF&G on the state's wolf management program. Some issues could not be agreed upon; the animal-rightists came to the table with nothing but demands. Included, however, was the agreement that in some instances some wolves could be controlled in small areas to protect or increase other wildlife populations. Shooting wolves from aircraft was one of the options.

Based on the planning team's report, ADF&G prepared the Strategic Wolf Management Plan which the BOG adopted in October, 1991. This plan was not a mirror image of recommendations of the planning team because consensus could not be reached on all issues, and the final plan had to comply with the state constitution's mandates, hunting/trapping regulations, and the department's logistic and financial capabilities.

The success of wolf control in 20A was ignored by the animal rightists.

In November, 1992, the BOG approved plans to kill wolves

annually over a five year period in three areas encompassing parts of several interior Alaska game management units, including 20A. The goal was to boost caribou and moose populations, and, with that, of course, to provide an increased food base for wolves. In 20A, and adjacent areas ADF&G personal were to kill the wolves from helicopters. Elsewhere hunters were to be allowed to land and shoot the wolves.

During public hearings on the plan animal rights groups testified they would "do whatever it takes" to stop the killing of wolves.

An editorial in *Wolftracks* magazine claiming that ADF&G was planning a mass wolf control program, and that parts of Denali National Park and Preserve were not to be immune, brought a flood of letters to the BOG and the governor's office.

An attorney representing Defenders of Wildlife, Wolf Haven International, The Sierra Club, and the Southeast Alaska Conservation Council testified before the BOG that "... they feel ADF&G has attempted to interpret, to co-opt, and to manipulate the Team's [Wolf Planning Team] recommendation to their own advantage, specifically to more extensively control wolf populations in Alaska under the guise of sound wildlife management."

They also threatened more litigation, imminent federal legislation, and claimed that ADF&G was incapable of being responsible stewards of wildlife which could result in the removal of ADF&G authority to do so.

Nearly every one of the eighty-plus Advisory Committees to the BOG and Board of Fisheries throughout the state (around 800 Alaska resident citizen advisers to the boards) supported the plan. The Alaska system is the most open-to-the-public wildlife management system in the U.S., and the BOG relies heavily on input from these advisory committees.

Support also came from various user groups in Alaska such as the Alaska Fish and Wildlife Conservation Fund, the Alaska Outdoor Council, and various sportsmen's groups. The Yukon [Canada] Fish and Wildlife Management Board supported the concept of rebuilding the Fortymile caribou herd, shared by Alaska and the Yukon. The herd once numbered nearly one half million, and roamed from Fairbanks to Whitehorse.

Animal rights and anti-hunting groups used misinformation and sensationalism to develop public support. Controversy, of course, is the bread and butter of these organizations. Cry "wolf" and the money pours in. Mailings included the usual words like "slaughter," "decimate," "kill thousands," "exterminate," "cruel," "barbaric."

Adds appeared in the *New York Times, Los Angeles Times*, and *USA Today*, paid for by Fund for Animals, Friends of Animals, and possibly others.

In an attempt to inform the public, ADF&G prepared an eight-page "Alaska Wolf Facts," which was distributed to the press and public. Probably because it didn't have any buzz words and didn't arouse emotions, was eight pages long, and didn't originate with animal rights or anti-hunting groups (which always get big play in the press), it didn't get much exposure.

"Wolf Facts" reported the number of wolves in Alaska was 5,900–7,200 (700–900 packs); gave the harvest rate (seventeen percent) and the fact that wolves can sustain a harvest rate of 25 to 40 percent; the fact that 70 percent of Alaska is federal lands where no wolf control is allowed; described the control areas where 300–400 wolves were to be killed (five to seven percent of the statewide population) in 1992–93, and 100 to 300 in three to five subsequent years; and last, predators consume around 85 percent of the moose and caribou that die in Alaska, while hunters take 2–7%. The remainder die of accidents, weather and disease.

Next step for the animal-rightists was to involve tourists. When pressured by animal-rightists, some tour groups indicated they wouldn't come to Alaska. The hoopla continued, and soon the Alaska Visitors Association estimated that if the boycott continued it would cost the state $64 million in lost revenue. This was questionable, for the same group predicted doom for Alaska tourism following the Exxon Valdez oil spill. Instead, tourism increased.

In major cities across the lower-48, where people are most susceptible to environmental extremism, demonstrators urged a boycott on Alaska. Made-for-television, the demonstrations—which extended into Canada and Europe—usually broke up after the TV cameras left. The resulting news-bites were carried on newscasts around the world.

Governor Walter J. Hickel invited fellow governors and wild-life, outdoors, and conservation groups to accept Alaska's wolves for introduction in other states. The offer had been in place for twenty two years without any takers. There was no interest in Hickel's bid to give wolves away in 1992.

Pressure built from animal rightists, and the Alaska tourism industry began to panic. An Oregon congressman said he would introduce legislation in the U.S. Congress to block the wolf kill. In early December, 1992, Hickel chose the politically expedient solution of calling a January, 1993 "Wolf Summit" in Fairbanks. The ADF&G was to invite national and international conservation and wildlife leaders and animal rights advocates.

Announcement of the summit didn't end the uproar. The Alaska Wildlife Alliance viewed the summit as a promotional effort by ADF&G to sell their program. Tina Lindgren, executive director of the Alaska Tourism Marketing Council, advised Hickel: "Look at the ramifications to the economy and the image of Alaska, rather than just looking at the issue biologically."

Fish and Game Commissioner Carl Rosier and Governor Hickel announced an end to wolf control for the year after more than 20,000 letters had arrived at Hickel's office opposing the control program, and an ultimatum from nine state and national groups threatening to boycott the summit unless wolf control was stopped before it took place.

Groups threatening to boycott were the Alaska Wildlife Alliance, Greenpeace, Sierra Club, Wilderness Society, Alaska Center for the Environment, Northern Alaska Environmental Center, Trustees for Alaska, Wolf Haven International, and National Parks and Conservation Society.

Hickel announced the summit would proceed, and he would attend. But since there would be no wolf control for the year, members of the BOG saw no need for the summit, realizing it would only prolong the controversy. The issue was now political, not biological. In essence, the BOG (which is an arm of the state legislature) had lost its authority as wildlife managers responsible for sustained production of wolves, moose, and caribou in the state.

Full-page ads in the *Fairbanks News-Miner* by The Alaska Wildlife Conservation Association proclaimed, "It's not about wolves. It is about . . . (1) Outsiders dictating Alaska's future, (2) Loss of state's rights, (3) Extortion, (4) Freedom and choice.

Alaska trappers, New York animal-rightists, field biologists, sportsmen, and the president of Holland America cruise lines—and a wide mix of other interests—attended. The proceedings were covered by local and national news media, including *The New York Times*.

Topics on the agenda included wolf biology, predator-prey relationships, different views on how Alaska's wolves should be managed, and wildlife's value to tourism. There were speeches, panel discussions and work groups.

It was ground that had been plowed many times, and has been repeatedly plowed since. Scientists presented the rational for wolf control, citing the success of 20A and other areas in Alaska where moose and caribou had increased after wolf numbers had been reduced. Animal-rightists brought demands that the nonsensical cruelty must stop, claiming that Alaska was wiping out her wolves. Travel-tourism interests said that wolves were too valuable to kill—their very presence attracts tourists who want to see Alaska as a pristine wilderness.

The only faction that seemed to recognize that wolves are a resilient renewable resource were the wildlife scientists, and rural and urban hunters and trappers. But their views were already known—they thought it was appropriate to manage wolves in some areas.

Some attendees at the summit were flown, with Governor Hickel, to the Athabaskan village of Minto, fifty miles west of Fairbanks, to hear the Minto peoples' views. Residents of Minto, like other rural residents of Alaska, depend upon hunting, fishing and trapping for food and money.

"Some of you are probably from New York or San Francisco and you've probably never even seen a wolf," said Charlie Titus Jr., a member of the tribal council. "But still, you condemn the way we live. I think that's wrong."

Kenny Charles, another village leader, told the visitors, "A few years ago animal-rights activists started talking about how it's not right to kill fur-bearing animals. For them to live in a city and say things like that about the way we live in Minto—which they've never even heard of—is a crock of bull."

"I was very surprised to hear that we are so much the enemy of the villagers," said Fran Stricker, a representative of the Sacramento, California-based Animal Protection Institute, after hearing Minto residents' critical comments on the animal-rights movement.

ONE OF THE SCIENTIFIC papers presented at the summit was prepared by Dr. Sam Harbo, representing the Alaska Outdoor

Council. Harbo, retired as Professor of Biometrics at the University of Alaska, Fairbanks, and the BOG chairman when I was a member, titled his paper "Environmental Sanity: Think Globally—Act Locally."

His paper compared the environmental impact of domestic meat production in the South 48 with that of producing wolves and moose in 20A.

Harbo pointed out that the food system in the United State uses nearly 17 percent of the total U.S. energy budget, with food processing and distribution accounting for 40 percent of that. The on-farm component of agriculture is energy consumptive and energy dependent, with nearly all energy coming from fossil fuels, for most farm work is accomplished with petroleum-using machinery.

Fertilizers and pesticides make up nearly one-third of the energy use on farms. Fossil fuel is nature's capital, a non-renewable resource—and we are burning it to produce and market agriculture products. Examples: one gallon of gasoline is used for every bushel of corn produced; on average, nearly ten calories of energy are burned for each calorie of food we consume. How long can we afford this?

For every bushel of Iowa corn produced, we lose five bushels of Iowa soil. In Eastern Washington, twenty bushels of topsoil are lost for every bushel of wheat harvested.

Animal husbandry is mostly designed to satisfy distant markets; transportation, processing, storage, and distribution of meats are all energy intensive. Most large dairy and beef operations are with penned animals. These plant eaters are efficient solar energy converters—but we don't use them efficiently. The hay and grains they eat are raised, using intensive and soil destroying methods, and then transported to feed the penned animals.

With that comes the problem of concentrated animal wastes, a significant source of pollution.

The reliance of the United States on energy intensive methods is at the root of many of our environmental problems, such as air pollution, soil erosion, ozone problems and water pollution.

How does all of this relate to moose and wolf management in Alaska?

Dr. Harbo pointed out that there were about 11,000 moose in 20A; at one time there were as many as 23,000.

He postulated that a temporary reduction in wolf numbers would allow moose to increase. A modest small-scale prescribed burning program could provide additional high quality moose habitat. Theoretically, a population of 20,000 moose could be supported in 20A.

In a plausible "let's suppose" scenario, Sam presumed a goal of maintaining a population of 350 wolves in 20A. In a nearly pure moose-wolf system, a ratio of one wolf to 30 moose can result in a near stable moose population, provided food is adequate and other sources of mortality are minor. However, 20A has caribou and Dall sheep, as well as black and grizzly bears. For ease in presentation, Dr. Harbo postulated that the additional predators would be offset by the additional prey animals.

Using a one wolf to thirty moose ratio, the 350 wolves could be supported by 10,500 moose, leaving 9,500 moose to produce a surplus for take by humans. In a productive situation, a harvest rate of 25 percent is sustainable. Hence, the 9,500 moose could produce a harvestable surplus of 2,375 moose annually, more than 2,000 animals greater than the then average harvest of about 250 moose. Assuming an average of 500 pounds of meat per moose, the increased is more than one million pounds greater than the then current harvest. In addition, the wolf population would have increased by more than 20 percent.

The health benefits of moose and other wild game meat, which is lean and low in cholesterol, compared with fatty, hormone-laced domestic-raised meat has been repeatedly pointed out by dietitians.

This scenario could be accomplished solely through predator management and modest habitat manipulation, both of which are ecologically and environmentally safe.

In such a managed wildlife system, the integrity of the natural ecosystem and the efficiency of the system's solar energy converters—the moose—would remain intact.

Such a system runs entirely on solar energy, without significant inputs of fossil fuel energy, without tillage that leads to soil erosion, and without fertilizers, herbicides, pesticides or growth hormones.

Further, local residents would benefit most, a strong incentive for Alaskans to manage such a system in a healthy, sustainable manner.

Pie in the sky thinking?

Not really. It's a biologically sound concept. Harbo painted a picture of an idealized, intensively managed, unfenced wolf/moose range.

Animal rightists pooh-poohed the idea, saying that such a

plan would benefit hunters only, that wilderness lovers wouldn't appreciate it.

They missed the point. Dr. Harbo was demonstrating the possibilities of intensive wildlife management, and that managing wolves and moose together has a favorable cost-benefit ratio, and is environmentally responsible. If the goal is a stable and abundant population of wild animals, non-hunters, wilderness lovers, animal lovers and wolf lovers all could in perpetuity benefit from modern game management, without adversely affecting the environment.

IN FEBRUARY, 1993, the Wildlife Society, a national organization of professional wildlife biologists, awarded the Wildlife Publications Award for one of the top wildlife papers of 1992 to "The Role of Predation in Limiting Moose at Low Densities in Alaska and Yukon and Implications for Conservation," a professional study (*Wildlife Monographs 120*, a supplement to the Journal of Wildlife Management published in January, 1992) by William C. Gasaway, Rodney D. Boertje, Daniel V. Grangaard, David G. Kelleyhouse, Robert O. Stephenson—all ADF&G wildlife biologists—and Douglas G. Larsen, a Yukon Territory (Canada) wildlife biologist.

Based on research in the Fortymile area near Tok and adjacent Yukon Territory during the 1980s, the study illustrated how predation by bears and wolves can keep moose populations at low levels.

There's an irony here; If a study of any kind about wolves had been published by animal rightists, with or without an award, it would have rated headlines, or at least the front page. As it was, the release about the award was buried in small columns on the back pages of the few Alaska newspapers that printed it. The scientific basis for wolf control in Alaska didn't rate the front page. But proposals to reduce wolf numbers always do.

"Speculation by a few individuals that the state's plans were flawed biologically should now be laid to rest," said David Kellyhouse, then director of the state Division of Wildlife Conservation, and one of the authors.

Bunde's resolution: Wolf consensus?

REN SMITH TELEPHONED me in late June, 1976. "Well Prof, you sure got me into trouble this time. Now I can't get rid of the woman," he said.

"What woman?" I asked. "Oh. You mean Pat York?" remembering when we were all together at Anaktuvuk Pass. "What do you mean, you can't get rid of her?"

"I married her," he said.

"My God, Ren. I just suggested you buy her a cup of coffee," I laughed. Then I added, "Congratulations, my friend. She's a real catch. I wish both of you every happiness."

"Thanks, Prof. Just thought I'd let you know," he signed off.

⌒

IN THE SPRING of 1993, Alaska State Representative Con Bunde, an Anchorage resident, a retired University of Alaska Professor, commercial pilot, and outdoorsman, introduced the following resolution in the Alaska House of Representatives. It is only partly tongue-in-cheek and is printed here with his permission.

. . . I don't fear, hate, or even dislike wolves. And it isn't about the rightness or wrongness of aerial wolf hunting that I speak. It is about truth, reality, respect and a struggle for power and domination. It is also about a new religion whose adherents worship animal rights, and who have mounted a serious assault on Alaska's wildlife resources.

Alaska's wildlife is the essence of what Alaska is all about for many of us. An assault is under way by well-meaning but misguided people, people who are involved in a power struggle for control of Alaska's wildlife. This struggle is between animal rights groups and sound scientific management of our wildlife resources. This issue is about more than wolf control. It is about who will have the power to control Alaska's access to our wildlife resources in particular and all of our natural resources in general.

The recent attempt at a boycott and threatened extortions of our tourist revenues showed just how serious this power struggle has become. I suppose it is only human nature that the farther people are from a problem, the more generous they are with their advice, and the less likely their advice is to be based on reality.

The lust for the power to control Alaska borders on religious zeal. Those who preach the animal rights philosophy are not swayed by logic or scientific evidence. They have assumed the moral high ground by labeling themselves as non-consumptive users of our wildlife resources.

There are no non-consumptive residents of this planet. If you exist, you consume. From the top of their wool ski hat to the soles of their Birkinstock sandals these animal rightists consume, if only indirectly, our wildlife resources. The cotton and wool of their clothing was grown on land that once supported wild animals. Be they vegetarian or macrobiotic they are part of a food chain. The production of this food displaces wildlife.

We are all part of a food chain that requires that other life forms die that we may live. Therefore, it is our responsibility when we participate in this food chain that we do it with respect and good stewardship toward other life forms. In other words we must promote and practice sound management of our wildlife. Sound management creates neither saint nor sinner out of any animal and doesn't elevate any species to the level of a deity, or give it the entire responsibility of being the symbol of our wilderness.

Many of these folk claim the wolf to them symbolizes the wilderness. This highly romanticized notion of the wolf is costing Alaskans a great many moose, sheep and caribou—a highly valuable, edible asset.

I think it only fair that we encourage these romantics, but there should be a price. They should reimburse Alaska for allowing them to live out their fantasies about the wilderness at our expense. In short, we should offer those who profess such a great concern for Alaska's wildlife an opportunity to put their money where their mouth is by establishing a license to advise us on how to manage our wildlife. Call it a wolf tax.

⌒

IN OCTOBER, 1993, ADF&G re-started the wolf control program in 20A. On October 2, David Sahadie, 36, of Tenafly New Jersey, left a message on Governor Hickel's answering machine, threatening to kill one of Hickel's family members for each wolf killed by the state. He pleaded guilty in a New Jersey federal court to threatening the governor over the state's wolf-control plan and was sentenced to five years probation and ordered to pay a $5,000 fine. He could have received five years in prison and a $250,000 fine.

As part of his probation, he was ordered to serve under house arrest for three months, perform 1,000 hours of community service, and write a letter of apology to Governor Hickel.

⌒

THE WOLF REMOVAL program in 20A in 1993–94 did not involve aerial shooting, the most humane, most efficient, and most economical method. Shotguns firing buckshot (large round lead pellets) at close range usually results in immediate death. Instead, as a compromise to appease animal-rights groups, the BOG directed wildlife biologists to use snares—a ground control method that calls for great skill and experience, with long man-hours of labor.

The results? Usually death by strangulation for wolves, and, unavoidably, occasionally other animals (including caribou and moose) that blunder into the snares. Sometimes poorly set snares catch and hold wolves by body parts other than the neck.'

On November 29, 1994, an animal rights advocate who apparently had been monitoring ADF&G biologists wolf snaring efforts, found a live wolf in a snare.

Rather than dispatching the wolf, or contacting the ADF&G to end its suffering, this person contacted an Anchorage television station and made plans to join a videotape crew and reporters who would helicopter up from Anchorage to record the suffering of the trapped wolf next day.

When the television cameraman, reporter, and animal rights advocate arrived at the site next day, more wolves had been caught.

While the crew was taping the animal rightist's comments about the inhumanity of trapping and wolf control to benefit hunters, the ADF&G biologist who set the snares arrived by helicopter.

His first concern was the trapped wolf. Hastily trying to humanely dispatch the most critically trapped wolf, the biologist allowed himself to be taped in a grisly inefficient attempt to put the wolf out of its misery. Later investigation revealed he had hastily chosen the wrong ammunition for his gun. The wolf endured five shots before dying. Three other wolves, still in snares, were photographed.

The next day the incident was nationally televised. The resultant public outrage was predictable. The videos of this unfortunate incident were widely distributed to television stations, and in the years since have frequently appeared on various Alaska stations, as well as those in the South 48.

Nothing could have aroused the Alaska public more; cruelty to animals is not acceptable. The wolf control program was halted by Governor Tony Knowles.

Anchorage Times editor Paul Jenkins placed the blame where it belonged in his "Wolf 'Consensus' not Worth the Effort," editorial of December 8, 1994 in the *Voice of The Times,* published in the *Anchorage Daily News,* reprinted here with permission of both:

While we're ankle-deep in the crocodile tears of animal rights activists all in a dither over errors made in the snaring of three wolves southwest of Fairbanks, let's at least try to remember recent history.

And let's not forget this: Animal activists and other assorted do-gooders flip-flopped, obstructed, weaseled and, ultimately, set the stage for the unfortunate mishap and share much of the blame for the wolves' suffering.

A few years back, after a lengthy, and very, very public process, the Alaska Wolf Management Planning Team—including everyone from fur buyers to animal activists—reached a tenuous consensus, or at least most of us thought it had. The team concluded that in some instances some of Alaska's 7,000 or so wolves could be controlled in small areas to protect or increase other game populations. Shooting wolves from aircraft was one of the options.

The Game Board ordered the team's June 1991 recommendations be used in crafting a Strategic Wolf Management Plan for Alaska. Using that plan, the board in the fall of 1992 adopted Area-Specific Management Plans for Game Units 20A, 20E and 13 which called for reducing the number of wolves in those areas. And the silly state guys actually wanted to use radio collars, guns and aircraft to get the job done efficiently, economically, and humanely.

That, ladies and gents, is when it hit the fan. All of a sudden, aghast animal crazies—whose idea of consensus is that they get their way, or else—were telling us the notion of predator control was a very big, nasty surprise to them. In truth, they saw an opportunity to cash in by misrepresenting what was happening.

They had little old ladies who never intended to visit Alaska fire off fistfuls of letters threatening they would avoid the state like the plague. They trotted out handfuls of useful idiots in a few cities and had them howl like wolves in front of the ever-obliging television cameras. Radio collars and aerial shooting, they said, were unfair—as if predator control were some kind of parlor game for sycophants and wildlife biology dilettantes.

The news media—as always—picked sides early on. They panted right along with the activists, hanging monikers like "Machinegun" on anybody backing the quickest, most efficient and humane method of culling wolves.

Then-Governor Walter Hickel pulled the plug on the program in the midst of the furor and called for a wolf summit in the middle of winter in Fairbanks, where—as far as most of us can tell—nothing actually was resolved.

The Board of Game shelved the controversial control effort, but a short time later opted to try a three-year experimental program with a narrower focus southwest of Fairbanks. The effort, now in its second year, was designed to help the Delta caribou herd recover. That herd in the 1980s numbered about 11,000 animals, but has declined to 3,500 or so.

And are wildlife biologists working in the experimental program allowed to use aircraft, radio collars and guns—the quickest and most humane method of thinning the packs? Get real. After the earlier craziness, the Game Board restricted Fish and Game to using snares, a passive and less efficient way to kill animals by strangulation.

And the results were sadly predictable, as was the cynical outcry that followed.

So, here we are with a public relations nightmare on our hands, and the very activists who set it up are poised again to profit from the fallout. When are we going to learn they do not have wildlife's interest at heart, that they're working from their own agenda?

As a state, we need to decide, and soon, whether we will allow scientific wildlife management or settle for management by letter-writing campaign. We need to decide whether we'll allow wolf control in some areas to save specific populations of moose and caribou—and eventually, the wolves themselves.

If we decide some wolves must be killed, it is incumbent that they be dispatched humanely and quickly. Snaring is not the best way to get the job done. It is nothing more than a sad compromise forced by those who desperately wanted, and went to great lengths to get, the videotape now being shown on national television.

Animal rights fanatics do not believe humans are predators, or a part of the food chain, or that they even have any business on this planet. They do not believe in hunting. They do not believe we should try to manage our wildlife resources. Instead, they believe in letting nature take its course, even if that means whole populations of animals being wiped out by starvation or disease.

Every time we play into their hands—every time we get suckered into another bogus "consensus" they can ignore at their convenience—this state takes it on the chin. Appeasing those who want—and need—predator control programs to fail is what got us into this mess in the first place.

If we've learned anything in this process, it should be this: Trying to compromise with zealots is a waste of time. And if we don't learn that pretty soon, this will be a vastly different state.

⁂

DURING HIS TWO TERMS in office (1994–2002), Governor Tony Knowles seemed to have little interest in backing his BOG and wildlife biologists of the ADF&G. Despite years of scientific study and abundant proof of the biological soundness and effectiveness of carefully planned wolf control, he refused to allow wolf control programs recommended by ADF&G and the BOG.

In a political tactic reminiscent of that of Governor Hickel's Wolf Summit, in 1995 Governor Knowles asked the National Academy of Sciences (NAS) to undertake a scientific and economic review of management of wolves and bears in Alaska. Until completion of the study there would be no wolf control.

The study was made by the National Research Council, the

operating arm of the NAS. It is a nonprofit organization that provides scientific research for the federal government as well as state governments.

The year-long study, mostly by academics from other states (although Dr. David Klein of the University of Alaska Fairbanks, a highly qualified Alaska scientist with five decades of wildlife studies, participated) started in July, 1996. The 207-page report *Wolves, Bears, and Their Prey in Alaska: Biological and Social Challenges in Wildlife Management*, was published in 1997.

The report summarized many wolf/bear/moose/caribou studies by Alaska's scientists, as well as those made elsewhere, and it discussed at some length relationships of predator and prey. It also reviewed social considerations in wolf management. Conclusions and recommendations of the study were predictable and nothing new to Alaska's wildlife scientists and others who had long followed the issue.

Conclusion number one of the report agreed with ADF&G scientists that, "Wolves and bears in combination can limit prey populations." Conclusion two stated that, "Wolf control has resulted in prey increases only when wolves were seriously reduced over a large area for at least four years."

I don't know what "seriously reduced" means. The original 1975 goal of Bob Hinman and his staff called for a much higher wolf kill than actually resulted in 20A. The removal in 20A by the state of an average of only twenty five wolves annually for seven years clearly resulted in an increase of moose and caribou. I don't think that could be defined as "seriously reduced." Yet it produced significant results.

If recommendations of the study were to be carried out, the number of state wildlife researchers and managers would have to be at least quadrupled, for they called for more evaluation of predator control programs, more benefit-cost analysis, more assessments of baseline of biological conditions, better data on habitat quality and bear ecology, more studies to determine status of predator and prey populations.

Most of these projects have been and are being carried out to the extent possible by the limited staff of the ADF&G.

Conclusion fifteen of the National Research Council's report, "Conflicts over management and control of predators are likely to continue indefinitely," brought shoulder shrugs and nods of agreement from most Alaskans who bothered to read the it.

The report, which cost the Alaska Department of Fish and Game $320,000 (from hunting and trapping license fees), didn't solve or change anything. It did make it clear that the Board of Game functions only at the whim of Alaska's governor, and that a governor who refuses to back the BOG (whose members he appoints) and ADF&G can usually find a political out when the pressure is on.

Was it worth continuing wolf removal efforts over the years while Alaska as a state, ADF&G staff, and BOG members, were harrased in court and out by animal rightists and die-hard wolf lovers? Because of this harrasment, supported largely by the news media, Alaska's national and international reputation as a responsible manager of wildlife suffered.

As a result, for more than three decades Alaska has assumed a defensive mode in its posture on wolf management. This has had broad implications in the management of all of Alaska's wildlife.

Would Alaska have been better off to have caved in to the demands of animal rightists and ended all wolf control?

Not in my view. Instead, if all of Alaska's governors since 1982 had had the backbone of Governor Jay Hammond and ignored special interests, and had backed the BOG and the ADF&G wildlife biologists, Alaska's wildlife populations—including wolves— would have fared better, as would have the state's reputation as a responsible manager of wildlife.

⌒

JIM DOUGLAS SMITH was born in Fairbanks in mid-March, 1977. Robert Dusty Smith was born in late 1978, and Hannah Patricia Smith arrived a year later.

Pat home-schooled all three children. Jim, like his father, entered the University of Alaska Fairbanks at the age of 16. His major was wildlife management. Today, with a B.S. in wildlife management from my old department at the U. of A, and with a Master of Science degree in wildlife management from Oregon State University, as well as a doctorate from Purdue in wildlife ecology, (he followed scholastically in his father's footsteps) he is a rising young biologist with ADF&G. For some reason he is especially fascinated with wolves, and he hopes eventually to become Alaska's leading wolf biologist by assuming the mantle long carried by his father.

I think he'll make it.

Robert Dusty Smith is the family's career aviator. He soloed on his sixteenth birthday and passed the examination for his private pilot's license. He also later easily passed the exam for commercial pilot, and has built his flying hours and experience as if he were born to it—which he was. He'll soon take over his grandfather's air taxi business at Wolverine so Dusty and Hannah can spend their winters in Hawaii where they now own a condominium. They'll summer in Alaska.

Hannah Patricia Smith, now 22, lives with her uncle Bill and his wife in Seattle where she is nearing her goal of becoming a pediatric orthopedist.

Ren retired from ADF&G in 1990, after twenty five years as the state's leading wolf biologist, and he and Pat moved from Fairbanks to Wolverine where they share the large, gracious Smith log home with Dusty and Hannah. For a time Ren helped Dusty with his flying, taking charters, and filling in on scheduled flights. But then his worldwide reputation as a wolf expert caught up with him.

He now spends much of his time as an adviser to national and international conservation organizations. Accompanied by Pat, he has been to Switzerland, Norway, India, Ottowa, Spain, India, Washington D.C. and I don't know where else, contributing his priceless wolf knowledge for the benefit of the wolf.

Between such trips, Alaska is their playground. Ren intimately knows the central arctic Brooks Range, and has the use of a dozen or more cabins scattered across these wild and beautiful mountains. Until his death in 1993, Lord Balmar arrived about once a year and the three of them flew to some far-off remote wilderness site where they hiked, caught a few fish, took pictures, and enjoyed the quiet of the wild land.

Pat has learned how to hunt, and much to Ren's amusement and joy, in the fall she often bags several caribou or a moose with which to fill their freezer. She has also earned a private pilot's license, and has her own prized Cessna 170B.

On occasion Ren and Pat visit me at my coastal Alaska home, and I take them fishing for halibut and salmon in my cabin cruiser. One recent summer day we talked as we drifted silently with baited hooks near bottom in the clear water, enjoying the glacier-hung Kenai Mountains, watching as arctic terns, kittiwakes, murres, puffins, and other seabirds busily searched for food.

"Pat, do you ever think of your life in Boston?" I asked.

"Not really. I've been so busy since Ren and I married I haven't had time to dwell on the past," she answered. She had lost her Boston accent some years earlier.

"And Ren," I asked, "do you miss working for the ADF&G?"

"I did at first," he replied thoughtfully. "I had the ideal job for me. I really enjoyed working with wolves. And, you know, I think I could have spent the rest of my life studying them and still not know everything about them. I must say, I don't miss the controversy.

"I think if I had to do it all over again I would try to develop a strong public education program, and maybe start with young kids in the schools. I'd like Alaskans to be the best educated people in the world on wildlife management. It is, after all, one of the last undeveloped lands of the world, with a wonderful variety of wildlife. If Alaskans take care and use science instead of emotions, our wildlife could be here forever. Unlike oil, our present economic darling, wildlife is perpetually renewable."

"You'd be fighting the propaganda of the animal rights groups. It would be facts vs. emotions. I wonder if the emotional side wouldn't win—as it has again and again," I suggested.

"Science versus emotional critics and advocates, resulting in an emotionally aroused but misinformed public. That's been the big battle, hasn't it?" he mused.

"Jay Long, one of my college professors warned that if the public doesn't support your program, you've lost before you even start," I said.

"I was a member of that public, if you'll recall," Pat commented. "I was absolutely convinced I was right, too."

"And how do you feel about wolves and wolf management now?" I asked.

"I still love wolves. But the wolf I know now isn't the wolf I imagined when I came to Alaska. I agree now there are situations when wolves should be controlled," she said, soberly.

"Believe it or not, Prof," Ren said with a wide grin, "Pat shot a wolf last winter."

"No," I exclaimed, laughing.

"It was attacking my sled dogs," she said. "I love those dogs. And I remembered what wolves did to Snow. Remember?" she asked me.

"Yes, I remember you telling me about Snow. Maybe that was when your views of wolves started to change," I suggested.

"Yes. I was terribly angry and felt betrayed by wolves at the moment," she mused. "Think about it. Here I was, a wolf lover, fresh from Boston, here to save the wolves, and the damned things come in and kill and eat my pet dog. On one side I was being paid to save wolves, on the other I was angry at them for killing my dog. No wonder I cried," she laughed.

"That was the first really good hug I got from Pat," Ren said. "Maybe the wolves that ate Snow did me a favor."

Then he added, "Pat has changed her mind about wolves and their management, but there is one thing she refuses to budge on."

"And what's that?" I asked.

"Have you ever managed to change a woman's mind about something she has sworn never to change?" he asked.

"Well, no," I admitted, glancing at my wife of thirty six years who sat near.

Then Ren suggested to Pat. "Tell Prof what you think now of aerial shooting of wolves?"

"I'm totally opposed to it and I will never change my mind." She said. She wasn't smiling.

E N D

Epilogue

THERE ARE MORE wolves in Alaska today than there were four decades ago when the state assumed management of its wildlife. State biologists estimate their numbers at 5,000 to 8,500, or more, which probably approximates the population of wolves found in Alaska in the 1930s and 1940s.

During the decade before statehood, wolves were appreciably thinned by poisoning, trapping, and aerial hunting by federal agents and the public. Under state management (starting in 1960) they recovered quickly from this abuse.

The wolf's natural distribution in Alaska has been little affected by human settlement and land use, and the animal is still found in virtually all of its original habitat. This includes most of the state except for some islands in Southeastern Alaska, Prince William Sound, and the Aleutian Islands, as well as Kodiak Island.

After statehood, Alaska classified the wolf as both a furbearer and a game animal, and management of the animal has been based on the constitutional mandate of sustained yield for the benefit of the resource and the people. The bounty was rescinded. Closed seasons and closed areas for the protection of wolves were established, as well as hunting bag limits where appropriate. Poison was banned. Aerial hunting for wolves by the public was halted in 1972.

These actions helped to produce the marked increase in wolves generally throughout the state that I have seen during my life.

Studies of Alaska's wolves by wildlife biologists before and since statehood have produced much solid information on the animal's life. This has helped the state to develop a sound wolf management program which parallels the management regimes of the many other valuable wildlife species in Alaska.

Wolves need about eight pounds of meat a day to thrive. Their principal food is deer in Southeast Alaska, moose and caribou in Interior and Central Alaska, and caribou in Arctic Alaska. Their diet may be supplemented with berries, fish, waterfowl, small mammals, sheep and goats—and whatever edible the animals can find or catch.

When food (prey) is abundant, wolf numbers may remain high. As prey decreases, so may wolves. At times, severe weather, or other factors, combined with wolf predation, may force a prey population into a downward trend. If this trend continues to the point where reproduction of the prey does not equal or exceed loss to predation, wolves can all but destroy their own food base, leaving a land with few prey animals, which in turn may support few wolves. Historic records suggest this situation can stagnate for decades—leaving a land with few prey animals and few wolves.

Most of Alaska's management and research biologists believe that before this point is reached, removal of enough wolves to allow prey numbers to rebuild can be in the best interest of man, as well as wolves. When the prey population recovers, it can support more wolves, as well as hunting and other uses by man. This knowledge can be used to maintain healthy numbers of moose, caribou, deer, and wolves. This, of course, is to the advantage of all who value good numbers of wild animals, whether it be for viewing, photography, hunting, or trapping, or simply knowing they exist.

This is basically the background of Alaska's various programs which have been aimed at removing a specified number of wolves. Annual removal of a relatively few wolves from 20A (Tanana Flats) over a quarter century (including ten years in which no wolves were removed by the state) revived a sagging moose population, and did no lasting damage to the wolf population.

The massive kills of wolves by federal agents during the 1950s in the Nelchina Basin and on the North Slope clearly resulted in a resurgence of caribou—but the cost in wolves from those operations would not be acceptable today.

A decrease of moose and or caribou due to predation cannot always be attributed to wolves. Alaska's bears, both black and grizzly, also prey on these animals. In-depth research in the Nelchina Basin demonstrated this. In this instance, grizzly bears, not wolves, were mostly responsible for moose calf mortality.

Clearly, wolf control should be undertaken only when research clearly demonstrates that removal of a designated number of the animals will benefit a population of moose or caribou (or both).

In the past half century, the American public's attitude toward wolves has swung 180 degrees, from "kill 'em all" to "don't kill any." Neither has its place in the science of modern wildlife management.

Will the Alaska public ever allow Alaska's wildlife managers to follow the state's constitutional requirement for management on a sustained yield for all species? For nearly three decades Alaska's wildlife managers have had an uphill battle in attempts to manage for sustained yield certain decimated moose/caribou populations that have been threatened by wolves. Though my account covers only the efforts for 20A, other Game Management Units in Alaska have seen attempts at wolf control similarly thwarted.

When based on good science, modern game management, including removal of a few wolves where indicated, does work—if given a chance.

Fictional characters and names

Acorn, Steve—ADF&G moose biologist at Fairbanks.

Alden—Aviation mechanic, Fairbanks.

Blanche—Ren Smith's sister. Wolverine resident.

Balmar, John—Trophy hunter and English Lord. Sponsor of conservation programs.

Bauer, Gracie—Representative of Wild Animal Lovers Association.

Cohen, Frederick—Testified at public hearing.

Foster, Davy—One of Pat York's 5th grade students.

Garth—Fairbanks racing dog musher.

Gates, Jim—Fairbanks FBI agent.

Grant, John—Preceded Pat York as National Wildlife Savers Foundation representative.

Hanson, Jerry—CEO of National Wildlife Savers Foundation, Boston.

Herman—Trapper in GMU 20A.

Johnson, Esau—Athapaskan resident of Stevens Village.

Johnson, Beth—Teacher who replaced Pat York in Boston school.

Kamerak, Eben—Testified at Board of Game public hearing at Fairbanks.

McCord, Bob—Early, greedy, bush pilot.

Molly, Aunt—Wife of Uncle Toby, village of Wolverine.

Olson, Lee—Translated Eben Kamerak's testimony at Board of Game public hearing.

Potter, Allen—Boston resident. One-time male friend of Pat York.

Rachel—Anaktuvuk Pass resident. Expert skin sewer. Made fur parka for Pat York.

Rainey, the Reverend Roland ("Pop")—Episcopal priest at village of Wolverine.

Rasmusson, Harry—Fairbanks racing dog musher.

Smith, Bill—Ren Smith's brother, a Seattle orthopedist.

Smith, Dusty—Wolverine village bush pilot. Ren Smith's father.

Smith, Hannah—Mother of Ren Smith.

Smith, Hannah Patricia—Daughter of Ren and Pat Smith.

Smith, Jim—Son of Ren and Pat Smith.

Smith, Ren—Our hero. ADF&G wolf biologist.

Smith, Robert Dusty—Son of Ren and Pat Smith.

The National Wildlife Savers Foundation (TNWSF)

Tepner, Julie—Quoted by newspaper as not believing wolves killed Fairbanks dogs.

Toby, (Uncle)—Ren Smith's uncle (mother's brother). Resident of Wolverine.

Wild Animal Lovers Association (WALA)

Wolf Lovers Association of Great Britain (WLAGB)

Wolverine (village)

York, Pat—Our heroine. Boston school teacher who travels to Alaska to save wolves.

Nonfiction characters

Adasiak, Allen—Reporter for several of Alaska's newspapers; Governor Walter Hickel's public relations rep; an editor for *ALASKA* magazine.

Ahgook, Bob—Anaktuvuk Pass Eskimo hunter.

Ahgook, Timothy—Anaktuvuk Pass resident. Son of Bob Ahgook.

Allen, Dr. Durward—Professor of Wildlife Ecology, Purdue University.

Anderson, Carl—Owner of dog team leased by federal government for Glaser's use.

Anderson, James L. (Andy)—One-time bush pilot in the Koyukuk valley. Retired in Pennsylvania. Author of as-told-to Jim Rearden book *Arctic Bush Pilot.*

Arctic John—Also known as *Italook.* Famed Eskimo hunter of the Brooks Range.

Baker, Mrs.—Resident of Healy in the 1920s.

Ballard, Warren B.—ADF&G wildlife biologist. Researched predation in the Nelchina basin.

Bauer, Dr.—Alaska Native Service doctor at Kotzebue in the 1940s.

Bernhardt, Tony—Teller resident who owned dog team hired by Frank Glaser. Member of Alaska Board of Fish and Game in early 1970s.

Billberg, Rudy—Long-time Alaska bush pilot. Author of as-told-to Jim Rearden book, *In the Shadow of Eagles.*

Billberg, Bessie—Wife of Rudy Billberg.

Bishop, George—One time trapper in Takotna/McGrath area.

Bojanich, George—Fairbanks resident who, in 1933, with Sam Hjorta, found remains of Moose John Millovich at Beaver Creek.

Bos, Greg—ADF&G wildlife biologist.

Brooks, James W.—Long-time wildlife biologist for ADF&G and FWS. Commissioner ADF&G. Wildlife management graduate of U of A, Fairbanks.

Buckmaster, Clint—Member of the Alaska Board of Game in 1970s. Resident of Sitka.

Bunde, Con—Member, Alaska House of Representatives. Retired Univ. of Alaska Professor, commercial pilot, outdoorsman.

Burke, Edmund—Alaska superior court judge.

Burkholder, Bob. U.S. Fish and Wildlife Service agent in Alaska during the 1940s and 1950s. Known for his work with wolves in the Nelchina district.

Burris, Oliver ("Bud")—ADF&G Regional Game coordinator at Fairbanks.

Butrovich, John—State senator from Fairbanks in 1970s.

Cade, Tom—Former student of wildlife management at University of Alaska, Fairbanks. Head, ornithology dept. at Cornell University.

Carbyn, Ludwig N.—Long-time Canadian Wildlife Service biologist.

Carlson, Hjalmar (Slim)—Long-time Minchumina trapper.

Charles, Kenny—Tribal leader, village of Minto.

Cisney, Doyle—FWS predator agent in Alaska during the 1950s.

Corbley, Louis—ranger at McKinley National Park in 1930s.

Crisler, Lois—Author of book *Arctic Wild.*

Crisler, Herb—Disney photographer. Photographed Alaska film *Arctic Wild* for Disney.

Day, Ed—Owner of Fairbanks dog livery in 1920s and 1930s.

Dimick, Roland E.—First head of the Department of Fish and Game at Oregon State College (now University).

Dubin, Sam—Early trader on Yukon River.

Dufresne, Frank—Executive Officer, Alaska Game Commission, 1930s and 1940s.

Edmonds, Debbie K.—Black Forest, Colorado, woman killed by two hybrid wolves.

Edwards, Mike—Writer for the *National Geographic* magazine in the 1970s.

Egan, Bill—Alaska's first governor after statehood. Served 1959–66 and 1970–74.

Eielson, Ben—Pioneer Alaska bush pilot.

Ellis, Bill—Registered big game guide and pilot at Nabesna, Alaska.

Farmen, Darrell—Long-time Alaska guide. Member Alaska Board of Game in 1970s.

Faro, Jim—Long-time ADF&G wildlife biologist. Retired.

Floyd, T.—Minnesota wolf researcher associated with Dr. L. David Mech.

Gabrielson, Ira—Nationally respected conservationist; Director of the FWS; influential in the development of scientific wildlife management in the U.S.

Glaser, Frank—Pioneer Alaskan market hunter/trapper. Federal predator control agent in Alaska 1937–55. Subject of book, *Alaska's Wolf Man* by Jim Rearden.

Glaser, Nellie—Wife of Frank Glaser.

Hammond, Jay. U.S.—FWS agent in Alaska in 1950s. Bush pilot, legislator, and Alaska's governor 1974–82.

Hanson, Jim—Builder of cabin on Prince Wales Island, Alaska.

Hanson, Ulrick—Builder of cabin on Prince Wales Island, Alaska.

Harbo, Sam, Dr.—Professor of Biometrics and Chairman of the Program in Wildlife and Fisheries at the University of Alaska, Fairbanks. Long-time chairman of the Alaska Board of Game. Retired.

Harris, Henry—Noatak resident who, with dog sled, hauled Glaser and his outfit back to Noatak Village from the upper Noatak River.

Harris, Buck—FWS agent during the 1940s and 1950s.

Hautop, Victor—One of four searchers who found remains of Crist Kolby on Prince of Wales Island.

Henning, Robert—Owner and publisher of *Alaska* magazine and Alaska Northwest Publishing Company.

Herning, Harold—McKinley National Park ranger in late 1930s and early 1940s.

Hickel, Walter J.—Governor of Alaska. 1966–1969 and 1990–1994.

Hinman, Bob—Graduate of Univ. of Alaska, Fairbanks in wildlife management. M.S. in wildlife from Univ. of Utah. Long-time wildlife biologist with ADF&G, including positions of Regional Director and Deputy Director of the Game Division.

Hjorta, Sam—Fairbanks resident who, in 1933, with George Bojanich, found remains of Moose John Millovich at Beaver Creek.

Huber, John—State senator from Fairbanks in 1970s.

Hugo, Ellen—Anaktuvuk Pass resident.

Huntington, Gilbert—Son of Sidney Huntington.

Huntington, Jimmy—Koyukon gunner for aerial wolf hunter Donald Stickman in 1956–57. Younger brother of Sidney Huntington. Representative in Alaska's legislature, and member of the Alaska Board of Fisheries.

Huntington, Sidney—Lifelong resident of Koyukuk region. Long-time member of Alaska Board of Fish and Game and Board of Game. Recipient of honorary doctorate from Univ. of Alaska, Fairbanks. Author of book *Shadows on the Koyukuk* as-told-to Jim Rearden.

Irwin, W. R. (Red)—A court-appointed investigator who searched for Crist Kolby on Prince of Wales Island.

Jackson, Sheldon, Dr.—General Agent for Education for Alaska. Introduced reindeer to Alaska in the late 1890s.

Jenkins, Paul—Editor, *The Anchorage Times.*

Johnson, Loyal—ADF&G wildlife biologist. Retired.

Kelly, Maurice—Director of predator control for the FWS in Alaska prior to statehood.

Kelleyhouse, David G.—ADF&G wildlife biologist, one time director of Wildlife Division.

Klein, David, Dr.—Long time Leader of the Alaska Cooperative Wildlife Research Unit at the University of Alaska, Fairbanks, and Professor Emeritus of Wildlife Management.

Knowles, Tony—Governor of Alaska, 1994–2002

Kolby, Crist—Trapper who died on Prince of Wales Island, Alaska. Searchers who found his remains believe he was killed by wolves.

Komak, John—Teller resident with dog team hired by Frank Glaser.

Kuhn, Lee W.—Emeritus Professor of wildlife management at Oregon State University.

Larsen, Douglas G.—Yukon Territory wildlife biologist.

Lee, Jack—Long-time Alaska registered guide/pilot.

Lidle, Janet—Editor and publisher of *Wolf!* a quarterly compendium of world news of wolves.

Liek, Harry—Superintendent of Mount McKinley National Park in the 1920s and 1930s.

Lindgren, Tina—Executive Director of the Alaska Tourism Marketing Council in 1992.

Long, Jay B.—Professor of wildlife management at Oregon State University.

Lund, Roy—Taxi and transport driver in Fairbanks in the 1930s.

Marshall, Robert—Author of classic 1933 book *Arctic Village.*

Marks, Mrs.—Co-owner of Teller trading post in 1940s.

Mayer, Dr. Lew—Anchorage physician who cared for Frank Glaser in his last days.

Mech, L. David, Dr.—Author of 1970 book *The Wolf.* Internationally recognized as one of the world's leading wolf scientist/researchers.

Mekiana, Justus—Anaktuvuk Pass hunter.

McIntyre, Dick—Owner of Frontier Sporting goods, Fairbanks.

McKay, Douglas—Secretary of Interior in 1955.

Mclroy, Carl—ADF&G wildlife biologist.

McMullen, Peter—Alaska game warden in the 1930s.

Miller, Sterling—ADF&G wildlife biologist. Associate of Warren Ballard on Nelchina basin predation study.

Miller, W. A.—One of four searchers who found remains of Crist Kolby on Prince of Wales Island.

Millovich, "Moose" John—Fairbanksan who trapped at Beaver Creek. Died at Beaver Creek in 1933. Body eaten by wolves. Some believe he was killed by wolves.

Miner, Joe—U.S. FWS predator agent in Alaska during the 1950s.

Mischa—Golovin resident, hired with his dog team by Frank Glaser.

Mitchell, Gordon—Noatak resident hired by Glaser to take him up the Noatak River.

Morry, Jack—Anaktuvuk Pass resident.

Mowat, Farley—Canadian author of book *Never Cry Wolf.*

Murie, Adolf—Wildlife biologist for the National Park Service. Author of 1944 book *The Wolves of Mt. McKinley.*

Murie, Olaus—Wildlife biologist for the Bureau of Biological Survey and FWS.

Nasholik, Henry—Unalakleet Eskimo hired with dog team by Frank Glaser.

Neuweiler, Phil—Big game trophy hunter from Pennsylvania.

Neuweiler, Cecille—Wife of Phil Neuweiler. Big game trophy hunter from Pennsylvania.

Newton—upper Tanana River trader.

O'Rear, Charles—Internationally known free-lance photographer.

Osborne, Calvin—Stepson of Frank Glaser.

Perkins, Jack—NBC News reporter.

Punyuk—Eskimo at Noorvik who, in the 1940s, was attacked by a rabid wolf.

Rausch, Robert A.—ADF&G biologist who necropsied 4,160 of Alaska's interior wolf carcasses obtained from trappers.

Rearden, Jim—Author and narrator of this volume. Also referred to as "Prof"—one-time professor of wildlife management at the University of Alaska Fairbanks.

Reed, Nathaniel— U.S. Wildlife and Parks Assistant Secretary in the 1970s.

Rhode, Clarence. Regional Director, FWS. Killed in plane crash in 1959.

Richardson, Wilds P.—U.S. Corp of Engineers officer responsible for early development of the Richardson Highway, which is named for him.

Rood, Sidney—Director of Alaska Native Reindeer Service at Nome.

Rosier, Carl—Commissioner of ADF&G 1990–94.

Sahadie, David—Resident of Tenafly New Jersey who threatened Alaska's Governor Hickel by telephone over wolf control program.

Schaller, George—Former student of fish and game management at the Univ. of Alaska Fairbanks. Affiliated with the New York Zoological Society. Author of popular accounts of the great apes, pandas, snow leopards, others.

Schwatka, Frederick—U.S. military officer who explored the Yukon River drainage inthe late 1800s.

Selfridge, W. R.—Author of "Wolves Killed Crist Kolby," published April 1943 by *The Alaska Sportsman* magazine.

Seton, Ernest Thompson—Naturalist/writer of the early 1900s.

Sheffield, Bill—Governor of Alaska 1982–86.

Sheldon, Charles—Prominent sportsman/hunter of early 1900s. One of the first whites to explore what was to become Mt. McKinley National Park.

Sherman, Enoch S.—Noatak resident who, with dog sled, hauled Glaser and his outfit back to Noatak Village from the upper Noatak River.

Shield, Saul—Noatak resident who, in winter, was to retrieve Glaser from upper Noatak.

Sigfried—Golovin, reindeer herd owner.

Skoog, Ron, Dr.—Long-time wildlife biologist. Graduate of Univ. of Alaska Fairbanks in wildlife management. PhD thesis on caribou U. of California. One-time Commissioner of ADF&G.

Spraker, Ted—ADF&G wildlife biologist. Associate of Warren Ballard on predation study in Nelchina basin.

Stalker, Austin—Noatak resident. Made tent stove for Glaser.

Stefansson, Vilhjalmur—Prominent arctic explorer of the early 1900s.

Stephenson, Robert O.—ADF&G wildlife biologist with decades of work with Alaska's wolves and other animals.

Stickman, Donald—Koyukon Athabaskan owner of an air taxi who, in 1956–57, used a small plane to hunt and kill wolves in the Koyukuk Valley.

Stricker, Fran—Representative of the Sacramento, California-based Animal Protection Institute. Attendee of 1993 Wolf Summit.

Swenson, Marge—Teacher/nurse at Noorvik in the 1940s.

Taylor, Ken—ADF&G wildlife biologist. Associate of Warren Ballard on predation study in Nelchina basin.

Tillion, Clem—Former Alaska legislator and "fish czar" who, while representing the governor's office, was influential in directing Alaska's commercial fisheries.

Titus, Charlie, Jr—Member of the tribal council of village of Minto.

Tobuk, David—Carried off by wolf as child. Captain of sternwheeler *Teddy H.*

Tondro, Frank—The "Malemute Kid," made famous by writings of Jack London.

Topkok, Maggie—Worker at Teller trading post.

Tremblay, Ray. Long-time FWS associate of Frank Glaser.

Valkenburg, Pat—Wildlife biologist for the Alaska Department of Fish and Game.

Van Bibber—Owner of Fairbanks dog livery in 1920s and 1930s.

Vogel, Oscar—Long-time trapper in Alaska's Talkeetna Mountains.

Vogler, Joe—Fairbanks gold miner. Ran for seat of Alaska governor under aegis of the Independent party.

Walker, Max—One of four searchers who found remains of Crist Kolby.

Waugaman, Bill—Long-time Alaska guide, resident of Fairbanks.

Wells, Michael—A court-appointed investigator who searched for the missing Crist Kolby on Prince of Wales Island.

Westlund, John—ADF&G biologist associate of Warren Ballard in processing captured grizzly bears during Nelchina predator study.

White, Sam—Alaska game warden in the 1930s and 1940s.

Wilkins, Hubert—Prominent Australian explorer of the early 1900s.

References

Ballard, W. B. 1991. T. H. Spraker, and K. P. Taylor. 1981. "Causes of moose calf mortality in Southcentral Alaska." *Journal of Wildlife Management* 45:335–42.

Ballard, W. B. 1991. "Management of predators and their prey: the Alaskan experience." Transactions of the North American Wildlife and Natural Resources Conference 56:527–38.

Ballard, W. B., J. S. Whitman, and C. L. Gardner. 1987. "Ecology of an exploited wolf population in south-central Alaska." *Wildlife Monographs* 98:1–54.

Ballard, W. B., T. H. Spraker, and K. P. Taylor. 1981. "Causes of moose calf mortality in southcentral Alaska." *Journal of Wildlife Management*, 45:335–42.

Ballard, W. B. and Miller, S. D. 1990. "Effects of reducing brown bear density on moose calf survival in southcentral Alaska." *Alces* 26:9–13.

Boertje, R. D., P. Valkenburg, and M. S. McNay. 1996. "Increases in moose, caribou, and wolves following wolf control in Alaska." *Journal of Wildlife Management* 60:474–89

Boertje, R. D. and R. O. Stephenson. 1992. "Effects of ungulate availability on wolf reproductive potential in Alaska." *Canadian Journal of Zoology* 70:2441–43.

Burkholder, B. L. 1959. "Movements and behavior of a wolf pack in Alaska." *Journal of Wildlife Management* 23:1–11.

Busch, Robert H. 1995. *The Wolf Almanac.* The Lyons Press, New York. 226 pp.

Crisler, Lois. 1956. *Arctic wild.* Harper and Bros. New York. 301 pp.

Errington, Paul L., *Of predation and life*. 1967. The Iowa State University Press, Ames, Iowa. 277 pp.

Floyd, T. J., L. D. Mech, and P. A. Jordan. 1978. "Relating wolf scat content to prey consumed." *Journal of Wildlife Management*. 42:528–32.

Gabrielson, Ira N. 1942. *Wildlife Conservation*. The Macmillan Company, New York. 250 pp.

Gasaway, W. C., R. O. Stephenson, J. L. Davis, P. E. K. Shepherd, and O. E. Burris. 1983. "Interrelationships of wolves, prey and man in Interior Alaska." *Wildlife Monographs* 84: 1–50.

Gasaway, W. C., R. D. Boertje, D. V. Grangaard, D. G. Kellyhouse, R. O. Stephenson, and D. G. Larsen. 1992. "The role of predation in limiting moose at low densities in Alaska and Yukon and implications for conservation." *Wildlife Monographs* 120: 1–59.

Gubser, Nicholas J. 1965. "The Nunamiut Eskimos; hunters of caribou." Yale University Press. 384 pp.

Harbo, Samuel J. Jr. 1993. "Environmental sanity: think globally, act locally." Paper presented at the Wolf Summit. Fairbanks Alaska, January 1993.

Harbo, Samuel J. Jr., and Frederick C. Dean. 1981. "Historical and current perspectives on wolf management in Alaska." *Canadian Wildlife Service Report Series* Number 45.

Harrington, Fred H., and L. David Mech. 1978. "Wolf howling and its role in territory maintenance." *Behavior* LXVIII 3–4.

Heimer, W. E. 1999. "Wolf management in Alaska's intact ecosystems: an observers reviews, critique, and functional prescription," pp. 311–32 in *Transactions 2nd North American Wild Sheep Conference*, 2,000, Reno, Nevada. 470pp.

Lidle, Janet. *WOLF!* Various volumes 1985–1991. Clifton Heights, PA.

Marquardt, Kathleen, with Herbert M. Levine and Mark LaRochelle. 1993. *Animal scam*. Regnery Publishing, Inc., Washington, D.C. 221 pp.

Mech, L. David. 1991. *The way of the wolf*. Swan Hill Press, Shrewsbury, England. 120 pp.

Mech, L. David. 1970. "The wolf. The ecology and behavior of an endangered species." The American Museum of Natural History, The Natural History Press, Garden City, New York. 384 pp.

Mech, L. David. 1966. "The wolves of Isle Royal." *Fauna of the National Parks of the United States* Series 7. 210 pp.

Mowat, Farley. 1963. *Never cry wolf.* Dell Publishing Co., New York. 176 pp.

Murie, A. O. 1944. *The wolves of Mount McKinley.* U.S. Natl. Park Serv. Fauna ser. 5. 238 pp.

National Research Council, 1997. *Wolves, bears, and their prey in Alaska.* National Academy Press. 207 pp.

Pimlott, D. H., Shannon, J. A., Kolenosky, G. B. 1969. "The ecology of the timber wolf in Algonquin Provincial Park." *Research Branch Report* (Wildlife) No. 87. Lands and Forests, Ontario.

Rausch, R. A. 1969. "A summary of wolf studies in southcentral Alaska, 1957–1968." *Transactions of the North American Wildlife and Natural Resource Conference* 34:141-157.

Rearden, Jim. 1998. *Alaska's wolf man; the 1915–55 wilderness adventures of Frank Glaser.* Pictorial Histories Publishing Co., Inc., Missoula, Montana. 330 pp.

Sheldon, Charles. 1930. *The wilderness of Denali.* Charles Scribners sons, New York. 412 pp.

Stephenson, R. O. W. B. Ballard, C. A. Smith, and K. Richardson. 1996. "Wolf Biology and management in Alaska 1981–91." L. N. Carbyn, S. H. Fritts, and D. R. Seip, eds. *Ecology and conservation of wolves in a changing world.* Canadian Circumpolar Inst., Univ. Alberta, Edmonton.

Strickland, Dan. 1981. "Wolf howling in parks—the Algonquin experience in interpretation." *Canadian Wildlife Service Report* Series Number 45.

Strickland, Dan, and Edward A. Goldman. 1994. *Mammals of Algonquin Provincial Park.* The Friends of Algonquin Park. 50 pp.

"Wolf Management in Selected Areas of North America." 1970. Eds. S. E. Jorgensen, C. E. Faulkner, L. David Mech. Proc. *Symposium, 35th Transactions of the North American Wildlife and Natural Resource Conference*, Chicago.

"Wolves in Canada and Alaska: their status, biology, and management." 1983. Ludwig N. Carbyn, ed. *Proceedings of the Wolf Symposium*, Edmonton, Alberta, May, 1981. Canadian Wildlife Service, Ser. 45, Ottawa.

Young, Stanley. 1946. *The wolf in North American history.* Caldwell Press, Caxton Printers. 149 pp.

Young, Stanley P., and Goldman, Edward A. 1944. *The wolves of North America.* The American Wildlife Institute, Washington, D.C. 636 pp.

About the author

A RESIDENT OF ALASKA for sixty years, Jim Rearden has written twenty-four books and more than five hundred magazine articles, mostly about Alaska. He has received many awards for his writing, including "Historian of the Year" from the Alaska Historical Society for his book *Alaska's Wolf Man*.

Rearden studied fish and game management at Oregon State College and the University of Maine, receiving degrees from both. In 2006 the University of Alaska Fairbanks awarded him an honorary doctor of science degree for his teaching, contributions to wildlife conservation, and writings.

In 1947 he was a Fishery Patrol Agent for the U.S. Fish and Wildlife Service at Chignik, Alaska. In 1950 he organized the Wildlife Department at The University of Alaska Fairbanks, and taught as head of that department for four years. He was the commercial fisheries Area Biologist in Cook Inlet for the Alaska Department of Fish and Game for ten years; served on the Alaska Board of Fish and Game for five years, and on the Alaska Board of Game for seven years. In 1976, President Gerald Ford appointed him to the National Advisory Committee on Oceans and Atmosphere where he served for a year and a half.

Rearden was the Outdoors Editor for *Alaska* magazine for twenty years, and simultaneously was a field editor for *Outdoor Life* magazine. He lives in Homer, Alaska, with his wife, Audrey, in a log house he built himself.